A Collection of Surveys on Market Experiments

A Collection of Surveys on Market Experiments

Edited by Charles N. Noussair and Steven Tucker

WILEY Blackwell

Registered Office
John Wiley & Sons Ltd, The Atrium, Southern Gate, Chichester, West Sussex, PO19 8SQ, United Kingdom

Editorial Offices
350 Main Street, Malden, MA 02148-5020, USA
9600 Garsington Road, Oxford, OX4 2DQ, UK
The Atrium, Southern Gate, Chichester, West Sussex, PO19 8SQ, UK

For details of our global editorial offices, for customer services, and for information about how to apply for permission to reuse the copyright material in this book please see our website at www.wiley.com/wiley-blackwell.

Library of Congress Cataloging-in-Publication Data:

A collection of surveys on market experiments / edited by Charles N. Noussair and Steven Tucker.
    pages cm
  Includes bibliographical references and index.
  ISBN 978-1-118-79071-7 (pbk.)
 1. Markets.   2. Game theory.   3. Experimental economics.   I. Noussair, Charles.   II. Tucker, Steven.
  HF5470.C627 2014
  332′.041501–dc23

                                                                                    2013034284

A catalogue record for this book is available from the British Library.

Cover image: Computer image © Myles McInnes. Bar chart © David Castillio Dominici.
Cover design by Workhaus

Set in 10/12pt Times by Aptara Inc., New Delhi, India
Printed in Malaysia by Ho Printing (M) Sdn Bhd

1   2014

CONTENTS

CONTENTS

1

A COLLECTION OF SURVEYS ON MARKET EXPERIMENTS

Charles N. Noussair

Tilburg University

Steven Tucker

University of Waikato

This special issue contains ten surveys of different streams of research on experimental markets. The literature on experimental markets has its origins in work on competitive markets and oligopoly with seminal contributions by Smith (1962), Fouraker and Siegel (1963), and Sauermann and Selten (1959). Over the last five decades, as laboratory experimental methods have gained acceptance in economics, the experimental literature on market behavior has branched out in many directions. Its evolution has been influenced by developments in theory, policy debates that have arisen, and the introduction of new tools for conducting experiments. This special issue includes surveys of some of the many productive lines of experimental research that have helped economists gain more understanding of how markets operate.

The first paper, by Casoria and Riedl (2013), considers experimental work on labor markets. Two special features typically characterize these markets. The first is that, unlike a market for a typical commodity, the seller of labor can take conscious actions that affect its value after a contract has been agreed. This creates the possibility of reciprocity, as for example a higher wage can be reciprocated with greater work effort. This had led to extensive experimental work, beginning with the work of Fehr *et al.* (1993) on the relationship between the contract under which an employee (a seller) is working and the effort or output he produces. The second special feature of a labor market is that the demand for labor is derived, typically from activity in the market for the output the labor is used to produce. The last part of the Casoria and Riedl article considers experiments with this feature, which typically involve an economy with markets for both output and labor in operation.

Interacting markets for labor and output are one type of general equilibrium structure. A focused but probing line of research has gone beyond the classical condition of a single market

A Collection of Surveys on Market Experiments, First Edition.
Edited by Charles N. Noussair and Steven Tucker. Chapters © 2014 The Authors.
Book compilation © 2014 John Wiley & Sons, Ltd. Published 2014 by John Wiley & Sons, Ltd.

operating in isolation with stable dynamic properties. The article by Crockett (2013) surveys various types of general equilibrium experiments. The first part of his article is concerned with price dynamics in experimental markets, both within and between market periods. The latter part considers multiple market economies, including some experimental studies focused on international, macro and monetary economics.

The experiments considered in the two previous articles are motivated by competitive theoretical models assuming price taking on the part of buyers and sellers. This assumption is recognized as unsatisfactory for oligopoly. In response to this problem, strategic game theoretic models have been developed for markets with a small number of firms. These models have been subject to extensive experimental investigation. The article by Potters and Suetens (2013) in this special issue surveys some of the more important developments in the experimental study of oligopoly since the year 2000. They survey work on simultaneous and sequential price and quantity competition, innovation, and price dispersion. They also discuss dynamics in oligopoly games and factors that influence sellers' ability to collude.

Another important application of game theory in economics has been in the study of auctions. An extensive experimental literature has investigated the behavioral properties of different auctions, motivated both by testing models of bidding behavior as well the development of auctions for use in policy applications. The article by Kwasnica and Sherstyuk (2013) considers a subfield of experimental research that has grown rapidly in recent years; that on multi-unit auctions. In such auctions, more than one unit is sold to a group of bidders. Kwasnica and Shestyuk discuss a number of important issues. They distinguish between settings with single and with multi-unit demand at the level of the individual buyer, which are very different in their properties. They discuss the effect of synergies in preferences and how auctions can be designed to realize efficient allocations in the presence of such synergies. They also discuss the impact of institutional details and factors that enhance and reduce collusion in multi-unit auctions.

Auctions are a type of competition in which those who commit the most resources and bid the most have the greatest chance of winning. The auctions considered in most of the literature, including the survey discussed in the last paragraph, have the feature that losing bidders do not incur any losses other than their opportunity cost of not winning the item. However, many types of competition have the feature that those who lose the competition are worse off than if they had not entered because they have expended resources that they cannot recover. Such situations are called contests. The survey of Sheremeta (2013) surveys experimental work in this area. He focuses on two dominant phenomena uncovered in this literature. These are the tendency to overbid, often so aggressively that bidders lose money in expectation, and the great heterogeneity in bidder behavior. He explores a number of potential drivers for each of the two patterns.

Market experiments have also been used for policy formulation in a number of countries. Friesen and Gangadharan (2013) survey developments in the area of policy experiments. They argue that experiments are particularly useful for understanding complex environments, for which theoretical modeling is intractable. They review experiments in environmental policy, focusing on emissions trading experiments in detail. They also review some work on experiments to develop markets for water use, resource conservation and agricultural policy.

The article by Camera *et al.* (2013) considers a potential source of friction in market operation. This is the fact that market participants interact with a particular other party infrequently, and interacting agents often have little information about each other. The authors survey a line of research that considers economies in which interacting pairs are formed at random each period in economies of indefinite duration. They review the means that have been used to create cooperation in such settings, for example peer punishment, the introduction of fiat money, and communication. They also report a new experiment that focuses on the effect of communication in a market with frictions.

Assets typically differ from other goods in one of the following two aspects. The first is that they have a life of more than one period. This allows scope for intertemporal speculation, and for this speculation to influence asset prices. Asset markets often also have a distinctive information structure, in which some traders have inside information about the value of the asset. Uninformed traders and market makers must take this information structure into account when trading. The article by Noussair and Tucker (2013) surveys several strands of research in asset markets. They focus on studies of market microstructure, pari-mutuel betting markets, and the connection between individuals' characteristics and their trading behavior.

One striking finding from experimental asset market research has been the discovery that prices in markets for long-lived assets tend to bubble and crash. This result was initially documented by Smith *et al.* (1988). The literature that this paper has inspired is the focus of the article of Palan (2013). In his survey, he describes the bubble and crash pattern and lists various factors that accentuate or mitigate price bubbles. These include trader characteristics and their expectations, the liquidity and quantity of the asset available, the time path of fundamentals, and the trading institutions in place.

Another avenue of experimental research on asset markets has been the literature on prediction markets, surveyed here by Deck and Porter (2013). A prediction market is an asset market in which contingent claims on future events are traded. The prices in the market yield a prediction of the likelihood of an event occurring or of the expected value of an outcome variable, such as the vote share of a political candidate in an election or a future stock price. Deck and Porter survey a number of applications of these markets and how experimental methods have been used to investigate factors that enhance or inhibit their ability to generate accurate predictions.

References

Camera, G., Casari, M. and Bigoni, M. (2013) Experimental markets with frictions. *Journal of Economic Surveys* 27(3): 536–553.

Casoria, F. and Riedl, A. (2013) Experimental Labor markets and policy considerations: incomplete contracts and macroeconomic aspects. *Journal of Economic Surveys* 27(3): 398–420.

Crockett, S. (2013) Price dynamics in general equilibrium experiments. *Journal of Economic Surveys* 27(3): 421–438.

Deck, C. and Porter, D. (2013) Prediction markets in the laboratory. *Journal of Economic Surveys* 27(3): 589–603.

Fehr, E., Kirchsteiger, G. and Riedl, A. (1993) Does fairness prevent market clearing? An experimental investigation. *Quart. J. Econ.* 108(2): 437–460.

Fouraker, L. and Siegel, S. (1963) Bargaining Behavior, McGraw-Hill Press, New York, USA.

Friesen, L. and Gangadharan, L. (2013) Environmental markets: what do we learn from the lab? *Journal of Economic Surveys* 27(3): 515–535.

Kwasnica, A. and Sherstyuk, K. (2013) Multi-unit auctions. *Journal of Economic Surveys* 27(3): 461–490.

Noussair, C. and Tucker, S. (2013) Experimental research on asset pricing. *Journal of Economic Surveys* 27(3): 554–569.

Palan, S. (2013) A review of bubbles and crashes in experimental asset markets. *Journal of Economic Surveys* 27(3): 570–588.

Potters, J. and Suetens, S. (2013) Oligopoly experiments in the current millenium. *Journal of Economic Surveys* 27(3): 439–460.

Sauermann, H. and Selten, R. (1959) Ein oligopolexperiment. *Zeitschrift für die gesamte Staatswissenschaft* 115: 427–471.

Sheremeta, R. (2013) Overbidding and heterogeneous behavior in contest experiments. *Journal of Economic Surveys* 27(3): 491–514.

Smith, V. (1962) An experimental study of competitive market behavior. *The Journal of Political Economy* 70(2): 111–137.

Smith, V., Suchanek, G. and Williams, A. (1988) Bubbles, crashes and endogenous expectations in experimental spot asset markets. *Econometrica* 56: 1119–1151.

2

EXPERIMENTAL LABOR MARKETS AND POLICY CONSIDERATIONS: INCOMPLETE CONTRACTS AND MACROECONOMIC ASPECTS

Fortuna Casoria and Arno Riedl

Maastricht University

1. Introduction

Experimental economics' focus on the functioning of labor markets has been growing over the years and the advantages of applying experimental economics methods to labor economics have been extensively discussed (see, e.g., Fehr *et al.*, 2009; Charness and Kuhn, 2011). Experiments allow for tight control over the many environmental factors that can affect behavior and render causal relations easier to infer. The possibility of controlling these factors implies the possibility of varying them and studying whether and to what degree the enforced changes affect decisions. This feature seems to be particularly suitable to analyze labor markets, where a large amount of labor-related available data are circumstantial, implying that it becomes difficult to exactly discern which factors play which role in the realization of outcomes.

The experimental labor economics literature is quite extensive with a wide range of issues addressed and this survey does neither intend nor pretend to cover the experimental labor literature in all its breath. We rather focus on two aspects that are important for a better understanding of labor market relations and their consequences for labor market policies. The first part of the survey is dedicated to papers that assess the prevalence of reciprocal considerations in incomplete labor contracts. The second part summarizes the relatively small but growing experimental literature exploring labor issues in macroeconomics and public finance studying the interaction between taxation and labor market outcomes. Readers interested in other aspects explored in experimental labor economics, such as work incentives or multitask problems, arbitration, job search, or gender differentials, are referred to the excellent reviews of Charness and Kuhn (2011) and Fehr *et al.* (2009).

A Collection of Surveys on Market Experiments, First Edition.

Edited by Charles N. Noussair and Steven Tucker. Chapters © 2014 The Authors.

Book compilation © 2014 John Wiley & Sons, Ltd. Published 2014 by John Wiley & Sons, Ltd.

Labor relations are often contractually incomplete in the sense that effort is typically not (fully) contractible or enforceable by a third party. This feature leaves room for reciprocal motivations to play a role in the work process as workers' general job attitudes become important (Fehr and Falk, 1999). The gift-exchange game, first implemented and introduced into the literature by Fehr *et al.* (1993), was designed to mimic precisely this situation. It tests the gift-exchange hypothesis of efficiency wage theory (Akerlof, 1982; Akerlof and Yellen, 1988, 1990), according to which there is a positive (i.e., reciprocal) relationship between the wages offered by firms and the effort exerted by workers. In a gift-exchange market wage offers are binding, while workers can discretionarily choose the amount of effort they exert. Experimental evidence has shown that a positive relation between wages and effort indeed emerges in such markets. Next to providing a survey of the main results related to the existence of this positive wage-effort relation, we also report on those studies that have tried to assess the implication of these findings for policy making. In addition, the robustness of the positive wage-effort relation is surveyed showing that while it survives many institutional variations and experimental conditions, there are also some environmental factors under which gift-exchange has difficulties to emerge.

The possibility of using laboratory experiments to better understand the functioning of markets has been mostly utilized for studying causal relationships at the micro level. However, lab experiments can also be a valuable research tool for gaining insights into the effects of alternative labor policies or institutions at a macro level. Indeed, the main strengths of the experimental method, control and replication, can be very useful in the domain of macroeconomics, which traditionally relies on circumstantial field data which may suffer from data non-availability, endogeneity, or measurement error. This implies that the causal impact of a given variable, for example, an increase of a labor tax, on economic performance may be difficult to assess. Experimental labor economics can be useful in such a macroeconomics context and help to overcome some of these problems. The second part of this survey focuses on the small but growing literature of laboratory labor market experiments in macroeconomics and public finance.

2. Experimental Gift-Exchange Labor Markets

2.1 *Common Features Across Experiments*

Most experiments described in this section are based on similar implementations of the gift-exchange game. At the beginning of an experimental session, subjects are randomly assigned the roles of either firms or workers and they keep their role during the whole session. In the first stage, firms offer a contract specifying the wage. In some experiments workers have to accept what is offered while in others the contract may be rejected in favor of some outside option. In the second stage, workers decide on the level of effort they want to exert, which is costly to them but profitable to the firm. Often this two-stage game is repeated for several periods with the same or changing firm-worker pairs. In the wage formation (first) stage commonly one of three institutions is explored: bilateral bargaining, one-sided auction, or double auction markets.

In bilateral bargaining, a firm is exogenously and randomly matched with a worker either only at the beginning of the experiment or at the beginning of each period. In each period, a firm proposes a wage only to the worker with whom it has been matched.

Table 1. Effort Levels and Costs of Effort.

Effort e	0.1	0.2	0.3	0.4	0.5	0.6	0.7	0.8	0.9	1
Cost $c(e)$	0	1	2	4	6	8	10	12	15	18

In one-sided auction markets, firms publicly announce their wage offers, which can be accepted by any worker. Firms are allowed to revise their offers, often according to an improvement rule, until they are accepted or the market closes. Workers cannot make counteroffers. In double auction markets both, firms and workers, can submit and accept wage offers at any time during the trading period. In both market institutions, after a wage contract is concluded the involved firm and the worker are removed from the market for that trading period. Firms and workers who do not strike a contract receive some reservation earnings. In the most common implementation at most one contract per period can be concluded and often there is an excess supply of labor.

In the basic implementation of the second stage, the worker's costly effort choice, firms can neither punish nor reward workers for their choice. Further, all institutional features are public knowledge, including the number of firms, workers, and periods, the matching mechanism, the feasible effort levels, the costs of effort, the wage range, and the payoff functions. Wage offers may be public or private depending on the chosen market institution, but a worker's effort choice is always private information. That is, it is only revealed to the firm with which the worker has concluded a contract. Identities of trading partners are usually not revealed.

2.1.1 Effort Levels and Cost Function

Most studies reviewed here adopt one of two effort-cost schedules. In one version, costs $c(e)$ are increasing and convex in effort e as, for example, in Table 1. In the other common version costs are linear in effort.

2.1.2 Payoff Functions

Regarding the payoff functions for firms and workers there are also two commonly implemented versions. Firms' payoff function is often a version of

$$\pi^F = (v - w)e + k \tag{1}$$

or

$$\pi^F = v - w + k \tag{2}$$

where v denotes an exogenously given redemption value, w the wage, e the effort chosen by the worker, and k some lump-sum transfer.

Workers' payoff function is mostly implemented as the difference between the accepted wage, w, the incurred effort cost, $c(e)$, and some fixed costs or transfer c_0:

$$\pi^W = w - c(e) - c_0 \tag{3}$$

The parameter values are chosen such that under the assumption of material self-interest workers will never choose an effort level higher than the minimum effort, irrespective of the accepted wage. Rational and profit-maximizing firms will anticipate this and, hence, offer the lowest positive wage satisfying workers' participation constraint. The predicted outcome is thus low wages, low efforts, and most importantly no positive relationship between wages and effort levels. Alternatively, the gift-exchange hypothesis (Akerlof, 1982) postulates a positive correlation between wage offers and effort provision and, in consequence, higher than minimum wages and higher than minimum effort levels.[1]

2.2 Fundamental Results

This section reviews some of the seminal gift-exchange labor market experiments and summarizes by now well-established empirical results on the wage-effort relation. First, early experiments are presented, where the gift-exchange hypothesis is tested in one-shot encounters. In these experiments firms and workers meet essentially only once, leaving no or little room for reputation concerns. Next, we survey papers where reputation may play a role due to repeated interactions between the same firm-worker pair. Finally, we present evidence on the role of negative reciprocity and wage attribution on the functioning of gift-exchange labor markets.

2.2.1 Gift-Exchange in One-Shot Interactions

Evidence on the presence of gift-exchange in experimental labor markets dates back to Fehr *et al.* (1993) who have been the first to use the above described setup to test for the validity of the fair wage-effort hypothesis. They model the labor market as a one-sided auction and frame it in good market terms: buyers and sellers who choose prices and quality, respectively. The authors observe clear evidence in favor of the gift-exchange hypothesis as wages and efforts are strongly positively correlated. Consequently, wages and effort are clearly above their respective minimum level and also do not show any tendency to decline with repetion.

In a second paper, Fehr *et al.* (1998b) check whether observed high wages are due to firms' unconditional preference to pay high wages or due to workers' willingness to reciprocate high wages with high effort levels. They compare two different treatments (reciprocity treatment and control treatment), which differ only in that in the control treatment effort levels are exogenously fixed at the lowest effort level, eliminating opportunities for gift-exchange, whereas in the reciprocity treatment workers are free in their effort choices. Since subjects participated in both treatments, it could be tested if the same firms change behavior or not. It is found that the very same firms which pay rather high wages when workers can reciprocate significantly lower their offers when the effort is fixed by the experimenter. This shows that it is mostly not firms' unconditional preference to pay high wages but that those are induced by experienced and anticipated low-effort responses to low wages and, consequently, low profits.

Fehr *et al.* (1998a) are the first to study the effect of competition among workers on wages. They conduct three different treatments: a one-sided auction, called gift-exchange market, a bilateral gift-exchange (BGE), where firms and workers are exogenously matched, and a complete contract market (CCM), where the maximum effort level is exogenously enforced. By comparing the wages in CCM and gift-exchange market it could be assessed whether the high wages in the latter as found by Fehr *et al.* (1993, 1998b) are indeed attributable to gift-exchange. Comparing wages in bilateral gift-exchange, where competition in the labor market cannot play any role, with those in gift-exchange market shows to what extent competition affects wage levels. The authors find that high wages are reciprocated by high efforts, both in gift-exchange market and bilateral gift-exchange, with no tendency for this positive correlation to decline over time. Importantly, already after a few periods wages in gift-exchange market and bilateral gift-exchange coincide, indicating that labor market competition does not affect wage formation. However, wages in gift-exchange market are significantly above wages in CCM, where firms constantly try to stipulate lower wages. This indicates that in gift-exchange market firms anticipate workers' reciprocal responses and that payment of noncompetitive wages generates higher profits. In consequence, firms are unwilling to enforce low wages when there is room for workers to reciprocate with effort.

2.2.2 *Gift-Exchange and Reputation*

Employment relationships are seldom characterized by one-shot transactions. Rather employers and employees often interact repeatedly over time, which creates incentives for reciprocation, even for materially selfish workers provided that they can expect (future) material gains from it. This potential reputation effect has been first explored in Gächter and Falk (2002). They compare behavior in a one-shot (OS) treatment and a repeated game (RG) treatment, where the same firm-worker pairs interact repeatedly. In line with earlier results they find that wages and effort levels are clearly above their minimum values. Importantly, for similar wages in the two treatments, workers are more reciprocal in RG than in one-shot: this shows that repeated interaction and reputation incentives strengthen the positive wage-effort relation. An individual level analysis further suggests that even selfish workers have a strong incentive to act reciprocally, because providing high effort in response to high wage offers improves reputation and gives access to attractive wage offers.

Brown *et al.* (2004) implement three treatment conditions in order to investigate how contractual incompleteness affects the nature of market interactions and the formation of relational contracts. In all treatments, the market for contracts is organized as a one-sided auction where contracts consist of a wage, a desired effort level, and the firm's ID number. In the complete contracts treatment (C), a firm's desired effort level is exogenously enforced by the experimenter. Under the incomplete contract condition (ICF), the worker can choose any effort in the feasible range. In both these treatments, firms and workers have fixed ID numbers throughout the whole experimental session implying that a firm can address its contract offer to a specific worker in consecutive periods. In the third incomplete contract treatment (ICR), firms and workers are randomly assigned a new ID number in each period, ruling out the possibility of entering long-term relations. In each trading period firms can make private or public offers, where private offers are only transmitted to the worker with whom a firm wants to trade while public offers can be observed and accepted by any worker in the market.

The authors find that in C traders are indifferent to their trading partners' identities, whereas firms strongly prefer to trade with the same worker over many consecutive periods in ICF. In the former case, contract offers are mostly public offers and the majority of trades take place in one-shot (OS) transactions. In contrast, in the latter case, trades are usually privately initiated and bilateral relationships emerge. In C firms pay relatively low wages and appropriate the largest share of the gains from trade, whereas in ICF they pay high wages and earnings from trade are distributed rather equally. Effort is significantly higher in ICF, while in ICR, average effort drops and workers choose the minimal effort level in most cases. An important insight from this paper is that firms use high wages, together with the threat of firing, to discipline selfish workers. They adopt a policy of contingent contract renewal where relatively high effort levels are rewarded with a new contract, while relations with workers providing low effort are terminated with high probability.

Brown *et al.* (2012) implement the same three treatments in a market characterized by excess demand for labor, to check whether relational contracts emerge even in the absence of the unemployment threat. What they find is that bilateral relations between firms and workers do emerge in these markets, with wages and effort higher in ICF than in ICR and C, but are more difficult to be sustained over time. Stronger competition among firms and the lower number of long-term relationships do not affect market performance, though: aggregate effort in ICF is almost identical to that under excess supply of labor. A main reason for that is that higher wages due to excess labor demand induces workers to provide more effort.

2.2.3 *Gift-Exchange, Negative Reciprocity, and Wage Attribution*

Some of the results surveyed above have been questioned because they are obtained in an environment that may favor workers' opportunity to exhibit positive reciprocity, that is, by responding to high wages with high effort levels. However, negative reciprocity, the willingness to incur costs to punish unkind actions, may also have a role in the wage formation with potential opposite effects, as low effort responses to low wages may unravel into even lower wages and efforts.

To study the role of negative reciprocity, Fehr and Falk (1999) compare double auction labor markets where effort is endogenous (main treatment) to others where effort is exogenously fixed (control treatment), with excess supply of workers in both cases. What distinguishes this experiment is the implementation of a modified cost function, according to which a selfish money-maximizing worker should always choose the maximum effort level, because lower levels are more costly. Results from the main treatment show that workers indeed react to low wage offers by choosing non-maximal effort levels. This negatively reciprocal behavior leads firms to pay higher wages in the main treatment, even if workers underbid each other's wage offers. In contrast, in the control treatment wages tend to decrease over time and come close to the competitive equilibrium level. These findings show that firms may be reluctant to push wages down toward the competitive level, if workers have the opportunity to punish them via their effort choices. Workers' negative reciprocity generates wages that are downwardly rigid.

Charness (2004) explores bilateral gift-exchange under three experimental conditions that differ in the wage-generating mechanism. First, wages are determined by the firm, second they are generated by a draw from a bingo cage, and, third, by an assignment by a third party, the experimenter. In all cases, workers are informed whether the received wage has been assigned by either the firm or one of the external processes. In all treatments, there is a positive relationship between wages and effort levels. However, at low wages, the effort level is lower when the wage is chosen by a firm than when it is exogenously generated, suggesting the presence of negative reciprocity. That is, workers never provide costly effort when a low wage can be attributed to the firm's intention but do so when the low wage comes from an exogenous source. At high wage levels, there is essentially no difference in effort levels across treatments.[2]

The results from Charness (2004) suggest that the mechanism according to which wages are formed has a non-negligible impact on workers' performances. Maximiano *et al.* (2013) make an important step in investigating this conjecture by studying wage attribution by means of a more complex gift-exchange environment, where ownership and control are separated. Specifically, owners do not directly set a worker's wage and the manager, who actually determines the wage, does not bear the full wage costs and does also not fully benefit from workers' higher efforts. The authors consider four treatments. The bilateral condition is a standard bilateral gift-exchange setting, with a firm consisting of a single owner–manager who is directly responsible for choosing the worker's wage. In the two trilateral conditions

(TC0 and TC25),[3] the firm is owned by a shareholder, who claims most of the firm's profit, but controlled by a manager, who chooses the worker's wage. In the fourth treatment, wages are randomly determined by the experimenter (cf. Charness, 2004). In all treatments, a gift-exchange wage-effort relationship is found. The higher the wage offered, the higher the average effort level chosen by workers, irrespective of the firm's composition and whether the manager receives part of the profits or not. Importantly, the wage-effort relationship is steepest when wages are determined by a member of the firm. The finding that the wage-effort relationship does not differ among the three endogenous treatments indicates that workers are not particularly sensitive to how ownership and control are divided within the firm, but are reciprocal toward the firm as a whole.

Table 2 shows the average wage, the average effort and the estimated wage-effort relation for some prominent papers surveyed in section 2.2.

2.3 *Gift-Exchange Labor Markets and Policy Instruments*

Despite the robustness and prevalence of gift-exchange wage-effort relationships, still relatively few experimental studies investigate policy implications of it. Among others, questions that could be asked are: Are (un)employment policies similarly (in)effective in gift-exchange and complete contract markets? Do optimal and redistributive tax policies have the predicted effects in gift-exchange labor markets? Here, we survey the experimental studies asking such important policy implications of gift-exchange in labor markets.

2.3.1 *Taxation*

Riedl and Tyran (2005) are the first to examine whether and to what extent statutory tax incidence affects the performance of efficiency-wage markets and whether Tax Liability Side Equivalence[4] (tax LSE) holds in gift-exchange labor markets. Theory predicts that tax LSE also holds in gift-exchange labor markets as long as participants are only concerned with net wages and profits. Yet, if workers make their effort choices on the basis of gross wages and consider taxation as exogenous to the gift-exchange relation, tax LSE breaks down. This alternative hypothesis is suggested by a study of Kerschbamer and Kirchsteiger (2000) who show that tax LSE may break down in bilateral bargaining environments.

In a one-sided auction environment, Riedl and Tyran (2005) implement two treatments, differing in the sequence of two distinct tax regimes. In one regime the tax is levied on firms while in the other regime workers are obliged to pay the tax. Each regime lasts for 16 trading periods.

The main results are that gift-exchange emerges and that tax LSE holds in the gift-exchange labor markets under study. None of the analyzed variables, net wages, worker efforts, and net earnings, significantly differs between regimes, not even in the short run. Net wages are almost the same in both tax regimes right from the very beginning. Similarly, workers' earnings as well as firms' profits are not different across nor within treatments, thus clearly supporting tax LSE.

2.3.2 *Competition and Wage Rigidity*

A main implication of gift-exchange is that wages may be downwardly rigid because firms have no incentive to lower wages as this would lead to low performance of workers and, hence, to low profits.

Table 2. Average Wage, Average Effort, and Gift-Exchange Relation for Selected Studies.

	Average Wage	Average Effort	Gift-Exchange
Fehr et al. (1993)	72	0.4	0.0078
	[26, 126]	[0.1, 1]	OLS
Fehr et al. (1998b)			
CT	215	–	
	[210, 290]		
RT	74	0.36	0.0087
	[30, 110]	[0.1, 1]	Tobit
Falk and Gächter (2002)			
RG	57.6	0.47	0.0111
	[20, 120]	[0.1, 1]	Tobit
Brown et al. (2004)			
C	33.3	9.3	–
	[1, 100]	[1, 10]	
ICF	40.1	6.9	0.14
	[1, 100]	[1, 10]	OLS
ICR	24.3	3.3	0.11
	[1, 100]	[1, 10]	OLS
Fehr and Falk (1999)			
CC	34.96	–	
	[20, 120]		
Charness (2004)			
Wage offer by employer	54.87	0.312	0.012
	[20, 120]	[0.1, 1]	Tobit
Wage offer by random	56.97	0.344	0.0088
	[20, 120]	[0.1, 1]	Tobit
Wage offer by third party	57.87	0.317	0.0085
	[20, 120]	[0.1, 1]	Tobit
Maximiano et al. (2013)			
BC	61.45	2.41	0.0283
	[0, 100]	[1, 10]	RE
TC0	67.24	2.77	0.0378
	[0, 100]	[1, 10]	RE
TC25	49.29	2.76	0.0039
	[0, 100]	[1, 10]	RE
BCexo	64.5	3.07	0.0118
	[0, 100]	[1, 10]	RE

Note: Brackets indicate the range of possible values; the variable "gift-exchange" measures the increase of effort for an infinitesimal increase in wage; OLS = ordinary least square regression; Tobit = Tobit regression; RE = random effects regression.

As mentioned above evidence for that has been provided by Fehr and Falk (1999) who investigate wage formation in a double auction market, which is considered as particularly competitive (see, e.g., Davis and Holt, 1993). Brandts and Charness (2004) analyze whether gift-exchange is affected by the relative number of firms and workers on the market. They implement a market with excess supply of labor and a market with excess supply of firms, with wage formation in a one-sided auction. They find that wage and effort are positively correlated and that this relation is not affected by competitive pressure. Specifically, wages do not significantly differ across treatments and are generally quite high. Hence, overall the gift-exchange relation appears to be robust to increased competition on the labor market.

2.3.3 *Minimum Wage Legislation*

Experimental evidence shows that changes in the level of the minimum wage strongly affect what is perceived by individuals as a fair wage, causing important effects on reservations wages, actual wages, and employment levels.

Brandts and Charness (2004) are the first to study the effect of a minimum wage on behavior of firms and workers in a gift-exchange context with excess supply of workers. They find that the imposition of a minimum wage has an adverse effect on effort exerted by workers. Although the relationship between wage and effort remains significantly positive, the impact on effort provision is negative. At all wages effort levels are lower with than without a minimum wage.

Falk *et al.* (2006) look at the effects of a minimum wage in an economy with complete contracts, where workers provide either zero effort, if they reject a wage offer, or automatically provide maximum effort, if they accept a wage offer. They find that, when minimum wages are introduced, workers' endogenous reservation wages increase to above the level of the minimum wage. This suggests that being paid exactly the minimum wage is viewed as unfair by workers. In addition, the introduction and removal of a minimum wage have asymmetric effects. If existing minimum wages are removed reservation wages only marginally decrease and remain substantially above those prevailing before the introduction of the minimum wage.

Owens and Kagel (2010) find partly contrasting results. They observe that the introduction of the minimum wage results in an increase in average wages but also that dropping the minimum wage leads to a decrease in both average wages and average effort. When a minimum wage is introduced the effects on effort levels differ depending on the wage rate. At lower wage rates and, in particular, in the neighborhood of the minimum wage, a reduction in effort is detected, while no systematic effects on effort levels are found for higher wages.

Overall the evidence of the effect of minimum wages on provided effort is mixed. Importantly, however, the surveyed studies show that on the one hand, the minimum wage increases average wages inducing reciprocal workers to exert more effort. On the other hand, the minimum wage may alter subjects' fairness perceptions perhaps due to a reference point effect (Kahneman and Tversky, 1979; Abeler *et al.*, 2011). Consequently, wages considered fair when there is no minimum wage tend to be perceived as less fair once there is a minimum wage. The net effect of the minimum wage on effort turns out to be ambiguous and depends on the relative size of these two counteracting effects (Fehr *et al.*, 2009).

2.3.4 *Sick Pay*

Duersch *et al.* (2012) experimentally study the interaction of sick pay provision and gift-exchange between firms and workers. The authors modify the standard gift-exchange design to specifically test two hypotheses: the "gift-exchange hypothesis," which claims that workers uniformly reciprocate sick pay, and the "selection hypothesis," according to which sick pay favors the matching between those firms who offer sick pay and those workers who appreciate and reciprocate it. In each of 10 periods, employers have to choose from a menu of five contracts each consisting of a wage, w, which is paid if the worker shows up for work, and a sick pay, s, which is paid otherwise. Workers' lowest effort is equivalent to (pretending to) being sick and not showing up at the workplace. Importantly, the lowest effort may also happen for reasons outside the workers' accountability. Firms, however, can only verify if workers show up or not. Two main treatments are compared. In treatment M (Monopsony) firms and workers are exogenously and anonymously matched in each period. In treatment S (Selection) firms compete for workers and are given the possibility of hiring more than one worker.

Gift-exchange results are replicated. Moreover, offering sick pay also increases effort. However, the experimental data also show that offering sick pay contracts is not always the most profitable option for firms. In M firms sometimes even suffer losses. Interestingly, when firms have to compete for workers they earn the highest profit when choosing a contract that offers only a partial sick pay. Firms realize this and most frequently choose the contract consisting of a partial sick pay. In both treatments, sick pay contracts induce self-selection and attract more reciprocal workers. In conclusion, in the presence of gift-exchange the effectiveness of sick pay is driven by competition in the labor market.

2.3.5 *Deferred Compensation*

Huck *et al.* (2011) experimentally test Lazear's (1979) model of deferred compensation and examine the relationship between a firm's wage offer and worker's effort provision in a three-period game.[5] Four treatments are implemented.

In the main Full Commitment Treatment (FCT), firms can fully commit to future wage offers. In FCT results are mixed for both, firms and workers. Deferred compensation is observed but not all firms offer the predicted wage pattern and some workers shirk although they are incentivized not to do. In order to better understand that pattern, the authors conduct two control treatments. In the No Commitment Treatment (NCT), firms can only make non-binding promises about future payments. In the computer firm treatment (CFT), firms' wage offers are generated by a computer in order to control for the effect of outcome inequality. When there is no commitment device workers' effort and efficiency are low, as predicted. Workers do not believe wage promises and do not reciprocate to promised high future wages. Actual wages are indeed lower than promised ones. Nevertheless, there is evidence for gift-exchange but mainly within a period. Therefore, the authors conclude that the best strategy to induce high effort is not to offer a low wage early and promise a high wage later but offer a high wage right at the beginning. In the Reputation Treatment (RT), firms' past history on wage promises and actual wages is made available to workers, in order to check for reputation effects. The authors find that actually paying high wages to old workers has indeed a reputation effect and reputation may work as a commitment device.

2.3.6 *Gift-Exchange, Incentive Schemes, and Contract Enforcement*

Laboratory gift-exchange experiments show that reciprocity is effectively increasing worker effort when contracts are incomplete. In the field, also material incentives are used to mitigate the enforcement problem. Therefore, the question of how explicit performance incentives and gift-exchange interact with each other has been subject of several studies.

Fehr *et al.* (1997) conduct three treatments involving competitive markets with more workers than firms. In each treatment, firms specify a wage, a desired effort level, and a fine imposed if a worker is detected shirking. In the no-reciprocity-treatment (NRT) contract terms are exogenously enforced by the experimenter; in the weak-reciprocity-treatment (WRT) workers who accept a contract choose an effort level, and a random device determines whether the firms are able to verify shirking; the strong-reciprocity-treatment (SRT) has an additional third stage in which firms can also respond reciprocally, by costly rewarding or punishing workers after they observe actual effort choices.

The results from WRT show that firms' behavior is affected by reciprocity considerations, as the number of generous offers is significantly higher than in the NRT. Nevertheless, shirking is also quite prevalent. In SRT firms demand and succeed in enforcing much higher effort levels than in WRT. They punish workers who shirk and reward both those who provide the desired or more effort. In response workers reciprocate high wages with high efforts. This leads to a higher aggregate monetary payoff, meaning that both workers and firms are better off in SRT.

Fehr and Gächter (2002) examine the possibility that explicit incentives may create a hostile atmosphere of threat and distrust undermining reciprocity-based extra effort. They conduct a gift-exchange experiment under two treatments, a trust treatment (TT), which resembles a standard gift-exchange game under the one-sided auction trading rules and an incentive treatment (IT) where firms can punish shirking workers.

In TT firms offer higher wages and demand higher effort levels than in IT, resulting in higher actual average effort. The authors observe that the lower effort levels in IT are not caused by lower wage offers but that low wages are a response to the reduction of the workers' willingness to reciprocate. Further, the data show that efficiency is lower in IT, due to the reduced effort levels. The authors conjecture that the negative incentive effect is due to framing the material inventive as punishment, which workers may perceive as unkind. To test this, an additional bonus treatment (BT) where a shirking worker, instead of paying a fine, does not receive a bonus if caught shirking, is conducted. The incentive structure is exactly the same in IT and BT. Nevertheless, large behavioral differences are observed in IT and BT. With the material incentive framed as bonus, effort levels are significantly higher than when it is framed as punishment.

Fehr et al. (2007) compare the performance of three types of contracts. In the incentive contract the principal offers a wage, a required effort level, and a fine paid in case the agent is caught shirking. If the principal invests in a verification technology, agents' effort choices are observed with the exogenous probability $p = 1/3$. In the trust contract, the principal offers a fixed wage to the agent and asks for high effort in return. Lastly, the bonus contract is similar to the trust contract, except that the principal announces that s/he might pay a bonus if the agent exerts more effort than required. The authors conduct a bilateral gift-exchange experiment with two treatments. In the trust-incentive treatment (TI) principals could choose between the trust contract and the incentive contract and in the bonus-incentive treatment (BI) all three contracts could be chosen. In TI it is found that incentive contracts are chosen by most principals and increasingly preferred over time as they perform better from the firm's perspective. Workers' effort levels and principals' payoffs are higher with incentive contracts than with trust contracts. In stark contrast, in the BI treatment bonus contracts are chosen much more often than the incentive contracts and the trust contract is never chosen. Hence, on the one hand, in TI fairness concerns are not powerful enough to contradict standard theory prediction that incentive contracts are preferred to trust contracts. On the other hand, when a non-binding promise to pay bonuses is introduced, the results contrast with what standard theory postulates.

In a subsequent paper, Fehr and Schmidt (2007) wonder whether combining a bonus and an incentive contract helps improving efficiency. Principals can choose between a pure bonus contract and a combined contract, which therefore offers both a fine paid in case of detected shirking and a voluntary bonus. Still, the authors find that the vast majority of principals prefer the pure bonus contract, which also turns out to be more efficient. These results seem to support the idea that, in many cases, explicit negative incentives may crowd out intrinsic motivation, as agents might perceive a fine as a hostile act and the choice of monitoring the agents as a signal of distrust.

Eriksson and Villeval (2012) study whether symbolic but costly reward ("respect" in the authors' words) for high effort affects gift-exchange. They find that the majority of employers do not send symbolic rewards. More symbolic rewards are sent when there is competition on the labor market than when it is balanced and they are mainly used to initiate longer-term relationships. Interestingly, receiving rewards induce higher efforts only when the market is balanced.

Fehr et al. (1996) study incentive effects on efforts in a different environment. Specifically, they test whether the predictions of the shirking version of the efficiency wage hypothesis (Shapiro and Stiglitz, 1984), namely that higher wages and lower effort requirements reduce shirking, are borne out by the data. In the Efficiency Wage Experiments (EWE) firms with different production technologies offer contracts consisting of a wage, a required effort level, and a penalty levied on the worker in case caught shirking. The results are then compared to a Market Clearing Experiment (MCE), where the incentive to pay efficiency wages is removed by allowing the imposition of a higher penalty. In the EWE it is observed that firms make a rational and selfish use of penalties, meaning that the great majority of the chosen penalties meet the standard theoretical predictions. However, wage offers and demanded effort levels tend to lie below the predicted values, suggesting that firms' choices might be affected by risk aversion. In the MCE the market converges to the predicted values. Most importantly, the authors find support for the efficiency wage hypothesis as an increase in wage offers reduces the probability of shirking and firms try to pay job rents to induce workers not to shirk. Finally, it is shown that the existence of efficiency wages leads to involuntary unemployment.

2.4 Robustness and Extensions of Gift-Exchange Labor Markets

Gift-exchange labor market experiments have been conducted under many environmental conditions and the strong positive relationship between wage and effort has been confirmed by a large number of papers. There are, however, some conditions where gift-exchange may break down. The experiments summarized in this section propose extensions of the basic gift-exchange game design and try to assess whether and to what extent changes in the environmental features affect gift-exchange.

2.4.1 Gift-Exchange, Multi-Worker Firms, and Social Comparisons

The external validity of experimental results gathered in relatively simple environments is a challenge for experimental economics in general and for gift-exchange labor market experiments in particular. For instance, the mostly used implementation of gift-exchange markets, where employment relationships involve one employer and one employee, may limit the validity of results for cases where employers can hire more than one worker.

Maximiano et al. (2007) compare a standard one-employer–one-worker (1–1) bilateral gift-exchange game with one in which each firm has four workers (1–4). In the latter case, the firm has to pay the same wage to all workers, who then simultaneously decide how much effort to provide without knowing the effort choices of their co-workers. In both treatments, workers choose, on average, a higher effort level the higher the offered wage and the difference between treatments is small and statistically not significant. Hence, overall the wage-effort relation is robust to an increased number of workers within a firm.

The previous paper is mainly concerned with the relationship between agents at different levels in the firm hierarchy. Charness and Kuhn (2007) examine how the horizontal relationship between workers and the observation of each other's wages may affect effort choices. They match two workers with different productivity levels (high and low) with one firm. Workers know that their productivity is different from their co-workers' but they do not know the direction of this difference. Firms can offer their workers different wages. The authors also vary, in a within-subjects design, whether wage offers are public (both workers know both wages) or private (workers know only their own wage). The data show that when a co-worker's wage is secret workers' effort choices respond very strongly to their own wage. Interestingly, the same holds when workers are informed of their co-workers' wage before choosing their own effort. Hence, workers seem to be mainly concerned with their own wage offer and horizontal comparisons are either not important or wage differences are perceived as justified because of the productivity differences.

Gächter and Thöni (2010) analyze horizontal pay comparison effects when workers are equally productive. In contrast to Charness and Kuhn (2007), they find that a worker who is paid less than a co-worker significantly reduces his/her effort relative to a situation where equal wages are paid. Gächter and Thöni (2010) further analyze whether the observed pay comparison effects actually come from wage differences or are due to an aversion to intentional wage discrimination. In an additional treatment, a random device chooses workers' wages on behalf of firms. It turns out that disadvantageous wage discrimination does not result anymore in reduced effort levels and, hence, intentionality is the source of reduced efforts in case of unequal wages.

Gächter et al. (2012) go a step further and investigate whether the possibility to compare both, pay and effort, influences reciprocal behavior. In a three-person gift-exchange game, the employer chooses a wage, which can be different for different workers. In the experiment employees first observe both wages and then choose sequentially an effort level. The worker who moves second (Employee 2), therefore, also receives information about the co-worker's effort choice. The authors find that in this setting pay comparisons do not affect effort choices. However, for a given wage combination, a worker's effort depends on the co-worker's effort decision. Employee 2 exerts high effort if Employee 1 does so and tends to choose low effort if the co-worker also chooses low effort. Hence, on average reciprocity toward the employer is weakened when effort comparison is possible.

Nosenzo (forthcoming) studies pay comparison effects in a gift-exchange game where one employer is matched with two symmetric employees, and compares effort choices under three treatments: in the "pay secrecy" treatment each employee only knows his/her own wage; the two "public wages" treatments, where both wages are known to both employees, differ in how wages are determined. In one treatment the employer can choose both wages, while in the other one wage is set exogenously. The data show that information about co-workers' wages can be detrimental for effort provision. In the pay secrecy treatment effort levels are higher than in the other two treatments because with public wages employees who are paid less exert less effort. Interestingly, this holds even when co-workers' wages are chosen exogenously.

In Abeler et al. (2010), two agents are matched with one principal who chooses a wage only after having observed the effort simultaneously chosen by the agents in the first stage of a gift-exchange game. In one treatment the principal has to pay the same wage to both agents, while in a second treatment she can set different wages for the two agents. The authors find that in the equal wage treatments effort levels are significantly lower than when agents are paid individually, suggesting that agents perceive equal wages for unequal performance as unfair. In the individual wage treatment principals seem to anticipate that and pay higher wages to agents who exert higher effort. Moreover, when wages are set equal by the employer, employees who initially work hard tend to reduce effort to the level of their low-performing co-workers. The opposite occurs when workers are paid individually: those workers who initially exert low effort align with the high performers.

Siang *et al.* (2010) also test for horizontal comparisons in a bilateral gift-exchange game, under both random and fixed matching, where workers are provided with either quantitative or qualitative information about the average wage in the market.[6] Overall, it is found that information about average wages has a decreasing effect on both wage and effort in the random-matching treatments, and the opposite effect under the fixed-matching protocol.

2.4.2 *Framing*

Charness *et al.* (2004) investigate whether providing experiment participants with a comprehensive payoff table has an effect on gift-exchange. They run a standard gift-exchange game under two different conditions. In both conditions subjects are given the payoff functions and in one treatment subjects are, in addition, given a complete payoff table reporting firms and workers' payoffs for all combinations of wages and effort. The authors find that the provision of such a table, although superfluous for subjects to be able to compute payoffs, does affect behavior. Gift-exchange is observed in both treatments but the inclusion of the payoff table decreases wages and effort. Further, with the payoff table the wage-effort relationship seems to be weakened over time, especially toward the end of the experiment suggesting strategic effort choices. The authors propose two main explanations for the lowered gift-exchange but leave the ultimate reason open. On the one hand, working through the table and focusing on it may have led workers somehow to regard their effort choices and firms' wage decisions as not linked to each other. On the other hand, the payoff table might have made the distributional consequences more salient, as firms' marginal benefit resulting from an increased effort decreases as wage increases, which might induce lower effort.

2.4.3 *Stake Levels*

Fehr *et al.* (2002) study the effect of high stakes on gift-exchange. They conduct two treatments of the gift-exchange market a normal-stake condition and a high-stake condition, where in the latter the stake level was 10 times higher than in the normal-stake condition, and (Russian) subjects' earnings amounted on average to up to three monthly incomes. The introduction of high stakes does not weaken the wage-effort relationship. Wages are above the competitive level and quite similar for normal and high stakes. The impact of increased stakes on effort is negligible as well. A comparison of behavior under normal stakes with Austrian subjects show that the reported results are not due to Russian subjects' characteristics. Overall, the results indicate that market institutions are more important in shaping behavior than stake size.

2.4.4 *Market Size*

The issue of how market size might affect behavior in a gift-exchange environment is addressed in Brandts *et al.* (2010). In the small market there are 7 traders (5 workers and 2 firms), while the large market has 21 trading agents (15 workers and 6 firms). In each market trades occur through two different market institutions: double auctions (DA) or bilateral negotiations (BN). The experiment lasts 30 periods in which during the first 10 rounds, subjects trade only through DA. In the successive 20 periods, at the beginning of each period, firms choose whether to enter the DA or privately negotiate with a worker. The worker, in turn, indicates whether or not s/he is willing to enter the BN. Thereafter, the game proceeds with wage offers and subsequent effort decisions. The authors report that gift-exchange is robust to the variation of the number of traders in the market. In both treatments effort and wages are positively correlated and wages and efforts in BN are higher than in DA. In both treatments aggregate surplus is considerably higher in periods 11–30 (when DA and BN coexist in the markets) than in the first 10 periods (with only DA). Hence, the market institution is more important in shaping behavior than the market size.

2.4.5 *Transparency*

In many employment relationships the amount of effort exerted by the workers is not perfectly observable by the employer, a factor that is ignored in standard gift-exchange experiments. The question arises if workers would still be reciprocal in a situation where hidden actions are possible and, consequently, if it is still profitable for firms to offer generous wages.

Irlenbusch and Sliwka (2005) address this issue by investigating how transparency of effort choices affects gift-exchange. In their experiment, a firm's payoff is given by the sum of a worker's effort and a random component. Two treatments are conducted. In the revealed-effort treatment, firms are perfectly informed about both components of their payoff, whereas in the hidden-effort treatment, firms only observe their payoff without any further detail. Their results show that the positive wage-effort relation is present in both treatments, but it is much stronger in the revealed effort treatment. When exploring the results in more detail the authors find that actual effort levels are similar across treatments, but that wages in the hidden effort treatment are higher. The hidden effort treatment is also characterized by much more heterogeneity in agents' behavior. It seems that some agents take advantage of the principal not being able to observe their effort while others are willing to exert even more than the efficient effort level in order to signal their willingness to reciprocate.

2.4.6 *Subject Pool*

Hannan *et al.* (2002) conducted two experiments with two different U.S. subject pools, MBAs and undergraduate students to explore the effect of work experience. They also compared their behavior to that of Austrian students in Fehr *et al.* (1998b) in order to investigate whether characteristics of the U.S. society (e.g., a more individualistic approach to work) leads to different results in terms of gift-exchange. The implemented gift-exchange labor markets consist of one-sided auctions and firms were either of high or low productivity. When comparing U.S. students, MBAs, and Austrian students, the authors find that all three subject pools exhibit reciprocal preferences, but that U.S. students are less reciprocal than MBAs and Austrian students. Similarly, MBAs' wage offers are found to be considerably higher than those of U.S. students. In order to explore whether U.S. students' weaker gift-exchange is due to not being familiar with gift-exchange labor markets, the authors conduct another treatment where firms have to submit also a desired effort level. In comparison to the first experiment U.S. students exert more effort, which suggest that different work experiences of undergraduates and MBAs may account for differences in their effort responses.

2.4.7 Gift-Exchange in Field Experiments

Some papers study gift-exchange in the field and provide evidence that social preferences identified in the laboratory map into fieldwork environments.

Gneezy and List (2006) hire people to perform two real-effort tasks, one involving work in a library and the other involving door-to-door fund-raising. In both cases, the participants know that it is a one-time employment. Two treatments per task are conducted. In both treatments a fixed wage per hour is promised. In the first one the promised wage is paid (noGift) and in the second, after the task has been explained, participants are told that they will be actually paid a higher wage (Gift). Consistent with the laboratory evidence, in the early hours of the task higher wages are reciprocated by higher effort levels, as effort in the Gift treatment is markedly higher than in the noGift treatment. This effect, however, vanishes over time. After a few hours, effort levels in the two treatments are statistically indistinguishable.

Kube *et al.* (2012) analyze how strongly workers reciprocate monetary and non-monetary gifts with higher productivity in a real-effort task. They hire students to enter data into a computer. In the benchmark treatment all students are paid an announced wage. In the cash treatment participants receive a monetary gift, while in the bottle treatment they are given a thermos bottle of equivalent monetary value. They also run additional control treatments. In one of them, the bottle's market price is explicitly mentioned, to rule out the possibility that workers might overestimate its market value. In the choice treatment, conducted to elicit preferences for receiving cash or the bottle, subjects can choose between the bottle and the money. Finally, in the origami treatment that is run to test whether the time and effort invested in the provision of gifts matter, the firm gives the workers money in the form of an origami.

The results show that the nature of gifts determines the strength of reciprocal behavior. The cash gift has only a statistically insignificant impact on workers' productivity, while the bottle starkly increases workers' performance and the effect remains large throughout the experiment. This result is closely replicated in the treatment where subjects are informed about the price of the bottle. Further, when workers can choose between gifts, almost all of them opt for the cash gift and workers' output is the same than in the no choice bottle treatment and, thus, higher than in the no choice money treatment. This suggests that time and effort the firm spends for a gift matter for the workers. Intriguingly, the data show that workers reciprocate a money gift of the same value as in the cash treatment but presented in origami form with an output level that is 30% higher.

In Kube *et al.* (forthcoming) workers are hired by a university library to catalog books. In the baseline treatment, workers are paid the announced wage. In two other treatments, workers are informed, right before performing their task, that they would be paid either less or more than announced, respectively. They find that, while unexpected wage cuts severely and persistently reduce productivity, analogous wage increases do not lead to higher output levels.

Hennig-Schmidt *et al.* (2010) hire students for updating a database. Next to the baseline treatment, where all workers are paid the same wage, the authors perform some treatments where workers receive an unexpected pay raise and some others where workers are also informed about the wage increase of a peer group.

They observe that neither increases in the own wage nor information on peers' wages seem to affect workers' effort. Hence, contrary to most laboratory and other field experiments no positive wage-effort relation is observed. The authors complement the analysis with a real-effort lab experiment, where employees either receive a flat wage or are exposed to an unexpected wage increase under two conditions, differing in whether the information about the employer's surplus from work effort is available or not. In the absence of surplus information there seems to be no positive relation between wage and effort. However, when surplus information is provided this relation is observed. In fact, the positive wage-effort relation is quite steep and a pay raise is profitable for employers. This result suggests that workers' being aware of the employer's surplus may be crucial for reciprocal inclinations to come into play.

2.5 *Summary*

Laboratory gift-exchange experiments have identified some broad regularities. Reputation incentives (help) discipline workers and induce them to provide higher effort (Gächter and Falk, 2002; Brown *et al.*, 2004, 2012). Effort responds to the mechanism underlying the wage formation process, at least at low wages, with stronger reactions when (low) wages are intentional (Charness, 2004), but not to the internal composition of the firm (Maximiano *et al.*, 2013). Effort decisions are affected by the introduction or the removal of a minimum wage. An increased minimum wage may induce more effort through higher wages. However, it also shifts subjects' reference point with counterproductive effects on effort once the minimum wage is dropped (Brandts and Charness, 2004; Falk *et al.*, 2006; Owens and Kagel, 2010).

Evidence on the effect of explicit incentives on effort provision is a bit mixed. On the one hand, the possibility for principals to punish or reward agents seems to increase effort levels (Fehr *et al.*, 1997). On the other hand, a decision by a principal to monitor or punish an agent can create an atmosphere of distrust and undermine gift-exchange, while nonbinding promises to pay bonuses for workers' performance can induce more effort and outperform explicit incentive contracts (Fehr and Gächter, 2002; Fehr *et al.*, 2007; Fehr and Schmidt, 2007). In case of deferred compensation contracts, however, unenforceable promises about future payments can reduce effort (Huck *et al.*, 2011).

Duersch *et al.* (2012) show that sick pay provision increases effort and attracts more reciprocal workers, even though offering sick pay contracts is a profitable option for firms only when they have to compete for workers.

Workers' effort choices can be driven by pay comparison considerations. When workers are characterized by different productivity levels wage differences do not affect effort decisions, suggesting that unequal wages for unequal performance are not perceived as unfair. A detrimental effect on effort is found when workers are all equally productive and principals offer different wages (Charness and Kuhn, 2007; Abeler *et al.*, 2010; Gächter *et al.*, 2012; Gächter and Thoni, 2010; Nosenzo, forthcoming). Workers' behavior can depend on co-workers' effort decisions when both effort and pay comparison information are made available (Gächter *et al.*, 2012).

The way decision tasks are presented in the laboratory may also affect behavior. The provision of a complete payoff table, for instance, significantly decreases wages and effort (Charness *et al.*, 2004). Impact of increased stakes on effort seems negligible (Fehr *et al.*, 2002) and so is the effect of the number of traders in the market (Brandts *et al.*, 2010). Effort choices may differ across subject pools (Hannan *et al.*, 2002).

Field experiments show that gift-exchange identified in the laboratory to a large extent map into field work environments (Gneezy and List, 2006). Effort also responds to the nature of gifts as workers exert more effort in response to a non-monetary gift (Kube *et al.*, 2012).

Laboratory results that pay comparison information may have little influence on effort choices are confirmed in the field (Hennig-Schmidt *et al.*, 2010). Finally, there is also strong field evidence of negative reciprocity when wages are cut (Kube *et al.*, forthcoming).

3. Experimental Labor Markets in Macroeconomics and Public Finance

Laboratory experiments can be a valuable research tool for investigating aggregate economic phenomena. In this section we survey papers that try to assess the impact of taxation on economic performance, mainly focusing on the relation between (labor) taxation and unemployment. In a series of studies, Riedl and van Winden (2001, 2007, 2012) show the existence of a vicious circle in the interaction between wage taxes and unemployment and suggest that shifting the tax burden from labor to sales or production can alleviate the unemployment-boosting effect of taxes. Blumkin *et al.* (2012) test the response of labor supply to various forms of taxation and argue that shifting taxation from labor to consumption increases labor supply, while Ortona *et al.* (2008) find the same effect on effort provision coming from destining taxes to insure subjects against risk and to finance public goods.

Riedl and van Winden (2001) are the first to use laboratory experiments to investigate the nexus between labor taxation and unemployment in a full-fledged economy. In particular, they study the effects of a wage tax (WT) system to finance unemployment benefits on the performance of an economy, mainly in reaction to tax adjustments due to a budget deficit or surplus. The economy under consideration is graphically depicted in Figure 1.

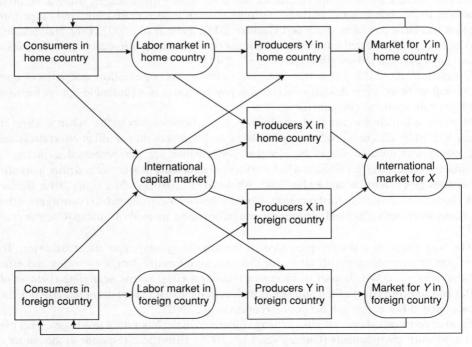

Figure 1. Flow Diagram of the Riedl and van Winden (2001, 2007, 2012) Economy.

It consists of two countries, a small "home" country and a large "foreign" country, where two inputs, capital K and labor L, and two outputs, X and Y, can be traded. In each country, goods X and Y are produced in two separate sectors with the help of inputs L and K. These inputs are, respectively, traded on a local labor market (separate in each country) and on an international capital market. Similarly, the market for commodity X is international, while the market for commodity Y is local. Consumers derive utility from leisure, the unsold units of labor, and the consumption of X and Y. They are endowed with some units of labor and capital, and they obtain an unemployment benefit for each unsold unit of their labor endowment. The government finances these benefits with the help of a tax on employed labor paid by producers. Two tax regimes are implemented in each country. During the first part of the experimental session, wage taxes are held constant. During the second part, the wage tax rate is adjusted to the previous period's deficit or surplus in the government budget.

Riedl and van Winden (2001) find that in the constant tax regime both countries experience a budget deficit in all periods, which does not decrease over time. They also show that, while unemployment levels converge to the equilibrium values, nominal wages are very low in both countries. A thorough analysis of consumers and producers behavior shows that the former supply too much labor at given prices, while the latter have a tendency to employ too few labor units. This supports the so-called risk-compensated price-adjustment hypothesis, which was first detected in pure commodity markets by Noussair *et al.* (1995). When producers make their input decisions market conditions, prevailing at the time consumers buy their products, are usually unknown, meaning that producers face uncertainty about the revenues they can make by selling their products. Given this price uncertainty, risk-averse producers demand less labor than predicted in equilibrium. Producers and consumers combined behavior leads to an upward trend of unemployment rates and drive nominal wages down, which explains the observed budget deficit. In the dynamic tax regime, an initial considerable increase in the tax rates is observed as the previous periods' budget is not balanced. Increased taxes help to decrease the budget deficit over time. However, it comes at the cost of strong negative effects on the performance of the economy as a whole. In both countries unemployment rates increase and real GDP sharply decreases.

In Riedl and van Winden (2007), the same setup is used to compare a closed with an international economy. Overall, the data confirm the earlier results. When the tax rate is constant, in all economies a budget deficit occurs already in early periods. The same excess supply of labor is observed, which is accompanied by producers' reluctance to buy inputs and a downward trend of wages. Together this accounts for the observed budget deficits. Once the dynamic tax regime is introduced, in all economies the deficit becomes smaller due to higher tax rates but the unemployment level increases, an effect that is due to the low employment of both factors (because of price uncertainty), which is exacerbated for labor through the wage tax.

These findings show that there exists a vicious circle in the interaction between wage tax and unemployment. This strongly suggests that shifting taxation from labor to consumption or sales may have beneficial effects on both production and employment. To explore this, Riedl and van Winden (2012) introduce a sales-tax-cum-labor-subsidy (STLS) system in the above described economy and compared it to a pure wage tax system. Two treatments are implemented. In the baseline treatment, in both the home country and the foreign country unemployment benefits are financed with a wage tax. In the alternative treatment, in the home country the wage tax system is substituted by the STLS system while the wage tax system prevails in the foreign country. Next to shifting the tax from labor to sales, in the STLS system producers also receive a subsidy equal to the unemployment benefit for each unit of labor they employ. Again, a constant tax regime is followed by a regime where the tax rate adjusts to previous periods' budget surpluses.

In the constant tax regime basically all quantities and prices as well as economic performance indicators, such as unemployment rate and real GDP, weakly converge to the theoretically predicted equilibrium values. In the small country the unemployment rate is initially higher when the STLS system is effective but tends to decrease over time, despite high sales taxes. Such a development is not observed under the wage tax system. Moreover, declining unemployment under the STLS system is associated with an increase in the budget surplus of the small country, while wage taxes are systematically accompanied by budget deficits. A similar pattern is observed for the real GDP. At the end of the constant tax regime the economies under the wage tax system face budget deficits, while budget surpluses are generated in the small country under the STLS system. Consequently, the transition to the variable tax regime is characterized by an increase in wage tax rates and by a decrease in sales taxes. The increasing tax rates in the wage tax system lead to increasing unemployment and a decrease in real GDP, while at the same time the burden from the budget deficit merely weakens. In stark contrast, in the alternative tax system the initial decline in sales tax rates reduces unemployment and boosts real GDP. In addition, the budget immediately balances and stabilizes over time. Overall, Riedl and van Winden's (2012) results show that the STLS system leads to a significantly better economic performance compared to the wage tax system. These differential results are mainly driven by producers' reluctance to incur upfront costs when they are uncertain about output prices. Importantly, producers seem to perceive uncertainty differently under the two tax systems because receiving a labor subsidy and paying taxes according to sales revenues basically gives producers the opportunity to share their risk with the government.

Blumkin et al. (2012) experimentally test the equivalence between consumption and wage taxes in a real-effort experiment where subjects have to decide how to allocate their time between labor and leisure. Subjects receive income according to their performance in a real-effort task, which they are then asked to allocate between two consumption goods. They also receive a payment for each unit of leisure consumed. The experiment consists of three parts: the first two are meant to measure and control for subjects' productivity and pretax labor-leisure preferences, respectively. Finally, in the third part in one treatment a labor income tax (IT) and in the other treatments a theoretically equivalent consumption tax (CT) is introduced.

Although theoretically equivalent, worker-consumers may work more and consume less leisure in presence of a consumption tax because of money illusion. That is, individuals may tend to think in nominal and not in real terms (for empirical evidence on money illusion see, e.g., Fehr and Tyran, 2001). In that case labor income taxes and consumption taxes may be perceived differently when the labor supply decision has to be made. When subjects make their decision the labor income tax is salient whereas the consumption tax is not. In consequence, subjects would work more in the consumption tax treatment than in the income tax treatment. This is indeed what the authors find. Specifically, those worker-consumers who reduce their labor supply when a tax is introduced, reduce it significantly more in the income tax treatment. In line with Riedl and van Winden (2012), this result suggests that shifting taxation from labor to consumption might potentially lead to welfare improvements, with higher utility for individuals and unchanged government tax revenues.[7]

Ortona et al. (2008) investigate the relation between labor supply and taxation when tax revenues are used for the production of public goods. They conduct a real-effort experiment and compare the labor supply in two states of the world. In a so-called state of nature (SN) there is a certain risk to lose part of the earned income and there are no taxes, insurance, and public goods. In a welfare state (WS) treatment, the same risk is partially insured and a proportional income tax and a public good exist. Their main result is that subjects work more under WS than under SN, which suggests that the fact that the returns from taxes are used to protect subjects against risk and provide public goods does not reduce labor supply and possibly increases it.

4. Conclusions

Laboratory experiments have entered labor economics and the generated results have significantly increased our knowledge on a variety of aspects. In this paper we have surveyed part of this literature and concentrated on two main areas. The first part has been devoted to the behavioral consequences of contractual incompleteness in a gift-exchange environment and in the second part more macroeconomics-oriented experiments have been presented, which mainly focus on the interaction between taxation and labor market performance.

Many employment relations are often contractually incomplete in terms of effort that workers are required to exert. In such contexts, workers' reciprocal inclinations play an important role in determining the overall surplus and profit of the firm. Laboratory experiments provide abundant evidence that a sizable share of people exhibits fairness concerns and show that reciprocity often can substitute for the absence of a formal contract enforcement device. It is now a well-established result that a positive relationship between the wages offered by firms and the effort exerted by workers exists, and that employers are actually willing to offer wages higher than the prevailing minimum to elicit higher effort.

The importance of gift-exchange in employer–employee relations has several policy implications. For instance, it has been shown that gift-exchange wages turn out to be downwardly rigid, speaking to Bewley's (1999) book title "Why wages don't fall during recessions." A consequence is that the introduction of a minimum wage may have unintended effects as it has been shown that a minimum wage may change workers' reference point of a fair wage and, hence, affect their effort provision. Further, the interaction between reciprocal inclinations and various incentive schemes has to be carefully taken into account as it does not necessarily hold that explicit incentives will have unambiguous positive effects on effort. In fact, explicit incentives may crowd out intrinsic motivation as agents may consider a fine or a punishment as a hostile act or being monitored as a signal of distrust, which may induce lower effort levels.

The positive relationship between wage and effort has been confirmed under a broad range of conditions. Nevertheless, the generalizability of gift-exchange results to more complex field environments has sometimes been questioned. Recently, scholars have started to study situations where employers can hire more than one worker, focusing in particular on the interplay between reciprocity and wage and effort comparisons. Overall also in these studies gift-exchange is observed. However, the strength of it may hinge on details of the environment. For instance, effort comparisons seem to have a stronger impact on workers' effort choices than wage comparisons.

Also, only recently field experiments have been used to investigate gift-exchange. The empirical results of the few studies are overall verifying the laboratory results, although some find only a weak wage-effort relationship. In the field, it seems that a wage cut has stronger effects than a wage increase and non-monetary gifts have a stronger effect than purely financial ones. An important open question is also the longevity of gift-exchange. As field experiments are almost always less controlled than laboratory setups, it is not clear yet what precisely is behind the larger variation in outcomes in field settings. It seems clear that much more research is required to filter out the institutional details that enhance or hamper gift-exchange in work relationships in the field.

The second part of this survey has been dedicated to the relatively small but important set of experiments aimed at assessing the impact of fiscal policies on the labor market and more general economic performance. These results show the existence of a vicious circle in the interaction between wage taxes and unemployment, because increasing labor taxes to balance budget deficits strongly and negatively affect overall economic performance. The findings suggest that shifting the tax burden from labor to sales or production might alleviate this effect. This research also explores conditions under which imposing a tax might foster effort provision. For instance, it is found that shifting taxation from labor to consumption increases labor supply. Overall, the number of laboratory experiments explicitly aiming at labor market questions traditionally belonging to macroeconomics and public finance is still very small. Interestingly, it is precisely these more traditional areas in economics that lately have been criticized by a skeptical public opinion. More experimental research in the laboratory (as well as the field) investigating such important questions as the perception of salience of different forms of labor taxation and the behavioral equivalence of theoretically equivalent policy interventions could be very informative for these fields too. Moreover, most of the experimental labor research takes place in a partial equilibrium setting where labor relationships and labor markets are assumed to operate on an isolated island. This has been an important and useful restriction in order to generate first clean results. Now the evidence and our knowledge have accumulated so much that time seems ripe to make the step out of the partial world and investigate more general market interactions in labor relations as it has already been done in international trade and other interactive markets experiments (Lei and Noussair, 2007; Noussair *et al.*, 1995, 2007).

Notes

1. The gift-exchange wage-effort relationship can be rationalized by assuming outcome-based social preferences (e.g., Fehr and Schmidt, 1999; Bolton and Ockenfels, 2000), intention-based reciprocal motives (Rabin, 1993; Dufwenberg and Kirchsteiger, 2004), and a mixture of both (Levine, 1998; Falk and Fischbacher, 2006).
2. Pereira *et al.* (2006) also find some evidence for negative reciprocity which may be caused by a framing effect similar to those observed in dictator allocation experiments (List, 2007; Bardsley, 2008).
3. In TC0 the manager is paid a fixed wage and in TC25 condition the manager earns 25% of the firm's profit.
4. Tax LSE states that "the statutory incidence (i.e., who legally pays a tax) is irrelevant for economic incidence (i.e., who bears the tax burden)" (Riedl and Tyran, 2005).
5. In deferred compensation contracts workers are underpaid in early years of their career and overpaid in later years. Theoretically, they induce higher effort because future payments within the firm always exceed future payment elsewhere (Lazear, 1979). However, since firms can renege on future payments, the optimality of deferred contracts depends on the existence of an effective commitment mechanism.

6. More precisely, workers are informed whether the employer offers a wage which is 5% larger or smaller than the average wage across markets.
7. A related salience effect of taxation is also found for consumer goods by Chetty *et al.* (2009).

References

Abeler, J., Altmann, S., Kube, S. and Wibral, M. (2010) Gift exchange and workers' fairness concerns: when equality is unfair. *Journal of the European Economic Association* 8: 1299–1324.

Abeler, J., Falk, A., Goette, L. and Huffman, D. (2011) Reference points and effort provision. *American Economic Review* 101: 470–492.

Akerlof, G.A. (1982) Labor contracts as partial gift exchange. *Quarterly Journal of Economics* 97: 543–569.

Akerlof, G.A. and Yellen, J.L. (1988) Fairness and unemployment. *American Economic Review* 78: 44–49.

Akerlof, G.A. and Yellen, J.L. (1990) The fair wage-effort hypothesis and unemployment. *Quarterly Journal of Economics* 105: 255–283.

Bardsley, N. (2008) Dictator game giving: altruism or artefact? *Experimental Economics* 11: 122–133.

Bewley, T.F. (1999) *Why Wages Don't Fall During a Recession*. Cambridge, MA: Harvard University Press.

Blumkin, T., Ruffle, B. and Ganun, Y. (2012) Are income and consumption taxes ever really equivalent? Evidence from a real-effort experiment with real goods. *European Economic Review* 56: 1200–1219.

Bolton, G. and Ockenfels, A. (2000) ERC: a theory of equity, reciprocity and competition. *American Economic Review* 90: 166–193.

Brandts, J. and Charness, G. (2004) Do labour market conditions affect gift exchange? Some experimental evidence. *Economic Journal* 114: 684–708.

Brandts, J., Gërxhani, K., Schram, A. and Ygosse-Battisti, J. (2010) Size doesn't matter! Gift exchange in experimental labor markets. *Journal of Economic Behavior & Organization* 76: 544–548.

Brown, M., Falk, A. and Fehr, E. (2004) Relational contracts and the nature of market interactions. *Econometrica* 72: 747–780.

Brown, M., Falk, A. and Fehr, E. (2012) Competition and relational contracts: the role of unemployment as a disciplinary device. *Journal of the European Economic Association* 10: 887–907.

Charness, G. (2004) Attribution and reciprocity in an experimental labor market. *Journal of Labor Economics* 22: 665–688.

Charness, G. and Kuhn, P. (2007) Does pay inequality affect worker effort? Experimental evidence. *Journal of Labor Economics*. 25: 693–723.

Charness, G. and Kuhn, P. (2011) Lab labor: what can labor economists learn from the lab? In *Handbook of Labor Economics* (Vol. 4A, pp. 229–330). North Holland: Elsevier.

Charness, G., Frechette, G. and Kagel, J. (2004) How robust is laboratory gift exchange?. *Experimental Economics* 7: 189–205.

Chetty, R., Looney, A. and Kroft, K. (2009) Salience and taxation: theory and evidence. *American Economic Review* 99: 1145–1177.

Davis, D.D. and Holt, C.A. (1993) Experimental Economics. Princeton, NJ: Princeton University Press.

Duersch, P., Oechssler, J. and Vadovic, R. (2012) Sick pay provision in experimental labor markets. *European Economic Review* 56: 1–19.

Dufwenberg, M. and Kirchsteiger, G. (2004) A theory of sequential reciprocity. *Games and Economic Behavior* 47: 268–298.

Eriksson, T. and Villeval, M.C. (2012) Respect and relational contracts. *Journal of Economic Behavior & Organization* 81: 286–298.

Falk, A. and Fischbacher, U. (2006) A theory of reciprocity. *Games and Economic Behavior* 54: 293–315.

Falk, A., Fehr, E. and Zehnder, C. (2006) Fairness perceptions and reservation wages. The behavioral effects of minimum wage laws. *The Quarterly Journal of Economics* 121: 1347–1381.

Fehr, E. and Falk, A. (1999) Wage rigidity in a competitive incomplete contract market. *Journal of Political Economy* 107: 106–134.

Fehr, E. and Gächter, S. (2002) Do incentive contracts crowd out voluntary cooperation? IEW Working Papers No. 034.

Fehr, E. and Schmidt, K.M. (1999) A theory of fairness, competition and co-operation. *Quarterly Journal of Economics* 114: 817–868.

Fehr, E. and Schmidt, K.M. (2007) Adding a stick to the carrot? The interaction of bonuses and fines. *American Economic Review* 97: 177–181.

Fehr, E. and Tyran, J.-R. (2001) Does money illusion matter? *American Economic Review* 91: 1239–1262.

Fehr, E., Kirchsteiger, G. and Riedl, A. (1993) Does fairness prevent market clearing? An experimental investigation. *Quarterly Journal of Economics* 108: 437–460.

Fehr, E., Kirchsteiger, G. and Riedl, A. (1996) Involuntary unemployment and non-compensating wage differentials in an experimental labour market. *Economic Journal* 106: 106–121.

Fehr, E., Gächter, S. and Kirchsteiger, G. (1997) Reciprocity as a contract enforcement device: experimental evidence. *Econometrica* 65: 833–860.

Fehr, E., Kirchler, E., Weichbold, A. and Gächter, S. (1998a) When social norms overpower competition: gift exchange in experimental labor markets. *Journal of Labor Economics* 16: 324–351.

Fehr, E., Kirchsteiger, G. and Riedl, A. (1998b) Gift exchange and reciprocity in competitive experimental markets. *European Economic Review* 42: 1–34.

Fehr, E., Fischbacher, U. and Tougareva, E. (2002) Do high stakes and competition undermine fairness? Evidence from Russia. IEW Working Paper No. 120.

Fehr, E., Klein, A. and Schmidt, K. (2007) Fairness and contract design. *Econometrica* 75: 121–154.

Fehr, E., Goette, L. and Zehnder, C. (2009) A behavioral account of the labor market: the role of fairness concerns. *Annual Review of Economics* 1: 355–384.

Gächter, S. and Thöni, C. (2010) Social comparison and performance: experimental evidence on the fair wage-effort hypothesis. *Journal of Economic Behavior & Organization* 76: 531–543.

Gächter, S., Nosenzo, D. and Sefton, M. (2012) The impact of social comparisons on reciprocity. *Scandinavian Journal of Economics* 114: 1346–1367.

Gneezy, U. and List, J.A. (2006) Putting behavioral economics to work: testing for gift exchange in labor markets using field experiments. *Econometrica* 74: 1365–1384.

Hannan, R., Kagel, J. and Moser, D. (2002) Partial gift exchange in an experimental labor market: impact of subject population differences, productivity differences, and effort requests on behavior. *Journal of Labor Economics* 20: 923–951.

Hennig-Schmidt, H., Rockenbach, B. and Sadrieh, K. (2010) In search of workers' real effort reciprocity – a field and a laboratory experiment. *Journal of the European Economic Association* 8: 817–837.

Huck, S., Seltzer, A. and Wallace, B. (2011) Deferred compensation in multiperiod labor contracts: an experimental test of Lazear's model *American Economic Review* 101: 819–843.

Irlenbusch, B. and Sliwka, D. (2005) Transparency and reciprocal behavior in employment relations. *Journal of Economic Behavior & Organization* 56: 383–403.

Kagel, J.H. and Owens, M.F. (2010) Minimum wage restrictions and employee effort in incomplete labor markets: an experimental investigation. *Journal of Economic Behavior & Organization* 73: 317–326.

Kahneman, D. and Tversky, A. (1979) Prospect theory: an analysis of decision under risk. *Econometrica* 47: 263–292.

Kerschbamer, R. and Kirchsteiger, G. (2000) Theoretically robust but empirically invalid? An experimental investigation into tax equivalence. *Economic Theory* 16: 719–734.

Kube, S., Maréchal, M.A. and Puppe, C. (2012) The currency of reciprocity – gift-exchange in the workplace. *American Economic Review* 102: 1644–1662.

Kube, S., Maréchal, M.A. and Puppe, C. (forthcoming). Do wage cuts damage work morale? Evidence from a natural field experiment. *Journal of the European Economic Association*.

Lazear, E. (1979) Why is There Mandatory Retirement? *Journal of Political Economy* 87: 1261–1284.

Lei, V. and Noussair, C.N. (2007) Equilibrium selection in an experimental macroeconomy. *Southern Economic Journal* 74(2): 448–482.

Levine, D.K. (1998) Modeling altruism and spitefulness in experiments. *Review of Economic Dynamics* 1: 593–622.

List, J.A. (2007) On the interpretation of giving in dictator games. *Journal of Political Economy* 115: 482–493.

Maximiano, S., Sloof, R. and Sonnemans, J. (2007) Gift exchange in a multi-worker firm. *Economic Journal* 117: 1025–1050.

Maximiano, S., Sloof, R. and Sonnemans, J. (2013) Gift exchange and the separation of ownership and control. *Games and Economic Behavior* 77: 41–60.

Nosenzo, D. (forthcoming). Pay secrecy and effort provision *Economic Inquiry*.

Noussair, C.N., Plott, C. and Riezman, R. (1995) An experimental investigation of the patterns of international trade. *American Economic Review* 85: 462–491.

Noussair, C.N., Plott, C. and Riezman, R. (2007) Production, trade and exchange rates in large experimental economies. *European Economic Review* 51: 46–76.

Ortona, G., Ottone, S., Ponzano, F. and Scacciati, F. (2008) Labour supply in presence of taxation financing public services. An experimental approach. *Journal of Economic Psychology* 29: 619–631.

Pereira, P., Silva, N. and Silva, J. (2006) Positive and negative reciprocity in the labor market. *Journal of Economic Behavior & Organization* 59: 406–422.

Rabin, M. (1993) Incorporating fairness into game theory and economics. *American Economic Review* 83: 1281–1302.

Riedl, A. and Tyran, J. (2005) Tax liability side equivalence in gift-exchange labor markets. *Journal of Public Economics* 89: 2369–2382.

Riedl, A. and Van Winden, F. (2001) Does the wage tax system cause budget deficits? A macro-economic experiment. *Public Choice* 109: 371–394.

Riedl, A. and Van Winden, F. (2007) An experimental investigation of wage taxation and unemployment in closed and open economies. *European Economic Review* 51: 871–900.

Riedl, A. and Van Winden, F. (2012) Input versus output taxation in an experimental international economy *European Economic Review* 56: 216–232.

Shapiro, C. and Stiglitz, J.E. (1984) Equilibrium unemployment as a worker discipline device. *American Economic Review* 74: 433–444.

Siang, C.K., Requate, T. and Waichman, I. (2011) On the role of social wage comparisons in gift-exchange experiments. *Economics Letters* 112: 75–78.

3

PRICE DYNAMICS IN GENERAL EQUILIBRIUM EXPERIMENTS

Sean Crockett

Baruch College, City University of New York

1. Introduction

General equilibrium (GE) theory has fallen out of fashion. Ominous epitaphs abound: "Still dead after all these years: Interpreting the failure of general equilibrium theory" (Ackerman, 2002), "The current non-status of general equilibrium theory" (Katzner, 2010), "The intrinsic limits of modern economic theory: The emperor has no clothes" (Kirman, 1989). Many economics Ph.D. programs have de-emphasized training in GE theory; a Google search of "general equilibrium theory" AND economics AND "qualifying exam" currently returns 403 results, the same search with "game theory" produces 46,400. Following a brief review of criticism that has contributed to GE's decline, this paper will argue that evidence from laboratory experiments during the past decade suggests the theory's weaknesses have been exaggerated and can be addressed.

Criticism of GE has centered on three themes: (1) *Homo economicus* is an implausible description of human behavior; (2) GE theory puts no testable structure on how prices and expectations become coordinated on equilibrium values; and (3) Even strong restrictions on individual preferences cannot rule out "perverse" aggregate excess demand functions that can induce multiple and/or unstable equilibria. Support for (1) is well documented. Individuals tend to be loss averse and overconfident, violate Bayes' rule, discount time hyperbolically, and are influenced by nonsubstantive framing.[1] However, while such behavior violates standard assumptions in GE theory, Kirman (1989) is entirely correct when he argues, "[I]t should be noted that provided the basic [behavioral] model is one in which individuals react in some continuous way to signals (prices) it is formally equivalent to the Arrow–Debreu model." (p. 127) Thus fallible *homo economicus* does not challenge the basic structure of GE theory, and there are many large-market contexts where agents reacting to prices is a more plausible model of behavior than agents reacting to other agents directly.

The missing coordination mechanism *is* a problem acknowledged by GE theorists (e.g., Fisher, 1983; Kirman, 1989). In the basic GE model prices are *assumed* to equate the quantities

A Collection of Surveys on Market Experiments, First Edition.
Edited by Charles N. Noussair and Steven Tucker. Chapters © 2014 The Authors.
Book compilation © 2014 John Wiley & Sons, Ltd. Published 2014 by John Wiley & Sons, Ltd.

supplied and demanded in all markets; GE theory has largely focused on conditions under which such equilibrium prices exist, are unique, and maximize social welfare. Equilibrium price coordination is left to abstraction, intuitively tied to the *tâtonnement* process in which the price of a good is adjusted downward (upward) if the good is in excess supply (demand). *Tâtonnement* is usually conceived as pledges of fictitious supply and demand at announced disequilibrium prices, with trade consummated only after convergence to equilibrium.

Walker (1987) argues that Walras actually favored an out-of-equilibrium exchange interpretation of tâtonnement, and there is a small GE theory literature on out-of-equilibrium exchange (e.g., Hahn and Negishi, 1962; Uzawa, 1962; Ledyard, 1974; Hurwicz *et al.*, 1975; Friedman, 1979; Fisher, 1983). However, theorists have largely maintained the fictitious trade interpretation of tâtonnement to keep GE theory institution-free and as general as possible. So in the 1960s and 1970s microfoundations were sought to guarantee "well behaved" aggregate excess demand functions that would ensure the stability of fictitious trade tâtonnement. If tâtonnement were found to be generally stable, perhaps its fictional nature could be forgiven.

But it turns out that even individuals with smooth, convex, monotonic preferences can produce multiple and unstable equilibria. Here the question of tâtonnement stability bumps into the famous Sonnenschein–Mantel–Debreu result: Standard neoclassical preferences only imply that excess demand functions be continuous, obey Walras' law, and are homogeneous of degree zero. Thus even strongly restricted preferences can result in "messy" excess demand functions in which the uniqueness and stability of equilibria are not assured. Committed to an abstract conception of exchange that is not generally stable in order to justify its focus on competitive equilibrium, GE theory has attracted a shrinking audience within the economics profession since the mid-1970s, despite maintaining a central role as the foundation of most models in macroeconomics and finance.

There is a fourth criticism of GE theory that is less frequently articulated, its lack of empirical validation. Without a plausible model of dynamics, the application of GE theory to field data requires the assumption that markets are in equilibrium. But through the Sonnenschein–Mantel–Debreu result we know that a vast array of excess demand functions may induce the observed (equilibrium) prices, so the choice of excess demand functions for identification purposes can have a huge impact on the comparative static analyses at the heart of applied work. Thus theory often does not place sufficient restrictions on the data to be very useful, resulting in low explanatory power and the risk of misspecification. Further, observed regularities in field data have not significantly influenced refinements of GE theory, so the "anything goes" character of Sonnenschein–Mantel–Debreu remains an impediment to the successful application of GE theory.

However, laboratory experiments have substantively informed the question of price dynamics. In these studies researchers exert control over preferences, endowments, attention, and institutions, providing structure to assist in the interpretation of market dynamics. These experiments have facilitated the development of theoretical solutions to the price coordination question. Plott (2001) makes this point powerfully in his Nobel Symposium address. GE theory does not *need* well-behaved aggregate excess demand functions to make strong predictions about market outcomes. Recent laboratory studies of the Scarf (1960) and Gale (1963) instability examples (Anderson *et al.*, 2004; Crockett *et al.*, 2011, respectively) confirm that even when excess demand functions are ridiculously perverse, there remain strong regularities in price and allocation dynamics which give clear hope for recovering a general structural model of aggregate behavior in large interconnected markets. A better understanding of market dynamics makes the Sonnenschein–Mantel–Debreu result considerably less daunting.

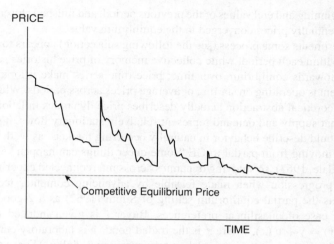

Figure 1. Sawtooth Pattern of Double Auction Prices.

2. Price Dynamics in Laboratory Exchange Economies

As the formal study of tâtonnement stability was heating up, a complementary pioneering approach to the same basic question was unveiled when Smith (1962) demonstrated the descriptive relevance of competitive equilibrium through the study of laboratory markets. Smith split human subjects into two groups, buyers and sellers of a fictitious good. Each buyer i received a card with a printed willingness to pay v_i, and each seller j received a card with a printed cost c_j. The set of all cards defined demand and supply correspondences for the experiment. To induce subjects to act as if their cards reflected their own values/costs in the market, Smith paid them for profitable trades: If a buyer and seller agreed to trade at price p, the buyer was paid in cash the amount $v_i - p$, and the seller was paid the amount $p - c_j$. Importantly, trade took place in an oral double auction.[2]

2.1 *Across-Period Dynamics*

Trade invariably took place at out-of-equilibrium prices in Smith's laboratory economy.[3] However, Smith developed an important conceptual insight for the theory of competitive equilibrium. In each session (i.e., an implementation with a new group of subjects) he studied several *periods* of exchange, each starting from the same initial endowment. After several periods, prices did indeed converge to competitive equilibrium values. This result turned out to be remarkably robust, and has been replicated hundreds if not thousands of times at laboratories around the world.

Plott (2008b) reports some emergent stylized facts from these induced value/cost double auction experiments, perhaps most importantly the "sawtooth" pattern of price convergence represented in Figure 1 (this figure has been reproduced from p. 17 of Plott and Smith (2008) with permission from the publisher).

The figure depicts transaction prices over time; a vertical line indicates a point in time at which one period ended and another began. In the first period prices initiated out-of-equilibrium and moved toward equilibrium without reaching it. In each subsequent period prices initiated between the beginning and end values of the previous period, and finished closer to equilibrium than before. Eventually prices converged to the equilibrium value.

In these experiments some process (see the following subsection) appears to guide prices to the Pareto set within each period, while collective memory of price histories serves to ratchet starting prices towards equilibrium over time; price time series make it look as if fictitious trade tâtonnement is operating on starting or average prices across periods. What seemed to be a convenient theoretical abstraction actually describes price dynamics in laboratory markets. To the extent that supply and demand represent relatively stationary flows, it's plausible this interpretation could describe behavior in naturally occurring markets, as well.[4]

However, in moving from partial to GE "some queer things can happen" even in the case of two goods (Gale, 1963), so studying dynamics across interconnected experimental markets was a natural progression when made feasible by advancing computer technology. Plott (2001) interprets the partial equilibrium setting of Smith (1962) as a 2-good GE economy for the special case of quasilinear preferences. Buyer i is given induced utility/payment function $u_i(x, y) = y + v_i(x)$, where x is the traded good, y is laboratory currency, and u is perhaps scaled by a constant to convert laboratory currency to dollars. For example, suppose $v_i(1) = 65$ and $p = 50$. Then the subject's induced utility is $u_i(x, y) = -50 + 65 = 15$, so the experimenter pays him for the difference between induced value and price. Similarly for sellers. Therefore the study of a special case of GE economies, where the set of induced utilities lay on a quasilinear grid, was already under way in the 1960s.

These quasilinear systems have proven to be remarkably stable across periods. Williams *et al.* (2000) extended this result to the case of CES preferences. Subjects were again sorted into buyers and sellers. But rather than being given induced values/costs for good x alone, buyers (sellers) were presented with a payoff (cost) table associated with buying (selling) various combinations of x and y, and the tables reflected CES utility. Buyers were also given an endowment of tokens in each period; these tokens were fiat money for buyers and worth a constant dollar amount for sellers. Double auctions for x and y were conducted simultaneously, with prices denominated in tokens. If each subject traded optimally at the unique competitive equilibrium price of x and y, all tokens would be held at the end of the period by sellers, and the aggregate supply of the two goods by sellers would equal the aggregate demand of the buyers. Similar to the quasilinear economies, Williams *et al.* report relatively strong convergence to competitive equilibrium prices.

Gjerstad (2013) also studied a 2-good CES economy with a unique competitive equilibrium. Two changes from Williams *et al.* reduced the cognitive load for subjects of participating in the experiment: Trade took place using commodity money, so that subjects only needed to transact in one market rather than two; and induced preferences were presented graphically (via indifference curves) as well as in table form, making profitable behavior more transparent. Gjerstad also increased the power of income effects in his parameterization relative to Williams *et al.*, potentially serving to destabilize prices. He reports convergence across periods toward the competitive equilibrium price in all sessions, although in some sessions prices had not (at least yet) converged.[5]

Thus laboratory economies *can* converge to competitive equilibrium across periods. But *must* they? And if there exist multiple equilibria, is there bias in the equilibrium selected? These are questions at the heart of GE theory. Experiments designed to answer these questions have focused on two alternative models of dynamics, Walrasian and Marshallian.

Walrasian adjustment, or tâtonnement, assumes some price p for good x at any time t, then treats the quantities demanded and supplied, $X_D(p)$ and $X_S(p)$, respectively, as functions of that price. Price adjustment over time is given by the equation

$$\frac{dp}{dt} = F\left(X_D(p) - X_S(p)\right),\tag{1}$$

where F preserves the sign of $X_D(p) - X_S(p)$. If prices converge the economy has reached a competitive equilibrium since the aggregate excess demand for each good is necessarily zero. Exchange only takes place in equilibrium. If prices converge from any initial condition the economy is *globally stable*, if prices converge within some range of prices the economy is *locally stable* on that range. In early work F was simply a constant; eventually increasing structure was placed on F in efforts to guarantee global stability. Smale (1976) showed that for any economy one can always construct F_x for each good x such that the economy is globally stable. However, the construction requires first and second-order derivatives of each agent's utility function in order to coordinate price movements across markets.

Marshallian adjustment, on the other hand, assumes some quantity q for good x at any time t, then treats the demand and supply price, $P_D(q)$ and $P_S(q)$, respectively, as functions of q. In other words, quantity is fixed and one considers the willingness to pay and willingness to accept of the marginal buyer/seller. Quantity adjustment over time is given by the equation

$$\frac{dq}{dt} = G\left(P_D(q) - P_S(q)\right),\tag{2}$$

where G preserves the sign of $P_D(q) - P_S(q)$. Thus Walras is a story of price adjustment, and Marshall is a story of quantity adjustment.

In a 2-good economy where the laws of supply and demand are satisfied, Walrasian and Marshallian adjustment are globally stable and converge to the unique interior competitive equilibrium. In Figure 2, consider demand curve D and supply curve S_1 (only one market need be considered by Walras' Law). For any price r greater than the equilibrium price it is true that $X_D(r) - X_{S_1}(r) < 0$, so tâtonnement prices changes are strictly decreasing until reaching the competitive equilibrium. For any price less than the equilibrium price, tâtonnement generates increasing prices until reaching equilibrium. Now consider Marshallian adjustment and any q greater than the equilibrium quantity. Then $P_D(q) - P_{S_1}(q) < 0$, so quantity is strictly

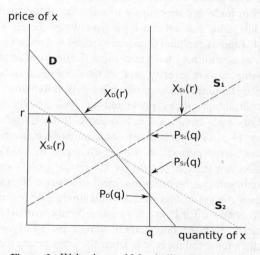

Figure 2. Walrasian and Marshallian Dynamics.

decreasing until reaching the competitive equilibrium. For any quantity less than equilibrium, Marshallian adjustment generates increasing quantities until convergence to equilibrium. Thus both processes are globally stable.

However, now consider the downward-sloping supply curve S_2, which can be derived from strong income effects or positive supply externalities as discussed below. The character of Marshallian dynamics are the same as for supply curve S_1, because the sign of $P_D(q) - P_{S_2}(q)$ equals the sign of $P_D(q) - P_{S_1}(q)$ for all q, so the competitive equilibrium remains stable. However, for all r the sign of $X_D(r) - X_{S_2}(r)$ is now the opposite of the sign of $X_D(r) - X_{S_1}(r)$ except at the equilibrium price, so the competitive equilibrium formed by the intersection of D and S_2 is unstable. Tâtonnement will cause prices to converge to a corner equilibrium, either to a price of 0 or a price equal to the y-intercept of the demand curve, depending on whether prices initiated below or above the equilibrium price, respectively.

A downward-sloping supply curve like S_2 can be implemented in a laboratory market by encouraging strong income effects through the appropriate choice of endowments and induced preferences/payoff functions. Plott (2001) introduced such income effects in a double auction, albeit with highly nonstandard payoffs,[6] and found powerful evidence for the Walrasian model across periods in all sessions. These laboratory economies always converged to a tâtonnement-stable equilibrium price that was unstable under Mashallian dynamics.

Crockett et al. (2011) fueled strong income effects with more conventional preferences by inducing the Gale (1963) economy in a laboratory double auction. In Gale's economy type 1 agents are endowed with a large (small) amount of good x (y), type 2 agents are endowed with a large (small) amount of good y (x), and all agents have type-dependent Leontief utility $u_i(x, y) = \min\{a_i x, y\}$, with $a_1 < 1$ and $a_2 > 1$.[7] Thus subjects were induced to view x and y as perfect complements with a strong taste for their predominantly endowed good, a recipe for large income effects. The net supply and demand curves for good x look similar to D and S_2 in Figure 2, but they are convex rather than linear and never cross the price axis. Thus the interior competitive equilibrium price is tâtonnement-unstable, and prices of 0 and ∞ serve as stable corner equilibrium prices albeit with nonzero excess demand.

As with Plott (2001), prices in each session which initiated in a tâtonnement-unstable region converged toward the corner equilibria.[8] Remarkably, corner equilibria in this economy imply that the gains from trade accrue entirely to one side of the market which is precisely what occurred in the lab, with one subject type typically securing 95% of the gains from trade. The Gale example (and a graphical predecessor due to Marshall himself) was viewed by contemporary theorists as a cautionary tale concerning the limits of aprioristic reasoning about markets because of its implausible severity, and yet tâtonnement turns out to do a remarkably good job of predicting the qualitative nature of across-period dynamics.

While graphs of transaction prices presented compelling visual evidence of corner convergence, the authors also conducted econometric tests of the Walrasian hypothesis. The Mann–Kendall $\tau \in [-1, 1]$ is an ordinal nonparametric measure of trend. Applied to weighted average prices across periods, τ was nearly equal to 1 (-1) in periods where the first observation initiated in a region of positive (negative) excess demand, supporting the simplest nonparametric interpretation of tâtonnement (that price changes share the same sign as excess demand). Session-level results were significant despite few observations. Similarly strong results were also obtained for Pearson's ρ, a cardinal correlation measure.

Interestingly, parametric tests of tâtonnement across periods were inconclusive. In the Gale example, the further removed a price is from the interior competitive equilibrium, the greater the absolute value of excess demand. But linear tâtonnement, where price changes are proportional to the size of excess demand (in absolute value), did not accurately describe the data. To make the gains from trade between subject types approximately zero-sum independent of price, the authors adopted a utility normalization that caused the forgone utility of unrequited demand/supply to decrease as the absolute value of excess demand increased. Thus there does appear to be a Marshallian influence on across-period dynamics, although the authors were not able to identify it parametrically. Clearly the Walrasian influence dominated as the interior competitive equilibrium was Marshallian-stable.

Anderson *et al.* (2004) and Hirota *et al.* (2005) found powerful evidence of across-period Walrasian dynamics in a double auction implementation of the 3-good economy of Scarf (1960). Type 1, 2, and 3 subjects were assigned Leontief payoffs over goods y and z, z and x, and x and y, respectively. Subjects were given a type-dependent endowment of one of the goods, and the ratio of preference between their two preferred goods was a function of their endowment to induce income effects. Good z served as commodity money with its price normalized to one, so price dynamics occurred in the (p_x, p_y) plane.

In all sessions there was a unique interior competitive equilibrium and five subjects of each type. Each paper adopted three treatments, using endowments and the set of preference ratio scalars as treatment variables. In Anderson *et al.* (2004), tâtonnement implies the treatments are characterized as (1) Globally stable interior competitive equilibrium, (2) Closed limit cycle of prices about the equilibrium in the clockwise direction, or (3) Closed limit cycle of prices about the equilibrium in the counter-clockwise direction. In Hirota *et al.* (2005), the three treatments are characterized as (1) Globally stable interior competitive equilibrium, (2) Explosive clockwise cycle of prices about the equilibrium that converges to (0,0) from greater to smaller values of x, and (3) Explosive counter-clockwise cycle of prices about the equilibrium that converges to (0,0) from greater to smaller values of y.

Tâtonnement describes qualitative across-period dynamics of each market session in both papers remarkably well. Convergence to the globally stable interior equilibrium was attained in each relevant session. In each interior-unstable session of both papers, mean prices across periods adjusted in the direction consistent with the tâtonnement phase space; the elliptical trajectory of prices in the (p_x, p_y) plane was unmistakable. In Anderson *et al.* (2004), no session completed more than one cycle of prices due to insufficient time to run more periods (sessions lasted about 3 h), and some sessions did not complete a full cycle. In Hirota *et al.* (2005), four of six sessions converged to a small neighborhood of (0,0) (small price floors for x and y were actually set to prevent zero period earnings), and the other two sessions were clearly moving toward (0,0) by the end of the session.[9]

Taken together, Anderson *et al.* (2004), Hirota *et al.* (2005), and Crockett *et al.* (2011) present the classic examples of tâtonnement instability in an entirely new light. The examples of Scarf (1960) and Gale (1963) were contemporaneously viewed as a call to arms for theorists to put additional structure on tâtonnement to guarantee its global stability, or to put restrictions on preferences so that tâtonnement-unstable environments could be eliminated. Both of these literatures are typically viewed to have ended in failure for GE theory. But these double auction experiments suggest that when strong income effects destabilize an economy theoretically under tâtonnement, they also destabilize its laboratory counterpart across periods in a remarkably similar fashion. The provocative but straightforward interpretation of this result is that under some conditions on preferences, the basin of attraction consistent with tâtaonnement dynamics is a more useful benchmark than competitive equilibrium. Importantly, the experiments plainly suggest long run dynamics even in tâtonnement-unstable economies may be robustly and transparently characterizable.

Before turning to within-period dynamics, it is important to note several limitations of tâtonnement to describe across-period dynamics in stationary multigood markets. First, while the sign of the mean price change from one period to the next is strongly predicted by the sign of excess demand at the current mean price, the specific functional form of tâtonnement has proven elusive (Hirota *et al.*, 2005, notwithstanding). Second, the results have been established using a double auction institution. Goeree and Lindsay (2012) successfully replicated Anderson *et al.* (2004) but report fast convergence to the interior (unstable) competitive equilibrium when they introduced a mechanism that required subjects to submit demand schedules and where trades were processed at one central price vector. Thus more work remains to compare institutional outcomes in laboratory GE economies.

Finally, Plott and George (1992) induced a downward-sloping supply curve similar to S_2 in Figure 2 through the use of positive externalities rather than income effects (the supply curve is "forward-falling" rather than "backward-bending"). Each individual supplier had an increasing marginal cost schedule, but his entire schedule was decreasing in aggregate supply. Under this condition, and within three different institutions (double auction, call auction, tâtonnement mechanism) prices tended to be sticky above but relatively near a Walrasian-unstable but Marshallian-stable interior competitive equilibrium. Plott and Smith (1999) studied upward-sloping demand curves generated through positive externalities (i.e., fads) along with forward-falling supply curves and reported strong evidence of across-period Marshallian stability in the double auction. Thus tâtonnement appears to be an excellent prediction of across-period sign changes in stationary multiple-good double auctions *except* in the presence of strong positive externalities in supply and/or demand.

2.2 *Within-Period Dynamics*

Most naturally occurring markets do not exhibit the extreme stationarity exhibited in the experimental markets reviewed above. Endowments need not be refreshed deterministically,[10] and individual market participants often enter and exit the market asynchronously. Thus what happens within a given period of a market is important.

Early papers in this area, the so-called "non-tâtonnement literature," imposed plausible restrictions on individual/aggregate behavior such that all trade operating under these restrictions would necessarily converge to the Pareto set. Exchange generally maintained the "institution-free" structure of GE theory, and there was no mention of laboratory experiments; this literature was written for consumption by theorists. Examples include Hahn and Negishi (1962), Uzawa (1962), Ledyard (1974), Hurwicz *et al.* (1975), Friedman (1979), and Fisher (1983).

Motivated by the increased availability of laboratory data, a number of papers shed the institution-free approach and developed theories of within-period dynamics committed specifically to the continuous double auction. Papers discussed in this survey are presented in Table 1.

These models focus on individual decision-making rather than aggregate market adjust-ments, perhaps reflecting the fact that each data point in a market experiment represents an individual action rather than an aggregated statistic as with across-period data. Nearly all of this work until quite recently has focused on partial equilibrium economies.

Friedman (1984) advised against characterizing the perfect Bayesian equilibria of double auctions, noting the difficulty of analyzing far simpler 2-person bargaining games with short time horizons and discrete intervals. Rather than describe specifically what agents in a continuous double auction must do, he instead specified what they cannot do; namely, leave (much) money on the table. He posited that agents are expected utility maximizers

Table 1. Summary of Within-Period Theories of Double Auction Dynamics.

Paper	Description
Friedman [1984]	No congestion equilibrium - No one would retroactively change her ending bid/ask after period ends.
Friedman [1991]	Bayesian agents view market actions by others as draws from exogenous distribution; rational but not strategic.
Easley and Ledyard [1993]	Assume reservation price strategy; bids/asks move towards value/cost by end of period.
Gode and Sunder [1993]	Zero intelligence - Agents make random utility-improving bids/asks; Pareto-efficiency requires minimal rationality.
Cason and Friedman [1996]	Laboratory test of extant models, limited support.
Gjerstad and Dickhaut [1998]	Game against nature as in Friedman (1991), but agents are frequentists not Bayesian. Improved fit.
Asparouhova, Bossaerts, and Ledyard [2011a]	Within-period adjustment is more Marshallian than Walrasian. Subjects are slow to react to price changes.
Gjerstad [2013]	Finds slow reaction to price changes in test of Hahn and Negishi (1962); income effects slow across-period learning.

who collectively play a *no congestion equilibrium*: If at the end of a period the market were to be reopened for one instant more, it must be true that no one would wish to change her standing bid or ask from the end of the period. Under this condition, a Nash equilibrium of the game must be 'nearly' Pareto optimal. Intuitively, as the end of the period approaches agents become increasingly willing to accept trades close to their reservation values/costs to mitigate the risk of leaving gains from trade on the table. This theory is consistent with the fact that in most periods of double auction experiments subjects do reach an approximately Pareto optimal allocation. However, many different learning rules that could lead to widely different allocations are consistent with the no congestion assumption.

Friedman (1991) proposed one such learning rule, where Bayesian agents perceive their participation in a double auction as a game against nature. More specifically, agents act as if the activity of others reflects draws from a distribution of actions unaffected by their own, and update their beliefs about this distribution after each observed action. Thus agents are rational but nonstrategic, giving the market a more Walrasian than Nash feel. Under these assumptions, agents have an optimal strategy to set an "aggressive reservation price strategy" at any point in time; they are willing to trade at any price between their own value/cost and this reservation price. Importantly, agents are also assumed to know at any point in time the expected number of new prices that will be posted in the market by the end of the period. Thus as the end of the period approaches, reservation prices will necessarily approach actual costs/values, and near-Pareto optimality will be achieved.

Friedman (1991) can be interpreted as providing a choice-theoretic rationale for Easley and Ledyard (1993), who simply assumed, rather than derived, that each agent has an aggressive reservation price strategy, and this reservation price moves towards his true value/cost by the end of the period if he has not yet transacted. The authors emphasized that the order of reservation prices across agents is not necessarily related to the order of true values/costs; such an outcome could potentially be supported within the Friedman (1991) framework through heterogeneous risk preferences.

Gode and Sunder (1993) developed an important insight with their "zero intelligence" (ZI) model of within-period dynamics. They assumed a buyer (seller) periodically bids (asks) on uniform random support between his induced value (cost) and some lower (upper) bound.[11] Agents transact when a new limit order crosses an existing one from the opposite side of the market. Markets populated by such minimally sophisticated agents necessarily converge to a Pareto optimal allocation in the absence of externalities given sufficient time, and extract most of the available surplus. Of course, such agents cannot exhibit across-period learning as human subjects collectively do.[12] However, ZI demonstrates that it does not take much sophistication to extract most of the available surplus from a market.

Unfortunately, these models do not imply all of the main features of double auctions data. Cason and Friedman (1996) tested the extant models (Friedman (1991), Gode and Sunder (1993), and a strategic game theoretic model of Wilson (1987)) in a series of experiments and found consistency on some dimensions but relatively weak fits overall. Gjerstad and Dickhaut (1998) subsequently developed a model that explains a bit more of the data. The model is related most closely to Friedman (1991), in that agents perceive the double auction nonstrategically, as a game against nature, but agents are frequentists rather than Bayesians. A buyer calculates the probability bid b will be accepted as $T(b)/(T(b) + R(b))$, where $T(b)$ is equal to the previous number of accepted bids and posted asks weakly less than b, and $R(b)$ is the number of rejected (untraded) bids weakly less than b. Buyer i also has a potentially limited memory of past market activity; he can only recall the previous L_i prior actions. Thus L_i becomes a free parameter to estimate. Seller behavior is modeled analogously.

A key implication of each of these models is that it is qualitatively consistent with the Marshallian dynamic described earlier. Recall that under Marshallian adjustment agents take quantity as given, report their marginal willingness to pay/cost, and then quantity adjusts in the direction of imbalance. Thus when markets are not in equilibrium, the Marshallian model assumes it is the marginal buyer and seller who drive adjustment. This feature is plainly implied by all of the models in Table 1, and is consistent with double auctions data going back to Smith (1962), who reported evidence favoring Marshallian over Walrasian within-period dynamics in the form of his "excess rent" hypothesis.

Asparouhova et al. (2011a) confirm the efficacy of focus on within-period Marshallian dynamics by testing Marshallian versus Walrasian models of exchange when competition is "in smalls." In most double auction experiments the bid-ask spread (the difference between the highest bid and lowest ask) is small, but a large market order will typically clear several limit orders, and the price of the "deepest" transacted limit order is worse for the market orderer than the first. Thus large orders tend to get worse average terms of trade than small orders. Institutional investors in naturally occurring markets face similar premia for large orders; see Rostek and Weretka (2011).[13]

Asparouhova et al. (2011a) capture "competition in smalls" in reduced form by modeling continuous exchange. In their local Walrasian model, each agent takes the price vector as given and (feasibly) maximizes the dot product of his current utility gradient with his local excess demand function at the current price. That is, he maximizes directionally the value of net trades. Price in each instant is assumed to be a local equilibrium, so that the sum of local excess demand functions conditional on this price is zero. Under standard conditions on preferences, this process necessarily converges to the Pareto set.

In their local Marshallian model, similar to Ledyard (1974) and Friedman (1979), one good serves as numeraire, and at each point in time each agent expresses a marginal (normalized) value for the other goods. A market price is given, and the key dynamics assumption is that the rate of demand/supply of any good by a given agent is proportional to the difference between his value and the good's market price. Optimality requires that the difference between the agent's value and price for a given good is proportional to the difference between his (normalized) marginal utility for that good and its price. Feasibility requires that net demands sum to zero, which pins down the price to an equilibrium value. This process necessarily converges to the Pareto set.

Both exchange processes are local equilibrium theories where agents nonstrategically take prices as given, and those prices are such that the actions of agents are collectively feasible. But in the Walrasian case trade for each agent follows excess demand, while in the Marshallian case net trade for a given good (which for the same price will have the same sign as local Walrasian trade) is weighted by the marginal utility of that good relative to the marginal utility of other agents. Under strong conditions the two processes can imply identical dynamics, but not in general. The authors also incorporate lagged prices to reflect the fact that prices can change while an individual is formulating and executing his action. Adding the lag improves the model's explanatory power but at the cost of Pareto optimality, although it does converge to the Pareto set in the special case of quasilinear preferences.

The authors ran several three-good quasilinear double auctions. Under the adopted parameters the fast and slow Marshallian dynamics operate on Walrasian excess demands through different functional relationships which could be tested (Walrasian excess demands enter into Marshallian adjustment but are weighted by marginal utility). The authors found that price changes are related to the slow rather than fast local Marshallian theory of adjustment. Further, the slow Marshallian theory also explains a feature of final allocations with a transparent CAPM interpretation: When payoff covariances are positive, violations of portfolio separation in final allocations are more extreme.

Gjerstad (2013) tested within-period Walrasian dynamics in a discrete version of Hahn and Negishi (1962) and also found that lagged prices added significantly to the explanatory power of the model. To incorporate across-period learning into the model, he assumed that the opening price of each period was uniform randomly distributed between the highest and lowest transaction price of the previous period. An interesting result in the paper is that income effects dramatically slowed across-period convergence to the competitive equilibrium. Combining income effects as a treatment variable with the local slow Marshallian adjustment model of Asparouhova et al. (2011a) is a natural next step in continuing to characterize within-period adjustment.

Plott et al. (2011) succinctly write in conclusion of a recent experiment:

> The two theories (Walrasian and Marshallian adjustment) are not simply inverses of each other but explain different features of the adjustment process. Marshall tells us who will trade and the speed at which trades will take place and that it will take place along the most efficient, wealth creating path. Walras tells us how prices will evolve when they do trade and that the ultimate prices will support equilibrium volumes and efficiency. Those theoretical principles are reflected in the data. (p. 15)

3. Further Experimental GE Applications

GE theory has left fundamental questions unanswered for the past several decades. Existing theories of adjustment are neither globally stable nor plausibly decentralized, and preferences cannot be credibly restricted so that even these centralized adjustment theories are stable. However, market experiments have begun to seriously address these shortcomings. These experiments suggest that market activity exhibits substantial predictability, and this predictability relates in a meaningful way to classical theories of out-of-equilibrium dynamics. New microfounded theories based on features of Walrasian and Marshallian dynamics continue to extend what we can learn from experimental data.

Despite its core issues GE theory has continued to be applied in many fields of economics, and is pervasive in macroeconomics and finance. Experiments have supported many of these applications; if anything, the study of experimental GE is accelerating. This paper concludes with a brief survey of GE experiments that weren't designed explicitly to inform the question of out-of-equilibrium dynamics.

Production and Comparative Advantage. In Goodfellow and Plott (1990) subjects were buyers, sellers, or producers. There was input L, output Z, and commodity money F. Sellers (buyers) had an induced cost (demand) schedule over L (Z) denominated in F, just as their namesakes in Smith (1962) but over type-dependent goods. Producers could convert L to Z through a production technology with decreasing returns to scale. Double auctions for L and Z were open simultaneously; producers participated in both markets. Endowments were refreshed in each period, with F-denominated earnings accumulating across periods and converted to dollars at the end of the session. Prices converged to a small neighborhood of the competitive equilibrium within several periods, a remarkable feat of decentralized coordination since total resources themselves were endogenous.

Noussair et al. (1995) extended production to two countries with distinct technologies over two output goods, and observed that decentralized coordination extended to the principle of comparative advantage. Subjects in each country were divided into producers and consumers of final goods Y and Z, and all subjects were endowed with good L (labor) and commodity money F. Consumers sold L to domestic producers, producers created Y and Z from L, and sold those goods on the world output markets. All exchange took place in a double auction. Producers in country 1 (2) had a comparative advantage in producing Y (Z). No one had intrinsic utility for L (it was thus supplied inelastically), producers had no intrinsic utility for Y and Z, and consumers converted their final holdings of Y and Z to F at a known concave rate at the end of each period.

In these experiments production, consumption, and prices converged towards their competitive equilibrium values across periods, and net trade between the countries converged to the equilibrium. The competitive equilibrium was a better predictor of outcomes than autarky, though prices in particular remained considerably distant. The biggest impediment to stronger convergence appears to have been the risk assumed by producers in acquiring labor prior to selling final goods in the output markets, a risk not present in equilibrium. The same comparative statics largely obtained when a tariff on imports of Z was imposed, though net trade of Z substantially underperformed its (new) equilibrium benchmark. In a second treatment, producers in both countries were induced with identical concave consumption preferences for two input goods (labor and capital) and had identical linear production technologies; thus inputs in this treatment were not exogenously and inelastically supplied as in the first. Factor prices in the two countries converged despite the segmented markets.

Noussair et al. (1997) instituted a similar environment but eliminated the input market and introduced foreign exchange. Consumers' induced utility was linear in domestic currency and concave in Y and Z. Producers' induced utility was linear in domestic currency and negative and convex in the production of Y and Z (costs were incurred at the point of sale). Goods had to be purchased in their country of origin with local currency, so consumers who wished to buy products abroad had to purchase foreign exchange in a currency market. As in Noussair *et al.* (1995), patterns of international trade followed the principle of comparative advantage, and prices (including exchange rates) converged over time towards the competitive equilibrium. However, the law of one price and purchasing power parity did not obtain, and appear to have been impeded by the exchange risk incurred by importing consumers; these individuals had to buy foreign currency they did not value in order to (hopefully) purchase goods in the foreign country.

Noussair *et al.* (2007) linked and extended the earlier papers to economies that included three countries, two inputs, three final goods, and foreign exchange. Each country included input suppliers, producers, and consumers. Inputs were restricted to the local market, outputs could be sold to foreigners but only in domestic currency. There were 40–60 subjects in each session, and each subject engaged in two of the three economic activities. Impressively, prices and economic activity converged towards their competitive equilibrium benchmarks over time, although once again, convergence appears to have been impeded by exchange and input risk.

In Crockett *et al.* (2009) all subjects were both producers and consumers of two output goods. Each subject was assigned a "house" and a "field" within a virtual village arranged about a chatroom. A subject chose output along her production possibilities frontier at the beginning of each period, causing goods to appear in her field as red or blue tiles. Subjects had induced utility over the tiles, and were informed that consumption occurred when goods were dragged and dropped into their houses. There were two production technologies in each economy. In each session subjects pooled into one or two groups: Those who produced and consumed in autarky, and those who specialized by comparative advantage and formed bilateral trade partnerships. Smaller groups were slower to discover the possibility of exchange, while larger groups found it more difficult to specialize and trade. Mirroring results in the previous papers, a major impediment to specialization and exchange appears to have been trading risk; goods were perfect complements in consumption which made specialization risky. This literature confirms the explanatory power of comparative advantage, and suggests that dynamic extensions where unused inputs, goods, and/or foreign carry forward to subsequent periods may improve economic efficiency.

Growth. Lei and Noussair (2002) implement the Ramsey–Cass–Koopmans growth model in a laboratory setting. The benchmark economy is home to an infinitely-lived representative agent who in each period must decide how much of his current allocation to consume and how much to invest; his allocation in the following period is, of course, increasing in his investment. The authors created a 5-subject version of this economy, in which the subjects' individual production and marginal utility schedules aggregated up to the representative agent's. Trade of capital for experimental currency took place in a double auction each period, after which consumption/investment decisions were made. The rate of time preference in the theoretical model was replaced by a period-continuation probability, which under the assumption risk-neutrality does not change the steady state equilibrium (a standard technique for studying infinite horizon models in laboratory experiments).

In each session of this experiment prices, the capital stock, and per capita consumption converged near their steady state values, and production was coordinated efficiently across subjects. A social planner treatment, where one subject made decisions as the representative agent, produced inferior convergence results. A planning agency treatment, where five subjects worked together as a social planner, converged near the steady state as in the decentralized market treatment but with greater variance. Capra *et al.* (2009) implemented the market treatment but added a threshold aggregate capital level above which individual productivity improved. This feature introduced two possible steady states, a socially optimal one that took advantage of the investment externality, and a low-growth "poverty trap." The baseline economies generally converged to the poverty trap. However, if given the opportunity to communicate by chatroom or to cast binding votes for capital levels, some economies escaped the poverty trap. If subjects were given both a chatroom and voting mechanism, their economies always converged near the socially optimal steady state.

Money and GE. Several experiments have focused on issues related to money in a GE setting. Duffy and Ochs (1999) and Duffy and Ochs (2002) studied the emergence of media of exchange in a laboratory implementation of the Kiyotaki–Wright model. Common to both experiments, there were three subject types and three goods. Each subject could produce one good but preferred to consume another. No pair of subject types shared a double coincidence of wants in produced goods. Subjects were randomly matched in each period. If they agreed to trade, they swapped current endowments. If the subject had his preferred good in inventory at the end of the period, he consumed it and immediately produced a unit of his production good; a subject thus always had one unit of one of his non-consumed goods in inventory. At the end of a period goods in inventory incurred a storage cost, where the cost of good 1 was less than the cost of good 2 which was less than the cost of good 3. The rate of time preference in the theoretical model was replaced by a period-continuation probability.

In one treatment of Duffy and Ochs (1999), parameters were chosen to induce two steady state equilibria, one *fundamental* and the other *speculative*. In the fundamental equilibrium, each subject would only be willing to trade for his consumption good or for a good with a lower storage cost than his current endowment. Thus the good with the lowest storage cost would emerge as a medium of exchange. In the speculative equilibrium, one subject type would be willing to trade for his nonconsumption good with the highest storage cost because it would sufficiently increase his probability of acquiring his consumption good in subsequent periods. In this treatment realized trade probabilities were far closer to the fundamental than speculative equilibrium. In another treatment, parameters were assigned such that a speculative equilibrium was the only steady state. In these sessions subjects persisted in trading for (against) the low (high) storage cost good relative to equilibrium frequencies. Thus subjects were biased towards trading for goods with low storage cost.

Duffy and Ochs (2002) introduced a fourth good, good 0, into this environment. Good 0 was intrinsically worthless to all subjects and was randomly assigned to a subset of them (in place of their production good) in the first period. In one treatment good 0 had the smallest storage cost and the economy admitted two steady state equilibria, one in which trading strategies were fundamental, and another in which good 0 would not be traded. Trade in good 0 did frequently take place, though a bit less than the equilibrium frequency. In another treatment that entailed a speculative steady state, speculation seldom took place, and subjects were *more* likely to trade for good 0 than equilibrium frequencies suggested. Thus Duffy and Ochs (2002) observed the endogenous adoption of fiat money, but again confirmed subject bias towards goods with low storage cost.

Duffy *et al.* (2011) extended study of fiat money adoption to the Lagos–Wright model. Subjects faced a stochastic horizon as in Kiyotaki–Wright, and each period had a decentralized and centralized subperiod. All subjects were endowed with intrinsically worthless but storable tokens in the first period. In the decentralized market subjects were randomly paired, and within a pair subjects were randomly assigned the role of producer or consumer. A producer could create a nonstorable good at cost but not consume it, and a consumer could consume the good but not produce it. Afterward in the centralized market, all subjects could produce and consume a second type of good. In one steady state equilibrium, producers sell the first good for fiat money in the decentralized market, and everyone uses the centralized market to rebalance fiat money holdings. In another steady state equilibrium which Pareto dominates the first, producers produce a fixed quantity in the first period and no one trades in the centralized market; this is a grim trigger "gift exchange" equilibrium with no role for money. Autarky constitutes a third equilibrium. Subjects did in fact mediate trade with money and used the centralized market to rebalance fiat money holdings. In a follow-up treatment with gift exchange but no money, efficiency deteriorated and was near autarkic levels, establishing that the existence of tokens in the baseline treatment did not destroy the gift exchange equilibrium through a demand effect.

Experiments have also shown little evidence of money illusion in response to fluctuations of the money supply. Lian and Plott (1998) studied a production economy similar to Goodfellow and Plott (1990) but with consumers and producers only, and fiat money F rather than commodity money. Consumers were endowed with constant L in each period and had concave induced utility over L and Z. Producers were endowed with F in period 1 and had concave induced utility over Z.[14] L and Z could be "consumed" (converted to dollars) at the end of the current period or carried to the subsequent period, but subjects rarely stored their goods so the economy was largely a static repetition across periods. In the final period F was converted to L and/or Z (and then consumed) at the average trading prices of the final period, so that subjects would be willing to hold fiat money throughout the experiment. In several sessions additional fiat money was injected into the system. The real price ratio of Z to L in all sessions converged to the competitive equilibrium value, and production and consumption approached their equilibrium values from below (but finished a bit short). Nominal effects of inflation were observed but there were no real effects.[15]

Dynamic GE. A growing body of experiments, in addition to those related to information aggregation and stochastic asset returns (discussed in other papers of this journal issue), have implemented dynamic economies where decisions in one period impact outcomes in subsequent periods. Some examples include Marimon and Sunder (1993), Bosch-Domenech and Silvestre (1997), Cipriani *et al.* (2012), Crockett and Duffy (2012), Asparouhova *et al.* (2011b), and Petersen (2012). The first paper focuses on money in an overlapping generations framework, the next two papers focus on credit within a GE setting, the following two implement a Lucas tree consumption-based asset pricing experiment, and the last explores monetary policy in a dynamic stochastic GE experiment. Space constraints limit further discussion of these papers, as the designs tend to be fairly complex.

Sunspots. A sunspot exists when extrinsic uncertainty (i.e., a draw from a distribution of outcomes with no relationship to economic fundamentals) plays a role in equilibrium outcomes. In the simplest possible setting, imagine there are two equilibrium outcomes, A and B, and extrinsic uncertainty takes the form of two possible states, "rain" and "shine." A sunspot is observed if all agents believe the outcome will be equilibrium A if it rains and B if it shines, and behave accordingly. Marimon *et al.* (1993) and Duffy and Fisher (2005) attempted to generate sunspots in the lab. From the former paper it appears to be the case that "neutral" extrinsic signals like "red" and "blue" make sunspot coordination difficult, while from the latter we learn that "context-rich" extrinsic signals like "high" and "low" facilitate sunspots.

Behavioral GE Theory. Bowles and Gintis (2000) and Kirman (1989) argue that GE theory can and should be extended to reflect robust deviations from standard neoclassical preference theory. Work in this area, both theoretical and experimental, has largely focused on the endowment effect[16] and reference-dependent preferences. Models of reference dependent preferences in a multi-good setting include Tversky and Kahneman (1991), Munro and Sugden (2003) and Kőszegi and Rabin (2006). Munro and Sugden (2003) and Crockett and Oprea (2012) explicitly derive GE consequences of such models. Knetsch (1989), List (2003), List (2004), Engelmann and Hollard (2010), Ericson and Fuster (2011), and Crockett and Oprea (2012) report evidence from multi-good exchange experiments. Consensus appears to be developing that the endowment effect disappears entirely across contexts in individuals with long-term trading experience, and diminishes rapidly within-context for inexperienced subjects who have had several opportunities to trade.

Acknowledgements

I thank Dan Friedman, Charles Plott, Stephen Spear, the editors, and an anonymous referee for useful comments.

Notes

1. See Camerer *et al.* (2003) for a survey of this literature, and Angner and Loewenstein (2012) for a brief history of its development.
2. See Friedman and Rust (1993) for a description of this institution and a survey of the related experimental literature. Chamberlain (1948) studied the same basic design as Smith but implemented trade via decentralized bilateral barter, which adversely impacted efficiency. The call auction is an informationally centralized alternative to the double auction, but tends to be less efficient (see Cason and Friedman, 1997).
3. Many papers surveyed in this subsection are summarized in Plott (2008a).
4. Joyce (1984) studied a tâtonnement exchange mechanism in which a price was publicly announced, subjects submitted tentative orders at that price, and orders were executed if quantity supplied equaled quantity demanded. If not, the next announced price was adjusted in the direction of the sign of excess demand. He reported that trade was quite efficient. Bronfman *et al.* (1996) replicated this result; when subjects were limited to trading only one unit per period and supply/demand was stationary as in Joyce (1984), markets were efficient after several periods. However, efficiency deteriorated and was well below levels observed for double auctions under comparable conditions if multiple units could be traded and supply/demand curves were manipulated from one period to the next.
5. Gode *et al.* (2004) and Crockett (2008) also induced CES preferences in markets with commodity money. However, Gode *et al.* only observed one period of trade per session, and Crockett studied 2-person economies, so neither contributes to understanding across-period convergence in large markets.
6. The payoff function for sellers was nonmonotonic and convex over a range of (x, y) combinations.
7. The authors also added a nonzero y-intercept term to encourage greater excess demand at a given price.
8. The discrete grid on which goods could be traded was relatively fine but did admit an interior equilibrium price cone that strictly contained the equilibrium price of the analogous continuous economy. In one of the eight sessions, prices initiated within the cone and never left, which is consistent with tâtonnement. In all other sessions prices initiated outside of the cone and converged to the nearest corner equilibrium.

9. Hirota *et al.* (2005) also report that scaling the excess demand for a good by its own price (or equivalently, positing that the percentage change in price is proportional to its excess demand) produces a better fit of across-period price dynamics than simple proportional tâtonnement. Anderson *et al.* (2004) test the same specification but do not report a strong difference in fit.

10. They could be stochastic and/or made endogenous through production or investment decisions. Research focused on such environments will be discussed later in this paper.

11. Gode *et al.* (2004) extend this intuition to convex two-good economies by assuming a buyer (seller) submits radian-denominated bids (asks) with uniform random support between his marginal rate of substitution and 0 ($\pi/2$).

12. Crockett *et al.* (2008) appended a simple learning constraint to ZI agents at the end of each period which guarantees convergence to a competitive equilibrium in convex exchange economies.

13. Trade in their model has a distinct Marshallian character as firms release their demand/supply in small orders, and those with the most surplus at stake transact more quickly.

14. To facilitate the opening of markets, consumers (producers) were also endowed with F (Z) in period 1.

15. In a price-setting game with strategic complements, Petersen and Winn (2012) investigated previous results interpreted as money illusion, and with new controls found money illusion actually played a small role in these results.

16. Individuals exogenously endowed with a good tend to value it substantially more than individuals who are not endowed with the good.

References

Ackerman, F. (2002) Still dead after all these years: interpreting the failure of general equilibrium theory. *Journal of Economic Methodology* 9: 119–139.

Anderson, C. M., Plott, C. R., Shimomura, K.-I., and Granat, S. (2004) Global instability in experimental general equilibrium: the Scarf example. *Journal of Economic Theory* 115: 209–249.

Angner, E. and Loewenstein, G. (2012) Behavioral economics. In Maki, U. (ed.), *Handbook of the Philosophy of Science: Philosophy of Economics* (pp. 641–690). Amsterdam: Elsevier.

Asparouhova, E., Bossaerts, P., and Ledyard, J. O. (2011a) Price formation in continuous double auctions; with implications for finance. Available at http://home.business.utah.edu/finea/decentPricing110531.pdf.

Asparouhova, E., Bossaerts, P., Roy, N., and Zame, W. (2011b) Experiments with the Lucas asset pricing model. Available at http://home.business.utah.edu/finea/Lucas.pdf.

Bosch-Domenech, A. and Silvestre, J. (1997) Credit constraints in general equilibrium: experimental results. *The Economic Journal* 107: 1445–1464.

Bowles, S. and Gintis, H. (2000) Walrasian economics in retrospect. *The Quarterly Journal of Economics* 115(4): 1411–1439.

Bronfman, C., McCabe, K., Porter, D., Rassenti, S., and Smith, V. (1996) An experimental examination of the walrasian tâtonnement mechanism. *The RAND Journal of Economics* 27(4): 681–699.

Camerer, C. F., Loewenstein, G., and Rabin, M., (eds), (2003) *Advances in Behavioral Economics*. Roundtable Series in Behavioral Economics. Princeton, NJ: Princeton University Press.

Capra, C. M., Tanaka, T., Camerer, C. F., Feiler, L., Sovero, V., and Noussair, C. N. (2009) The impact of simple institutions in experimental economies with poverty traps. *The Economic Journal* 119: 977–1009.

Cason, T. N. and Friedman, D. (1996) Price formation in double auction markets. *Journal of Economic Dynamics and Control* 20: 1307–1337.

Cason, T. N. and Friedman, D. (1997) Price formation in single call markets. *Econometrica* 65(2): 311–345.

Chamberlain, E. H. (1948) An experimental imperfect market. *Journal of Political Economy* 56(2): 95–108.

Cipriani, M., Fostel, A., and Houser, D. (2012) Leverage and asset prices: an experiment. Working paper, Federal Reserve Bank of New York.

Crockett, S. (2008) Learning competitive equilibrium in laboratory exchange economies. *Economic Theory* 34(1): 157–180.

Crockett, S. and Duffy, J. (2012) A dynamic general equilibrium approach to asset pricing experiments Available at http://aux.zicklin.baruch.cuny.edu/crockett/crockett_duffy.pdf.

Crockett, S. and Oprea, R. (2012) In the long run we all trade: reference dependence in dynamic economies Available at http://aux.zicklin.baruch.cuny.edu/crockett/crockett_oprea.pdf.

Crockett, S., Oprea, R., and Plott, C. R. (2011) Extreme Walrasian dynamics: the gale example in the lab. *The American Economic Review* 101: 3196–3220.

Crockett, S., Smith, V. L., and Wilson, B. J. (2009) Exchange and specialisation as a discovery process. *The Economic Journal* 119: 1162–1188.

Crockett, S., Spear, S., and Sunder, S. (2008) Learning competitive equilibrium. *Journal of Mathematical Economics* 44(7): 651–671.

Duffy, J. and Fisher, E. O. (2005) Sunspots in the laboratory. *The American Economic Review* 95(3): 510–529.

Duffy, J., Groskopf, B., and Puzzello, D. (2011) Gift exchange versus monetary exchange: experimental evidence Available at http://www.economicdynamics.org/meetpapers/2011/paper_1153.pdf.

Duffy, J. and Ochs, J. (1999) Emergence of money as a medium of exchange: an experimental study. *The American Economic Review* 89(4): 847–877.

Duffy, J. and Ochs, J. (2002) Intrinsically worthless objects as media of exchange: experimental evidence. *International Economic Review* 43(3): 637–673.

Easley, D. and Ledyard, J. O. (1993) Theories of price formation and exchange in double oral auctions. In Friedman, D. and Rust, J., (eds), *The Double Auction Market: Institutions, Theories, and Evidence* (pp. 63–97). Reading, MA: Addison-Wesley.

Engelmann, D. and Hollard, G. (2010) Reconsidering the effect of market experience on the endowment effect. *Econometrica* 78(6): 2005–2019.

Ericson, K. M. M. and Fuster, A. (2011) Expectations as endowments: evidence on reference-dependent preferences from exchange and valuation experiments. *Quarterly Journal of Economics* 126(4): 1879–1907.

Fisher, F. M. (1983) *Disequilibrium Foundations of Equilibrium Economics*. Econometric Society Monographs in Pure Theory, No. 6. New York, NY: Cambridge University Press.

Friedman, D. (1979) Money-mediated disequilibrium processes in a pure exchange economy. *Journal of Mathematical Economics* 6: 149–167.

Friedman, D. (1984) On the efficiency of experimental double auction markets. *The American Economic Review* 74(1): 60–72.

Friedman, D. (1991) A simple testable model of double auction markets. *Journal of Economic Behavior and Organization* 15: 47–70.

Friedman, D. and Rust, J., (eds), (1993) *The Double Auction Market: Institutions, Theories, and Evidence*. Proceedings Volume XIV in the Santa Fe Institute Studies in the Sciences of Complexity. Reading, MA: Addison-Wesley.

Gale, D. (1963) A note on global instability of competitive equilibrium. *Naval Research Logistics Quarterly* 10: 81–87.

Gjerstad, S. (2013) Price dynamics in an exchange economy. *Economic Theory* 52(2): 461–500.

Gjerstad, S. and Dickhaut, J. (1998) Price formation in double auctions. *Games and Economic Behavior* 22(1): 1–29.

Gode, D. K., Spear, S. E., and Sunder, S. (2004) Convergence of double auctions to Pareto optimal allocations in the Edgeworth box. Available at http://papers.ssrn.com/sol3/papers.cfm?abstract_id=1280707.

Gode, D. K. and Sunder, S. (1993) Allocative efficiency of markets with zero intelligence (zj) traders: market as a partial substitute for individual rationality. *Journal of Political Economy* 101: 119–137.

Goeree, J. K. and Lindsay, L. (2012) Stabilizing the economy: market design and general equilibrium Available at http://papers.ssrn.com/sol3/papers.cfm?abstract_id=2146695.

Goodfellow, J. and Plott, C. R. (1990) An experimental examination of the simultaneous determination of input prices and output prices. *Southern Economic Journal* 56(4): 969.

Hahn, F. H. and Negishi, T. (1962) A theorem on non-tâtonnement stability. *Econometrica* 30(3): 463–469.

Hirota, M., Hsu, M., Plott, C. R., and Rogers, B. W. (2005) Divergence, closed cycles and convergence in scarf environments: experiments in the dynamics of general equilibrium systems. Working Paper 1239, Division of the Humanities and Social Sciences, California Institute of Technology.

Hurwicz, L., Radner, R., and Reiter, S. (1975) A stochastic decentralized resource allocation process. Part I. *Econometrica* 43(3): 187–222.

Joyce, P. (1984) The walrasian tâtonnement mechanism and information. *The RAND Journal of Economics* 15(3): 416–425.

Katzner, D. W. (2010) The current non-status of general equilibrium theory. *Review of Economic Design* 14: 203–219.

Kőszegi, B. and Rabin, M. (2006) A model of reference-dependent preferences. *Quarterly Journal of Economics* 121(4): 1133–1165.

Kirman, A. (1989) The intrinsic limits of modern economic theory: the emperor has no clothes. *The Economic Journal* 99: 126–139.

Knetsch, J. L. (1989) The endowment effect and evidence of nonreversible indifference curves. *The American Economic Review* 79(5): 1277–1284.

Ledyard, J. O. (1974) Decentralized disequilibrium trading and price formation. Working paper 86 of The Center for Mathematical Studies in Economics and Management Science, Northwestern University.

Lei, V. and Noussair, C. N. (2002) An experimental test of an optimal growth model. *The American Economic Review* 92(3): 549–570.

Lian, P. and Plott, C. R. (1998) General equilibrium, markets, macroeconomics and money in a laboratory experimental environment. *Economic Theory* 12(1): 21–75.

List, J. A. (2003) Does market experience eliminate anomalies? *Quarterly Journal of Economics* 118(1): 41–71.

List, J. A. (2004) Neoclassical theory versus prospect theory: evidence from the marketplace. *Econometrica* 72(2): 615–625.

Marimon, R., Spear, S. E., and Sunder, S. (1993) Expectationally driven market volatility: an experimental study. *Journal of Economic Theory* 61: 74–103.

Marimon, R. and Sunder, S. (1993) Indeterminacy of equilibria in a hyperinflationary world: experimental evidence. *Econometrica* 61(5): 1073–1107.

Munro, A. and Sugden, R. (2003) On the theory of reference-dependent preferences. *Journal of Economic Behavior and Organization* 50(4): 407–428.

Noussair, C. N., Plott, C. R., and Riezman, R. G. (1995) An experimental investigation of the patterns of international trade. *The American Economic Review* 85(3): 462–491.

Noussair, C. N., Plott, C. R., and Riezman, R. G. (1997) The principles of exchange rate determination in an international finance experiment. *Journal of Political Economy* 105(4): 822–862.

Noussair, C. N., Plott, C. R., and Riezman, R. G. (2007) Production, trade, prices, exchange rates and equilibration in large experimental economies. *European Economic Review* 51(1): 49–76.

Petersen, L. (2012) Nonneutrality of money, preferences and expectations in laboratory new Keynesian economies. Available at http://sigfirm.ucsc.edu/pdfs/WPS-2012/WPS.

Petersen, L. and Winn, A. (2012) The role of money illusion in nominal price adjustment Available at http://www.sfu.ca/econ-research/RePEc/sfu/sfudps/dp12-19.pdf.

Plott, C. R. (2001) Equilibrium, equilibration, information and multiple markets: from basic science to institutional design. In *Nobel Symposium on Behavioral and Experimental Economics*, Stockholm, Sweden.

Plott, C. R. (2008a) Principles of market adjustment and stability. In Plott, C. R. and Smith, V. L., (eds), *Handbook of Experimental Economics Results* (pp. 214–227). North-Holland: Elsevier.

Plott, C. R. (2008b) Properties of disequilibrium adjustment in double auction markets. In Plott, C. R. and Smith, V. L., (eds), *Handbook of Experimental Economics Results* (pp. 16–21). North-Holland: Elsevier.

Plott, C. R. and George, G. (1992) Marshallian vs. Walrasian stability in an experimental market. *The Economic Journal* 102(412): 437–460.

Plott, C. R., Roy, N., and Tong, B. (2011) An experimental test of marshall's basic principle of entry, volume, and efficiency seeking market dynamics. Social Science Working Paper 1345, California Institute of Technology.

Plott, C. R. and Smith, J. (1999) Instability of equilibria in experimental markets: Upward-sloping demands, externalities, and fad-like incentives. *Southern Economic Journal* 65(3): 405–426.

Plott, C. R. and Smith, V. L., (eds), (2008) *Handbook of Experimental Economics Results*. North-Holland: Elsevier.

Rostek, M. and Weretka, M. (2011) Dynamic thin markets. Available at http://www.ssc.wisc.edu/~mrostek/Term_structure.pdf.

Scarf, H. (1960) Some examples of global instability of the competitive equilibrium. *International Economic Review* 1(3): 157–172.

Smale, S. (1976) A convergent process of price adjustments and global Newton methods. *Journal of Mathematical Economics* 3: 1–14.

Smith, V. L. (1962) An experimental study of competitive market behavior. *The Journal of Political Economy* 70(2): 111–137.

Tversky, A. and Kahneman, D. (1991) Loss aversion and riskless choice: A reference dependent model. *Quarterly Journal of Economics* 106(4): 1039–1061.

Uzawa, H. (1962) On the stability of Edgeworth's barter process. *Econometrica* 3(2): 218–232.

Walker, D. A. (1987) Walras's theories of tatonnement. *Journal of Political Economy* 95(4): 758–774.

Williams, A. W., Smith, V. L., Ledyard, J. O., and Gjerstad, S. (2000) Concurrent trading in two experimental markets with demand interdependence. *Economic Theory* 16: 511–528.

Wilson, R. (1987) On equilibria of bid-ask markets. In Feiwel, G. R. (ed.), *Arrow and the Ascent of Modern Economic Theory* (pp. 375–414). Houndmills: MacMillan Press.

4

OLIGOPOLY EXPERIMENTS IN THE CURRENT MILLENNIUM

Jan Potters and Sigrid Suetens

Tilburg University, Center, TILEC

1. Introduction

"Oligopoly is a market form in which a market or industry is dominated by a small number of sellers (oligopolists). Because there are few sellers, each oligopolist is likely to be aware of the actions of the others. The decisions of one firm influence, and are influenced by, the decisions of other firms." (cited from Wikipedia)

Oligopoly experiments have a long history. Around the same time that Vernon Smith published his 1962 article showing that double auction markets quickly converge to the competitive equilibrium, the first controlled oligopoly experiments were published. In these experiments quantity-setting sellers were treated as strategic decision-makers, playing a "game," and the demand side was simulated and directly built into the payoff matrix (Hoggatt, 1959; Sauermann and Selten, 1959; Fouraker *et al.*, 1961; Fouraker and Siegel, 1963).[1] Since then oligopoly has never disappeared from the attention of experimentalists – like it never has from the attention of theorists either – and it still makes up a major part of experimental industrial organization.

In this paper, we provide an overview of oligopoly experiments published in the current millennium. Roughly speaking, we distinguish three broad themes, and these themes correspond to the three sections in this paper: (1) oligopoly competition from a static perspective, (2) dynamics, (non-)convergence and learning processes, and (3) collusion and policy.

2. Oligopoly Competition from a Static Perspective

Most studies that take a static perspective on behavior in oligopoly either focus on the effect of a certain institution on competitiveness (e.g., price/cost margins, deviation from static equilibrium predictions) or evaluate the performance of comparative static predictions made by a specific theoretical model.

A Collection of Surveys on Market Experiments, First Edition.
Edited by Charles N. Noussair and Steven Tucker. Chapters © 2014 The Authors.
Book compilation © 2014 John Wiley & Sons, Ltd. Published 2014 by John Wiley & Sons, Ltd.

2.1 *Simultaneous-Move Quantity and Price Competition*

2.1.1 *Quantity Versus Price Competition*

Among the two main workhorse models of oligopoly, Bertrand markets are traditionally viewed as more competitive than Cournot markets in the sense that they lead to a lower price/cost margin in equilibrium. The reason is that for the same market demand, residual demand is more elastic under Bertrand competition than under Cournot competition. Huck *et al.* (2000) show that this is indeed the case in an experiment where four sellers compete in oligopoly markets with differentiated products, and where the nature of competition is varied across treatments keeping demand and cost conditions controlled. Experimental outcomes reported by Altavilla *et al.* (2006) and Davis (2011) are less conclusive on this issue, and suggest that prices can even be higher in Bertrand markets than in Cournot markets. Overall, however, Cournot markets typically exhibit higher prices than Bertrand markets (Engel, 2007).

A related but different question is whether Cournot and Bertrand markets differ in a behavioral sense, particularly, whether behavior and market outcomes in both types of markets deviate from the static NE in a similar way. Almost 20 years ago, Holt (1995) suggested that prices in price-setting experiments tend to be above equilibrium prices, and quantities in quantity-setting experiments above equilibrium quantities, which would imply that Bertrand markets are in a sense less competitive, or more conducive to collusion – taking NE as the natural behavioral benchmark – than Cournot markets. Holt's intuition is corroborated in the meta-study of Engel (2007), who reports that outcomes in price-setting experiments are indeed less competitive than equilibrium, whereas in quantity-setting experiments they are typically more competitive. Similarly, Suetens and Potters (2007), who pooled data from experiments that included both treatments with Cournot markets and treatments with Bertrand markets,[2] show that behavioral outcomes in Cournot markets tend to be more competitive relative to equilibrium as compared to those in Bertrand markets.

These aggregate results seem to come from a combination of two different behavioral mechanisms. One mechanism is that in some periods sellers are guided by the incentive to imitate the competitor that earned the highest payoff in the previous trading period. Such imitation incentives have a stronger impact in Cournot markets than in Bertrand markets in the sense that they drive behavior further away from NE toward the perfectly competitive outcome (more on imitation is in Section 3.3). Another mechanism is that Cournot and Bertrand markets generate different incentives for profit-maximizing sellers to follow moves by their competitors. Most oligopoly experiments use substitutable product markets with linear demand and costs. Under these conditions, quantity competition is characterized by strategic substitutability meaning that quantity-setters have an incentive to decrease production as the competitors' production increases. In contrast, price-setters increase their price as the price of competitors increases because prices are strategic complements. A price increase will thus be followed under price-setting, but a quantity increase will be offset under quantity-setting, and thus make markets in the aggregate more competitive under quantity- than under price-setting (see Potters and Suetens, 2009, for experimental evidence).

2.1.2 *Quantity and Price Competition*

If firms decide about production capacity before they set prices rather than – as under Bertrand competition – after demand is determined, the equilibrium price is the same as under Cournot competition (Kreps and Scheinkman, 1983). A number of experiments have been inspired by the Kreps–Scheinkman model. Typically, these experiments include treatments where a stage game is repeated among the same sellers who first set capacity, and then, after having received feedback about other sellers' capacity decisions, choose which price to set. The focus is on how well behavior corresponds to the Kreps–Scheinkman predictions, and, particularly, on the role of experience and learning.[3]

A robust finding is that experience and learning matter a lot in markets with quantity and price competition.[4] For one, experienced sellers – sellers who have experience with repeatedly playing the stage game with another seller – choose capacities closer to the Cournot quantity as compared to inexperienced sellers. Capacities chosen by inexperienced sellers are typically above the Cournot quantity, so more competitive (Muren, 2000; Anderhub et al., 2003; Goodwin and Mestelman, 2010; Hampton and Sherstyuk, 2012; Le Coq and Sturluson, 2012). Also, inexperienced sellers learn to set prices closer to the market clearing price level if they get the chance to learn the consequences of their prices, that is, if capacity choices are fixed for a number of rounds (Anderhub et al., 2003).[5]

2.2 Sequential-Move Games, Timing and Commitment

2.2.1 Exogeneous Timing

If decision-making is sequential rather than simultaneous, firms are predicted to behave according to the Stackelberg model. In the Stackelberg model one firm – the Stackelberg leader – chooses her production quantity or price first, and after observing this choice, the other firm – the Stackelberg follower – chooses her production quantity or price. If the follower observes the leader's action (perfect observability), outcomes differ quite substantially from those with simultaneous decision-making. These outcomes are referred to as Stackelberg outcomes. If it is costly for the follower to observe the leader's action or if the leader's action is observed with noise (imperfect observability), outcomes may differ from but may also be similar to those under simultaneous decision-making (Bagwell, 1995; van Damme and Hurkens, 1997). Experiments have been designed to test whether and under what conditions Stackelberg outcomes occur.

Overall, experimental outcomes are closer to Stackelberg than to Cournot or Bertrand outcomes if decision-making is sequential and leader and follower roles are appointed ex ante. This is shown for the case of perfect observability by Huck et al. (2001) and Kübler and Müller (2002). Specifically, Huck et al. (2001) find that total production quantity of firms in duopoly competing in quantities is higher under sequential than under simultaneous decision-making, and find behavioral support for the predicted first-mover advantage. Kübler and Müller (2002) find that with price competition sequential decision-making increases prices as compared to simultaneous decision-making and leads to a second-mover advantage.[6] Huck and Müller (2000) and Morgan and Várdy (2004) implement games with imperfect observability. In these games, Stackelberg outcomes occur more frequently than Cournot outcomes as long as the level of noise or cost of observation is not too high.

2.2.2 Endogenous Timing

If the timing of moves among ex ante symmetric firms is endogenous either simultaneous-move or Stackelberg outcomes may arise (Saloner, 1987; Hamilton and Slutsky, 1990).[7]

Whether one of the outcomes is predicted as a unique equilibrium depends on whether the timing of the competitor can be observed at the moment that firms decide on their price or quantity.

In general, in experiments where both simultaneous-move or Stackelberg outcomes can arise in equilibrium, Stackelberg leadership does not emerge easily (see Huck *et al.*, 2002a; Fonseca *et al.*, 2005; Müller, 2006, for experiments with quantity leadership). For one, subjects have difficulties coordinating the timing of their moves and sometimes prefer to delay, potentially, in order to avoid strategic uncertainty. Also, rather than playing BR, followers often reciprocate by producing a higher (lower) quantity, the higher (lower) the quantity produced by the leader. Even if the Stackelberg outcome is predicted as a unique equilibrium (as in the observable delay model with price-setting by Hamilton and Slutsky, 1990), Datta Mago and Dechenaux (2009) show in a price-setting experiment that quite a substantial degree of firm size asymmetry is needed to get price leadership in posted-offer markets. However, if the simultaneous-move outcome is predicted as a unique equilibrium (as in the observable delay model with quantity-setting by Hamilton and Slutsky, 1990), the majority of outcomes corresponds closely to the (predicted) equilibrium after learning, as shown in the experiment with quantity setting in Fonseca *et al.* (2006).

2.3 Innovation and Competition

2.3.1 R&D Investment and Patent Races

A substantial part of the theoretical industrial organization literature has focused on modeling oligopolistic firms that on a first stage invest in cost-reducing R&D and on a second stage compete in the product market. Several experiments have been inspired by this literature.

A number of experiments have studied the effect of technological spillovers on R&D investment, mostly motivated by theoretical models that point out that technological spillovers – the degree to which returns from R&D cannot be appropriated – are an important determinant of R&D investment. In particular, firms are predicted to invest less in R&D, the lower the level of appropriability, which is exactly the opposite as what is socially optimal. Jullien and Ruffieux (2001) find partial support for this prediction in an experiment where the investment stage is followed by a double auction. Suetens (2005) and Halbheer *et al.* (2009) find support for this prediction in experiments where firms are simulated to be Cournot competitors in the product market.[8] Moreover, as predicted, allowing firms to jointly decide on R&D if it is insufficiently appropriable helps to increase investment and bring it closer to the socially optimal level (Suetens, 2005). The intuition is that by cooperating in R&D, technological spillovers are internalized. If R&D is fully appropriable, however, R&D cooperation has the opposite effect and decreases investment, or slows down the rate of innovation (see Silipo, 2005, for evidence on the latter effect). The intuition is that with fully appropriable R&D, R&D cooperation serves as a means to economize on R&D investment rather than to internalize technological spillovers.

R&D investment has also been studied in experiments where firms are asymmetric, for example because they have *ex ante* different unit costs (Halbheer *et al.*, 2009), or because they are ahead/lag behind in a dynamic winner-take-all race (Zizzo, 2002; Silipo, 2005). One of the main predictions in such context is that the (low-cost) leader invests more than the (high-cost) follower. Silipo (2005), Halbheer *et al.* (2009), and Sacco and Schmutzler (2011) find support for this prediction, and Zizzo (2002) provides partial support in the sense that in his experiment leaders only invest more than followers when the gap is sufficiently large, but do not do so in general.

2.3.2 *Effect of Competition on R&D Investment*

A longstanding research topic in the theoretical and empirical IO literature is the effect of market power and competition on R&D investment and incentives to innovate. It is not clear *a priori* what this relation should look like. On the one hand, some degree of competition seems to stimulate firms to innovate more than a monopolist would. On the other hand, in order to avoid completely destroying temporary monopoly profits due to innovation, some degree of market power seems to be necessary. Pinning down the relation using field data is not straightforward due to, for example, endogeneity problems. Innovation and successful R&D investments may create market power and thus have an effect on the level of competition in a market. This problem is much less of an issue in laboratory experiments, where competition can be clearly defined and exogenously implemented.

"Competition" has been defined in many different ways in the experimental literature. Silipo (2005) measures the extent of collusion or market power as the size of a "prize" that can be obtained after an R&D race. He finds that a firm's willingness to cooperate in an R&D race depends positively on the size of this prize. Given that cooperation with fully appropriable R&D tends to decrease R&D investment, these results suggest that market power decreases R&D investment. Darai *et al.* (2010) define competition as the number of firms that operate in the product market or the nature of competition in the product market (Bertrand versus Cournot). They find, in line with the predictions, that R&D investment decreases as the number of firms increases from two to four. They also find that a shift from Cournot to Bertrand competition increases investment, which is only predicted for duopolies. Bertrand competition turns the investment stage into an R&D race and leads to overinvestment as compared to the static equilibrium. Sacco and Schmutzler (2011) define competition as the degree of product differentiation (the lower, the more competitive) and recover the predicted U-relation in the lab quite closely: as the degree of product differentiation decreases, R&D investment first decreases and then increases. Finally, Cason and Gangadharan (2013) show that without communication sellers invest much less in cooperative research (implemented as a stochastic threshold public good game) when the investment stage is followed by a double auction in which sellers realize the cost reduction of successful research than when not followed by a double auction. With communication, however, sellers invest in cooperative research irrespective of whether the cost reduction is realized in a double auction or not.[9]

2.3.3 *R&D Cooperation and Tacit Collusion*

Whereas R&D cooperation helps to solve the problem of underinvestment if returns to R&D cannot be fully appropriated, it may also facilitate tacit collusion in the product market. Suetens (2008), for example, observes more tacit price collusion among duopolists that explicitly engage in cost-reducing R&D cooperation – by signing binding R&D contracts – than among duopolists that do not do so, or do not have the option to do so. In the same spirit, Nicklisch (2012) finds a positive correlation between *implicit* cooperation in investment in product innovation and the extent to which price-setting duopolists tacitly collude. If competition in the product market is sufficiently fierce, however, as is the case in the double auction markets in

Cason and Gangadharan (2013), cooperation in R&D does not seem to spill over to cooperation in the product market.

2.4 *Price Dispersion*

Although the "law of one price" prescribes that identical products are priced at one and the same price, in reality there exists persistent price dispersion. Theorists have suggested a number of reasons for why the "law of one price" may fail in practice (e.g., capacity constraints, product differentiation, costly buyer search). One advantage of laboratory experimentation for studying price dispersion is that the relevance of each of these reasons can be studied in a controlled way. More importantly, in the lab products can be induced to be genuinely identical, such that some potential confounds can be excluded by design.

2.4.1 *Capacity Constraints and Product Differentiation*

Price dispersion can be rationalized if one takes sellers to be capacity-constrained. This assumption is often maintained in posted-offer pricing experiments and has as a consequence that rather than pricing at marginal costs, sellers use a mixed strategy in equilibrium (see, for example, Davis and Wilson, 2000, 2006, 2008b; Davis *et al.*, 2002, 2009; Davis, 2009; Fonseca and Normann, 2013). Alternatively, products may look identical at the surface, but are in fact differentiated due to, for example, differences in location, advertising or customer service. Under spatial price competition, for example, firms are typically predicted to randomize their pricing strategies as well (at least, under certain conditions), and experimental evidence supports these predictions (Orzen and Sefton, 2008; Peeters and Strobel, 2009; Barreda-Tarrazona *et al.*, 2011).[10]

2.4.2 *Costly Buyer Search*

Price dispersion may also stem from information asymmetries between buyers and sellers that make it costly for buyers to search for the product with the lowest price. For example, if with some probability buyers observe a sample of the available prices and it is costly to obtain information about the other prices, Burdett and Judd (1983) show that the unique NE is one in mixed strategies. Intuitively, the equilibrium lies in between one of two extremes (see Cason and Friedman, 2003, for a streamlined version of the model). In one extreme all buyers observe all prices and have zero search costs – resulting in Bertrand NE – and in the other extreme all buyers observe just one price and have positive search costs – resulting in monopoly pricing (Diamond, 1971).[11] Cason and Friedman (2003) find that the range of prices observed in experimental posted-offer markets inspired by this search model is predicted quite well, and so are comparative statics (i.e., the impact of sample size and search costs), particularly if buyers are simulated. Along the same lines, Morgan *et al.* (2006a) find support for the predicted comparative statics in an experiment with informed (price-sensitive) and uninformed (price-insensitive) consumers inspired by the model of Varian (1980). They find that an increase in the fraction of informed consumers decreases prices, and an increase in the number of firms in the market leads to more price dispersion.[12]

   A unique equilibrium in mixed strategies is also predicted in models with costly buyer search where firms choose whether to advertise their prices (to make prices public to buyers). And also here, comparative static predictions are supported by experimental evidence. For example, in experiments with *ex ante* or *ex post* heterogeneous buyers, Morgan *et al.* (2006b), Cason and Datta (2006), and Cason and Mago (2010) find that as advertising costs increase, sellers advertise less frequently and prices are higher.

The leitmotif across many of the above-mentioned studies is that comparative statics are very much in line with mixed-strategy predictions. However, outcomes often differ quite substantially from point predictions, particularly if buyers are human players rather than computerized robots (see Cason and Mago, 2010; Barreda-Tarrazona *et al.*, 2011). For example, sellers in Morgan *et al.* (2006b), Cason and Datta (2006), and Cason and Mago (2010) typically overadvertise, which may lead to lower than predicted prices. And prices are particularly low if buyers are human.[13] It has been suggested that allowing for noisy play à la QRE – where players "do not always choose best responses, but they are more likely to choose better responses than worse responses" (cited from Cason and Mago, 2010) – on the part of sellers and, if applicable, buyers, may help to explain price and other *levels*. In fact, Baye and Morgan (2004) show that introducing bounded rationality à la QRE in a simple pricing game (as suggested by Dufwenberg and Gneezy, 2000) helps to explain price levels and price dispersion observed in experiments with homogeneous products, where buyers can perfectly observe price and do not incur search costs.

At the individual level, however, the models typically break down: observed prices are correlated in time rather than randomly distributed (see, e.g., Cason and Friedman, 2003). This suggests that the factors that potentially influence behavioral dynamics (e.g., information conditions) may play a crucial role for determining which (static) outcome is converged too. This is the topic of Section 3.

Finally, price dispersion can also arise due to sellers attempting to induce high prices, and can thus be seen as a consequence of uncoordinated collusive pricing (see Durham *et al.*, 2004; Davis *et al.*, 2010). In this interpretation, sellers communicate or try to do so through their prices. They use prices as signals to induce high prices by other sellers, or as responses to other sellers' past prices. For example, Durham *et al.* (2004) report that price signals by sellers in posted-offer markets have a significantly positive effect on subsequent average prices in the market. In a similar vein, Bruttel (2009) shows that when information about prices is public, sellers in randomly matched Bertrand duopolies set high prices to induce high prices by potential future competitors. More on such attempts to collude can be found in Section 4.1.

3. Dynamics, (non-)Convergence, and Learning Processes

Most models in industrial organization are static models (for example, Cournot, Bertrand, Stackelberg model). Since they are meant to describe field settings in which firms interact repeatedly, an important question is whether or not firms and industries evolve toward the static predictions over time. Experiments are an excellent tool to study dynamics and convergence properties of oligopolistic markets because they allow to abstract from "disturbing" influences such as demand shocks, or, on the contrary, to isolate the effect of certain influences such as demand shocks or information conditions.

3.1 *Stability and Convergence of Cournot Markets*

A characteristic of Cournot markets with multiple firms is that stability conditions and conditions under which learning dynamics converge to the NE are generally more stringent than is the case for Bertrand markets.[14] For example, in the textbook case with homogeneous products, linear demand and constant marginal cost, a process where firms best-respond one-by-one to the rivals' past actions – adaptive best-response (BR) – does not converge to the NE in Cournot markets with more than three firms (Theocharis, 1960), while it does so under Bertrand competition. Intuitively, because under Cournot competition actions are strategic substitutes, all firms best-responding to the rivals' previous production quantity results in overshooting as compared to the NE, which leads to sharp fluctuations of alternating zero and maximum production quantity. The BR dynamic under Bertrand competition, on the contrary, is not characterized by oscillations because of strategic complementarity, and generally converges more easily to the NE.[15] Whether markets converge and, if so, to which outcome is ultimately a behavioral question.

A number of laboratory experiments have studied whether stability of NE helps organizing and explaining behavior in Cournot markets. Most of these experiments vary between treatments whether the Cournot NE is stable or not (whether the BR dynamic converges to NE or not), for example, by implementing different cost structures. A number of these studies find that stability properties have a substantial impact on behavior. Cox and Walker (1998), for example, report results from an experiment that varies across treatments whether BR curves "cross in the correct way," by varying the extent of asymmetry in marginal costs between Cournot duopolists. Duopolists compete during 30 rounds and are randomly re-matched. Aggregate behavior in the experiment ends up being close to NE only in treatments where BR curves cross correctly (where NE is stable and interior). In treatments where BR curves do not cross correctly, behavior does not converge to an equilibrium (even though it is stable). In a similar vein, Rassenti *et al.* (2000) find that in asymmetric five-seller Cournot markets with a unique and unstable NE that are repeated 75 times, behavior does not converge but instead exhibits substantial intertemporal and cross-sectional variation. Also related is Davis *et al.* (2003) who present results from an experiment with randomly re-matched triopolies and a unique NE that varies across treatments the steepness of marginal costs. They find that the percentage of NE choices in the final rounds is higher when marginal costs are steep – and the NE is stable – than when they are flat – and the NE is closer to being unstable.[16]

Other treatment variations that affect stability in Cournot markets are the presence of inertia and the degree of horizontal product differentiation. Huck *et al.* (1999) show that introducing inertia can stabilize the BR dynamic and make it converge to NE. Huck *et al.* (2002b) compare repeated Cournot quadropolies with and without inertia in a laboratory experiment. In the treatment with inertia but not so in the treatment without inertia, participants keep the choice from the previous period with a probability of one third. The observed frequency distribution of individual quantities across all periods is somewhat more peaked with than without inertia, but in both treatments there is a clear move toward NE, and subjects best-respond to a similar extent. Also Davis (2011), who varies stability of the Cournot NE by varying the degree of product differentiation in repeated four-seller markets, does not find differences in convergence between stable and unstable treatments, neither before or after an exogenously induced nominal shock. In both of his treatments, quantities oscillate substantially but also move toward NE.

3.2 *Cycles under Price Competition*

Whereas dynamics under quantity competition are predicted and observed to oscillate heavily – in most applications, quantities are strategic substitutes – dynamics under price competition are typically much smoother due to strategic complementarity. In markets with homogeneous goods, for example, the BR for a firm is to slightly undercut the price charged by competitors.

As long as the combined capacity of all firms is sufficient to fulfill demand, this process converges to the Bertrand NE. However, if the price is so low that capacity constraints are hit, the BR is to charge the monopoly price. In the latter case, the dynamic process does not converge but leads to an Edgeworth cycle – a cycle of undercutting and jumping up to a higher price. Maskin and Tirole (1988) show that in an infinitely repeated game framework Edgeworth cycles may result if firms take turns choosing prices, even when they are not capacity constrained.

Laboratory studies on price competition have reported evidence of price cycles (see Davis and Wilson, 2008a, for an overview of pre-2000 studies). Bruttel (2009a) and Leufkens and Peeters (2011), for example, find that subjects who alternately set prices typically first collude or try to do so, then enter a phase of undercutting, and after a number of low-price periods turn back to collusion. Interestingly, similar patterns seem to appear in simultaneous-move experiments (see Durham *et al.*, 2004; Bruttel, 2009; Peeters and Strobel, 2009; Davis, 2011; Leufkens and Peeters, 2011) which suggests that some inertia is present also in simultaneous-move settings. For example, Durham *et al.* (2004) report that subjects who post a high price are likely to maintain it in subsequent periods.

Price cycles that have some flavor of Edgeworth cycles are also reported by Cason *et al.* (2005), who ran an experiment where it is costly for buyers to search for the seller with the lowest price. Perhaps the strongest evidence for Edgeworth cycles comes from a Bertrand pricing experiment reported by Fonseca and Normann (2013). Fonseca and Normann vary the extent of excess capacity and number of firms in the market (2 and 3) and show that as capacity decreases, dynamics correspond closer to Edgeworth price cycles.

3.3 *Feedback, Information and Learning Processes*

Clearly, convergence or non-convergence results highly depend on the nature of the learning process. Fictitious play, for example, which attributes weight to the entire history of competitors' play, BR and other adaptive learning rules are known to converge to NE under strategic complementarity (Milgrom and Roberts, 1990). The imitation dynamic, however, where players imitate the competitor who was most successful in the previous period (the "best performer"), converges to the competitive (Walrasian) outcome rather than to NE (Vega-Redondo, 1997).[17] The nature of the learning process, in turn, highly depends on the information firms have at their disposal and the type of feedback they get about past behavior of competitors. For example, if no information is available about one's profit function, it is basically impossible to BR to past actions of others. Or if information about past performance of competitors is hidden, it is difficult to imitate the firm that performed best. Several experiments have studied how different types of information affect behavioral dynamics and, consequently, market outcomes.

3.3.1 *Information About Own Payoff Function*

Intuitively, firms may more often turn to simple imitation rules, the more complicated the decision environment or the less information they have about the decision environment. This intuition has been a motivation to run experiments where no information about the payoff function is provided, or where the level of information about one's own payoff function varies across treatments, and where feedback is given about past actions and payoffs of competitors.[18]

Huck *et al.* (1999), for example, vary the level of information from detailed information about the market (with payoff- and BR-calculator) to no information (without payoff- or BR-calculator) in repeated Cournot quadropolies. Bosch-Domènech and Vriend (2003), on the contrary, run randomly re-matched duopolies and triopolies and give all subjects the necessary information to calculate one's payoff and BR but vary the level of complexity of calculating them. In their least complicated treatment subjects have a convenient profit table and in their most complicated treatment they only have the minimally necessary ingredients available. Selten and Apesteguia (2005) let subjects compete on a circle with locational product differentiation and do not provide any information about the payoff function (except that it is constant throughout all rounds).

Overall, the experimental results provide clear evidence that imitation of the best performer is an important force in environments where no information is available to calculate one's own payoff (of course, provided that one gets information about past actions and payoffs of competitors). The consequence is that, in the end, market outcomes are more competitive if no information is provided about one's payoff function than if such information is provided.[19] Selten and Apesteguia (2005) show that the imitation effect may even overrule a numbers effect. In line with imitation equilibrium (due to Selten and Ostmann, 2001) they observe higher prices in four- or five-firm markets than in three-firm markets in which firms compete on a circle.[20] However, the results by Bosch-Domènech and Vriend (2003) suggest that if information needed to calculate one's payoff or BR is available, additional calculation complexity does not induce subjects to imitate the best performer more often.

3.3.2 *Feedback About Competitors*

A number of experiments vary the level of feedback about past actions and performance of competitors. Huck *et al.* (2000), Davis (2002), and Altavilla *et al.* (2006), for example, include treatments where subjects who compete in Cournot or Bertrand markets are informed about past aggregate actions of competitors (total quantity or average price) and treatments where subjects are (on top of aggregate outcomes) informed about past individual actions and payoffs of competitors. Huck *et al.* (1999) include two such treatments and focus on Cournot markets. Offerman *et al.* (2002) also focus on Cournot markets and include a third treatment with an intermediate level of feedback: feedback about aggregate and individual actions (but not payoffs). Bigoni (2010) lets subjects in Cournot markets choose which information to obtain.

Results from experimental Cournot markets largely point in the same direction. If only aggregate information is available about past actions, outcomes end up being close to NE. In some experiments this is due to subjects playing BR (e.g., Huck *et al.*, 1999; Bigoni, 2010), but this is not clear for all experiments. The most important general tendency is that feedback about competitors' past actions and payoffs – whether provided by the experimenter or chosen by the subject – induces subjects to imitate the best performer more often than when no feedback about competitors' payoff is provided. The consequence is that aggregate quantity is higher than the NE quantity and, in line with Vega-Redondo (1997), closer to the competitive (Walrasian) quantity.[21]

In Bertrand markets there is not much of a difference in average prices between settings with feedback about individual prices and payoffs and settings with only feedback about the market price – average prices are typically close to the Bertrand NE, at least after learning (see also Bruttel, 2009; Boone *et al.*, 2012) – but this is not that surprising given that Bertrand NE predictions are typically close to (with differentiated products) or even the same as (with homogeneous products) the competitive price. This does not necessarily imply that under price competition subjects do not imitate the best performer. In fact, in an experiment with price competition and increasing marginal costs Abbink and Brandts (2008) show that imitation of the best performer serves as a coordination device – it helps to coordinate on one of the multiple equilibria – particularly in three- and four-seller markets.

The experimental studies also show that there is substantial heterogeneity in individual learning processes. Subjects tend to follow a hybrid of different learning rules. For example, Offerman *et al.* (2002) show that rather than imitating the best performer some subjects tend to imitate the "exemplary firm" – the one who produced least in the previous period – if they have the necessary information to do so, particularly if no information about competitors' past payoff is provided. And Bigoni (2010) shows that subjects who are free to choose which information to obtain are mostly interested in viewing past individual quantities and profits – so have all the ingredients to imitate the best performer – but still a majority of them plays BR.

3.3.3 *Feedback About Other Markets*

Another type of feedback that potentially has quite a substantial effect on behavior in oligopolistic markets is feedback about other markets. Evolutionary models have shown that if firms use average profitability across all markets as an aspiration level – and do not change their action as long as they do not fall behind their aspiration – prices or quantities move from NE toward more joint-profit maximizing outcomes (Dixon, 2000; Oechssler, 2002). Altavilla *et al.* (2006) provide evidence for such effect for Cournot duopolies with random matching but not for Bertrand duopolies.

In related experiments by Dufwenberg and Gneezy (2000, 2002) and Bruttel (2009) prices stay well above NE in randomly matched homogeneous-goods Bertrand duopolies when subjects receive feedback about all submitted prices in all markets.[22] In particular, prices are higher, on the one hand, as compared to the case where feedback is limited to only "winning" prices across all markets and, on the other hand, as compared to the case where feedback is limited to the price of the competitor in one's own market. These results indicate that sellers realize they can affect the distribution of prices observed by potential future competitors, and at least some of them use this opportunity to signal their willingness to increase their price. The combination of such signaling behavior and BR to the expected population price explains dynamics quite well (Bruttel, 2009).[23]

4. Collusion and Policy

Whether and when firms are able to collude is a classic topic in IO and also in the current millennium numerous experimental papers have been devoted to it. The current section reviews the results.

4.1 *Tacit Collusion*

Tacit collusion (or conscious parallelism) occurs when firms coordinate strategies in order to raise prices and profits without explicitly agreeing to do so. It is difficult to identify such conduct with field data because it is usually unknown what "non-collusive" prices and profits are. An advantage of the lab is that at least it is known what the static noncooperative equilibrium is. Therefore, experimental markets are typically taken to be collusive if aggregate outcomes are less competitive than in the static equilibrium (Holt, 1995).[24] Here we review some of the factors that may affect the incidence of tacit collusion in experiments with repeated interaction (fixed matching).

4.1.1 *Market Conditions*

The scope for tacit collusion is strongly affected by the number of competitors. Basically, implicit coordination on a joint-profit maximizing price is frequently observed in markets with two sellers, rarely in markets with three sellers, and almost never in markets with four or more sellers.[25] This effect has been observed in posted-offer markets (Brandts and Guillen, 2007; Davis, 2009; Ewing and Kruse, 2010; Fonseca and Normann, 2012), under Bertrand competition (Abbink and Brandts, 2005, 2008; Orzen, 2008), as well as Cournot competition (Huck *et al.*, 2004b).[26]

Another supply factor that has been shown to impact collusion is the cost structure. Premillennium experiments had shown that cost asymmetries may hinder collusion (Mason *et al.*, 1992; Mason and Phillips, 1997) in Cournot duopolies. Argenton and Müller (2012) extend the analysis to asymmetric Bertrand duopolies with convex costs, which have mixed strategy equilibria. They find, remarkably, that cost asymmetries facilitate collusion. The authors speculate that under asymmetry the low cost firm acts as a price leader who is followed by the high cost firm.

Anderson *et al.* (2010) compare price setting duopolies with substitute products (so that prices are strategic complements) to price setting duopolies with complementary products (where prices are strategic substitutes). They find that, in the aggregate, the former markets are more collusive than the latter. This is remarkable, at least for us, since it goes against the suggestion that games with strategic complements are not as competitive as games with strategic substitutes (Potters and Suetens, 2009). It is not entirely clear what drives this difference. Possibly, it is related to (the absolute value of) the slope of the BR function, which affects the force of BR dynamics in pulling the outcome toward NE. A somewhat related issue is studied by Bruttel (2009a) when she compares price setting duopolies with and without product differentiation. Her aim is to examine whether the analysis of the critical discount factor for the sustainability of cooperation in infinitely repeated games (Friedman, 1971) is relevant for tacit collusion in finitely repeated games as well. This seems to be the case indeed, as she finds less collusion with differentiated products than with homogeneous products.

Also demand conditions are important. Abbink and Brandts (2009) study collusion in Bertrand duopolies under dynamic demand conditions. In one treatment demand grows over time; in the mirror treatment demand declines over time. The results show that collusion is more frequent when demand grows than when it shrinks. The authors conjecture that the prospect of declining profits exerts a disciplining effect and discourages defection. Another demand factor that seems important in Bertrand markets is how demand is determined in case both firms offer the same price. Puzzello (2008) shows that collusion is easier if demand is shared equally than in case total demand is randomly allocated to either one of the two firms in case of a tie. The effect is particularly strong when the price space is rather coarse.

4.1.2 *Facilitating Institutions*

An institution that seems of central importance for the scope for collusion is the possibility to monitor competitors' conduct, especially when price is a noisy signal of that conduct due to unobservable demand shocks. In line with the theoretical literature, which dates back to Stigler (1964), Feinberg and Snyder (2002) show that it is more difficult to collude when there is uncertainty about rival's actions (see also Aoyagi and Fréchette, 2009). For Cournot triopolies, Offerman *et al.* (2002) find that collusion is more frequent when firms receive information about each competitor's quantity rather than just about aggregate quantity. In case a market is not hospitable to collusion in the first place, matters are more subtle (see Section 3.3).

Another facilitating institution that has drawn considerable interest are price matching guarantees (PMGs). The predominant view in IO is that PMGs are anticompetitive since they reduce the incentives of firms to undercut their rivals. There are other perspectives though, such as the role of PMGs as credible price signals or as price discrimination devices. Field studies on the matter are rather scarce and inconclusive in all. Such a state of affairs calls for experiments and several researchers have picked up on that call lately. The way PMGs are typically implemented in the lab is that a firm issues a price offer but that its effective price is equal to the lowest price offer in the market.

The experimental evidence suggests that such PMGs lead to higher prices, above the noncooperative level. Fatas and Manez (2007), for example, find that in a duopoly with differentiated goods prices are close to the collusive level if both firms implement a PMG, whereas prices are close to the noncooperative level if neither firm implements a PMG. The potential loss of being undercut by rival's price offer is entirely eliminated with a PMG in this setting. This anticompetitive effect holds both with homogeneous and with differentiated goods (Mago and Pate, 2009). Moreover, it does not seem to matter much whether the PMG is imposed exogenously or whether it is chosen by the firms themselves. In simple settings most subjects seem to realize very quickly that opting for a PMG is a profitable thing to do (Fatas and Manez, 2007), although in more complex settings this seems less obvious (Deck and Wilson, 2003).

It appears that the collusion facilitating effect of PMGs is robust to products being homogeneous rather than heterogeneous (Dugar, 2007; Mago and Pate, 2009), to the market having two, three, or four firms (Deck and Wilson, 2003; Dugar, 2007), to firms having asymmetric costs (Mago and Pate, 2009), and to a design with strangers or partners matching (Dugar, 2007). There are other factors though which can substantially reduce the collusive effect of PMGs. One is the presence of hassle costs, due to which it is costly for buyers to effectuate a PMG (Dugar and Sorensen, 2006). In the experiment, (simulated) buyers with hassle costs buy from the firm which directly charges the lowest price, which puts a premium on competitive pricing even when other firms implement a PMG. Another relevant factor is the use of a more aggressive price beating guarantee which ensures that a lower price of a competitor is not matched but undercut (Fatás *et al.*, 2005, 2013). Finally, using a relatively elaborate design with both human sellers and buyers, Yuan and Krishna (2011) show that when buyers need to search for price information and informed buyers have more elastic demand than uninformed buyers, PMGs may even be procompetitive as they increase buyers' incentives to search. So, experiments have generated many useful insights, but the jury is still out on whether or not PMGs are predominantly collusive.

Finally, one recent paper studies capacity coordination. In case of an unexpected negative demand shock an argument in favor of capacity coordination is that it will prevent the duplication of fixed but avoidable costs. The risk, however, is that it will facilitate tacit price collusion. Hampton and Sherstyuk (2012) implement a repeated Kreps–Scheinkman two-stage capacity and price-setting game in which halfway there is a demand shock and they compare treatments with and without explicit capacity coordination. They find, first, that explicit capacity coordination is not necessary for a quick adjustment of capacities after the shock, and, second, that explicit capacity coordination has a pronounced effect on collusion. The net effect of capacity coordination on welfare is clearly negative.

4.2 *Cartels and Competition Policy*

From experimental papers dating as far back as Friedman (1967) we know that firms will use communication opportunities to conspire. Moreover, communication is often found to be effective in raising profits, whether the main decision variable is price, quantity, or location (Brown Kruse and Schenk, 2000). An interesting question which is, remarkably, only picked up recently is whether and how the impact of communication varies with the number of firms in a market. Fonseca and Normann (2012) explore the difference between explicit and tacit collusion in Bertrand oligopolies with various numbers of firms, and find that the profit gain of being able to talk is non-monotonic in the number of firms, with medium-sized markets realizing the biggest increase over tacit collusion. Duopolies do not need communication to collude and large markets are unable to collude even with communication. Medium-sized industries are rather competitive without communication and the ability to talk enables them to maintain some degree of collusion.

Usually, in experiments decisions are made by individual subjects. Gillet *et al.* (2011) compare repeated Bertrand games in which the decision whether or not to enter a cartel is determined either by an individual or by a group. In the latter case, they distinguish three different decision rules: majority rule, consensus, or dictatorship. The results show that the frequency at which cartels form is independent of who makes the decision, individual or group. As far as the cartel prices are concerned though, they find that dictators ("CEOs") set the highest prices.[27]

It seems intuitive that antitrust fines discourage the formation of cartels. Andersson and Wengström (2007) use repeated Bertrand duopolies to explore this basic intuition. They compare a treatment in which firms can freely communicate to one in which sending messages bears costs (due to antitrust). The results show that costs reduce the number of messages, but also enhance their effectiveness in sustaining collusion. The combined effect leads to higher prices on average. The fact that talk is no longer cheap (literally), seems to enhance its commitment value. Bigoni *et al.* (2012) study a setting in which the cost of communication is not fixed, like in Andersson and Wengström (2007), but stochastic. If firms decide to form a cartel, there is a fixed probability that the cartel is detected and a fine is issued. Despite the many differences in design, also Bigoni *et al.* (2012) also find that the presence of antitrust fines leads to fewer but more effective cartels.

To destabilize cartels many authorities have implemented leniency policies, hoping to encourage whistle-blowing by offering a cartel member (partial) immunity from fines or even a bonus when reporting the cartel to the authorities. The idea is very intuitive but not uncontested. Leniency could also turn whistle blowing into an effective punishment against defectors who wish to undercut the cartel price. A number of recent experiments suggests that the latter concern may be overstated. Apesteguia *et al.* (2007a) study one-shot Bertrand triopolies in which firms can choose to communicate and form a cartel. The design implements treatments with and without leniency. The results show that leniency can significantly reduce the prevalence of cartels. However, to deter cartels it is important just to be lenient and not to actually reward whistle blowing.

Also in repeated interactions, which arguably give more leeway for a potential negative effect, leniency seems to discourage the formation of cartels. Whether the cartels that still form are destabilized by leniency or not seems to depend on the details of the schemes. Also the negative effect of rewarding whistle blowers rather than just granting immunity from fines seems to be less robust. It may depend on whether the interaction is one-shot or repeated, and on the timing of cartel formation and whistle-blowing (Hinloopen and Soetevent, 2008; Hamaguchi *et al.*, 2009; Bigoni *et al.*, 2012).

4.3 *Regulation*

4.3.1 *Price Ceilings and Price Floors*

Price ceilings are another common regulatory instrument. The claim that if they are not binding they cannot harm competition either, is challenged in the IO literature with reference to their possible role as focal points. Engelmann and Normann (2009) and Engelmann and Müller (2011) study price caps in an environment which seems to be more favorable for finding a collusive effect than some earlier experiments from the 1980s in which the incentives to collude were very low. In Engelmann and Normann (2009) two firms interact repeatedly, under conditions of asymmetric costs such that they disagree on the preferred collusive price and could benefit from a coordination device. By colluding at the price ceiling firms can increase profits by 31%. Still, in spite of this hospitable environment, the experimental results indicate that price ceilings are not able to move prices toward more collusion.

An interesting and somewhat counterintuitive effect of price floors is that they may actually be procompetitive in price-setting oligopoly markets. In the standard Bertrand equilibrium, a firm's profit function is completely flat and any price greater than or equal to marginal cost gives the same profit of zero. There is no cost of deviating from the equilibrium, and that may be why firms often deviate from equilibrium in experiments and choose (very) high prices. A price floor restores a nonnegligble cost of deviating from the equilibrium, since the positive expected profit at the price floor may get lost. Dufwenberg *et al.* (2007) show that in a duopoly market a price floor reduces average prices indeed. The result, however, does not carry over to quadropolies where price floors do not seem to affect average prices.

4.3.2 *Resticted Entry*

In some markets, entry needs to be restricted for technical or economic reasons. Limited spectrum size, for example, precludes free entry in mobile telecoms, and natural monopoly properties constrain entry into energy transportation. A number of mechanisms have been proposed to solve, at least in theory, the resulting tension between cost efficiency and market power. Often a crucial assumption is that firms refrain from collusion. Experiments can be used to explore how the mechanisms fair in practice.

A common way to regulate entry is to auction off the market positions to the highest bidders. Since the entry fees are sunk it is hypothesized that they will not affect postentry market prices. The experiment by Offerman and Potters (2006) challenges that hypothesis. They implement an entry auction in which four candidates bid for two positions in a repeated symmetric price-setting duopoly market. They find that postentry market prices are higher with this entry auction than they are in case the two market positions are given away for free. In particular, postentry collusion is more prevalent with than without entry fees. This is reminiscent to other papers that find a significant effect of sunk costs on prices in oligopoly markets (Buchheit and Feltovich, 2011; Durham *et al.*, 2004).

Yardstick competition is a regulatory scheme that introduces competition between local monopolists and is very similar to oligopoly. The essence is that the price level of each firm is determined by the cost level of the other firm(s). Yardstick competition works best with high-powered incentives to curtail costs. Potters *et al.* (2004) implement yardstick competition between two symmetric local monopolists who interact repeatedly for a finite number of periods. Since price is regulated, firms only choose effort to reduce cost. They compare a low-powered scheme (where price depends on both firms' cost) to a high-powered scheme (where price depends only on the other firm's cost level). Contrary to the theoretical prediction, in the experiment the low-powered scheme outperforms the high-powered scheme. The reason is that collusion is much more prevalent in the latter case. It seems that low noncooperative profits are an important plus factor for collusion. This is reminiscent of the analysis of the critical discount factor for infinitely repeated games, in which the difference between noncooperative and cooperative profits plays a central role.

5. Concluding Remarks

It is hard to summarize the results or insights from such a broad collection of papers, and we will not attempt to do so. Rather we wish to conclude with a number of thoughts that came up while writing this survey.

Oligopoly experiments exemplify many of the key advantages of laboratory experiments. One is the mere possibility of observation, which is essential, for instance, for studying the formation, sustenance, and impact of explicit cartels. Another is knowledge of the key market parameters, which is important for theory testing but also for studying phenomena like convergence or tacit collusion which are defined in relation to a theoretical benchmark. Finally, there is the possibility to create a counterfactual which allows for a clean, ceteris paribus, assessment of the impact of particular conditions (e.g., incomplete information) or institutions (e.g., price matching).

The last issue reminds us of an important remark by Holt (1995), namely "that contractual practices in unregulated markets are endogenous, so the effects of exogenously imposed laboratory rules should be interpreted with care" (p. 416). At the time, Holt (1995) notices, there were almost no studies with endogenous institutions. There are quite a few now. For example, Andersson and Wengström (2012) and Gillet *et al.* (2011) give firms the choice whether or not to communicate and conspire, Fatás *et al.* (2005) allow firms to opt for a price beating guarantee rather than imposing it, and Lindqvist and Stennek (2005) endogenize the occurrence of mergers. There are other domains where endogeneity may be important though. For example, the provision of feedback about competitors' conduct is often harmless or may even have procompetitive effects when imposed by itself; at the same time it is found to be crucial to sustain explicit cartels. Hence, if information exchange between firms is endogenous it may well be a consequence of (explicit) collusion rather than a cause of (tacit) collusion (Potters, 2009).

A question that is often raised in relation to experiments, and to IO experiments in particular, is whether the results generalize to the setting of interest outside the laboratory. There are several dimensions to this concern. One is that decision-makers in firms are not students (Frechette, 2011). Another is that decisions of firms are usually not made by one individual acting on her or his own account. Importantly, some experiments have started to explore whether individual decisions are similar to those made by an agent provided with incentives by a principal (Huck *et al.*, 2004a); others have begun to explore the decisions by groups of individuals (boards) and how these depend on the decision-making procedure in the group (Bornstein *et al.*, 2008; Raab and Schipper, 2009; Gillet *et al.*, 2011). In some cases, individuals seem to act very differently from groups, whereas in other cases few differences are found. It is too early for general insights, and we expect to see more such studies.

Finally, let us mention what we think is a main shortcoming of this review. Besides the lack of depth and detail, an omission is a discussion of the insights from experiments with bi-matrix games such as the prisoner's dilemma. Several issues which play a role in these games, such as the impact of certain types of feedback information on learning and cooperation, or the role of repetition, have direct relevance for oligopoly as well. Hopefully, a future review, can pay due attention to the insights of such studies.

Acknowledgements

Suetens acknowledges financial support from the Netherlands Organization for Scientific Research (NWO). The authors thank Charles Noussair and participants in an internal TILEC seminar for their valuable comments.

Notes

1. See Bosch-Domènech and Vriend (2008) for a detailed overview of these early Cournot experiments.
2. Data from Fouraker and Siegel (1963), Huck *et al.* (2000), Davis (2002), and Altavilla *et al.* (2006) were included.
3. Another experiment where sellers choose both quantity and price is reported by Brandts and Guillen (2007). Because it focuses on collusion, we discuss it in Section 4.
4. In market with quantity competition only, as shown by Goodwin and Mestelman (2010), inexperienced players choose quantities close to the Cournot quantity from the start. Experienced players end up choosing quantities somewhat below the Cournot quantity.
5. Muren (2000) uses triopoly markets and the journals use duopoly markets.
6. Although comparative statics are largely in line with theoretical predictions, the Stackelberg model does not organize behavior perfectly. For example, due to reciprocal behavior – followers often respond with an increase in quantity to an increase in the leader's quantity – the estimated BR of followers typically has a higher slope than predicted, particularly when subjects play a repeated game (cf. fixed matching). In fact, the "behavioral" slope of the BR curve turns out to be positive in some cases, even under Stackelberg quantity competition.
7. In Saloner (1987) firms simultaneously decide on their production quantity in each of two consecutive periods. In the action commitment model by Hamilton and Slutsky (1990) firms simultaneously decide in period 1 to commit to an action or delay their action to period 2, then observe the journal firm's move in period 1, and then decide on their action in period 2. In the model with observable delay by Hamilton and Slutsky (1990) firms simultaneously announce their timing (period 1 of 2) and decide on price or quantity after observing the timing chosen by the journal firm.
8. In fact, the result goes all the way back to Isaac and Reynolds (1988).

9. When there is no opportunity to coordinate easily in the research phase (e.g., by means of communication), the double auction thus seem to hamper coordination on an efficient equilibrium.

10. In the same vein, Collins and Sherstyuk (2000) report that location choices correspond quite well to predicted mixed strategies in a fixed-price location experiment. See also Huck *et al.* (2002a) and Camacho-Cuena *et al.* (2005) for experiments on spatial competition.

11. See Abrams *et al.* (2000) for an experiment that compares these two extremes.

12. In an experiment where sellers can track buyers' search history and price discriminate, Deck and Wilson (2006) find that (informed) buyers with a search-intensive history are charged lower prices than (uninformed) buyers who search less.

13. The introduction of human buyers can also have the opposite effect, and increase prices. Kalayci and Potters (2011) show that sellers may make it more difficult for buyers to compare the quality of different products in order to reduce the price elasticity of demand and increase market power. Such strategies only have an effect with human buyers, but not with rational computerized buyers.

14. See Vives (1999) for a theoretical rationale and Davis (2011) for experimental evidence.

15. For Bertrand competition the general result obtained by Milgrom and Roberts (1990) applies: in games with strategic complementarities any adaptive learning dynamic (e.g., BR, fictitious play and Bayesian learning) eventually converges to the (set of) NE.

16. Davis *et al.* (2003) include treatments with fixed matching and do not find any effect of steepness of marginal costs there. This suggests that journal (repeated-game) incentives might overrule the effect of stability.

17. Remarkably, Duersch *et al.* (2010) show that as compared to a number of journal learning dynamics (BR, fictitious play, reinforcement learning, trial and error) imitation is the only learning algorithm which is not exploitable.

18. In the Cournot markets of Friedman *et al.* (2004) subjects are not informed about their payoff function, nor about competitors' actions or payoffs. The result is that behavior does not converge and exhibits sharp oscillations, even after thousands of periods of play (in near-continuous time).

19. In a similar vein, Davis *et al.* (2009) show that in posted-offer triopolies where subjects have information about their costs, prices are lower if they also have information about aggregate supply and demand than if they have no such information.

20. They also observe attempts to collude.

21. Apesteguia *et al.* (2010) show that this imitation result – although theoretically sensitive – is behaviorally robust to small asymmetries in costs.

22. In three- or four-seller markets, prices move toward NE, even when information is provided about all submitted prices (Dufwenberg and Gneezy, 2000).

23. Apesteguia *et al.* (2007b) find that if subjects receive information about *one* journal subject in anjournal group, quantities in a (simplified) Cournot triopoly are close to NE, as predicted by Schlag (1998).

24. Since intentions are hard to identify it is not obvious that such outcomes are always due to 'conscious' collusion. Sometimes it seems clear that subjects try to induce collusion by raising their price – and use prices as signals – but such attempts are neither necessary nor sufficient for collusion (Durham *et al.*, 2004; Davis *et al.*, 2010).

25. Results from merger experiments are less straightforward, perhaps because mergers induce asymmetries (Davis, 2002; Davis and Wilson, 2005; Huck *et al.*, 2007; Fonseca and Normann, 2008). See Lindqvist and Stennek (2005) for a study on endogenous merger

formation, and Goette and Schmutzler (2009) for an excellent survey of the experimental literature on mergers.

26. In some cases, prices increase as the number of firms increases (e.g., Morgan *et al.*, 2006a), but only so under random matching and if the underlying NE predicts this to occur. Dufwenberg and Gneezy (2000) is an example of an experiment with random matching where prices decrease as the number of firms increases.

27. The effect of group decision-making is less clear for tacit collusion (see Bornstein *et al.*, 2008; Raab and Schipper, 2009).

References

Abbink, K. and Brandts, J. (2005) Price competition under cost uncertainty: a laboratory analysis. *Economic Inquiry* 43(3): 636–648.

Abbink, K. and Brandts, J. (2008) Pricing in Bertrand competition with increasing marginal costs. *Games and Economic Behavior* 63(1): 1–31.

Abbink, K. and Brandts, J. (2009) Collusion in growing and shrinking markets: empirical evidence from experimental duopolies. In Hinloopen, J. and Normann, H.-T., (eds), *Experiments and Competition Policy* (pp. 34–60). Cambridge, UK: Cambridge University Press.

Abrams, E., Sefton, M. and Yavas, A. (2000) An experimental comparison of two search models. *Economic Theory* 16: 735–749.

Altavilla, C., Luini, L. and Sbriglia, P. (2006) Social learning in market games. *Journal of Economic Behavior and Organization* 61(4): 632–652.

Anderhub, V., Güth, W., Kamecke, U. and Normann, H.-T. (2003) Capacity choices and price competition in experimental markets. *Experimental Economics* 6(1): 27–52.

Anderson, L., Freeborn, B. and Holt, C. (2010) Tacit collusion in price-setting duopoly markets: experimental evidence with complements and substitutes. *Southern Economic Journal* 76(3): 577–591.

Andersson, O. and Wengström, E. (2007) Do antitrust laws facilitate collusion? Experimental evidence on costly communication in duopolies. *Scandinavian Journal of Economics* 109(2): 321–339.

Andersson, O. and Wengström, E. (2012) Credible communication and cooperation: experimental evidence from multi-stage games. *Journal of Economic Behavior and Organization* 81(1): 207–219.

Aoyagi, M. and Fréchette, G. (2009) Collusion as public monitoring becomes noisy: experimental evidence. *Journal of Economic Theory* 144(3): 1135–1165.

Apesteguia, J., Dufwenberg, M. and Selten, R. (2007a) Blowing the whistle. *Economic Theory* 31(1): 143–166.

Apesteguia, J., Huck, S. and Oechssler, J. (2007b) Imitation-theory and experimental evidence. *Journal of Economic Theory* 136(1): 217–235.

Apesteguia, J., Huck, S., Oechssler, J. and Weidenholzer, S. (2010) Imitation and the evolution of walrasian behavior: theoretically fragile but behaviorally robust. *Journal of Economic Theory* 145(5): 1603–1617.

Argenton, C. and Müller, W. (2012) Collusion in experimental Bertrand duopolies with convex costs: the role of cost asymmetry. *International Journal of Industrial Organization* 30: 508–517.

Bagwell, K. (1995) Commitment and observability in games. *Games and Economic Behavior* 8: 271–280.

Barreda-Tarrazona, I., García-Gallego, A., Georgantzís, N., And aluz-Funcia, J. and Gil-Sanz, A. (2011) An experiment on spatial competition with endogenous pricing. *International Journal of Industrial Organization* 29(1): 74–83.

Baye, M. and Morgan, J. (2004) Price dispersion in the lab and on the internet: theory and evidence. *RAND Journal of Economics* 35(3): 449–466.

Bigoni, M. (2010) What do you want to know? Information acquisition and learning in experimental Cournot games. *Research in Economics* 64(1): 1–17.

Bigoni, M., Fridolfsson, S., Le Coq, C. and Spagnolo, G. (2012) Fines, leniency and rewards in antitrust. *RAND Journal of Economics* 43: 368–390.

Boone, J., Larrain Aylwin, M., Müller, W. and Chaudhuri, A. (2012) Bertrand competition with asymmetric costs: experimental evidence. *Economics Letters* 117: 134–137.

Bornstein, G., Kugler, T., Budescu, D. and Selten, R. (2008) Repeated price competition between individuals and between teams. *Journal of Economic Behavior and Organization* 66(3-4): 808–821.

Bosch-Domènech, A. and Vriend, N. (2003) Imitation of successful behaviour in Cournot markets. *Economic Journal* 113(487): 495–524.

Bosch-Domènech, A. and Vriend, N. (2008) The classical experiments on Cournot oligopoly. In Charles R. Plott and Vernon L. Smith (eds), *Handbook of Experimental Economics Results* Vol. 1, Chapter 18 (pp. 146–152). Amsterdam: North-Holland.

Brandts, J. and Guillen, P. (2007) Collusion and fights in an experiment with price-setting firms and advance production. *Journal of Industrial Economics* 55(3): 453–473.

Brown Kruse, J. and Schenk, D. (2000) Location, cooperation and communication: an experimental examination. *International Journal of Industrial Organization* 18(1): 59–80.

Bruttel, L. (2009a) The critical discount factor as a measure for cartel stability? *Journal of Economics/Zeitschrift fur Nationalokonomie* 96(2): 113–136.

Bruttel, L. (2009b) Group dynamics in experimental studies – the Bertrand paradox revisited. *Journal of Economic Behavior and Organization* 69(1): 51–63.

Buchheit, S. and Feltovich, N. (2011) Experimental evidence of a sunk-cost paradox: a study of pricing behavior in Bertrand-Edgeworth duopoly. *International Economic Review* 52(2): 317–347.

Burdett, K. and Judd, K. (1983) Equilibrium price dispersion. *Econometrica* 51: 955–969.

Camacho-Cuena, E., García-Gallego, A., Georgantzís, N. and Sabater-Grande, G. (2005) Buyer-seller interaction in experimental spatial markets. *Regional Science and Urban Economics* 35(2): 89–108.

Cason, T. and Datta, S. (2006) An experimental study of price dispersion in an optimal search model with advertising. *International Journal of Industrial Organization* 24: 639–665.

Cason, T. and Friedman, D. (2003) Buyer search and price dispersion: a laboratory study. *Journal of Economic Theory* 112: 232–260.

Cason, T., Friedman, D. and Wagener, F. (2005) The dynamics of price dispersion, or Edgeworth variations. *Journal of Economic Dynamics and Control* 29: 801–822.

Cason, T. and Gangadharan, L. (2013) Cooperation spillovers and price competition in experimental markets. *Economic Inquiry*, Forthcoming.

Cason, T. and Mago, S. (2010) Costly buyer search in laboratory markets with seller advertising. *Journal of Industrial Economics* 58(2): 424–449.

Collins, R. and Sherstyuk, K. (2000) Spatial competition with three firms: an experimental study. *Economic Inquiry* 38(1): 73–94.

Cox, J. and Walker, M. (1998) Learning to play Cournot duopoly strategies. *Journal of Economic Behavior & Organization* 36: 141–161.

Darai, D., Sacco, D. and Schmutzler, A. (2010) Competition and innovation: an experimental investigation. *Experimental Economics* 13(4): 439–460.

Datta Mago, S. and Dechenaux, E. (2009) Price leadership and firm size asymmetry: an experimental analysis. *Experimental Economics* 12(3): 289–317.

Davis, D. (2002) Strategic interactions, market information and predicting the effects of mergers in differentiated product markets. *International Journal of Industrial Organization* 20(9): 1277–1312.

Davis, D. (2009) Pure numbers effects, market power and tacit collusion in posted offer markets. *Journal of Economic Behavior and Organization* 72(1): 475–488.

Davis, D. (2011) Behavioral convergence properties of Cournot and Bertrand markets: an experimental analysis. *Journal of Economic Behavior and Organization* 80(3): 443–458.

Davis, D., Holt, C. and Villamil, A. (2002) Supra-competitive prices and market power in posted-offer markets. In Isaac, R. and Holt, C., (eds), *Experiments Investigating Market Power, Research in Experimental Economics* (pp. 121–138). Amsterdam: JAI Press.

Davis, D., Korenok, O. and Reilly, R. (2009) Re-matching, information and sequencing effects in posted offer markets. *Experimental Economics* 12(1): 65–86.

Davis, D., Korenok, O. and Reilly, R. (2010) Cooperation without coordination: signaling, types and tacit collusion in laboratory oligopolies. *Experimental Economics* 13(1): 45–65.

Davis, D., Reilly, R. and Wilson, B. (2003) Cost structures and Nash play in repeated Cournot games. *Experimental Economics* 6(2): 209–226.

Davis, D. and Wilson, B. (2000) Firm-specific cost savings and market power. *Economic Theory* 16:545–565.

Davis, D. and Wilson, B. (2005) Differentiated product competition and the antitrust logit model: an experimental analysis. *Journal of Economic Behavior and Organization* 57(1): 89–113.

Davis, D. and Wilson, B. (2006) Equilibrium price dispersion, mergers and synergies: an experimental investigation of differentiated product competition. *International Journal of the Economics of Business* 13(2): 169–194.

Davis, D. and Wilson, B. (2008a) Mixed strategy Nash equilibrium predictions as a means of organizing behavior in posted-offer market experiments. In C. R. Plott and V. L. Smith (eds), *Handbook of Experimental Economics Results*, Chapter 7 (pp. 62–70). Amsterdam: North-Holland.

Davis, D. and Wilson, B. (2008b) Strategic buyers, horizontal mergers and synergies: an experimental investigation. *International Journal of Industrial Organization* 26(3): 643–661.

Deck, C. and Wilson, B. (2003) Automated pricing rules in electronic posted offer markets. *Economic Inquiry* 41: 208–223.

Deck, C. and Wilson, B. (2006) Tracking customer search to price discriminate. *Economic Inquiry* 44(2): 280–295.

Diamond, P. (1971) A model of price adjustment. *Journal of Economic Theory* 3: 156–168.

Dixon, H. (2000) Keeping up with the Joneses: competition and the evolution of collusion. *Journal of Economic Behavior & Organization* 43: 223–238.

Duersch, P., Kolb, A., Oechssler, J. and Schipper, B. (2010) Rage against the machines: how subjects play against learning algorithms. *Economic Theory* 43(3): 407–430.

Dufwenberg, M. and Gneezy, U. (2000) Price competition and market concentration: an experimental study. *International Journal of Industrial Organization* 18(1): 7–22.

Dufwenberg, M. and Gneezy, U. (2002) Information disclosure in auctions: an experiment. *Journal of Economic Behavior & Organization* 48(2): 431–444.

Dufwenberg, M., Gneezy, U., Goeree, J. and Nagel, R. (2007) Price floors and competition. *Economic Theory* 33: 211–224.

Dugar, S. (2007) Price-matching guarantees and equilibrium selection in a homogenous product market: an experimental study. *Review of Industrial Organization* 30(2): 107–119.

Dugar, S. and Sorensen, T. (2006) Hassle costs, price-matching guarantees and price competition: an experiment. *Review of Industrial Organization* 28(4): 359–378.

Durham, Y., McCabe, K., Olson, M., Rassenti, S. and Smith, V. (2004) Oligopoly competition in fixed cost environments. *International Journal of Industrial Organization* 22(2): 147–162.

Engel, C. (2007) How much collusion? A meta-analysis of oligopoly experiments. *Journal of Competition Law and Economics* 3(4): 491–549.

Engelmann, D. and Müller, W. (2011) Collusion through price ceilings? In search of a focal-point effect. *Journal of Economic Behavior and Organization* 79(3): 291–302.

Engelmann, D. and Normann, H.-T. (2009) Price ceilings as focal points? An experimental test. In Hinloopen, J. and Normann, H.-T. (eds), *Experiments and Competition Policy* (pp. 61–80). Cambridge University Press, Cambridge, UK.

Ewing, B. and Kruse, J. (2010) An experimental examination of market concentration and capacity effects on price competition. *Journal of Business Valuation and Economic Loss Analysis* 5(1): 1–14.

Fatás, E., Georgantzís, N., Manez, J. and Sabater, G. (2013) Experimental duopolies under price guarantees. *Applied Economics* 45(1): 15–35.

Fatás, E., Georgantzís, N., Manez, J. and Sabater-Grande, G. (2005) Pro-competitive price beating guarantees: experimental evidence. *Review of Industrial Organization* 26(1): 115–136.

Fatas, E. and Manez, J. (2007) Are low-price promises collusion guarantees? An experimental test of price matching policies. *Spanish Economic Review* 9(1): 59–77.

Feinberg, R. and Snyder, C. (2002) Collusion with secret price cuts: an experimental investigation. *Economics Bulletin* 3: 1–11.

Fonseca, M., Huck, S. and Normann, H.-T. (2005) Playing Cournot although they shouldn't: endogenous timing in experimental duopolies with asymmetric cost. *Economic Theory* 25(3): 669–677.

Fonseca, M., Müller, W. and Normann, H.-T. (2006) Endogenous timing in duopoly: experimental evidence. *International Journal of Game Theory* 34(3): 443–456.

Fonseca, M. and Normann, H.-T. (2008) Mergers, asymmetries and collusion: experimental evidence. *Economic Journal* 118: 387–400.

Fonseca, M. and Normann, H.-T. (2012) Explicit vs. tacit collusion – the impact of communication in oligopoly experiments. *European Economic Review* 56: 1759–1772.

Fonseca, M. and Normann, H.-T. (2013) Excess capacity and pricing in Bertrand-Edgeworth markets: experimental evidence. *Journal of Institutional and Theoretical Economics* Forthcoming.

Fouraker, L. and Siegel, S. (1963) *Bargaining Behavior*. London: McGraw-Hill.

Fouraker, L., Shubik, M. and Siegel, S. (1961) Oligopoly bargaining: the quantity adjuster models. Research Bulletin, Pennsylvania State University, Department of Psychology.

Frechette, G. (2011) Laboratory experiments: professionals versus students. Working Paper, Department of Economics, New York University.

Friedman, E., Shor, M., Shenker, S. and Sopher, B. (2004) An experiment on learning with limited information: nonconvergence, experimentation cascades and the advantage of being slow. *Games and Economic Behavior* 47: 325–352.

Friedman, J. (1967) An experimental study of cooperative duopoly. *Econometrica* 35: 379–397.

Friedman, J. (1971) A non-cooperative equilibrium for supergames. *Review of Economic Studies* 38:1–12.

Gillet, J., Schram, A. and Sonnemans, J. (2011) Cartel formation and pricing: the effect of managerial decision-making rules. *International Journal of Industrial Organization* 29(1): 126–133.

Goette, L. and Schmutzler, A. (2009) Merger policy: what can we learn from experiments? In Hinloopen, J. and Normann, H.-T. (eds), *Experiments and Competition Policy* (pp. 185–216). Cambridge, UK: Cambridge University Press.

Goodwin, D. and Mestelman, S. (2010) A note comparing the capacity setting performance of the kreps-scheinkman duopoly model with the Cournot duopoly model in a laboratory setting. *International Journal of Industrial Organization* 28(5): 522–525.

Halbheer, D., Fehr, E., Goette, L. and Schmutzler, A. (2009) Self-reinforcing market dominance. *Games and Economic Behavior* 67(2): 481–502.

Hamaguchi, Y., Kawagoe, T. and Shibata, A. (2009) Group size effects on cartel formation and the enforcement power of leniency programs. *International Journal of Industrial Organization* 27(2): 145–165.

Hamilton, J. and Slutsky, S. (1990) Endogenous timing in duopoly games: Stackelberg or Cournot equilibria. *Games and Economic Behavior* 2: 29–46.

Hampton, K. and Sherstyuk, K. (2012) Demand shocks, capacity coordination and industry performance: lessons from an economic laboratory. *RAND Journal of Economics* 43(1): 139–166.

Hinloopen, J. and Soetevent, A. (2008) Laboratory evidence on the effectiveness of corporate leniency programs. *RAND Journal of Economics* 39: 607–616.

Hoggatt, A. (1959) An experimental business game. *Behavioral Science* 4: 192–203.

Holt, C. (1995) Industrial organization: a survey of laboratory research. In Kagel, J. and Roth, A., (eds), *The Handbook of Experimental Economics* (pp. 349–444). New Jersey: Princeton University Press.

Huck, S., Konrad, K., Müller, W. and Normann, H.-T. (2007) The merger paradox and why aspiration levels let it fail in the laboratory. *Economic Journal* 117(522): 1073–1095.

Huck, S. and Müller, W. (2000) Perfect versus imperfect observability – an experimental test of Bagwell's result. *Games and Economic Behavior* 31: 174–190.

Huck, S., Müller, W. and Normann, H.-T. (2001) Stackelberg beats Cournot: on collusion and efficiency in experimental markets. *Economic Journal* 111(474): 749–765.

Huck, S., Müller, W. and Normann, H.-T. (2004a) Strategic delegation in experimental markets. *International Journal of Industrial Organization* 22(4): 561–574.

Huck, S., Müller, W. and Vriend, N. (2002a) The east end, the west end and King's cross: on clustering in the four-player Hotelling game. *Economic Inquiry* 40: 231–240.

Huck, S., Normann, H.-T. and Oechssler, J. (1999) Learning in Cournot oligopoly – an experiment. *The Economic Journal* 109(3): C80–C95.

Huck, S., Normann, H.-T. and Oechssler, J. (2000) Does information about competitors' actions increase or decrease competition in experimental oligopoly markets? *International Journal of Industrial Organization* 18(1): 39–57.

Huck, S., Normann, H.-T. and Oechssler, J. (2002b) Stability of the Cournot process – experimental evidence. *International Journal of Game Theory* 31(1): 123–136.

Huck, S., Normann, H.-T. and Oechssler, J. (2004b) Two are few and four are many: number effects in experimental oligopolies. *Journal of Economic Behavior and Organization* 53(4): 435–446.

Isaac, R. and Reynolds, S. (1988) Appropriability and market structure in a stochastic invention model. *Quarterly Journal of Economics* 103(4): 647–671.

Jullien, C. and Ruffieux, B. (2001) Innovation, avantages concurrentiels et concurrence. *Revue d'Economie Politique* 76: 121–150.

Kalayci, K. and Potters, J. (2011) Buyer confusion and market prices. *International Journal of Industrial Organization* 29(1): 14–22.

Kreps, D. and Scheinkman, J. (1983) Quantity precommitment and Bertrand competition yield Cournot outcomes. *Bell Journal of Economics* 14(3): 326–337.

Kübler, D. and Müller, W. (2002) Simultaneous and sequential price competition in heterogeneous duopoly markets: experimental evidence. *International Journal of Industrial Organization* 20(10): 1437–1460.

Le Coq, C. and Sturluson, J. (2012) Does opponents' experience matter? Experimental evidence from a quantity precommitment game. *Journal of Economic Behavior and Organization* 84: 265–277.

Leufkens, K. and Peeters, R. (2011) Price dynamics and collusion under short-run price commitments. *International Journal of Industrial Organization* 29(1): 134–153.

Lindqvist, T. and Stennek, J. (2005) The insiders' dilemma: an experiment on merger formation. *Experimental Economics* 8(3): 267–284.

Mago, S. and Pate, J. (2009) An experimental examination of competitor-based price matching guarantees. *Journal of Economic Behavior and Organization* 70(1-2): 342–360.

Maskin, E. and Tirole, J. (1988) A theory of dynamic oligopoly, II. Price competition, kinked demand curve and Edgeworth cycles. *Econometrica* 56(3): 571–599.

Mason, C. and Phillips, O. (1997) Information and cost asymmetry in experimental duopoly markets. *Review of Economics and Statistics* 79: 290–299.

Mason, C., Phillips, O. and Nowell, C. (1992) Duopoly behavior in asymmetric markets: an experimental evaluation. *Review of Economics and Statistics* 74: 662–670.

Milgrom, P. and Roberts, J. (1990) Rationalizability, learning and equilibrium in games with strategic complementarities. *Econometrica* 6: 1255–1277.

Morgan, J., Orzen, H. and Sefton, M. (2006a) An experimental study of price dispersion. *Games and Economic Behavior* 54(1): 134–158.

Morgan, J., Orzen, H. and Sefton, M. (2006b) A laboratory study of advertising and price competition. *European Economic Review* 50: 323–347.

Morgan, J. and Várdy, F. (2004) An experimental study of commitment in Stackelberg games with observation costs. *Games and Economic Behavior* 49(2): 401–423.

Müller, W. (2006) Allowing for two production periods in the Cournot duopoly: experimental evidence. *Journal of Economic Behavior and Organization* 60(1): 100–111.

Muren, A. (2000) Quantity precommitment in an experimental oligopoly market. *Journal of Economic Behavior and Organization* 41(2): 147–157.

Nicklisch, A. (2012) Does collusive advertising facilitate collusive pricing? Evidence from experimental duopolies. *European Journal of Law and Economics* 34: 515–532.

Oechssler, J. (2002) Cooperation as a result of learning with aspiration levels. *Journal of Economic Behavior & Organization* 49: 405–409.

Offerman, T. and Potters, J. (2006) Does auctioning of entry licences induce collusion? An experimental study. *Review of Economic Studies* 73(3): 769–791.

Offerman, T., Potters, J. and Sonnemans, J. (2002) Imitation and belief learning in an oligopoly experiment. *Review of Economic Studies* 69(4): 973–997.

Orzen, H. (2008) Counterintuitive number effects in experimental oligopolies. *Experimental Economics* 11(4): 390–401.

Orzen, H. and Sefton, M. (2008) An experiment on spatial price competition. *International Journal of Industrial Organization* 26(3): 716–729.

Peeters, R. and Strobel, M. (2009) Pricing behavior in asymmetric markets with differentiated products. *International Journal of Industrial Organization* 27(1): 24–32.

Potters, J. (2009) Transparancy about past, present and future conduct: experimental evidence on the impact on competitiveness. In Hinloopen, J. and Normann, H.-T., (eds), *Experiments and Competition Policy* (pp. 81–104). Cambridge, UK: Cambridge University Press.

Potters, J., Rockenbach, B., Sadrieh, A. and Van Damme, E. (2004) Collusion under yardstick competition: an experimental study. *International Journal of Industrial Organization* 22(7): 1017–1038.

Potters, J. and Suetens, S. (2009) Cooperation in experimental games of strategic complements and substitutes. *Review of Economic Studies* 76(3): 1125–1147.

Puzzello, D. (2008) Tie-breaking rules and divisibility in experimental duopoly markets. *Journal of Economic Behavior and Organization* 67(1): 164–179.

Raab, P. and Schipper, B. (2009) Cournot competition between teams: an experimental study. *Journal of Economic Behavior and Organization* 72(2): 691–702.

Rassenti, S., Reynolds, S., Smith, V. and Szidarovszky, F. (2000) Adaptation and convergence of behavior in repeated experimental Cournot games. *Journal of Economic Behavior and Organization* 41(2): 117–146.

Sacco, D. and Schmutzler, A. (2011) Is there a U-shaped relation between competition and investment? *International Journal of Industrial Organization* 29(1): 65–73.

Saloner, G. (1987) Cournot duopoly with two production periods. *Journal of Economic Theory* 42: 183–187.

Sauermann, H. and Selten, R. (1959) Ein oligopolexperiment. *Zeitschrift für die gesamte Staatswissenschaft* 115: 427–471.

Schlag, K. (1998) Why imitate and if so, how? *Journal of Economic Theory* 78: 130–156.

Selten, R. and Apesteguia, J. (2005) Experimentally observed imitation and cooperation in price competition on the circle. *Games and Economic Behavior* 51(1): 171–192.

Selten, R. and Ostmann, A. (2001) Imitation equilibrium. *Homo Oeconomicus* 43: 111–149.

Selten, R. and Stoecker, R. (1986) End behavior in sequences of finite prisoner's dilemma supergames. *Journal of Economic Behavior and Organization* 7: 47–70.

Silipo, D. (2005) The evolution of cooperation in patent races: theory and experimental evidence. *Journal of Economics* 85(1): 1–38.

Stigler, G. (1964) A theory of oligopoly. *Journal of Political Economy* 72: 44–61.

Suetens, S. (2005) Cooperative and noncooperative R&D in experimental duopoly markets. *International Journal of Industrial Organization* 23(1–2): 63–82.

Suetens, S. (2008) Does R&D cooperation facilitate price collusion? An experiment. *Journal of Economic Behavior and Organization* 66(3–4): 822–836.

Suetens, S. and Potters, J. (2007) Bertrand colludes more than Cournot. *Experimental Economics* 10(1): 71–77.

Theocharis, R. (1960) On the stability of the Cournot solution on the oligopoly problem. *Review of Economic Studies* 73: 133–134.

van Damme, E. and Hurkens, S. (1997) Games with imperfectly observable commitment. *Games and Economic Behavior* 21: 282–308.

Varian, H. (1980) A model of sales. *American Economic Behavior* 70: 651–659.

Vega-Redondo, R. (1997) The evolution of Walrasian behavior. *Econometrica* 65: 375–384.

Vives, X. (1999) *Oligopoly Pricing: Old Ideas and New Tools*. Cambridge: MIT Press.

Yuan, H. and Krishna, A. (2011) Price-matching guarantees with endogenous search: a market experiment approach. *Journal of Retailing* 87(2): 182–193.

Zizzo, D. (2002) Racing with uncertainty: a patent race experiment. *International Journal of Industrial Organization* 20: 877–902.

5

MULTIUNIT AUCTIONS

Anthony M. Kwasnica

The Pennsylvania State University

Katerina Sherstyuk

University of Hawaii at Manoa

1. Introduction

In a multiunit auction, multiple identical (homogeneous) or distinct (heterogeneous) objects are to be allocated to bidders. Multiunit auctions are widely used in both the public and private sector for agricultural products, construction procurement, electromagnetic spectrum, environmental projects, electricity distribution and generation, gas leases, government securities, real estate, and timber among others. The growing practical relevance of multiunit auctions has motivated substantial theoretical, empirical, and experimental research on the topic. The purpose of this survey is to provide an overview of experimental research on multiunit auctions with an emphasis on the topics or themes that may be of a unifying interest to experimental, as well as theoretical and empirical economists. A number of common research themes arise across methodologies and include: static multiunit auctions (including pay-your-bid and uniform-price auctions), dynamic auctions, combinatorial auctions and efficient auction design, bidder asymmetry, common values, endogenous entry, and collusion in auctions (see Ausubel, 2008; Bajari, 2008; Perrigne and Vuong, 2008). We explore many of these areas in this survey.

There are a number of earlier surveys of experimental auctions. Kagel 1995 surveys early (pre-1995) research and Kagel and Levin (unpublished data, 2011) examine experimental auction research since 1995; Roth (unpublished data, 2012) discusses the history and the influence of auction experiments on the design of the Federal Communications Commission (FCC) electromagnetic spectrum auctions. Sherstyuk (2008) reviews demand reduction and bidder collusion is ascending multiunit auctions. Normann and Ricciuti (2009) review experiments on economic policy making, including auctions and emission permits. Bajari and Hortacsu (2004) and Ockenfels *et al.* (2006) survey Internet auctions. Given the existing

A Collection of Surveys on Market Experiments, First Edition.
Edited by Charles N. Noussair and Steven Tucker. Chapters © 2014 The Authors.
Book compilation © 2014 John Wiley & Sons, Ltd. Published 2014 by John Wiley & Sons, Ltd.

surveys, other contributed articles to this special issue, and space constraints, we do not review environmental and online auctions, as well as electricity, water, and gas markets specifically. For the topics that are reviewed but have overlap with the existing surveys, such as comparison of auction formats, auction design, demand reduction, and collusion, we try to minimize the overlap and provide a different perspective on the research.

We begin by reviewing a few basic multiunit auction institutions. As with single-unit auctions, auction formats differ in whether the auction is static (or sealed bid), or dynamic. In static sealed-bid (SB) auctions, the bids are submitted only once, and the prices and allocations are then immediately determined. Dynamic auctions involve multiple rounds of price and demand adjustments, or continuous price changes, with a specified stopping rule. Dynamic auctions may be either ascending (increasing price) or descending (decreasing price). The auction formats further differ in how the prices for the units are determined once the bidding stops. The most commonly discussed multiunit auction formats are generalizations of English, Dutch, first-price sealed-bid (FPSB), and Vickrey second-price sealed-bid (SPSB) auctions. Suppose k units of a homogeneous good are offered for sale. Under the ascending uniform-price English clock (EC) auction, the price starts low, and then rises, either continuously or in certain increments, with bidders having an option to irreversibly reduce their demand (drop out on units) at each price. The clock stops with the last dropout when the total number of units demanded reduces to k, the number supplied. The price where the clock stops determines the uniform selling price for all k units. Smith (1967) refers to this pricing rule as "competitive" as such a price would presumably prevail in a competitive market. Examples of real-world clock auctions are auctions for diamonds, electricity, gas, and emission allowances in Europe (Cramton *et al.*, 2012). An SB analog of this institution is the uniform-price sealed-bid (UPSB) auction where k highest bids are accepted, and the price equals to the highest rejected bid; this corresponds to the Vickrey SPSB auction in the single-unit case. There is also the UPSB auction where the price equals to the lowest accepted bid. Such a pricing rule is presently used in the U.S. Treasury auctions. In a k-unit discriminative SB auction (the multiunit analog of the FPSB auction), the k highest bidders buy the goods at the prices equal to their submitted bids; this auction procedure is used by the European Central Bank and many other countries to sell government securities, and was used by the U.S. Treasury pre-1992 (Abbink *et al.*, 2006). The dynamic analog of the discriminative auction is the simultaneous Dutch descending price auction, where the prices start high on each of the units offered for sale, and then decrease on all units at the same pace; the bidder who is the first to stop the clock on a given unit buys the unit at the corresponding price. Furthermore, when goods are heterogeneous, they may be sold in separate auctions run either simultaneously or sequentially. Many more auction institutions emerge when there are synergies or other interdependencies in buyer values across the goods. We will introduce these auction formats as we discuss them later in the paper.

In most studies, the auction institutions are evaluated and compared against several performance criteria, the most prominent of which are allocative efficiency and seller revenue. Efficiency is typically measured as the percentage of the sum of the values of the winning units relative to the maximal feasible sum of the values of the units. Other performance criteria include bidder profits and auction duration.

The rest of the survey is organized as follows. Section 2 reviews auctions where each bidder demands only one unit. Section 3 discusses auctions with multiunit demand with additive valuations. Section 4 takes up the issues of auctions with synergies and package bidding. Specific institutional issues relevant to many multiunit auction environments are discussed in Section 5. Section 6 reviews experiments examining collusion. Section 7 discusses sequential as opposed to simultaneous auctions. Finally, we present conclusions and some open issues in Section 8.

2. Multiunit Auctions, Single-Unit Demand

We first study settings where there are several objects offered for sale, but each bidder is constrained to buy at most one unit. As Krishna (2002) discusses, the fact that bidders demand only a single unit greatly reduces the difficulties of the auction design process from a strategic standpoint and, therefore, many results from standard (single-unit) auction theory can be extended to this context. One of the earliest studies in this setting is Cox *et al.* (1984) who are the first to report that bidding tends to be greater than the risk-neutral Nash equilibrium level in multiunit discriminative auctions, thus extending the similar finding from single-unit, first-price sealed auctions. Cox *et al.* (1984) also point out that the extent of overbidding relative to the risk-neutral Nash equilibrium prediction depends on the number of bidders relative to the number of units, with a higher ratio of bidders to units leading to more overbidding. Experimental evidence from many studies that followed suggests that this ratio is indicative of auction competitiveness and affects how aggressively bidders behave across a wide range of auction environments, as we discuss below.

2.1 *Comparison of Auction Formats Motivated by Spectrum Sales*

Government electromagnetic spectrum sales gave a boost to experimental research on multiunit auctions. Several studies are motivated by the 3G spectrum auctions in countries such as Great Britain and the Netherlands, where each bidder was constrained to buy at most one license. Much of the motivation comes from Klemperer (2002) who argues that encouraging entry and competition are the key elements in good auction design. Klemperer further suggests that adding the element of an FPSB auction to an ascending auction may increase competition in "uncompetitive" environments by giving new entrants a greater chance of winning, and further help bidders to avoid the winner's curse in settings with a common value component. In view of these arguments, several experimental papers compare the performance of simultaneous ascending auctions (SAAs) with FPSB, descending auction formats, or hybrids.

Abbink *et al.* (2005) report on experiments that were conducted in preparation for the 2000 British 3G auctions. In the experiments, four homogeneous units were auctioned off to four incumbent (strong) bidders, and four new entrant (weak) bidders, with the incumbents more likely to have their value drawn from a distribution with a higher support. The underlying bidder values included both private and common values components. Three auction mechanisms were compared: discriminatory and uniform-price variants of the Anglo-Dutch auction, and a traditional English auction. The Anglo-Dutch format proceeded as the English auction until only five (of the original eight) bidders remain; the last stage then proceeded as an SB, with the four highest bidders winning the units. In the uniform-price auction, all winning bidders paid the fourth highest bid, whereas in the discriminatory auction, the bidders paid their own bids. In the English auction, the price paid by the four highest bidders equaled the fifth highest bid. The authors report very little difference among the three auction formats with respect to efficiency (which was around 70% under all auction formats), revenue, avoidance of the winner's curse, and chances of winning by new entrants. The new entrants (weak bidders) bid somewhat more aggressively in the English auction than in either of the hybrids, giving them a slightly better chance of winning under this format; however, some entry was inefficient.[1] This lack of differences between formats may be attributed to the relatively high competitiveness of the environment, with eight bidders competing for four licenses.[2]

Goeree *et al.* (2006) study an "uncompetitive" setting motivated by the Dutch spectrum auctions, with three heterogeneous units offered for sale to only four bidders. In an SAA, all units are offered for sale simultaneously. At each price, bidders indicate which unit they want to buy, and the price rises on units which are demanded by more than one bidder; as the price rises, bidders can switch their bid to different objects. The SAA is compared with three first-price auction formats: (1) simultaneous FPSB auction, where all bidders simultaneously submit bids for every unit; (2) sequential FPSB auction, where units are sold one at a time; and (3) simultaneous descending auction (SDA), which is a Dutch clock where the clock starts at the same price and drops at equal speed for all units, and a bidder who is the first to stop the clock for a given unit buys this unit at the price where they stopped the clock. Each auction format is studied across four environments of different complexity: symmetric or asymmetric bidders, and private values or values with an added uncertain common value component. Under asymmetry, there are three strong bidders (incumbents) and one weak bidder (entrant); the weak bidder's values are drawn from a distribution with a lower support. There is also a treatment with an endogenous entry decisions of the weak bidder. The SAA is found to be the most efficient (resulting in up to 98% efficiency), but yielded the revenue which was around 10% lower, and also more variable, than that in the first-price auctions. The revenue was the highest in the sequential FPSB auctions where the most valuable item was auctioned first ("the best foot forward" strategy). Consistent with Klemperer (2002)'s claims, the simultaneous FPSB auction offered weak bidders a higher chance to win, and resulted in higher entry; it also showed the lowest incidence of the winner's curse.[3] The authors conclude that in low-competition environments, the choice between auction formats depends on whether efficiency or revenue is a more important performance criterion.

2.2 *Other Single-Unit Demand Auctions*

Olson and Porter (1994) is an early study that compares SB Vickrey-Leonard (Leonard, 1983) and ascending DGS (Demange *et al.*, 1986) auctions, along with two nonmonetary mechanisms, to solve the assignment problem where each bidder is constrained to buy at most one of a set of heterogeneous objects. The Vickrey–Leonard (VL) is the SPSB auction extended to the heterogeneous goods environment, whereas the DGS is unlike the SAA explained above, in that it requires bidders to indicate all their most desired items at a current vector of prices; the prices are then increased on the items that are "overdemanded." Both low-contention ("easy") and high-contention ("hard") value environments are considered. Olson and Porter (1994) find that, unlike the nonmonetary mechanisms, both the VL and the DGS auctions result in close to full efficiency, as most bidders reveal their demands truthfully (although they are less likely to report all indifferences between objects under the DGS than under the VL auction). In contrast, in a recent study, Andersson *et al.* (2012) report that the DGS auction performs worse than the VL auction in terms of truthful demand revelation, efficiency, and seller revenue. Andersson *et al.* (2012)'s findings largely contradict the rest of the literature, which shows that dynamic auctions tend to outperform SBs in terms of efficiency; their results merit robustness checks, as the authors consider only one value setting, repeated across only 10 periods.

Barut *et al.* (2002) compare all-pay (AP) and winner-pay (WP) SB auctions in multiple identical units settings with two or four objects. Unlike WP auctions where only winning bidders pay, in AP auctions bidders pay whether they win a unit or not. The authors suggest allocation of A's on a grading curve, or assigning of identical jobs in a hierarchy, as examples of multiunit AP auctions. The recent emergence of "penny auctions" online can also be seen as an example of AP auctions. Barut *et al.* (2002) report that, as in the single-unit case, AP SB auctions lead to overdissipation of rent, thus generating higher revenue than the Nash equilibrium prediction. They find similar revenue in the AP and WP SB auctions, but higher efficiency in WP auctions,[4] providing a rationale why AP auctions are rarely used in the field to sell goods.

Damianov *et al.* (2010) study auctions with variable supply, where the seller decides how many customers with unit demand to serve after observing their bids. The authors suggest that the variable supply auctions are quite frequent in reality and include auctions for electricity, Treasury bills, and initial public offerings. There are two bidders who have a commonly known value for the good, but who are uncertain about the seller's constant marginal cost. Damianov *et al.* (2010) compare a uniform (lowest accepted bid) and a discriminatory-price auction theoretically and experimentally. In their experiment, the seller is computerized and is programmed to sell all units that, given bids, yield a nonnegative profit. The data from both auctions are consistent with the theoretical predictions: the uniform-price auction raises more revenue and is more efficient. Intuitively, bids are higher in the uniform-price than in the discriminatory auction, as raising a bid in the discriminatory auction ultimately leads to a higher transaction price for that bidder; in the uniform-price auction, a bidder is able to raise his chances of winning, but not necessarily the price he pays.

A related earlier study, Shogren *et al.* (2001), compares demand-revealing properties of the SPSB auction with those of the "random *n*th price" auction. The latter may be interpreted as a uniform-price auction with random supply (realized after the bids are submitted). In this auction, the uniform cutoff price *n* is randomly determined and may be equal to any number from two up to the total number of bidders. The authors find, in a private values setting, that both auction formats were demand-revealing in aggregate. However, the random *n*th price auction leads to more sincere bidding by "off-margin" bidders (with extremely high or low valuations), since everyone has a chance to win, but less so for "on-margin" bidders. The comparison with the second-price auction is constrained to the demand-revealing properties of the institutions as the differing supply conditions of the second-price and random *n*th price auction make revenue and efficiency noncomparable.

Merlob *et al.* (2012) consider an auction designed by the Centers for Medicare and Medicaid Services (CMS) to procure medical supplies and equipment. The CMS auction is a uniform-price auction that employs two unorthodox rules. First, the selling price is set at the median of the winning bids. Second, bids are nonbinding, meaning bidders can withdraw their bids once the prices are determined; the median price is not recalculated. Merlob *et al.* (2012) compare the CMS auction with the standard uniform-price auction where the price equals to the first rejected bid, and bids are binding. The standard first rejected bid auction performs well, leading to high efficiency (93.7%), perfect procurement (all seven units were procured in every period) and close to competitive prices. In contrast, the CMS auction created incentives for bidders to "lowball" bids, leading to median prices so low (as low as 33.4% of the competitive level in some treatments) that many sellers could not afford selling and eventually withdrew their bids. This resulted in low procurement (on average, between two and four units out of seven) and low overall efficiency of the auction (as low as 37.2%). By systematically varying particular CMS auction rules, the authors further show that both the first rejected bid pricing and the binding bids rules are important to guarantee efficiency, and thus the CMS auction cannot be easily remedied by changing only one of these unorthodox rules. This study presents a fine example of a policy experiment that demonstrates how misguided auction design may lead to poor economic outcomes.

Goeree *et al.* (2004) and Efiaz *et al.* (2008) study bidders' choice auctions that are popular in the sales of real estate such as condominiums, as well as antiques and jewelry. These are multistage auctions of heterogeneous goods, in which the highest bidder in each stage wins the right to choose the good first. Goeree *et al.* (2004) consider sequences of ascending bidders' choice auctions, comparing them to standard simultaneous auctions, whereas Efiaz *et al.* (2008) compare sequential second-price bidder choice auctions with standard sequential SPSB auctions. In both studies, each bidder had only one preferred object, with other objects having very little or no value to him. In Goeree *et al.* (2004), there were two objects and four bidders, and bidders were equally likely to prefer each object. In Efiaz *et al.* (2008), there were four objects and eight bidders, but each object was desired by only two bidders. While the Revenue Equivalence Theorem implies that, under risk-neutrality, bidders' choice auctions should yield the same expected revenue as their studied alternatives, both studies show that bidders' choice auctions resulted in revenues higher by 10–25%, thus effectively "creating competition out of thin air." Efiaz *et al.* (2008) show that this increased competition is due to the bidders behaving as if they faced more competition than they actually did. Salmon and Iachini (2007) study a "pooled" auction as an alternative to the SAA.[5] The former is a version of a multiple-unit SB auction and is similar to a bidders' choice auction in that the highest bidder wins the right to choose the good. The key difference is that it is a single-stage mechanism, with the second-highest bidder picking after the first one and so on; all winning bidders pay their bids. Salmon and Iachini (2007) consider a relatively competitive environment with seven bidders competing for five objects, and all bidders having the same preference rankings over the objects. They report very aggressive bidding resulting in up to 40% higher revenue in the pooled auction than in the SAA. The pooled auction also yielded persistent losses for the bidders. Salmon and Iachini (2007) explain such aggressive overbidding by attentional bias, with the subjects focusing their attention on their best two or three items, and ignoring the possibility of winning other items.

In sum, research on multiunit auctions with single-unit demand has mainly focused on the comparison of various auction formats in terms of revenue and efficiency. The studies show that ascending auctions are often more efficient, but FPSB auctions yield higher revenue, which is a finding that will reemerge in other, more complex settings. Using misguided pricing rules or allowing nonbinding bids may lead to performance failures in both revenue and efficiency. On the other hand, bidder biases in perception or attention may be used to increase competition in uncompetitive environments.

3. Multiunit Demand, No Synergies

In multiunit demand settings, a bidder has value for more than one unit of a homogeneous or heterogeneous good. In this section, we review settings where bidder valuations for the goods are additively separable, that is, the value of acquiring several goods is equal to the sum of the goods' valuations. Motivating real-world examples are Treasury bill auctions, initial public offerings, and spectrum auctions in countries, such as the USA, where each bidder is allowed by the rules to acquire more than one license. While in spectrum auctions, bidder values for multiple licenses may exhibit synergies, they often exhibit decreasing returns as well (see Kagel and Levin, 2001). We consider the additively separable values case in this section. An alternative setting (where synergies may exist) is reviewed in Section 4.

The first experiment with multiunit demands was Smith (1967). Motivated by Treasury auctions, he compared the behavior of discriminative and uniform-price auctions for a homogeneous good. Smith hypothesized that under a uniform-price auction with the highest rejected bid pricing rule, the average bid, the variance of bids, and seller revenue would exceed those under a discriminative auction in an identical environment. He found that the variance of bids under the uniform-price rule was indeed consistently greater than the variance of discriminative bids. However, whether the bids and revenue were higher in uniform-price auctions depended on the proportion of rejected bids, that is, the ratio of excess demand beyond the quantity offered for sale to the sale quantity. The bids and revenue increased with the proportion of rejected bids in discriminative auctions, but not in uniform-price auctions.

3.1 Demand Reduction under Uniform-Price Auctions and Institutional Remedies

Uniform-price auctions that are frequently used to sell homogeneous goods, such as Treasury bills, are theoretically demand-revealing under single-unit demand setting (Vickrey, 1961). Yet, under multiunit demands the uniform-price rule gives rise to demand reduction incentives: a bidder may want to reduce her bids on lesser-valued units in an attempt to lower the price at which she buys higher valued units. Smith (1967) did not observe demand reduction attempts in his experiment as he studied competitive settings with a large number of bidders (13–17). Because demand reduction may lead to inefficient allocations and low revenue in less competitive environments, in recent years experimentalists have carefully addressed two questions. First, does demand reduction occur under uniform-price open and SB auctions? Second, do alternative institutions safeguard against this phenomenon and lead to more efficient allocations and higher seller revenues? As many experimental studies on demand reduction have been reviewed in detail in earlier surveys (Sherstyuk, 2008; Kagel and Levin, unpublished data, 2011), we give a relatively short summary of these studies, and focus on the latest contributions. Unless mentioned otherwise, all the studies below assume private values, and investigate simple environments with two-unit demand, where the equilibrium predictions can be derived for all institutions of interest, and where demand reduction incentives may also be more transparent to experimental participants.

The first experimental study on demand reduction is Alsemgeest *et al.* (1998), who compare multiunit EC auctions and SB auctions with lowest-accepted-bid pricing, in both single-unit and two-unit demand environments. Consistent with the theoretical predictions, they observed a considerable amount of underrevelation on the lower valued unit in EC auctions. However, they observed no underrevelation in the SB auctions. Kagel and Levin (2001) compare uniform price EC and SB auctions with dynamic Vickrey, or Ausubel auctions (Ausubel, 2004), which are theoretically demand-revealing.[6] In their design, a human subject with a flat demand for two units competed with a number of computer rivals with single-unit demands. Kagel and Levin observe substantial demand reduction in both EC and SB auctions, but more so in the EC than in the SB: only 11.4% of all second-unit bids affected market price in EC, as compared to 31% in the SB (with the equilibrium prediction of 0%); the authors demonstrate that observing the drop-out prices of other bidders helped bidders in EC to learn demand reduction strategies. The Ausubel auction eliminated demand reduction incentives and yielded higher efficiency (over 99% in Ausubel as compared to around 97% in SB and EC), but resulted in less revenue than the uniform-price SB auction due to frequent overbidding under the latter.

List and Lucking-Reiley (2000) compare two-bidder UPSB and Vickrey SB auctions in a field experiment involving sports trading cards, and report significant underbidding on the second unit in the UPSB auction as compared to the Vickrey auction. Engelbrecht-Wiggans *et al.* (2006) show that this phenomenon persists in three- and five-bidder auctions.[7] Porter and Vragov (2006) compare Vickrey and UPSB with the EC auctions in a setting with two human bidders. They also find that EC results in more demand reduction than UPSB, but also observe significant overbidding under both Vickrey and UPSB. Engelmann and Grimm (2009) compare uniform EC, uniform SB, Ausubel, Vickrey SB, and FPSB (discriminative) auctions. They also find the most demand reduction under uniform EC, higher efficiency under Ausubel, and significant overbidding on the first unit (and consequently higher revenue) under all SB formats.

Several papers compare the Vickrey SB auction with its ascending clock version, the Ausubel auction. Theoretically, both auction institutions are demand-revealing. Manelli *et al.* (2006) compare Vickrey and Ausubel mechanisms in a three-unit supply environment with three bidders in both private value and common value component environments. They report significant overbidding on the first unit in both Vickrey and Ausubel auctions under private values, with more overbidding and higher revenues in Vickrey. Efficiency was comparable between the two institutions (around 85%) and neither auction was close to full efficiency, as bidders under Ausubel sometimes bid on all three units lowering efficiency.[8] Kagel and Levin (2009) compare Vickrey SB with dynamic Ausubel auctions in a setting with four human bidders with a supply of two or three units. They find substantially more sincere bidding under the Ausubel auction, and significantly more overbidding on both units under the Vickrey SB format. The Ausubel auction also resulted in higher efficiency, which averaged over 98%, as compared to around 96% under SB. The authors further study the modified Ausubel auction without drop-out price information, and conclude that the superior performance of the Ausubel auction over the Vickrey SB is due to the superior feedback (on the drop-out prices) inherent in dynamic auctions.

The above studies give a consistent picture: uniform-price auctions are confirmed to exhibit demand reduction behavior where it is predicted in equilibrium, but more so under clock auctions than under SB variants. Furthermore, SB auctions are characterized by a substantial amount of overbidding on the first unit as compared to the equilibrium prediction. This is true for Vickrey SB as well as UPSB auctions, and leads to higher revenue under SB than under clock auctions. In fact, Engelmann and Grimm (2009) claim that "in clear contrast to the theory, the auctioneer's revenues do not primarily depend on the pricing rule but on whether the auction is open or sealed-bid" (p. 877). The dynamic Ausubel auction performs best in terms of demand revelation and efficiency, as it eliminates demand reduction incentives in theory, and is also more transparent for bidders than the (theoretically demand-revealing) Vickrey SB auction. Thus, a closer conformity to equilibrium behavior under dynamic ascending clock than under SB auctions is observed to generalize from single-unit to multiunit auction settings.[9]

3.2 *Extensions to Asymmetric Bidders and Common Values*

Goeree *et al.* (2013) compare a uniform-price clock auction with a discriminatory (first-price) SB auction in a setting with three bidders each having a flat demand for three units and a supply of six units. The authors enrich the well-studied two-unit demand setting with symmetric bidders in several nontrivial ways. First, the bidders are asymmetric: there are two incumbents and one entrant, who differ only in that the incumbents suffer a fixed externality cost (representing increased competition in the product market) if the entrant is successful in buying any number of units, whereas the entrant does not bear any such cost. Thus, the entrant has an *ex ante* cost advantage over the incumbents.[10] Furthermore, the symmetric bidders setting (zero externality cost) is compared with those with moderate and high externality cost. The ascending auctions in this setting allow for two types of equilibria: the demand reduction equilibrium, where all three bidders reduce their demands and buy two units each at zero prices, resulting in zero revenue; and the preemptive bidding equilibrium where the incumbents engage in aggressive bidding in an attempt to keep the entrant from buying any units. The discriminative SB auction does not have a symmetric demand reduction equilibrium. Goeree *et al.* (2013) report that demand reduction in ascending auctions was quite prevalent under all levels of the externality cost, thus leading to low and more variable revenue (with a mode of zero for all levels of externality costs) and lower efficiency (around 88% in ascending auctions as compared to 96% in discriminative SB under zero and low externality costs); the revenue in discriminative auctions was significantly higher and consistent with the preemptive equilibrium prediction. The study presents clear evidence that in ascending auctions, bidders are likely to coordinate on a higher payoff tacit collusion equilibrium rather than on the low-payoff competitive preemptive bidding equilibrium. This conclusion is very much in line with Kwasnica and Sherstyuk (2007) (to be discussed in Section 6 later).[11]

In contrast to the above findings on uniform-price ascending auctions, there is little evidence that uniform-price SB auctions may result in low revenue. Motivated by Treasury auctions, Abbink *et al.* (2006) consider multiunit demand auctions in a common values setting.[12] Abbink *et al.* (2006) compare revenue-raising properties of three SB auction formats that are used in Treasury auctions: uniform-price, discriminatory and a "Spanish" auction, which is a hybrid of the first two auctions. Under the latter format, adopted by the Bank of Spain, the winning bidders are charged the average winning bid for all bids above this average, while all winning bids that fall below the average are fully paid. In the experiments, both the uniform-price and the Spanish auction raised significantly more revenue than the discriminatory auction, allowing the authors to suggest that the uniform-price and the Spanish auctions may be "interesting alternatives" to the widely used discriminatory auction format (p. 298).[13] Furthermore, on average, winning bidders in this experiment do not bid above value, and thus do not fall prey to the winner's curse. This may be attributed to the less competitive environment than the usual single-unit common values settings: eight bidders, with two-unit demand each, competed for seven objects offered for sale. In fact, the authors suggest that in the early rounds of experiment, the bidders tried to suppress competition, which then increased toward the later rounds. Furthermore, the bidders submitted downward-sloping demands on their two units, which may be interpreted as evidence of (apparently unsuccessful) demand reduction attempts.

Superior revenue-raising properties of the uniform-price SB auction are also documented by Zhang (2009), who compares fixed-price offerings with uniform-price SB auctions in an experimental common values setting motivated by initial public offerings. There is a large number of homogeneous units available for sale to three "informed" buyers (who receive a signal about the value of the good), and one "uninformed" buyer (who does not receive a signal). Under the fixed-price offering, the price is exogenously set so that all units are sold in equilibrium. Under the uniform-price auction, bidders submit (possibly multiple) bids that are price-quantity pairs, and the price is determined by the highest price where demand exceeds supply. Uniform-price auctions are characterized by a multiplicity of equilibria, including "tacit collusion equilibria" (TCE), which are similar in spirit to demand reduction equilibria, and result in all bidders splitting the quantity supplied at a low price. Zhang (2009) finds no evidence that such TCE are played in the experiment. The uniform-price auctions lead to significantly higher selling prices and revenues than fixed-price offerings.

In summary, demand reduction is a well-documented phenomenon in uniform-price ascending bid auctions with a small number of bidders (two); in contrast, SBs result in higher revenue in such environments. However, the revenue-raising properties of uniform-price auctions, as compared to other formats, in environments with a higher number of bidders still warrant further investigation.

4. Synergies and Package Bidding

When bidders demand multiple units their valuations may exhibit "synergies" meaning the value for the combination of the objects is greater than the sum of the valuations for the individual components.[14] When this is the case, the auctioneer may want to allow bidders to place bids for packages of objects where the bid indicates that they are to be allocated all or none of the items in the package. Auctions that allow such bidding are known as combinatorial auctions and the complexity of the auction problem is greatly increased for both the auctioneer and the bidders. The designer faces new choices of auction rules that were previously irrelevant, and the bidders may find the task of selecting a good bid cognitively difficult.

With the exception of the simplest environments, theory is difficult and frequently untractable so the experimental laboratory has played a critical role. In many cases, theory is used as a "guide" where the theoretical results from simple environments are examined in the laboratory to see whether they also apply to the more complex, practical settings.

Combinatorial auction designs have been proposed and experimentally examined for a variety of applications such as airport landing slots (Rassenti et al., 1982), space shuttle load allocation (Banks et al., 1989), transportation services (Ledyard et al., 2002), and road painting (Lunander and Nilsson, 2004). Most recent research on combinatorial auction design has been at least in part motivated by the FCC's highly publicized electromagnetic spectrum auctions.

Most of the experimental literature focuses on one or both of the following issues associated with auctions in the presence of synergies. First is the examination of the aggregate performance of various auction designs in environments often designed to mimic practical applications. Second is the examination of bidder behavior that may impact overall auction performance.

4.1 Vickrey–Clarke–Groves (VCG) Auctions

One auction with well-known theoretical properties is the SB VCG auction, which is an extension of the SPSB auction to this more complex environment. As in simpler environments, it is a weakly dominant strategy for bidders to reveal their valuations and the auction outcomes should be efficient. A natural question is how well the VCG actually performs when synergies are present. Isaac and James (2000) examine the VCG auction in a simple environment with three bidders and two objects. Across a number of information conditions and valuation structures (subadditive versus superadditive values) they find that bidders rarely truthfully report their valuations. Despite this, Isaac and James (2000) report that the VCG is more efficient than two simultaneous SPSB auctions achieving an average efficiency of 96% compared to 89% for the nonpackage bidding auction.

Chen and Takeuchi (2010) consider the VCG in an environment with three bidders and four objects. In many sessions, single bidders compete against two computer-simulated bidders in order to mitigate difficulties potentially created by strategic uncertainty. The authors find that bidders frequently fail to bid on all objects they have values for in the VCG, and they are more likely to bid on higher valued objects. This might impact the efficiency results since, due to the complexity of the problem, it is possible that efficiency might dictate that a bidder win an object with a relatively low valuation. Furthermore, as opposed to well-known results in second-price auctions for a single object, 73% of bidders tend to underreport their valuations. Scheffel *et al.* (2011) examine the VCG in a range of environments, which included as few as three objects and as many as 18. As in Chen and Takeuchi (2010) they find that in the VCG there is both underbidding but also a substantial portion of the bidders who bid above valuation when they decide to bid. Furthermore, many positively valued packages are not bid on, and the percentages of positively valued packages bid on decreases as the number of objects increases.

4.2 *Exposure and Threshold Problems*

As it became clear early on that, in practice, VCG auctions may not lead to full demand revelation, experimentalists considered alternative auction mechanisms. Two potential strategic issues have emerged and played a significant role in the development of auction designs in environments with synergies. Bykowsky *et al.* (2000) provide a detailed explanation of the "exposure" and "threshold" problems. The exposure problem provides a rationale for the inclusion of package bidding; a bidder whose values exhibit synergies may, if package bidding is not allowed, be forced to bid above her value for an individual object thereby incurring a risk of losses if she fails to obtain other objects. This exposure to losses might ultimately encourage more conservative behavior and lower efficiency. The threshold problem is the counter to the exposure problem and suggests that package bidding may be avoided; if package bidding is allowed larger (global) bidders might enjoy a benefit over smaller (local) bidders since those bidders must coordinate to displace the bid of the large bidder. While it may be efficient for the small bidders to win, each bidder would prefer that the other bidder be the one that raises the bid thus creating a sort of "free-rider" problem[15] where the large bidder wins resulting in inefficiency.

Bykowsky *et al.* (2000) demonstrate that the performance of the SAA,[16] adopted by the FCC, is negatively impacted by the exposure problem. They suggest an alternative auction, Adaptive User Selection Mechanism (AUSM) with a "stand by queue" to allow for small bidder coordination that seems to avoid the threshold problem.[17] A number of studies that followed provide a more systematic examination of the problems by examining simpler environments where these behaviors can be captured formally.

Kagel and Levin (2005) provide an important formalization of the potential impact of the exposure problem by considering an environment where all but one of the bidders value one unit of the homogeneous good and one global bidder values two units and has a synergy associated with obtaining a second unit.[18] They theoretically and experimentally examine both the UPSB auction and a uniform-price ascending (clock) auction. Both auctions exhibit competing incentives for the large bidder: as outlined in Section 3 there is a demand reduction incentive, but there is also the risk of losses. In an experiment where the single-unit bidders are computerized, they find that bidding behavior is more often consistent with theoretical predictions under the ascending auctions, but in both cases the potential impact of exposure to losses is a strong demand reduction effect. Bidder profits are 6.7%[19] higher on average in the ascending auction but are still lower than theory predicts, seller revenue is 9.6% higher on average in the SB auction, and efficiency is not significantly impacted.

Englmaier *et al.* (2009) provide a straightforward examination of the exposure problem by studying two SB auction formats. In their environment, there are two bidders and three homogeneous objects and bidders have a strong value synergy for obtaining the second unit but no value for the third unit. In the SB auction they term a "chop stick auction" (CSA), the highest bidder wins two units at the per unit price of their bid whereas the second bidder receives only one unit. Both the CSA and the well-known SPSB auction (where two objects are sold as a bundle) have an efficient and revenue equivalent equilibrium. In the CSA, bidders face some risk of losses (the chance they are the lower bidder and win only one unit), but the SPSB does not force bidders to risk losses. Englmaier *et al.* (2009) find that efficiency is higher under the SPSB and revenue is greater than predicted by theory. Under the CSA, the revenue starts high but decreases over time presumably because bidders are taking more conservative strategies to avoid losses.

Katok and Roth (2004) compare the performance of a Dutch (descending clock) auction to an ascending auction without package bidding. Two homogeneous units are for sale in both auctions but one bidder has increasing returns for obtaining a second object; the other two bidders only value one unit. Since, in the Dutch auction, the auction can be ended for both objects simultaneously, the global bidder only faces an exposure problem in the ascending auction. The authors find that the Dutch auction always performs at least as well in terms of efficiency and revenue.

Chernomaz and Levin (2012) examine the threshold problem in the FPSB auction with and without package bidding. They consider a model with two objects, one global bidder who has a synergy for obtaining both objects, and two local bidders (Krishna and Rosenthal, 1996). Theoretically, when package bidding is allowed, the global bidders should bid more aggressively than the local bidders who will, as a result of the threshold problem, place lower relative bids. In environments with and without synergies, Chernomaz and Levin (2012) consider three different auctions: no package bidding is allowed, package bidding is allowed and the global bidder can only bid on the package, and package bidding is allowed and the global bidder can bid on both the package and individual items. The efficiency results are qualitatively consistent with the theory. Allowing package bidding lowers efficiency (weakly) without synergies but increases it with synergies. Similar qualitatively consistent results are obtained for revenue and bidder profits. An interesting and important behavioral result is the differences between the two package bidding auctions. In theory, when stand-alone bids are allowed for the global bidder, he should figure out that it is optimal to place zero bids on these individual objects. However, experimentally, global bidders fail to realize this benefit and consistently bid on the individual items, which has the impact of mitigating some of the negative effects on seller revenue from allowing package bidding. In contrast to experiments on the VCG where bidders failed to bid on all packages as they should in equilibrium, here it is the global bidder's excessive bidding (relative to equilibrium) that makes the package bidding auction (with stand-alone bids) perform better than expected.

4.3 *Comparison of Alternative Auction Mechanisms*

Since the FCC has primarily conducted SAA, many studies use some variant of SAA as a baseline for comparison with alternative formats. Under SAA, package bidding is not allowed, but bidders are permitted to bid on each object repeatedly in an English-style auction that is conducted either iteratively (over multiple rounds)[20] or in continuous time.[21] The key feature is that bidders desiring to obtain a package of items must be the high bidder on all individual items in the package.

Porter *et al.* (2003) present and evaluate a simple package bidding auction that has become a commonly considered alternative to the SAA. The Combinatorial Clock (CC) auction allows package bidding but raises prices in automatic, set increments based upon demand for the objects. In short, if more than one bidder demands a particular object, the price goes up, otherwise, it remains fixed. As such, an attractive feature of the CC is that it might eliminate potential strategic complications associated with placing a specific bid on a package such as jump bidding (see Section 5) since bidders are simply deciding what packages are profitable given current prices. Noussair (2003) provides a description of how the CC may have more desirable strategic properties over other auctions such as AUSM. Porter *et al.* (2003) report increased efficiency from the CC relative to the SAA and an alternative combinatorial auction proposed by Charles River & Associates (CRA) to the FCC; the CC was allocatively efficient in all but 2 (of 22) auctions compared to 6 (of 10) for SAA and 18 (of 21) for CRA. Banks *et al.* (2003) also examine the CRA auction in comparison to the SAA. They find that CRA generates similar results to the SAA in additive environments but higher efficiency and lower revenue in environments with synergies. However, average auction duration increases significantly under the CRA from 8.9 rounds per auction under SAA to 29.3 rounds under CRA. This is perhaps driven by the fact that the CRA provides little price guidance and does not restrict bidding.

The importance of information feedback in the CC is examined by Adomavicius *et al.* (2012). They consider the CC auction under three information environments which increase from simply observing bids placed, to also observing winning allocation and price information. They find that efficiency increases as more information is provided; however, the difference between the two most generous information conditions is not significant.

Kwasnica *et al.* (2005) present an auction design known as the Resource Allocation Design (RAD) that allows package bidding, is iterative, and provides feedback to bidders via single-items prices. The main innovation of the RAD design is to suggest a method for determining single-item prices that mimic competitive equilibrium prices when possible (Bikhchandani and Ostroy (2002) show the impossibility of finding anonymous competitive equilibrium prices) and provide a guide for bidders to determine future winning bids and hopefully avoid the threshold problem. The RAD design was compared to the SAA as well as AUSM. When examining performance for the objects with synergies, both RAD and AUSM significantly outperform the SAA in terms of efficiency (90% for RAD, 94% for AUSM, 67% for SAA), bidder profits ($4.23, $5.68, −$7.73), and net revenue (revenue minus revenue from bidder losses) (74%, 69%, 61% of maximal revenue). For the additive objects, RAD, AUSM, and SAA achieve similar results. Under both environments, RAD auctions were shorter, averaging 3.32 rounds to completion, than the SAA, averaging 16.2 rounds, in contrast to earlier reported results with the CRA auction.

Brunner *et al.* (2010) build on the previous two studies and directly compare RAD and CC along with the SAA and an alternative package bidding auction that bares similarities to RAD but uses "XOR" bidding (exactly one package bid per bidder can win) and a different pricing rule that bases current iteration prices on previous iteration prices whereas RAD prices were determined anew every round and therefore could be nonmonotonic. Relatively complex environments with eight bidders and 12 objects are considered with value structures that increase complementarities (synergies) and overlap between bidders so as to examine progressively more difficult settings. Overall, the authors find that RAD yields higher efficiency than the three other auctions. When synergies are high, the SAA only averages 84% efficiency whereas all three combinatorial auctions average efficiencies 90% or greater. The CC yields seller revenue that is 10–15% greater (as percent of maximal revenue) than the other institutions. Likewise, bidder profits are 13–15% lower under the CC.

Finally, Goeree and Holt (2010) present a new design known as the hierarchical package bidding (HPB) which limits the types of packages that can be bid on thereby making computational issues less severe. This design builds on the important work of Rothkopf *et al.* (1998) who show that by limiting the set of admissible packages the winner determination problem for the auctioneer can be greatly simplified. Goeree and Holt (2010) demonstrate that such a simplification also makes the pricing problem, which is a central concern in designs like RAD, substantially easier. Goeree and Holt (2010) compare HPB to the SAA and an auction similar to RAD. While both package bidding auctions obtain higher efficiency than the 85.1% achieved by the SAA, the HPB performs even better, with average efficiency of 92.9% as compared to 89.7% for RAD. A similar result holds for seller revenues (as a percentage of maximum revenue) with 65.6% (SAA), 70.8% (RAD), and 76.6% (HPB). Bidder profits are more difficult to rank with similar profits for small (local) bidders across auctions but higher profits for the big (global) bidder under the package bidding institutions.

Chen and Takeuchi (2010) consider the iBundle Extend & Adjust (*i*BEA) auction originally proposed by Parkes and Ungar (2002). The *i*BEA auction is a clock-type auction in which it has been shown that a myopic best-response strategy (similar to straightforward bidding where bidders place bid on packages that are most profitable given current prices) is an *ex post* Nash equilibrium. Assuming that bidders follow these equilibrium strategies, *i*BEA should be efficient. As noted earlier, they also examine the VCG in a simple environment with some bidders being simulated. Chen and Takeuchi (2010) find that while the VCG achieves approximately 14% higher seller revenue, the *i*BEA achieves approximately 24% greater bidder profits and is more likely to be efficient.

Scheffel *et al.* (2011) examine many of the auctions previously discussed in environments specifically chosen to test auction performance. In most treatments, four bidders participated in one of four auction designs: VCG, CC, *i*BEA, and RAD,[22] in environments with 3–18 objects. Overall, the authors find that there are very few significant differences in allocative efficiency between auctions and environments. However, seller revenue tends to be lower under the VCG (in contrast to Chen and Takeuchi (2010) discussed above) and auction duration is longer under *i*BEA than both RAD and CC.[23]

What general results can be drawn from these studies? First, the theoretically attractive VCG auction does not perform as well as ascending combinatorial auctions. This is likely because of the need, due to the complexity of the bidding problem, for the auction to provide guidance for bidders about profitable opportunities.[24] Second, it is clear that most auction designs achieve similar results when there are no synergies. Likewise, while most reasonable combinatorial auctions seem to perform well in terms of efficiency, differences are most likely to come from either environmental differences that are better or worse for one design or the other or interest in other performance measures beyond efficiency such as seller revenue and auction duration.

On the behavioral side, bidder behavior is rarely consistent with theory when there are concrete predictions. Interestingly, underbidding (in terms of values and objects bid on) seems common but is also countered by times when bidders bid on objects that theory predicts they should not. It seems that bidders adopt heuristic strategies that are only occasionally consistent with theory. It would be worthwhile considering whether behavioral models that either account for bounded rationality or other nontraditional preferences can better predict behavior. Rothkopf (2007) goes as far as to suggest that decision analysis may be preferable to game theory.[25] While given the complexity of the environment it makes sense that bidders might resort to simpler strategies, bidders also show a remarkable level of sophistication in some settings as is outlined in Section 6 when considering bidder collusion.

Kagel *et al.* (2010) provide a particularly interesting combination of behavioral theory and auction performance. They theoretically examine sufficient conditions on package bids to obtain efficient or core outcomes. Under the assumption that bidders will only bid on a subset of all profitable packages, they show that there are environments that should be more or less difficult for combinatorial auctions. They then validate these predictions by comparing performance of the CC to the SAA in environments of varying difficulty. The CC outperforms the SAA in terms of efficiency in the simpler setting (95.5% versus 82.9%), but the results are reversed when the environment is sufficiently difficult (90.3% versus 93.4%). While the environments were specifically designed to "stress test" the CC, it provides an important proof of concept that relatively straightforward theory and simulations may help in the design process. In a subsequent paper, Kagel *et al.* (2012) examine other features of the auction environment that might impact performance. For example, they find that whether the efficient combination of bids corresponds to the "named" packages of each bidder (those that each bidder naturally is expected to have a higher valuation for) can impact auction performance. Obvious next steps are to address whether or not the applied environment of interest is simple or hard and whether there are alternative price-guided combinatorial auctions that might perform better than the CC in these difficult settings.[26]

5. Role of Specific Institutional Features

Fine institutional details that govern auction dynamics can significantly impact performance. Here, we discuss activity and ending rules that can impact ascending auction performance across a range of settings, including single-unit or multiunit demand, and environments with or without synergies.

5.1 Bid Withdrawal and Eligibility Rules

A practice allowed in the SAA conducted by the FCC was the withdrawal of bids; by allowing bid withdrawal (with a penalty) the intention was to mitigate some of the adverse effects of the exposure problem in auctions without package bidding. Porter (1999) considers the impact of bid withdrawal in a continuous version of the SAA in two environments. Interestingly, allowing bid withdrawal increases auction efficiency and seller revenue but actually increases bidder losses and thus lowers overall bidder surplus.[27] This seems to be in contrast to some of the intended impact of bid withdrawal shielding bidders from the exposure problem; the author attributes this to the increased difficulty in bidder coordination (e.g., avoiding the threshold problem) caused by bid withdrawal. In comparison, in settings without synergies, the lack of commitment caused by allowing bid withdrawal after the auction close is documented to have pronounced negative impact on auction efficiency and revenue (see Merlob *et al.* (2012) discussed in Section 2).

Another feature of the FCC SAA auctions was that bidders had a certain "eligibility" which limits the number of objects that they can bid on. The purpose of such a rule is twofold. First, as in procurement, eligibility could represent a judgment by the auctioneer as to the number of objects the bidder can service if they win. Second, eligibility is generally coupled with a "use-it-or-lose-it" rule whereby failure to bid on a sufficient number of objects in the previous round will result in a decline in eligibility in future rounds thereby encouraging early bidding by bidders despite the obvious cheap talk features. Banks *et al.* (2003) consider SAA with different variants of the eligibility rule under environments with and without synergies. Not surprisingly, eligibility has little impact on auction performance in additive environments, but in environments with synergies efficiency is increased by 8.2–15.4% depending on the treatment by allowing for a flexible eligibility rule that permits bidding on more units than the bidder is eligible for on occasion. Similarly, seller revenue is improved by both flexible eligibility rules and unequal eligibility that requires more eligibility for some objects. On the other hand, flexible eligibility tends to increase auction duration.

5.2 *Ending Rules*

Ariely *et al.* (2005) study ending rules and "sniping" in single-unit auctions modeled after online auctions. They show that a "hard" closing rule where an auction ends after a fixed period of time can create incentives for bidders to wait for the last moments of the auction to bid whereas a soft closing rule always provides the opportunity for rebidding thereby reducing the incentive to snipe. Sherstyuk (2009) extends the analysis to auctions for multiple heterogeneous goods with independent valuations, with four objects and four bidders. She compares FPSB auctions, SAA with the hard closing rule, and SAA with the soft closing rule. The FPSB auctions resulted in revenues 30% higher than the hard closing rule auction and 13% higher than the soft closing rule auction, as bidders tend to bid above the risk-neutral equilibrium predictions. On the other hand, just as discovered in Ariely *et al.* (2005) for single-unit settings, SAA with the hard closing rule lead to the lowest and most variable revenues, and to approximately 5% lower efficiency than the other auction formats, due to a significant amount of late bidding caused by the hard closing rule.

In more complex multiunit auctions with synergies, the choice of a closing rule can be important since the high number of objects may make auctions last for a very long time. On the other hand, the cost of delay, bidding, and winner determination may provide incentives for the auctioneer to select an ending rule that ensures that the auction ends in a reasonable period of time. In fact, in the pioneering study that developed, experimentally tested, and implemented a combinatorial auction for the procurement of transportation services, Ledyard *et al.* (2002) state: "A critical, if seemingly innocuous, part of the auction design is the stopping rule. The stopping rule for an auction is absolutely crucial to its performance, both in the final cost of acquisition and in the time to completion, because it affects the incentives and the information of the bidders." Ledyard *et al.* (2002) report the successful use of a rule that ended the auction if revenue from the winning bids did not increase by a certain percentage between rounds. All subsequent experimental studies that we are aware of have opted for more conservative ending rules that do not end the auction until no new bids are placed or at least the seller's revenue does not increase. Unfortunately, there are no systematic studies of how these rules might impact auction performance and the seemingly small differences in ending rules between experimental studies are often relegated to an afterthought.

5.3 *Jump Bidding*

In (nonclock) ascending auctions, bidders may place jump bids, that is, bids that are significantly greater than the minimum acceptable bid increment. This sort of bidding behavior is common in both the field and the laboratory; the potential for inefficiencies due to jump bidding has been used as justification for clock ascending auctions Banks *et al.* (2003).

The motivation for jump bidding can come from signaling, irrationality, strategic bidding, and impatience. Isaac *et al.* (2005) provide a review of these competing theories and an experimental examination in a single-unit setting that suggests that strategic bidding and impatience appear to be the most likely motivations for jump bidding.[28]

In the multiunit context, Plott and Salmon (2004) propose a model of bidding behavior in SAAs, based on the principles of surplus maximization and bid minimization, that would allow the auctioneer to predict the length of the auction as well as final prices.[29] They test their model using both lab experiments and data from the 2000 British 3G auctions, using a private values framework. They confirm predicted convergence to equilibrium prices and high levels of efficiency in the lab auctions. This is despite the fact that they observe substantial jump bidding (7–32% of all bids in their experiments) in both settings, which is inconsistent with the model. Therefore, they conclude that jump bidding is most likely due to impatience and an attempt to speed the pace of the auction.

Isaac and Schnier 2005 consider both field and lab data on charity silent auctions. In such auctions, multiple, heterogeneous units are for sale simultaneously, the auctions all end at a fixed time, the auctions are somewhat geographically dispersed (thus increasing monitoring costs), and jump bidding is permitted and common. The authors conclude that, "there is persistent support for the conjecture that bidders jump bid because they are impatient" (p. 772). As opposed to single-unit auctions, auction efficiency is somewhat lower than expected, but the lack of full efficiency may also be impacted by the relatively limited bidding time and high number of objects.

While the experimental literature on jump bidding in multiunit auctions is still somewhat limited, the results all seem to point toward bidder impatience as being the driving force behind observed jump bids, with minimal impact on auction performance. Yet, jump bidding in multiunit settings may also be an indicator of signaling and retaliation by colluding bidders, as we discuss in the next section.

6. Collusion

Concerns about bidder collusion have been prominent in the studies of auctions for a long time, but when highly publicized spectrum auctions resulted in clear evidence of coordinated attempts by bidders to avoid raising prices (Klemperer, 2002) these concerns became even more pressing. The notion of collusion is closely related to that of demand reduction, but is not restricted to uniform-price auctions, and may refer to a coordinated attempt by bidders to engage in anticompetitive behavior under a wide range of environments and institutions. Compared to a single-unit auction, the multiunit nature of sale may facilitate collusion, as the bidders may split the objects, much like sellers may split the market in other industrial settings. However, the multiobject nature may also make the environment more complex and create new coordination problems for bidders in reaching explicit or tacit cooperative agreements. Experimental research investigates the following questions: Can collusion be successful in multiobject settings? Does collusion occur to the same degree under different auction formats? What types of collusive strategies are adopted by bidders? Does the presence of a large number of bidders preclude collusion? And, for auction formats that are susceptible to collusion, what institutional features may facilitate or safeguard against collusion?

Traditionally, collusion has implied conspiracies (i.e., explicit communication among bidders). Recently, a significant amount of research has been drawn to tacit collusion, where bidders coordinate on low-revenue (and often lower efficiency) outcomes without explicit communication but as the result of equilibrium play. We review studies of explicit conspiracies first, and then move to studies of tacit collusion.

6.1 *Collusion with Explicit Communication*

Communication greatly facilitates cooperation among economic agents in a variety of settings. When studying conspiracies in multiunit auctions, experimental researchers focus on the effect of institutions and their collusion-facilitating and collusion-destroying features, and on the analysis of collusive agreements that emerge among bidders.

Many studies are motivated by real-world settings where concerns about bidder collusion exists. Phillips *et al.* (2003) study collusive practices in sequential multiunit English ascending auctions for homogeneous goods modeled after cattle auctions. Perhaps the most surprising finding is that the bidders were able to sustain collusion successfully in auctions with six, as well as with two bidders; the prices in these auctions were about half of the competitive norm, and consistently lower than in auctions without communication. Communication was the key collusion-facilitating feature in the six-bidder auctions, whereas knowing the quantity for sale was the key in the two-bidder auctions. One reason for successful collusion is the low competitiveness of the environment (modeled after the real-world setting of interest), with a large number of units (between 19 and 30) available for sale in each auction. With communication, the bidders successfully coordinated on simple bid rotation schemes to split the objects. "Our explanation for collusion being successful, when there are six players, is a simple bid sharing plan that lets bidders alternate taking the low bid is focal" (Phillips *et al.*, 2003, p. 977).[30]

Sade *et al.* (2006) study Treasury auctions, employing both students and finance industry professionals as experimental participants. The authors compare discriminatory and uniform-price formats with communication in a multiunit common publicly known values setting with five bidders competing for 26 units. Whereas the discriminatory auction has a unique equilibrium with competitive pricing, the uniform-price auction admits a lower-price equilibrium. In the experiments, however, the discriminatory auction was more susceptible to collusion and thus raised less revenue (by around 4%) than the uniform-price auction. This result is in agreement with the earlier findings of Smith (1967) and Abbink *et al.* (2006) on the revenue rankings of uniform-price and discriminative auctions without communication (see Section 3). The authors claim that these findings are consistent with the recent switch to uniform pricing by the U.S. Treasury. Furthermore, Sade *et al.* (2006) demonstrate that the seller's ability to reduce supply after observing bidders' demands in uniform-price auctions leads to higher revenue as compared to the fixed supply setting.

Burtraw *et al.* (2009) compare, in the context of environmental markets, three auction formats in terms of susceptibility to collusion: uniform-price (UPSB) and discriminatory SB auctions, where bidders submitted sealed bids on blocks of pollution permits, and multiround ascending-clock auctions, where bidders were asked to state the number of blocks demanded at each price. Six bidders competed for 30 homogeneous units, in auctions with or without communication; this is compared to the competitive baseline where 12 bidders competed for 60 units. The authors report that the prices were below the competitive benchmark both with and without communication, but communication further reduced auction revenues under all formats (by around 16%). The clock auction was the most collusive and produced the lowest revenue; with communication 38% of the clock auctions stopped at the reserve price of $2.00, yielding the average price of $2.29, as compared to $2.77 under UPSB, $2.83 under the discriminatory SB, and the competitive benchmark of $3.60. The authors suggest that the sequential nature of the clock auction appears to facilitate successful collusion, as it allows bidders to focus on one dimension of cooperation (quantity) rather than two dimensions (price and quantity) under the SB formats. A similar observation is made by Sherstyuk and Dulatre (2008) who compare bidder conspiracies in simultaneous and sequential ascending multiobject auctions. They report that bidders were able to reach and sustain collusive agreements more often under the sequential format than the simultaneous format. They attribute the result to the lower complexity of sequential auctions, which allow bidders to focus on one object at a time. It is interesting to note that bidders tendency to focus on one or a few objects manifests itself across a variety of multiobject settings, but has different effects depending on the setting. It causes overly aggressive bidding in pooled auctions (see Salmon and Iachini, 2007 discussed in Section 2), may result in bidding on only a subset of all profitable packages in combinatorial auctions (see Kagel *et al.*, 2010, discussed in Section 4), and facilitates collusion in sequential auctions, as discussed here.

Mougeot *et al.* (2011) adopt the framework of Burtraw *et al.* (2009) to consider whether introducing speculators (bidders who have no value for the objects except that they can resell them) may be used as a collusion-breaking device, as bidding rings may be harder to establish with such "outsiders." They compare the UPSB auction with the ascending clock auction and find that, in the UPSB, the presence of speculators makes other bidders bid aggressively, raising auction revenue. The effect is quite different in the more collusive clock auction; bidders accommodate speculators, letting them buy permits in the auction, and buying their necessary permits on the secondary market. They also observe that opening the auction to speculators deteriorates efficiency (from close to 100% without speculators to around 86% with speculators).

A number of papers study collusion in procurement auctions. Davis and Wilson (2002) investigate conspiracies in multiunit auctions under posted offer institution, where sellers specify quantity as well as the asking price, and find a strong effect of communication. Lunander and Nilsson (2006) consider procurement auctions for two goods with scale economies, and suggest that a combinatorial auction makes bidders less likely to collude than the standard SB auction.

Kwasnica (2000) studies collusive mechanisms in five-object, five-person SB auctions. He reports that bidders largely adopt collusive mechanisms that are incentive compatible[31] and payoff-superior to the simple random assignment scheme.[32] Furthermore, Kwasnica (2000) observes that whether bidders restrict themselves to incentive compatible strategies depend on the informational feedback available in the auction, and on whether bidders are symmetric. In an environment with symmetric bidders and bids tied to bidder identities, bidders select linear bid reduction strategies that are payoff maximizing, but are not incentive compatible. However, asymmetry or decreased information leads bidders to choose incentive compatible collusion mechanisms.

6.2 Tacit Collusion

In repeated or ascending price auctions, collusive low-price outcomes may be supported as equilibria even without communication, using signaling to allocate goods and the threat of retaliation to deter deviations. Experimental literature on tacit collusion, nearly all of which has emerged in the last 10–15 years,[33] investigates whether existing or newly adopted real-world auction institutions, such as the SAA, are susceptible to collusion, and how collusion may be remedied.

Kwasnica and Sherstyuk (2007) investigate bidder collusion in SAA modeled after the FCC spectrum auctions. Cramton and Schwartz (2002) provide evidence of collusion via signaling in FCC auctions, where bidders split markets at low prices. Brusco and Lopomo (2002) show that such low-price signaling outcomes may be supported as equilibria, and that such equilibria may be sustained even in the presence of large but common complementarities between objects. Kwasnica and Sherstyuk (2007) study experimental auctions for two goods with two or five bidders, and find a large amount of collusion in two-bidder markets without complementarities or with moderate complementarities; up to one-half of all markets with no complementarities and about one-third of the markets with moderate complementarities had prices below 50% of the competitive prediction. Moreover, just as predicted by the theory, they observe both signaling among bidders, and retaliation in response to deviators, often in the form of jump bids. There is strong evidence that bidders chose collusive schemes that were more efficient and payoff-superior than randomly splitting markets. Without complementarities, signaling preferred objects was used to split the markets as efficiently as possible among the bidders; with complementarities, bid rotation across periods was used to capture the complementarity term. However, collusion was never observed in two-bidder markets with large complementarities, or in five-bidder markets, indicating that large complementarities, and a low object to bidder ratio, tend to hinder collusion.

Sherstyuk (1999, 2002) study the role of bid improvement rules in ascending auctions. If the bidders are allowed to match each other's bids in open auctions, they can sustain low-price collusive equilibria where all bidders submit low equal bids, and the goods are allocated randomly among the bidders. These equilibria are observed in such "weakly ascending" experimental auctions under both common (known) values and under private values with three bidders with single-unit demand and two goods for sale. In the common value setting, the average price in the weakly ascending auction was 25.6 cents, as compared to 64.5 cents under the UPSB run in the identical environment, and the competitive prediction of 100 cents. Bid matching was observed in 89.7% of all weakly ascending auction outcomes; it served as an equivalent mechanism to random assignment, allowing all bidders an equal chance to buy the good at a low price. These results indicate that a strict improvement rule (disallowing tie bids) is a necessary element for enhancing competition.

Li and Plott (2009) study conditions for tacit collusion facilitation and prevention, and show that collusion may occur even with a large number of bidders. They create a "collusion incubator" environment which results in perfect collusion in experimental auctions under the standard SAA format with eight objects and eight bidders. The environment is characterized by "symmetrically folded and item-aligned preferences" (p. 425). Essentially, each bidder has a different best-preferred item, for which he has the highest value among all bidders, and faces serious competition for this item from only one other bidder. The preferences structure was publicly known, and the experimental auctions evolved toward perfectly collusive outcomes, with each buyer buying their preferred item at the reserve price, thus resulting in zero seller revenue but full efficiency.[34] Moreover, once collusion is established, it persists even when bidder identifiers are removed, the information about preferences is no longer public (but the preference structure remains unchanged), and even if some items are removed from sale. Competition is only restored when the preference structure is changed (without public announcement) in a way that creates head-to-head competition between two agents. Brown *et al.* (2009) further demonstrate that tacit collusion that emerges under the SAA is effectively destroyed by switching to the SDA. The reason is that, unlike the ascending auction, retaliation against deviators under the descending auction is costly to other bidders: every bid in the SDA is final, and punishing deviators typically involves bidding at a loss. The punishment thus rarely occurs.

The above two papers establish the following important regularities. First, forming common beliefs about cooperative behavior is a key factor in establishing successful collusion. Once the common beliefs are established, some institutional features (such as displaying bidder identifiers) that are important in sustaining collusion in theory, become unimportant in practice.[35] The second important factor in establishing and sustaining collusion is the ability to punish deviators. If this ability is nonexistent or very costly, as under SDAs, collusion is destroyed and competitive bidding prevails.

In summary, experimental studies document that collusion can and does occur with communication, or when it is supported as a low-price equilibrium, enhanced by repeated play. A large number of bidders does not necessarily preclude collusion, as long as the number of objects is large enough to share among bidders. Bidders gravitate toward collusive strategies that are payoff-maximizing, rather than simple random assignment. Sequential and multiround auctions appear to be especially conducive to bidder conspiracies. However, SAAs are also susceptible to collusion, and the presence of synergies does not always eliminate the phenomenon. There is some (but not enough) evidence that allowing combinatorial bids may break collusion. In the homogeneous goods setting, open ascending clock auctions have also been documented to be subject to collusion in the form of demand reduction (Section 3). Competitive pressures (measured by the object-to-bidder ratio) appear to be one of the most important factors for breaking collusion. Sellers may also counter collusion by reducing supply in response to low pricing, which may lead to higher auction revenue.

7. Sequential Bidding

We now briefly review experimental studies that consider sequential sales.

7.1 Auction Formats and Sequencing of Sales

A number of papers compare simultaneous and sequential auction formats. Lunander and Nilsson (2004) report that when bidders are asymmetric and have nonlinear average costs of winning more than one contract, SB combinatorial auctions are more efficient and have lower procurement costs, as compared to either simultaneous or sequential auctions. In their experiment, combinatorial auctions resulted in 91% efficiency,[36] as compared to 70% under simultaneous FPSB and 68% under sequential FPSB auctions, and a 4% lower procurement cost. In contrast, in a setting with single-unit demands (see Section 2) Goeree et al. (2006) find that the revenue is higher, by about 6%, in the sequential FPSB auctions where the most valuable item is auctioned first ("The best foot forward" strategy), whereas efficiency is the highest in the SAA, exceeding other auction formats by up to 15%. The simultaneous FPSB auctions give a higher chance of winning to weak bidders, and generate more entry on their part. Grether and Plott (2009) consider revenue-maximizing sequencing in a field experiment on sequential automobile auctions. Interestingly, they report that the worst performing sequence is for the seller to order vehicles from highest to lowest values. Unlike Goeree et al. (2006), Grether and Plott (2009) study a setting with seller competition, where several sellers simultaneously sell vehicles in sequential ascending price auctions.

Leufkens *et al.* (2012) compare first-price and SPSB sequential auctions for two goods, when the winner of the first auction receives a positive synergy from the second good. However, the value of the second object is not known at the time of bidding for the first object; an example of such a setting is expertise that is created during the first project and may be used in the second project. In this environment, bidding in the first auction involves bidding not only for the first object itself, but also for the option value of being in the favorable position in the second auction. However, because the option value may not be realized, bidders face an exposure problem (as explained in Section 4). Leufkens *et al.* (2012) find that the auctions are not different in terms of efficiency, but the first-price auction yields about 4% more revenue than the second-price auction, and also results in less frequent *ex post* bidder losses when positive synergies are present. These findings contradict the theoretical predictions, and are explained by bidders not fully incorporating the option value in the bid for the first object. The authors claim that the "results ... support the common use of the first-price auctions in governmental and business-to-business procurements" (p. 25).

Brosig and Reiss (2007) study bidder strategies in FPSB sequential auctions for two units, when both bidders are constrained (due to capacity) to win only one object. Bidder costs are drawn independently for both units. Due to the capacity constraint, the presence of the second unit presents an opportunity cost for a bidder, as winning the first unit would preclude the bidder from winning the second unit. Theoretically, a bidder should not always participate in the auction for the first unit,[37] and if they do, they should bid less aggressively than they would in a singe-unit auction. The experimental results confirm both of these phenomena in the lab. For the second unit, theory predicts that both bidders should bid more aggressively, provided they still face competition from the other bidder (which happens if they both forego the first unit).[38] This second phenomenon is not observed in the lab, and bidding on the second unit is indistinguishable from bidding in single-unit auctions. The strength of this paper is an in-depth analysis of bidder behavior. An interesting addition would be to take a viewpoint of an auctioneer offering two units for sale, and compare the sequential and simultaneous auctions with respect to efficiency and revenue.

Several papers consider nonauction alternatives to sequential sales. Salmon and Wilson (2008) study auctions with second-chance offers, where a loser of a single-unit English auction is given a take-it-or-leave-it offer to buy another unit, and find that such an auction/bargaining hybrid generates more revenue than two sequential English auctions. Fevrier *et al.* 2007 study two-unit, two-buyer sequential auctions with or without a buyer option, which allows the winner of the first unit to buy the second unit at the same price. Theoretically, whether the buyer option has an effect on bidding behavior depends on the auction format, and on whether the individual demands are increasing or decreasing. The authors compare four standard auction institutions: English, Dutch, FPSB and SPSB, in environments with decreasing, flat and increasing demands for two units, and report that the buyer option was used correctly in most cases. However, they do not compare revenues between auctions with and without the buyer option.[39]

7.2 *Price Trends in Sequential Auctions*

Several experimental studies explore price trends in sequential auctions. Milgrom and Weber (1982) show, theoretically, that if a number of identical units are sold one after the other to risk-neutral bidders, then the resulting expected prices should be constant. In contrast, many empirical studies document a "declining price anomaly" where prices decline for later items

Ashenfelter (1989). Keser and Olson (1996) observe declining price trends in sequential first-price auctions for homogeneous goods with single-unit demands. Neugebauer and Pezanis-Christou (2007) show that declining price trends may be exacerbated by supply uncertainty, as the latter causes more aggressive bidding in early stages in the auction, as compared to a setting where the supply is certain.[40] This finding is in agreement with the studies discussed in Section 6, which find that varying supply may be used by the auctioneers to counter bidder collusion. Deltas and Kosmopoulou (2004) suggest that increasing variance in bids and a decreasing probability of sale, observed in a field experiment with sequential book sales, may be due to a reduction in attention of mail-in bidders, rather than bidder strategic behavior.

In summary, sequential multiunit auctions, that are quite frequent in real-world settings, have not been studied by experimentalists as much as simultaneous auctions. There is some evidence, consistent with findings on simultaneous auctions, that FPSB auctions raise more revenue than other auction formats. The presence of synergies, or option values, affects bidding in early rounds. Some studies suggest that sequential auctions may be particularly vulnerable to bidder collusion (see Section 6). Many issues deserve further investigation including: choice of the auction format; sequencing of sales for heterogeneous goods; comparison with simultaneous auctions, or with other alternatives (such as bargaining) when applicable; and explaining price and sales trends. Bidder bounded rationality (such as limited attention span) is likely to play a role in explaining bidder behavior, much as in other complex multiobject settings.

8. Conclusions and Open Questions

In conclusion, we identify a few themes that cut across the various sections as well as discuss some areas that, in our opinion, warrant further experimental examination.

8.1 *Comparison of Auction Formats and Alternative Mechanisms*

By far the most common theme of experimental research on multiunit auctions is the comparison of various auction formats. While the efficacy of one auction format over another depends critically on the environment and performance measure, a few general trends can be identified. SB auctions tend to generate higher seller revenue in environments with both single and multiple unit demand without synergies. In environments with synergies, the SB auction, with the exception of VCG, has been studied much less, and the revenue results for the VCG are mixed depending on the study (Chen and Takeuchi, 2010; Scheffel *et al.*, 2011). On the other hand, ascending auction formats appear to be uniformly attractive in terms of efficiency. The dynamic, feedback rich nature of ascending auctions seems to be important to generate efficient outcomes in the more complex multiunit setting. The downside of the ascending auction is that it might also foster collusion and demand reduction. Interestingly, it might be the ability of the ascending auction to allow bidders to coordinate their behavior that makes the ascending auction work so well in environments with synergies. However, it is also evident that specific design elements of ascending combinatorial auctions such as price-guidance (RAD) or limited bidding combinations (HPB) might be important to further simplify the complex decision process for bidders. Unfortunately, we do not know theoretically (and experimentally) why these features usually work.

In practice, auctions rarely exist in a vacuum. Most experimental research on multiunit auctions has focused on auctions in isolation from other institutions. While this is important to allow us to understand issues of auction performance, it might limit the practicality of many experimental results. For example, in procurement settings, it is frequently the case that some procurement contracts are written outside of an auction whereas others are the result of an auction. Engelbrecht-Wiggans and Katok 2006 investigate a mechanism that combines auctions with such noncompetitive contracts. There are a number of papers that look at hybrids of auctions with other mechanism. Second chance offers and buyer options (Fevrier *et al.*, 2007; Salmon and Wilson, 2008) were discussed in Section 7. Evans *et al.* (2009) study a hybrid allocation mechanism that combines features of auctions and lotteries for publicly provided goods.

As is evidenced by the protracted debate over the adoption of package bidding for FCC auctions, the decision to conduct and design of auctions frequently exists within a political or business decision-making context. The process of decision making and the preferences of those decision makers needs to be considered when examining ultimate auction outcomes. Likewise, auctions are just one possible allocation mechanism; Banks *et al.* (1989) provide a comparison of various allocation mechanisms in addition to auctions for a problem that involved a traditionally bureaucratic decision.[41] Given the complexity of the multiunit environment, it is worth considering the performance of alternative mechanisms that may greatly simplify the allocation process or satisfy different performance measures.[42]

8.2 *Asymmetric Bidders, Entry, and Competition among Auctions*

As discussed by Klemperer (2002), encouraging entry and participation is considered to be one of the key elements of successful auction design. In many applications, such as procurement auctions, it is reasonable to perceive entrants as "weak" bidders, having either cost or information disadvantages compared to larger or more established incumbents. Indeed, a number of experiments consider environments with asymmetric bidders, typically modeling weak bidders as having a stochastic cost disadvantage (Abbink *et al.*, 2005; Goeree *et al.*, 2013). In contrast, Goeree *et al.* (2006) model entrants as having a fixed-cost advantage over incumbents. Studies of environments with synergies explore bidder asymmetries in terms of objects demanded where local bidders demand only one objects and global bidders demand multiple objects thereby affording global bidders a strategic advantage (Katok and Roth, 2004; Kagel and Levin, 2005; Chernomaz and Levin, 2012). With the exception of Zhang (2009), informational asymmetries in the multiunit auction setting remain largely unexplored.[43]

Very few laboratory studies on multiunit auctions, with the exception of Goeree *et al.* (2006), consider endogenous entry decisions, where bidders bear a cost (direct or opportunity) for entering the auction. In a single-unit auction setting with bidder choice over auction format, Ivanova-Stenzel and Salmon (2004, 2008) show that ascending clock auctions are preferred by bidders and result in more entry as compared to FPSB auctions.[44] Buchanan *et al.* (2012) show that uncertainty about the number of competitors (as well as about the number of units for sale) increases revenue in a multiunit, uniform-price Dutch auction. Carpenter *et al.* (2008) provide field evidence that entry and participation play an important role in the revenue-raising properties of auctions. They compare first-price and SPSB auctions with AP SB auctions in a multiobject charity auction field experiment. The authors find that the first-price auction raises more revenue than second-price or AP auctions, largely because they lead to more participation than the other two auction formats.[45]

Although we do not cover Internet auctions in our survey, there are many issues in auction design, such as choice of auction format, encouraging entry and increasing competition, that are relevant to both non-Internet and Internet auctions, and we expect both strands of research to benefit from each other's findings more in the future. For example, it is common on the Internet for there to be many auctions or auction sites offering essentially equivalent products. Using a field experiment, Ely and Hossain (2009) show that bidders may use squatting (early bidding), rather than sniping (late bidding), to deter entry of competitors.[46] Competition between auction sites in terms of charging policies (e.g., fees to sellers and bidders) remains largely unexplored experimentally.

Finally, auctions may be used to create competition for the right to participate in a subsequent economic activity, which may greatly enhance the participants' performance in this activity. Van Huyck *et al.* (1993) show that auctioning off the rights to play a median effort coordination game remedies coordination failure and leads to coordination on the efficient high-output equilibrium of the game. Offerman and Potters (2006) demonstrate that auctioning off entry licenses in an oligopoly industry leads to higher prices as it facilitates tacit collusion among the sellers. This powerful role of auctioning off participation rights in enhancing performance has not been investigated enough and deserves more attention.

8.3 *Behavioral Models of Bidding*

Many experiments in the multiunit auction setting have identified cognitive costs and observed limitations to rationality as key features in auction outcomes. Some examples are impatience (Plott and Salmon, 2004), cognitive costs of bidding for multiple items at the same time (List and Lucking-Reiley, 2002; Isaac and Schnier, 2005), attention fatigue (Deltas and Kosmopoulou, 2004), attention bias (Salmon and Iachini, 2007), and not bidding for all items or bidding for too many items (Olson and Porter, 1994; Chen and Takeuchi, 2010; Chernomaz and Levin, 2012). These behavioral features are no doubt important to take into account in auction design, and they deserve further investigation.

Recently, there has been significant progress in applying "behavioral" models of bidder behavior to single-unit auctions. Crawford and Iriberri (2007) demonstrate how a level-k model of boundedly rational bidders can explain bidding behavior in various single-unit auction environments. Likewise, anticipated regret is frequently identified as a salient feature in auctions and can explain overbidding in simple auctions (Filiz-Ozbay and Ozbay, 2007; Engelbrecht-Wiggans and Katok, 2008). While it has been suggested that, due to the inherently asymmetric outcomes (one winner) of auctions, the issues of equity and reciprocity may not matter as much as in the other settings (Bolton and Ockenfels, 2000), the multiunit environment may make equity and fairness concerns more relevant. For example, equity concerns might reinforce collusive behavior since, under some strategies, bidder payoffs are less unequal than under competition. The application of models of social preferences (both theoretically and experimentally) to the multiunit setting might provide improved explanations of observed bidder behavior as well as new normative insights regarding auction design.

Acknowledgements

We would like to thank Charles Noussair, Steven Tucker, an anonymous referee, John Kagel and Charles Plott for valuable comments and suggestions. Sherstyuk is grateful for the support by the Ministry of Education and Science of Russia, project 14.B37.21.0263.

Notes

1. In the epilogue, the authors report that the elements of the first-price auction were not implemented in the British 3G auctions, which proceeded under the SAA format; a fifth license was added and reserved exclusively for new entrants.
2. Sutter *et al.* (2009) adopt the values design of Abbink *et al.* (2005) to consider whether teams may bid differently than individuals in an ascending multiround, uniform-price auction. They report that teams behaved more competitively than individuals, and, consequently, made smaller profits and suffered more often from the winner's curse. The authors explain this by the prevalence of the "winning" motive in teams. Interestingly, such competitive behavior also resulted in higher auction efficiency with teams. However, the authors do not report on the demographics of the subject pool; it is possible that the observed higher competitiveness of teams is specific for college-aged participants, but may be mitigated in teams of more seasoned experts bidding in real-world auctions.
3. This observation is curious since, in the context of single-unit auctions, Levin *et al.* (1996) demonstrate that ascending auctions have advantages over the SB formats in alleviating the winner's curse because of the informativeness of drop-out prices. In Goeree *et al.* (2006), however, because of the low competitiveness, the auction ends with the first drop-out, and hence the drop-out price information cannot be of use to the remaining three bidders.
4. For four-object auctions, Pareto efficient allocations were achieved in 46.8% of AP auctions, as compared to 67.1% for WP auctions; the average efficiency was 96.6% in AP as compared to 97.9% in WP.
5. Salmon and Iachini (2007) point out that the SAA (used by the FCC to allocate spectrum) may take prohibitively long to run in many settings, and consider the pooled auction as an alternative format.
6. The dynamic Ausubel auction works similarly to the EC ascending price auction, except winning bidders in the Ausubel auction do not pay a common price, but the price at which they have "clinched" an item (see Ausubel, 2004 for details). Thus, a bidder in the dynamic Ausubel auction cannot affect the price he pays for one unit by misrepresenting demand for another unit. In equilibrium, the auction results in full demand revelation and full efficiency.
7. An informative, if unanticipated finding in the latter study concerns the first-unit bids. Whereas List and Lucking-Reiley (2000) observed significant overbidding on the first unit in the two-bidder uniform-price as compared to the Vickrey auctions, Engelbrecht-Wiggans *et al.* (2006) show that this effect disappears with three and five bidders; thus increased competition causes behavior to move closer to equilibrium predictions. Bidding true value on the first unit is a weakly dominant strategy under both Vickrey and uniform price auction formats. Therefore, no differences in bid levels should be expected on the first unit.
8. Such efficiency-disturbing aggressive behavior under Ausubel is not reported in any other study and may deserve further investigation.
9. See Kagel (1995) for a discussion of closer conformity of open auctions than of SBs to equilibrium in single-unit auctions, and Kagel and Levin (2009) for generalizations to multiunit settings.
10. This is unlike Abbink *et al.* (2005) and Goeree *et al.* (2006) who model entrants as weak bidders, with their values drawn from a distribution with a lower support than those of the

incumbents (see Section 2). In the current study, all bidders' independent private values are drawn from the same distribution, and the only difference between the incumbents and the entrant is the fixed externality cost that the incumbents bear if the entrant enters.

11. Although Goeree *et al.* (2013) do not give direct evidence that coordinating on demand reduction equilibria resulted in increased payoffs for bidders (as compared to the preemptive equilibrium predictions, or to the actual payoffs in the discriminative auctions), they do mention that "the weak appeal of the preemptive bidding equilibrium might be related to the fact that this equilibrium potentially results in the worst-case scenario for an incumbent." The latter would occur if preemptive bidding is unsuccessful and the incumbent ends up buying units at above cost and paying the externality cost caused by the entrant. However, such loss-aversion argument does not explain the prevalence of demand reduction equilibria under zero externality cost (the symmetric bidder case), where losses cannot occur in the competitive equilibrium as bidding stops at value. The prevalence of the demand reduction equilibrium is thus more likely explained by the payoff-dominance argument.

12. A common value framework is modeled in the standard way: bidders are uncertain about the common value, but each receives a private signal about the value (see Kagel, 1995).

13. These findings on the comparison between uniform-price and discriminatory auctions are, to a large extent, consistent with Smith (1967), who conducted such a comparison 39 years earlier; see the beginning of Section 3 for a review of Smith (1967).

14. Synergies for homogeneous goods may be the result of increasing returns.

15. The threshold problem is frequently termed the free-rider problem, but as described by Bykowsky *et al.* (2000), is more like a battle of the sexes game where there are multiple equilibria and the difficulty in coordinating behavior may result in inefficiency.

16. See a detailed description of the SAA in Sections 2 and 4.3.

17. The AUSM originally reported by Banks *et al.* (1989) is a continuous-time ascending auction that allowed package bids but did not provide price feedback. The stand by queue is a feature that allows bidders to publicly propose currently nonwinning bids (e.g., those that do not raise auction revenue by themselves). Other bidders then could propose their own bids that would pair with these bids and together become winning bids in the auction.

18. Many papers consider environments closely related to that analyzed originally by Krishna and Rosenthal (1996) where one or more bidders are global bidders who value more than one object (possibly with synergies) and other bidders are local bidders who only value one object.

19. Since the average human bidder profits are occasionally negative, we compare the profits differences as a percentage of the human bidder's value for one object, which was fixed in each treatment.

20. Such an SAA is often referred to as the simultaneous multiround (SMR) auction.

21. Variations in the auction rules of the SAA can be achieved by changing rules related to auction ending rules, minimum bid increments, or bidding activity requirements and will only be discussed to the extent that they are relevant for the experimental results presented.

22. Slightly different versions of RAD and *i*BEA were utilized for these experiments.

23. The VCG is an SB auction so auction duration comparisons are not particularly meaningful.

24. The need for such guidance has been understood since the very early years of multiunit auction design. Banks *et al.* (1989) state their choice of iterative ascending bid procedure

for the allocation problem with complementarities was motivated by " . . . the feeling, based on experimental evidence, that in an environment in which the basis for common knowledge are little understood and controlled, iterations with commitment allow subjects to 'feel their way . . . '."

25. Santamaría (2012) reports theory and experiments that uses decision analysis to generate predicted behavior and arrives at results similar to those reported by Chernomaz and Levin (2012).

26. Auctions such as RAD and HPB were not evaluated although the suggestion of this approach is that these environments will also be difficult for these auctions.

27. It is worth noting that the only efficiency result that meets most standard definitions of statistical significance with a p-value below 0.1 is in the homogeneous environment.

28. Kwasnica and Katok (2007) also show that jump bidding is impacted by timing concerns. Isaac et al. (2005) largely confirm the theory proposed by Isaac et al. (2007) and find that jump bidding does not significantly impact auction efficiency or seller revenue. Interestingly, they find that only the prohibition of jump bidding impacts auction performance; when jump bidding is not allowed many bidders drop out of the auction before reaching their value.

29. Such behavior is frequently referred to as straightforward bidding.

30. In a later paper, Phillips and Menkhaus (2009) study repeated English auctions with advanced production of the good by sellers. The sellers in this experiment often reduce units supplied to the auction in response to low bids by buyers, thus destabilizing conspiracies among bidders. This result confirms the observation by Sade et al. (2006) (discussed later) that the seller's ability to reduce supply may increase auction revenue.

31. A collusive mechanism is incentive compatible if it is in the best interest of each bidder to reveal their true valuation.

32. In particular, the ranking mechanism of Pesendorfer (2000) and the serial dictator mechanism were adopted frequently.

33. Kagel (1995) writes that " . . . outright collusion among bidders has not been reported under standard experimental procedures." A notable exception is Burns (1985) who observed some unstable collusion attempts in a multiunit sequential English auction with three bidders.

34. A curious observation is that such a preference structure is reminiscent of that studied in Efiaz et al. (2008) in the context of sequential bidder choice auctions, where the opposite result was observed, and the auction format created "competition out of thin air." They key differences between the auction institutions and the environment studied in Efiaz et al. (2008) and Li and Plott (2009) are: bidder choice auction as compared to simultaneous auction; private as compared to public information; and lower object to bidder ratio (four objects for eight bidders as compared to eight objects for eight bidders.)

35. Thus repetition with the same cohort of bidders appears essential for establishing these common beliefs, which is an observation that is also supported by the results of Phillips et al. (2003) and Kwasnica and Sherstyuk (2007).

36. The reported efficiency measure is normalized to the random assignment efficiency benchmark.

37. A bidder should skip bidding for the first unit if the cost of the first object is high enough relative to that of the second object.

38. This is because the presence of both bidders in the second auction indicates that both have a significant cost advantage in the second unit over the first one.

39. The authors do compare revenues across auction formats though, and report that the revenue ranking for the four auction institutions was the same as in single-unit auctions.
40. Neugebauer and Pezanis-Christou (2007) investigate longer series of repetitions than Keser and Olson (1996), and do not observe declining price trends in the treatment with certain supply, but only because subjects with high values wait until later stages to bid, whereas subjects with low values bid more aggressively, which is inconsistent with theory.
41. See also Olson and Porter (1994).
42. Such comparisons have appeared outside of experimental research. For example, Park *et al.* (2011) empirically compare spectrum auctions with beauty contests.
43. Andreoni *et al.* (2007) consider informational asymmetries about rival types that may exist between incumbents and new entrants in a single-unit auction setting.
44. See Kagel and Levin (unpublished data, 2011) for a broader discussion of experiments related to entry.
45. The authors estimate that " ... *ceteris paribus* and relative to second-price auctions, bidders are 14% more likely to participate in first-price auctions and 24% less likely to participate in all-pay auctions" (p. 104).
46. Davis *et al.* (2012) examines a similar type strategy, as identified by Bulow and Klemperer (2009), in a single-unit auction with sequential arrivals. They find that, while early arriving bidders place preemptive bids, these bids do not sufficiently deter competition.

References

Abbink, K., Irlenbusch, B., Pezanis-Christou, P., Rockenbach, B., Sadrieh, A. and Selten, R. (2005) An experimental test of design alternative for the British 3G/UMTS auction. *European Economic Review* 49(2): 505–530.

Abbink, K., Brandts, J. and Pezanis-Christou, P. (2006) Auctions for government securities: a laboratory comparison of uniform, discriminatory and Spanish designs. *Journal of Economic Behavior & Organization* 61(2): 284–303.

Adomavicius, G., Curley, S.P., Gupta, A. and Sanyal, P. (2012) Effect of information feedback on bidder behavior in continuous combinatorial auctions. *Management Science* 58(4): 811–830.

Alsemgeest, P., Noussair, C. and Olson, M. (1998) Experimental comparisons of auctions under single- and multi-unit demand. *Economic Inquiry* 36(1): 87–97.

Andersson, C., Andersson, Ola and Andersson, T. (2012) Sealed bid auctions versus ascending bid auctions: an experimental study. *Review of Economic Design*, forthcoming. http://link.springer.com/article/10.1007/s10058-012-0129-3

Andreoni, J., Che, Y.-K. and Kim, J. (2007) Asymmetric information about rivals' types in standard auctions: an experiment. *Games And Economic Behavior* 59(2): 240–259.

Ariely, D., Ockenfels, A. and Roth, A.E. (2005) An experimental analysis of ending rules in Internet auctions. *RAND Journal of Economics* 36(4): 890–907.

Ashenfelter, O. (1989) How auctions work for wine and art. *The Journal of Economic Perspectives* 3(3): 23–36.

Ausubel, L.M. (2004) An efficient ascending-bid auction for multiple objects. *The American Economic Review* 94(5): 1452–1475.

Ausubel, L.M. (2008) Auctions (theory). In S.N. Durlauf and L.E. Blume (eds.), *The New Palgrave Dictionary of Economics*. Basingstoke: Palgrave Macmillan.

Bajari, P. (2008) Auctions (applications). In S.N. Durlauf and L.E. Blume (eds.), *The New Palgrave Dictionary of Economics*. Basingstoke: Palgrave Macmillan.

Bajari, P. and Hortacsu, A. (2004) Economic insights from Internet auctions. *Journal of Economic Literature* 42(2): 457–486.

Banks, J., Olson, M., Porter, D., Rassenti, S. and Smith, V. (2003) Theory, experiment and the Federal Communications Commission spectrum auctions. *Journal of Economic Behavior & Organization* 51(3): 303–350.

Banks, J.S., Ledyard, J.O. and Porter, D.P. (1989) Allocating uncertain and unresponsive resources: an experimental approach. RAND Journal of Economics 20(1): 1–25.

Barut, Y., Kovenock, D. and Noussair, C.N. (2002) A comparison of multiple-unit all-pay and winner-pay auctions under incomplete information. *International Economic Review* 43(3): 675–708.

Bikhchandani, S. and Ostroy, J.M. (2002) The package assignment model. *Journal of Economic Theory* 107(2): 377–406.

Bolton, G.E. and Ockenfels, A. (2000) ERC: a theory of equity, reciprocity, and competition. *American Economic Review* 90(1): 166–193.

Brosig, J. and Reiss, P.J. (2007) Entry decisions and bidding behavior in sequential first-price procurement auctions: an experimental study. *Games and Economic Behavior* 58(1): 50–74.

Brown, A.L., Plott, C.R. and Sullivan, H.J. (2009) Collusion facilitating and collusion breaking power of simultaneous ascending and descending price auctions. *Economic Inquiry* 47(3): 395–424.

Brunner, C., Goeree, J.K., Holt, C.A. and Ledyard, J.O. (2010) An experimental test of flexible combinatorial spectrum auction formats. *American Economic Journal-Microeconomics* 2(1): 39–57.

Brusco, S. and Lopomo, G. (2002) Collusion via signalling in simultaneous ascending bid auctions with heterogeneous objects, with and without complementarities. *Review of Economic Studies* 69(2): 407–436.

Buchanan, J.A., Gjerstad, S. and Porter, D.P. (2012) Information effects in multi-unit Dutch auctions. Working Papers 12-08, Chapman University, Economic Science Institute.

Bulow, J. and Klemperer, P. (2009) Why do sellers (usually) prefer auctions? *American Economic Review* 99(4): 1544–1575.

Burns, P. (1985) Market structure and buyer behaviour: price adjustment in a multi-object progressive oral auction. *Journal of Economic Behavior & Organization* 6(3): 275–300.

Burtraw, D., Goeree, J., Holt, C.A., Myers, E., Palmer, K. and Shobe, W. (2009) Collusion in auctions for emission permits: an experimental analysis. *Journal of Policy Analysis and Management* 28(4): 672–691.

Bykowsky, M.M., Cull, R.J. and Ledyard, J.O. (2000) Mutually destructive bidding: the FCC auction design problem. *Journal of Regulatory Economics* 17(3): 205–228.

Carpenter, J., Holmes, J. and Matthews, P.H. (2008) Charity auctions: a field experiment. *Economic Journal* 118(525): 92–113.

Chen, Y. and Takeuchi, K. (2010) Multi-object auctions with package bidding: an experimental comparison of Vickrey and iBEA. *Games And Economic Behavior* 68(2): 557–579.

Chernomaz, K. and Levin, D. (2012) Efficiency and synergy in a multi-unit auction with and without package bidding: an experimental study. *Games and Economic Behavior* 76(2): 611–635.

Cox, J.C., Smith, V.L. and Walker, J.M. (1984) Theory and behavior of multiple unit discriminative auctions. *The Journal of Finance* 39(4): 983–1010.

Cramton, P. and Schwartz, J. (2002) Collusive bidding in the FCC spectrum auctions. *Contributions to Economic Analysis & Policy* 1(1): 1078–1078.

Cramton, P., Filiz-Ozbay, E., Ozbay, E.Y. and Sujarittanonta, P. (2012) Discrete clock auctions: an experimental study. *Experimental Economics* 15: 309–322.

Crawford, V. and Iriberri, N. (2007) Level-k auctions: can a nonequilibrium model of strategic thinking explain the winner's curse and overbidding in private-value auctions? *Econometrica* 75(6): 1721–1770.

Damianov, D.S., Oechssler, J. and Becker, J.G. (2010) Uniform vs. discriminatory auctions with variable supply–experimental evidence. *Games and Economic Behavior* 68(1): 60–76.

Davis, A., Katok, E. and Kwasnica, A.M. (2012) A laboratory comparison of auctions and sequential mechanisms.Unpublished.

Davis, D.D. and Wilson, B.J. (2002) Collusion in procurement auctions: an experimental examination. *Economic Inquiry* 40(2): 213–230.

Deltas, G. and Kosmopoulou, G. (2004) 'Catalogue' vs 'order-of-sale' effects in sequential auctions: theory and evidence from a rare book sale. *Economic Journal* 114(492): 28–54.

Demange, G., Gale, D. and Sotomayor, M. (1986) Multi-item auctions, *The Journal of Political Economy* 94(4): 863–872.

Efiaz, K., Offerman, T. and Schotter, A. (2008) Creating competition out of thin air: an experimental study of right-to-choose auctions. *Games and Economic Behavior* 62(2): 383–416.

Ely, J.C. and Hossain, T. (2009) Sniping and squatting in auction markets. *American Economic Journal-Microeconomics* 1(2): 68–94.

Engelbrecht-Wiggans, R. and Katok, E. (2006) E-sourcing in procurement: theory and behavior in reverse auctions with noncompetitive contracts. *Management Science* 52(4): 581–596.

Engelbrecht-Wiggans, R. and Katok, E. (2008) Regret and feedback information in first-price sealed-bid auctions. *Management Science* 54(4): 808–819.

Engelbrecht-Wiggans, R., List, J.A. and Reiley, D.H. (2006) Demand reduction in multi-unit auctions with varying numbers of bidders: theory and evidence from a field experiment. *International Economic Review* 47(1): 203–231.

Engelmann, D. and Grimm, V. (2009) Bidding behaviour in multi-unit auctions – an experimental investigation. *Economic Journal* 119(537): 855–882.

Englmaier, F., Guillén, P., Llorente, Onderstal, L.S. and Sausgruber, R. (2009) The chopstick auction: a study of the exposure problem in multi-unit auctions. *International Journal of Industrial Organization* 27(2): 286–291.

Evans, M.F., Vossler, C.A. and Flores, N.E. (2009) Hybrid allocation mechanisms for publicly provided goods. *Journal of Public Economics* 93(1–2): 311–325.

Fevrier, P., Linnemer, L. and Visser, M. (2007) Buy or wait, that is the option: the buyer's option in sequential laboratory auctions. *RAND Journal of Economics* 38(1): 98–118.

Filiz-Ozbay, E. and Ozbay, E.Y. (2007) Auctions with anticipated regret: theory and experiment. *American Economic Review* 97(4): 1407–1418.

Goeree, J.K. and Holt, C.A. (2010) Hierarchical package bidding: a paper & pencil combinatorial auction. *Games and Economic Behavior* 70(1,SI): 146–169.

Goeree, J.K., Plott, C. and Wooders, J. (2004) Bidders' choice auctions: raising revenues through the right to choose. *Journal of the European Economic Association* 2(2–3): 504–515.

Goeree, J.K., Offerman, T. and Sloof R. (2013), Demand reduction and preemptive bidding in multi-unit license auctions. *Experimental Economics* 16(1): 52–87.

Goeree, J.K., Offerman, T. and Schram, A. (2006) Using first-price auctions to sell heterogeneous licenses. *International Journal of Industrial Organization* 24(3): 555–581.

Grether, D.M. and Plott, C.R. (2009) Sequencing strategies in large, competitive, ascending price automobile auctions: an experimental examination. *Journal of Economic Behavior & Organization* 71(2): 75–88.

Huyck, J.B. Van, Battalio, R.C., and Beil, R.O. (1993) Asset markets as an equilibrium selection mechanism: coordination failure, game form auctions, and tacit communication. *Games and Economic Behavior* 5(3): 485–504.

Isaac, R.M. and James, D. (2000) Robustness of the incentive compatible combinatorial auction. *Experimental Economics* 3(31–53).

Isaac, R.M. and Schnier, K. (2005) Silent auctions in the field and in the laboratory. *Economic Inquiry* 43(4): 715–733.

Isaac, R.M., Salmon, T.C. and Zillante, A. (2005) An experimental test of alternative models of bidding in ascending auctions. *International Journal of Game Theory* 33(2): 287–313.

Isaac, R.M., Salmon, T.C. and Zillante, A. (2007) A theory of jump bidding in ascending auctions. *Journal of Economic Behavior & Organization* 62(1): 144–164.

Ivanova-Stenzel, R. and Salmon, T.C. (2004) Bidder preferences among auction institutions. *Economic Inquiry* 42(2): 223–236.

Ivanova-Stenzel, R. and Salmon, T.C. (2008) Revenue equivalence revisited. *Games and Economic Behavior* 64(1): 171–192.

Kagel, J.H. and Levin, D. (2005) Multi-unit demand auctions with synergies: behavior in sealed-bid versus ascending-bid uniform-price auctions. *Games and Economic Behavior* 53(2): 170–207.

Kagel, J.H. (1995) Auctions: a survey of experimental research. In J.H. Kagel and A.E. Roth (eds.), *The Handbook of Experimental Economics* (chapter 7, pp. 501–535). Princeton, NJ: Princeton University Press.

Kagel, J.H. and Levin, D. (2001) Behavior in multi-unit demand auctions: experiments with uniform price and dynamic Vickrey auctions. *Econometrica* 69(2): pp. 413–454.

Kagel, J.H. and Levin, D. (2009) Implementing efficient multi-object auction institutions: an experimental study of the performance of boundedly rational agents. *Games and Economic Behavior* 66(1): 221–237.

Kagel, J.H. and Levin, D. (2011) Auctions: a survey of experimental research, 1995–2010. Unpublished.

Kagel, J.H., Lien, Y. and Milgrom, P. (2010) Ascending prices and package bidding: a theoretical and experimental analysis. *American Economic Journal-Microeconomics* 2(3): 160–185.

Kagel, J.H., Lien, Y. and Milgrom, P. (2012) Ascending prices and package bidding: further experimental analysis. Unpublished.

Katok, E. and Roth, A.E. (2004) Auctions of homogeneous goods with increasing returns: experimental comparison of alternative "Dutch" auctions. *Management Science* 50(8): 1044–1063.

Keser, C. and Olson, M. (1996) Experimental examination of the declining-price anomaly. *Contributions to Economic Analysis* 237: 151–176.

Klemperer, P. (2002) What really matters in auction design. *Journal of Economic Perspectives* 16(1): 169–189.

Krishna, V. (2002) *Auction Theory*. Burlington, MA: Academic Press.

Krishna, V. and Rosenthal, R.W. (1996) Simultaneous auctions with synergies. *Games and Economic Behavior* 17(1): 1–31.

Kwasnica, A.M. (2000) The choice of cooperative strategies in sealed bid auctions. *Journal of Economic Behavior & Organization* 42(3): 323–346.

Kwasnica, A.M. and Katok, E. (2007) The effect of timing on bid increments in ascending auctions. *Production and Operations Management* 16(4): 483–494.

Kwasnica, A.M. and Sherstyuk, K. (2007) Collusion and equilibrium selection in auctions. *Economic Journal* 117(516): 120–145.

Kwasnica, A.M., Ledyard, J.O., Porter, D. and DeMartini, C. (2005) A new and improved design for multiobject iterative auctions. *Management Science* 51(3): 419–434.

Ledyard, J.O., Olson, M., Porter, D., Swanson, J.A. and Torma, D.P. (2002) The first use of a combined value auction for transportation services. *Interfaces* 32(5): 4–12.

Leonard, H.B. (1983) Elicitation of honest preferences for the assignment of individuals to positions. *The Journal of Political Economy* 91(3): 461–479.

Leufkens, K., Peeters, R. and Vorsatz, M. (2012) An experimental comparison of sequential first- and second-price auctions with synergies. *B E Journal of Theoretical Economics* 12(1): Article 2.

Levin, D., Kagel, J.H. and Richard, J.F. (1996) Revenue effects and information processing in English common value auctions. *American Economic Review* 86(3): 442–460.

Jin, Li and Plott, C. (2009) Tacit collusion in auctions and conditions for its facilitation and prevention: equilibrium selection in laboratory experimental markets. *Economic Inquiry* 47(3): 425–448.

List, J.A. and Lucking-Reiley, D. (2000) Demand reduction in multiunit auctions: evidence from a sportscard field experiment. *American Economic Review* 90(4): 961–972.

List, J.A. and Lucking-Reiley, D. (2002) Bidding behavior and decision costs in field experiments. *Economic Inquiry* 40(4): 611–619.

Lunander, A. and Nilsson, J.E. (2004) Taking the lab to the field: experimental tests of alternative mechanisms to procure multiple contracts. *Journal of Regulatory Economics* 25(1): 39–58.

Lunander, A. and Nilsson, J.E. (2006) Combinatorial procurement auctions: a collusion remedy?. *Rivista di Politica Economica* 96(1): 65–90.

Manelli, A.M., Sefton, M. and Wilner, B.S. (2006) Multi-unit auctions: a comparison of static and dynamic mechanisms. *Journal of Economic Behavior & Organization* 61(2): 304–323.

Merlob, B., Plott, C. and Zhang, Y. (2012) The CMS auction: experimental studies of a median-bid procurement auction with nonbinding bids. *Quarterly Journal of Economics* 127(2): 793–827.

Milgrom, P.R. and Weber, R.J. (1982) A theory of auctions and competitive bidding. *Econometrica* 50(5): 1089–1122.

Mougeot, M., Naegelen, F., Pelloux, B. and Rulliere, J.L. (2011) Breaking collusion in auctions through speculation: an experiment on CO_2 emission permit markets. *Journal of Public Economic Theory* 13(5): 829–856.

Neugebauer, T. and Pezanis-Christou, P. (2007) Bidding behavior at sequential first-price auctions with(out) supply uncertainty: a laboratory analysis. *Journal of Economic Behavior & Organization* 63(1): 55–72.

Normann, H.T. and Ricciuti, R. (2009) Laboratory experiments for economic policy making. *Journal of Economic Surveys* 23(3): 407–432.

Noussair, C. (2003) Innovations in the design of bundled-item auctions. *Proceedings of the National Academy of Sciences*, 100(19): 10590–10591.

Ockenfels, A., Reiley, D.H. and Abdolkarim, S. (2006) Online auctions. Technical Report 12785, NBER Working Paper.

Offerman, T. and Potters, J. (2006) Does auctioning of entry licences induce collusion? an experimental study. *Review of Economic Studies* 73(3): 769–791.

Olson, M. and Porter, D. (1994) An experimental examination into the design of decentralized methods to solve the assignment problem with and without money. *Economic Theory* 4(1): 11–40.

Park, M., Lee, S.W. and Choi, Y.J. (2011) Does spectrum auctioning harm consumers? lessons from 3G licensing. *Information Economics and Policy* 23(1): 118–126.

Parkes, D. and Ungar, L. (2002) An ascending-price generalized Vickrey auction. *Proceedings of 2002 Stanford Institute for Theoretical Economics Workshop on The Economics of the Internet*, Stanford, CA.

Perrigne, I. and Quang, V. (2008) Auctions (empirics). In S.N. Durlauf and L.E. Blume (eds.), *The New Palgrave Dictionary of Economics*. Basingstoke: Palgrave Macmillan.

Pesendorfer, M. (2000) A study of collusion in first-price auctions. *The Review of Economic Studies* 67(3): 381–411.

Phillips, O.R. and Menkhaus, D.J. (2009) Maintaining tacit collusion in repeated ascending auctions. *Journal of Law & Economics* 52(1): 91–109.

Phillips, O.R., Menkhaus, D.J. and Coatney, K.T. (2003) Collusive practices in repeated English auctions: experimental evidence on bidding rings. *American Economic Review* 93(3): 965–979.

Plott, C. and Salmon, T.C. (2004) The simultaneous, ascending auction: dynamics of price adjustment in experiments and in the UK3G spectrum auction. *Journal of Economic Behavior & Organization* 53(3): 353–383.

Porter, D.P. (1999) The effect of bid withdrawal in a multi-object auction. *Review of Economic Design* 4: 73–97.

Porter, D. and Vragov, R. (2006) An experimental examination of demand reduction in multi-unit versions of the Uniform-price, Vickrey, and English auctions. *Managerial and Decision Economics* 27(6): 445–458.

Porter, D., Rassenti, S., Roopnarine, A. and Smith, V. (2003) Combinatorial auction design. *Proceedings of the National Academy of Sciences* 100(19): 11153–11157.

Rassenti, S.J., Smith, V.L. and Bulfin, R.L. (1982) A combinatorial auction mechanism for airport time slot allocation. *Bell Journal of Economics* 13: 402–417.

Roth, A. (2012) Experiments in market design. Unpublished.

Rothkopf, M.H. (2007) Decision analysis: the right tool for auctions. *Decision Analysis* 4(3): 167–172.

Rothkopf, M.H., Pekeč, A. and Harstad, R.M. (1998) Computationally manageable combinational auctions. *Management Science* 44(8): 1131–1147.

Sade, O., Schnitzlein, C. and Zender, J.F. (2006) Competition and cooperation in divisible good auctions: an experimental examination. *Review of Financial Studies* 19(1): 195–235.

Salmon, T.C. and Iachini, M. (2007) Continuous ascending vs. pooled multiple unit auctions. *Games and Economic Behavior* 61(1): 67–85.

Salmon, T.C. and Wilson, B.J. (2008) Second chance offers versus sequential auctions: theory and behavior. *Economic Theory* 34(1): 47–67.

Santamaría, N. (2012) Competing against oneself in sealed-bid combinatorial auctions. Working Papers, SSRN Working Paper., http://dx.doi.org/10.2139/ssrn.1941814

Scheffel, T., Pikovsky, A., Bichler, M. and Guler, K. (2011) An experimental comparison of linear and nonlinear price combinatorial auctions. *Information Systems Research* 22(2): 346–368.

Sherstyuk, K. (1999) Collusion without conspiracy: an experimental study of one-sided auctions. *Experimental Economics* 2(1): 59–75.

Sherstyuk, K. (2002) Collusion in private value ascending price auctions. *Journal of Economic Behavior & Organization* 48(2): 177–195.

Sherstyuk, K. (2008) Some results on anti-competitive behavior in multi-unit ascending price auctions. In C.R. Plott and V.L. Smith (eds.), *Handbook of Experimental Economics Results* (Vol. 1, pp. 185–198). Amsterdam: North-Holland.

Sherstyuk, K. (2009) A comparison of first price multi-object auctions. *Experimental Economics* 12(1): 42–64.

Sherstyuk, K. and Dulatre, J. (2008) Market performance and collusion in sequential and simultaneous multi-object auctions: evidence from an ascending auctions experiment. *International Journal of Industrial Organization* 26(2): 557–572.

Shogren, J.F., Margolis, M., Koo, C. and List, J.A. (2001) A random nth-price auction. *Journal of Economic Behavior & Organization* 46(4): 409–421.

Smith, V.L. (1967) Experimental studies of discrimination versus competition in sealed-bid auction markets. *Journal of Business* 40(1): 56–84.

Sutter, M., Kocher, M.G. and Strauss, S. (2009) Individuals and teams in auctions. *Oxford Economic Papers-New Series* 61(2): 380–394.

Vickrey, W. (1961) Counterspeculation, auctions, and competitive sealed tenders. *The Journal of Finance* 16(1): 8–37.

Zhang, P. (2009) Uniform price auctions and fixed price offerings in IPOs: an experimental comparison. *Experimental Economics* 12(2): 202–219.

Two references, Kagel and Levin (2011) and Roth (2012), have been reinstated in this version of the article published on 14 March 2012 after initial publication on 6 March 2013. The references were removed in error during the proofing process.

6

OVERBIDDING AND HETEROGENEOUS BEHAVIOR IN CONTEST EXPERIMENTS

Roman M. Sheremeta

Argyros School of Business and Economics
Chapman University

1. Introduction

Many examples of competition have the property that multiple agents exert costly irreversible efforts while competing for a prize but only one agent receives the prize. Such costly competitions between economic agents are often portrayed as contests. Examples include rent-seeking contests, R&D competitions between firms, patent races, and competitions for promotion. These environments have attracted the attention of many prominent theorists and have yielded a number of interesting theoretical predictions; for a comprehensive review of theoretical literature, see Konrad (2009). Some of these predictions have been tested empirically using field data (Prendergast, 1999; Szymanski, 2003). Most of the empirical studies, however, focus solely on investigating whether the pattern of outcomes in contests is consistent with the comparative static predictions, since it is difficult to measure the actual effort expended by players in the field (Ericsson and Charness, 1994).

Controlled laboratory experiments give researchers the ability to measure the actual effort in contests, while controlling for relative abilities of contestants and the amount of noise in the contest.[1] Almost all experimental studies are based on three canonical models – contests (Tullock, 1980), rank-order tournaments (Lazear and Rosen, 1981), and all-pay auctions (Hirshleifer and Riley, 1978; Nalebuff and Stiglitz, 1982; Hillman and Riley, 1989). For a comprehensive review of a rapidly growing experimental literature on contests, all-pay auctions and tournaments, see Dechenaux *et al.* (2012). Although certain assumptions underlying the three canonical models are different, all three models assume that (i) players exert costly irreversible efforts while competing for a prize and (ii) an individual player's probability of winning the prize depends on the players' relative expenditures.

Contests, all-pay auctions and tournaments have traditionally been applied to different areas of economic analysis. Contests have been commonly used in the study of R&D races and

A Collection of Surveys on Market Experiments, First Edition.
Edited by Charles N. Noussair and Steven Tucker. Chapters © 2014 The Authors.
Book compilation © 2014 John Wiley & Sons, Ltd. Published 2014 by John Wiley & Sons, Ltd.

political or rent-seeking competitions (Millner and Pratt, 1989; Davis and Reilly, 1998; Potters *et al.*, 1998; Sheremeta, 2010, 2011; Sheremeta and Zhang, 2010; Price and Sheremeta, 2011, 2012; Morgan *et al.*, 2012). The commonly observed finding from contest experiments, first documented by Millner and Pratt (1989), is that there is significant overbidding relative to the standard Nash equilibrium prediction. Such overbidding is not desirable, since in the context of rent-seeking competitions where contests have often been applied, a welfare maximizing social-planner seeks to minimize socially wasteful expenditures (Tullock, 1980).[2]

Rank-order tournaments have been used in the principal-agent, contract design and labor literatures (Bull *et al.*, 1987; Schotter and Weigelt, 1992; Harbring and Irlenbusch, 2011; Sheremeta and Wu, 2011; Agranov and Tergiman, 2013; Eisenkopf and Teyssier, 2013). Contrary to contest experiments, the common finding from tournament experiments, which was first documented by Bull *et al.* (1987), is that the average effort levels in tournaments are well predicted by theory. Such efforts in rank-order tournaments are usually viewed as valuable because they contribute to the firm's output.

Finally, all-pay auctions have been used in the auction literature and in lobbying and military applications (Barut *et al.*, 2002; Noussair and Silver, 2006; Gneezy and Smorodinsky, 2006; Lugovskyy *et al.*, 2010; Kovenock *et al.*, 2010; Deck and Sheremeta, 2012; and Chowdhury *et al.*, 2013). Similarly to contest experiment, all-pay auction experiments find significant overbidding relative to the Nash equilibrium prediction. Also, as in contests, overbidding in all-pay auctions is not desirable.

In this paper, we restrict our attention mostly to contests (Tullock, 1980). The main reasons we focus on contests are that (i) contests have attracted most attention from experimental researchers and (ii) the results and phenomena observed in contest experiments are very robust and demand rigorous and comprehensive explanations. This paper attempts to provide such explanations.

We begin by introducing a simple theoretical contest model in Section 2. In Section 3, we provide an overview of experimental literature on contests and point out the two main phenomena observed in almost all contest experiments: (i) *overbidding* relative to the standard Nash equilibrium prediction and (ii) *heterogeneous behavior* of *ex ante* symmetric contestants. In Section 4 we provide explanations for the overbidding phenomenon, including bounded rationality, utility of winning, other-regarding preferences, probability distortion, and the shape of the payoff function. We also suggest mechanisms that can reduce overbidding. In Section 5 we provide explanations for heterogeneous behavior of contestants based on differences in preferences toward winning, inequality, risk and losses, and demographic differences. We also discuss several mechanisms that can reduce heterogeneity of individual behavior. Section 6 concludes and suggests directions for future research.

2. A Simple Contest Model

Perhaps the simplest contest model is a lottery contest proposed by Tullock (1980). In such a contest, there are n identical risk-neutral players competing for a prize value of v. The probability that player i wins the prize depends on player i's effort e_i and the efforts of all other $n - 1$ players. Specifically, player i's probability of winning the prize is defined by a contest success function (CSF):

$$p_i(e_i, e_{-i}) = \frac{e_i}{\sum_{j=1}^{n} e_j} \tag{1}$$

Given CSF (1), the expected payoff for player i is

$$E(\pi_i(e_i, e_{-i})) = p_i(e_i, e_{-i})v - e_i \tag{2}$$

That is, the probability of winning the prize $p_i(e_i, e_{-i})$ times the prize value v minus the cost of effort $c(e_i) = e_i$. Differentiating (2) with respect to e_i and accounting for the symmetric Nash equilibrium leads to a standard solution (Tullock, 1980):

$$e^* = \frac{(n-1)}{n^2}v \tag{3}$$

There are no asymmetric equilibria in the lottery contest and the symmetric equilibrium (3) is unique (Szidarovszky and Okuguchi, 1997). Given (3), the probability of winning in the equilibrium is $1/n$ and the expected payoff is $E(\pi^*) = v/n^2$. In a classic formulation of a Tullock contest efforts are considered as wasteful rent-seeking expenditures. The Pareto optimal level of effort is $e^{PO} = 0$. In such a case, the probability of winning is still $1/n$, but the expected payoff is $E(\pi^{PO}) = v/n$.

3. Experimental Findings on Contests

The first attempt to examine a lottery contest using a laboratory experiment dates back to Millner and Pratt (1989). In their experiment, subjects are placed in groups of two (i.e. $n = 2$) and the composition of the groups changes from period to period. Each period, subjects submit their efforts (bids) in order to win a prize of $8 (i.e. $v = 8$). Given these parameters, the unique equilibrium effort from equation (3) is $e^* = v(n - 1)/n^2 = 2$. The two main findings of Millner and Pratt (1989) are that (i) average effort is significantly higher than the risk-neutral Nash equilibrium prediction (*overbidding*) and (ii) there is a high variance in individual efforts (*heterogeneous behavior*).[3]

Since Millner and Pratt (1989), many other experiments have replicated the phenomena of overbidding and heterogeneity of efforts. Table 1 presents a summary of lottery contest experiments with symmetric players. Two main conclusions can be made regarding over-bidding. First, overbidding is a widespread phenomenon observed in almost all experimental contest studies. Out of 30 studies, 28 studies document statistically significant overbidding. The median overbidding rate, defined as $(e - e^*)/e^*$, is 72%, and in some studies the overbidding rate is so high that subjects on average earn negative payoffs (Abbink *et al.*, 2010; Sheremeta and Zhang, 2010; Price and Sheremeta, 2011, 2012; Chowdhury *et al.*, 2012; Lim *et al.*, 2012; Morgan *et al.*, 2012). Second, the overbidding rate across the 28 studies that find significant overbidding is quite different, ranging from 10% to 256%. From a first glance it is difficult to ascertain what causes such differences in overbidding rates. However, it is clear that there are many procedural and design differences that may be important. For example, most experiments employ either fixed or random matching protocols (Andreoni and Croson, 2008). When subjects face the same opponents for a number of periods (fixed matching) they may learn how to collude by reducing their efforts (Lugovskyy *et al.*, 2010).[4] Also, before participating in the contest, subjects are usually endowed with a certain amount of experimental currency that allows them to exert efforts (make bids) in the contest (Price and Sheremeta, 2011, 2012). In some studies, the endowment is higher than the prize value (i.e. Millner and Pratt, 1989) and in other studies it is lower (Shogren and Baik, 1991). Finally, it is possible that the overbidding rate depends on the number of contestants.

SHEREMETA

Table 1. Summary of Lottery Contest Experiments.

Study	Year	Treatment name	Matching	Endowment	Prize value v	Number of players n	Predicted effort e^*	Actual effort e	Overbidding rate $(e-e^*)/e^*$
Millner and Pratt	1989	Lottery	Random	12	8	2	2.00	2.24	12%
Millner and Pratt	1991	Less risk-averse	Random	12	8	2	2.00	2.45	23%
Shogren and Baik	1991	Lottery	Fixed	24	32	2	8.00	8.11	1%
Davis and Reilly	1998	Lottery	Fixed	Cash balance	200	4	37.50	54.97	46%
Potters et al.	1998	Lottery	Random	15	12	2	3.00	5.05	68%
Anderson and Stafford	2003	Homogeneous	One shot	5	5	2	1.25	2.42	94%
			One shot	5	5	3	1.11	2.00	80%
			One shot	5	5	4	0.94	2.25	139%
			One shot	5	5	5	0.80	2.85	256%
			One shot	5	5	10	0.45	1.33	196%
Schmitt et al.	2004	Static	Random	150	120	2	30.00	52.70	76%
Schmidt et al.	2005	Single-prize	One shot	20	72	4	13.5	9.4	−30%
Herrmann and Orzen	2008	Direct repeated	Random	16	16	2	4.00	8.20	105%
Kong	2008	Less loss averse	Fixed	300	200	3	44.44	80.56	81%
Fonseca	2009	Simultaneous	Random	300	200	2	50.00	100.08	100%
Abbink et al.	2010	1:1	Fixed	1000	1000	2	250	513	105%
Sheremeta	2010	One-Stage	Random	120	120	4	22.5	34.1	52%
Sheremeta and Zhang	2010	Individual	Random	120	120	4	22.5	43.8	95%
Ahn et al.	2011	Individual	Fixed	Cash balance	1000	2	250	342.5	37%
Deck and Jahedi	2011	Baseline	One shot	5	5	2	1.25	2.05	64%
Price and Sheremeta	2011	P treatment	Random	120	120	4	22.5	42.8	90%
Sheremeta	2011	GC	Random	60	120	4	22.5	30.0	33%
		SC	Random	60	60	2	15.0	19.7	31%
Cason et al.	2012	Individual	Fixed	60	60	2	15.0	18.96	26%
Chowdhury et al.	2012	PL	Random	80	80	4	15.0	26.2	75%
Fallucchi et al.	2012	Own-Stochastic	Fixed	1000	1000	3	222	368.5	66%
Faravelli and Stanca	2012	LOT	Random	800	1600	2	400	440.8	10%
Lim et al.	2012	N = 2	Random	1200	1000	2	250	325	30%
		N = 4	Random	1200	1000	4	187.5	302	61%
		N = 9	Random	1200	1000	9	98.8	326	230%
Mago et al.	2012	NPNI	Fixed	80	80	4	15.0	29.1	94%
Masiliunasy et al.	2012	N1S1	Random	16	16	2	4.00	4.98	25%
Morgan et al.	2012	Small prize	Fixed	100	50	2	12.5	21.5	72%
			Fixed	100	50	3	11.1	16.1	45%
			Fixed	100	50	4	9.4	21.7	131%
Price and Sheremeta	2012	Gift	Random	120	120	4	22.5	43.2	92%
Ke et al.	2013	Baseline	Random	250	450	3	100	150	50%
Kimbrough and Sheremeta	2013	Baseline	Random	60	60	2	15.0	29.3	95%
Savikhin and Sheremeta	2013	Baseline	Fixed	80	80	4	15.0	33.5	123%

We examine what factors can explain differences in overbidding rates across the 30 studies reported in Table 1 by estimating a simple OLS regression (a unit of observation is an average over an entire study), where the dependent variable is the *overbidding rate* $(e - e^*)/e^*$ and the independent variables are the relative (to the prize value) size of *endowment*, the number of contestants n, a dummy-variable for the *fixed* matching protocol, and a *constant*.[5] The estimated regression (with ** and *** indicating significance at 0.05 and 0.01 level and standard errors in parentheses) is

$$\text{overbidding rate} = \underbrace{0.43^{**}}_{(0.21)} \text{ endowment} + \underbrace{0.20^{***}}_{(0.04)} n - \underbrace{0.08}_{(0.17)} \text{fixed} - \underbrace{0.41^{**}}_{(0.27)} \text{constant}$$

(4)

This simple model explains 45% of variation in the sample (adjusted R-squared is 0.45). The regression shows that the overbidding rate increases (i) in the relative size of endowment (p-value $= 0.04$) and (ii) in the number of contestants (p-value < 0.01). The coefficient on the dummy-variable for the fixed matching protocol is negative (as one would expect from collusion) but it is not significant (p-value $= 0.65$). Based on the estimation results presented in (4), the experimenters should expect an average overbidding rate of about 22% when using the endowment equal to the prize value (*endowment* $= 1$) in a two-player contest ($n = 2$) with random matching (*fixed* $= 0$).

Overall, the summary of the 30 experimental studies on contests reported in Table 1 and the estimation results of a simple OLS regression pose a number of interesting questions: Why do subjects overbid relative to the standard Nash equilibrium prediction? Why does overbidding increase in the relative size of endowment and the number of players? The next section provides explanations to these questions.

4. Overbidding in Contests

4.1 *Bounded Rationality*

We begin by discussing perhaps one of the most commonly cited explanations for overbidding – bounded rationality. Potters *et al.* (1998) conjecture that most subjects are likely to make mistakes, which add noise to the Nash equilibrium solution and thus may cause overbidding. Sheremeta (2011) tests this conjecture by applying the quantal response equilibrium (QRE) developed by McKelvey and Palfrey (1995). In the Nash equilibrium, players must only put positive probability on playing strategies that are best responses to other players' equilibrium strategies. In the QRE, player i plays a mixed strategy σ_i in which the probability of playing a pure strategy e_i is increasing in the expected payoff $E(\pi_i(e_i, \sigma_{-i}))$ of that strategy e_i given that others are playing the equilibrium mixed strategy σ_{-i}. The most commonly used specification of the QRE is the logistic QRE, where the player i's equilibrium probability of playing e_i is given by

$$\sigma_i(e_i) = \frac{\exp\left(E\left(\pi_i\left(e_i, \sigma_{-i}\right)\right)/\mu\right)}{\int_e \exp\left(E\left(\pi_i\left(e, \sigma_{-i}\right)\right)/\mu\right)}$$

(5)

where $\mu > 0$ is a parameter that describes the level of noise in the decision-making process. If $\mu \to 0$, then the Nash equilibrium effort e^* is chosen with probability one. If $\mu \to \infty$, then each effort e_i between 0 and the maximum allowed effort level (endowment in Table 1) is equally likely to be chosen.

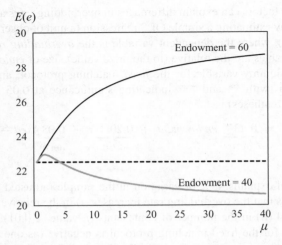

Figure 1. Endowment and the Expected Average Effort at the QRE.

An implication of the QRE is that subjects who have higher endowments (and thus larger strategy space to make mistakes) are more likely to overbid. The intuition is simple. Consider a subject who is completely confused and does not understand the rules of the game (i.e. $\mu \to \infty$). According to the QRE, such a subject should make his decision by randomly choosing any effort level e_i between 0 and the *endowment* level. So, the higher is the endowment, the more likely it is that the confused subject chooses an effort that is higher than the Nash equilibrium.[6] On the contrary, the lower the endowment, the lower is the probability that the confused subject overbids.

Sheremeta (2011) explicitly tests the predictions of the QRE model by conducting two experimental treatments. In each treatment, four subjects ($n = 4$) compete in a lottery contest for a prize value of $v = 120$. In one treatment, subjects receive the endowment of 60 and in the other treatment subjects receive the endowment of 40. Note that the endowment is not binding relative to the Nash equilibrium of 22.5 (i.e. $e^* = v(n - 1)/n^2 = 22.5$). Figure 1 displays the expected average effort at the QRE as a function of μ and *endowment*. When $\mu \to 0$, the behavior is consistent with the Nash equilibrium. When $\mu \to \infty$, players move closer to a random play, and thus the average effort approaches 30 (overbidding) for the *endowment* of 60 and it approaches 20 (underbidding) for the *endowment* of 40. Therefore, if subjects make substantial level of mistakes, then the average effort should be significantly higher in the treatment with the endowment of 60. Sheremeta (2011) finds that the actual average effort is 29.3 when the endowment is 60 and it is 21.0 when the endowment is 40, consistent with the predictions of the QRE.[7]

The findings of Sheremeta (2011) can explain why only 2 out of 30 studies reported in Table 1 do not find significant overbidding (i.e. Shogren and Baik, 1991; Schmidt et al., 2005). In both of these studies, the endowment is very small relative to the prize value. In Shogren and Baik (1991) subjects cannot exert efforts higher than 24, while the prize value is 32. In Schmidt et al. (2005) subjects can exert efforts only up to 20, while the prize value is 72. Therefore, it is not surprising that these two studies do not find overbidding.

Bounded rationality can also explain why overbidding increases in the number of players. Lim et al. (2012) use the QRE to show that overbidding increases in the number of players

n and find support for this prediction in a laboratory experiment. Specifically, they find that when there are two players ($n = 2$) in a contest, the overbidding rate $(e - e^*)/e^*$ is 30%. When the number of players increases to 4 and then to 9, the overbidding rate increases to 61% and then further to 230%.[8] Therefore, it appears that bounded rationality can explain why the overbidding rate increases (i) in the relative size of endowment and (ii) in the number of contestants.

4.2 Utility of Winning

In addition to bounded rationality, another oft-cited explanation for overbidding is a non-monetary utility of winning. The theoretical predictions in Section 3 are based on the assumption that subjects care only about the monetary value of the prize (i.e. v). However, subjects also may care about winning itself. Schmitt et al. (2004) argue that the persistent overbidding in numerous experimental studies (including their own) suggests that such behavior is not merely the result of subjects' mistakes or misunderstanding of the experimental environment. They propose that winning may be a component in a subject's utility. Sheremeta (2010) tests this hypothesis by directly eliciting such a utility from subjects. In the experiment, subjects participated in 30 periods of play in a four-player contest (i.e. $n = 4$) with a prize value of 120 (i.e. $v = 120$). At the end of the experiment, subjects were asked to submit their efforts for a prize value of 0 (i.e. $v = 0$). Subjects were explicitly told that they would have to pay for their efforts and that they would not receive any monetary benefit in case they won.

If subjects value only monetary payoffs, they should not exert any effort when the monetary prize value is zero. However, if subjects derive utility from winning itself, they may choose to exert positive efforts even when there is no monetary prize.[9] Sheremeta (2010) finds that more than 40% of subjects exert positive efforts in the contest with a prize value of zero. Moreover, efforts in a contest with a zero prize are correlated with efforts in contests with a strictly positive prize. Figure 2 displays the correlation between an effort for a prize of $v = 0$ and an average (over 30 periods of play) effort for a prize of $v = 120$. According to the theoretical prediction, the Nash equilibrium effort is $e^* = v(n - 1)/n^2 = 22.5$ when the prize is $v = 120$,

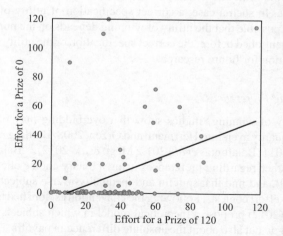

Figure 2. Utility of Winning.
Note: The data are taken from Sheremeta (2010).

and $e^* = 0$ when the prize is $v = 0$. Figure 2 shows that there is substantial heterogeneity in efforts, and subjects who exert higher efforts for the prize of 0 also exert higher efforts for the prize of 120 (Spearman's correlation coefficient is 0.31, p-value < 0.01). Therefore, it appears that in addition to monetary utility, some subjects derive non-monetary utility of winning and such a utility can partially explain overbidding.

Although the findings of Sheremeta (2010) have been replicated by other studies (Price and Sheremeta, 2011, 2012; Brookins and Ryvkin, 2011; Cason *et al.*, 2011; Mago *et al.*, 2012), there is still more scope for future research. For example, when eliciting utility of winning there may be several confounds, such as an experimenter demand effect (Zizzo, 2010) – subjects may feel obligated to submit efforts for the prize of value zero because the experimenter has asked them to do so. It may be also the case that subjects who make errors in assessing their effort strategies for a prize of positive value (see the discussion in Section 4.1) are also likely to make errors in bidding for a prize of value zero. Finally, even if subjects derive a utility of winning, the exact specification of such a utility function is not clear.

One way to incorporate the utility of winning into a contest model described in Section 3, is to assume that in addition to the prize value v, individuals also have an additive utility of winning w (Sheremeta, 2010). Therefore, the updated expected payoff (2) of player i can be written as

$$E_w\left(\pi_i\left(e_i, e_{-i}\right)\right) = p_i\left(e_i, e_{-i}\right)(v + w) - e_i \tag{6}$$

Differentiating (6) with respect to e_i and accounting for the symmetric Nash equilibrium gives us a new equilibrium effort, which is a function of both a monetary (v) and a non-monetary (w) component:

$$e_w^* = \frac{(n-1)}{n^2}(v + w) \tag{7}$$

From (7) one can easily verify that $\partial e_w^*/\partial w = (n-1)/n^2 > 0$. An implication of this result is that compared to the standard Nash equilibrium effort e^* described by (3), equilibrium effort e_w^* described by (7) implies overbidding (i.e. $e_w^* > e^*$).

It is possible that the utility of winning is not additive and is not invariant to the value of the monetary prize v. In such a case, a correct specification of utility of winning would be $w = w(v)$. It is also possible that the utility of winning depends on the number of contestants, i.e. $w = w(n)$. As mentioned before, the correct specification of the utility of winning function is an important question for future research.

4.3 *Other-Regarding Preferences*

Related to the utility of winning, studies show that overbidding may be driven by spiteful preferences and inequality aversion (Herrmann and Orzen, 2008; Bartling *et al.*, 2009; Fonseca, 2009; Cason *et al.*, 2011; Balafoutas *et al.*, 2012; Mago *et al.*, 2012).[10] Balafoutas *et al.* (2012), for example, elicit other-regarding preferences using a binary choice elicitation procedure of Bartling *et al.* (2009), and find that spiteful and inequality-averse subjects exert significantly higher efforts in real-effort contests. Following the convention established in evolutionary game theory, Mago *et al.* (2012) propose a theoretical model in which subjects care not only about the utility of winning w but also about the absolute difference in payoffs, i.e. $E\left(\pi_i\left(e_i, e_{-i}\right)\right) - s\frac{1}{n}\sum_j E\left(\pi_j(e_j, e_{-j})\right)$, where s is the interdependent social payoff parameter. Accounting for the behavioral factors captured by w and s, the expected utility for a risk-neutral player i is given by

$$U_i(e_i, e_{-i}) = E_w(\pi_i(e_i, e_{-i})) - s\frac{1}{n}\sum_j E_w(\pi_j(e_j, e_{-j}))$$

$$= (p_i(e_i, e_{-i})(v + w) - e_i) - s\frac{1}{n}\sum_j (p_j(e_j, e_{-j})(v + w) - e_j) \tag{8}$$

The utility function (8) is most commonly used in evolutionary contest theory (Leininger, 2003; Hehenkamp *et al.*, 2004; Riechmann, 2007). The idea is that the objective of a contestant is not necessarily to maximize the expected payoff $E_w(\pi_i(e_i, e_{-i}))$, but to 'survive' by outperforming all rivals. This quest to seek a higher payoff relative to others is an evolutionary stable strategy, and it is also consistent with 'spite' (Hamilton, 1970). Mago *et al.* (2012) interpret $s > 0$ as status-seeking behavior, i.e. contestants strive to obtain a higher relative payoff within the group. Herrmann and Orzen (2008) interpret $s > 0$ as aversion toward disadvantageous inequality. The utility function (7) also can capture pro-social behavior if $s < 0$, i.e. contestants have preferences to increase the payoff of the entire group.

Differentiating (8) with respect to e_i and accounting for the symmetric Nash equilibrium gives the equilibrium effort

$$e^*_{ws} = \frac{(n-1)}{n(n-s)}(v + w) \tag{9}$$

The equilibrium effort (9) increases in the utility of winning w (i.e. $\partial e^*_{ws}/\partial w > 0$) and increases in the status-seeking parameter s (i.e. $\partial e^*_{ws}/\partial s > 0$).

In their experiment, Mago *et al.* (2012) find that 51% of subjects indicate positive utility of winning ($w > 0$) and 67% of subjects behave as status-seekers ($s > 0$). These findings suggest that overbidding in contests can also be explained by a combination of a utility of winning and relative payoff maximization.

4.4 *Probability Distortion*

Baharad and Nitzan (2008) illustrate theoretically how probability distortion of the CSF (1) can lead to overbidding. Building on the theory of Tversky and Kahneman (1992), Baharad and Nitzan use an inverse S-shaped probability weighting function. According to this theory, individuals assign a distorted value $d(p)$ to the objective probability p. Thus, instead of CSF (1), subject's perceived probability of winning is given by

$$d(p) = \frac{p^\beta}{(p^\beta + (1-p)^\beta)^{1/\beta}} \tag{10}$$

Figure 3 illustrates the distortion function (10), assuming $\beta = 0.61$, as in Tversky and Kahneman (1992). When facing relatively small probabilities ($p < 0.33$) the individual is optimistic, since the distorted probability of winning $d(p)$ is higher than the objective probability p. When facing relatively large probabilities ($p > 0.33$) the individual is pessimistic, since p is underestimated.

Given the distortion function (10), the expected payoff for an individual i is

$$E_d(\pi_i(e_i, e_{-i})) = d(p_i(e_i, e_{-i}))v - e_i \tag{11}$$

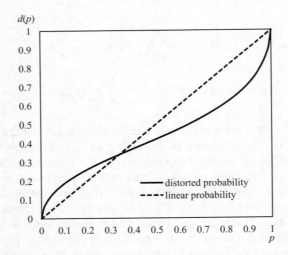

Figure 3. Probability Distortion.

Differentiating (11) with respect to e_i and accounting for the symmetric Nash equilibrium gives the equilibrium effort

$$e_d^* = \frac{(n-1)}{n^\beta(1+(n-1)^\beta)^{1/\beta}} \left(\beta - \frac{1-(n-1)^{\beta-1}}{1+(n-1)^\beta} \right) v \quad (12)$$

When comparing e_d^* described by (12) to a standard Nash equilibrium effort e^* described by (3), we find that the overbidding rate $(e_d^* - e^*)/e^*$ depends on the number of contestants n. For a relatively small number of contestants, probability distortion may result in underbidding. For example, with $n = 2$ and $\beta = 0.61$, the equilibrium effort (12) with distorted probability (10) is $e_d^* = 0.13v$, while the equilibrium effort (3) with no distortion is $e^* = 0.25v$. The intuition is that with only two contestants, the relatively high winning probabilities are underestimated and this substantially reduces the incentive to exert efforts in the contest.[11] However, when the number of contestants is relatively large, probability distortion implies overbidding relative to the standard Nash equilibrium (i.e. $e_d^* > e^*$). For example, with $n = 15$ and $\beta = 0.61$, the equilibrium effort (12) with distorted probability is $e_d^* = 0.07v$, while the equilibrium effort (3) with no distortion is $e^* = 0.06v$. Note that the fact that overbidding increases in the number of players (due to distorted probabilities) can also help explain different overbidding rates reported in Table 1, and the estimation results reported in (4).

Parco et al. (2005) and Amaldoss and Rapoport (2009) apply the distorted probability function (10), combined with a utility of winning, to explain the pattern of the data observed in their contest experiments. They find that behavior of contestants can be well explained by a combination of a utility of winning and a distorted probability function.

4.5 The Shape of the Payoff Function

Subjects participating in a contest experiment are usually inexperienced. Therefore, it may be difficult for them to understand the precise incentives underlying the game. As described in Section 4.4, subjects may have distorted perception of probabilities (Tversky and Kahneman,

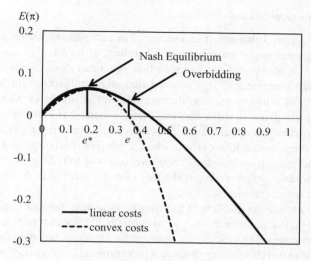

Figure 4. Linear versus Convex Costs.

1992). They may also find it difficult to calculate the exact expected payoff, since the feedback they receive after each repetition of the contest game is very noisy: a subject either wins the prize or not. Moreover, it can be shown that the payoff function (2) is relatively flat around the Nash equilibrium. Figure 4 shows the expected payoff in a four-player contest ($n = 4$) as a function of effort e, given that the opponents play the Nash equilibrium e^* (the value of the prize v is normalized to 1). Given these parameters, the effort that maximizes the expected payoff is $e^* = 0.18v$. It is easy to verify that even when the overbidding rate is 100% (i.e. $(e - e^*)/e^* = 1$) subjects can still make almost 50% of the equilibrium payoff.

Chowdhury *et al.* (2012) design an experiment aimed at examining how individual behavior is impacted by the specification of the payoff function (2). In a two-by-two design, they vary whether the prize is assigned probabilistically (i.e. efforts determine the probabilities of winning the prize) or proportionally (i.e. efforts determine the shares of the prize) and whether the cost function is linear or convex (see Figure 4), while holding the risk-neutral Nash equilibrium effort level constant. They find that compared to the probabilistic CSF, the proportional rule results in effort levels that are closer to the risk-neutral prediction.[12] The variance in individual efforts is also lower under the proportional rule and the distribution of individual efforts converges toward Nash equilibrium over time. Combining the proportional rule with a convex cost function further strengthens these results.

Fallucchi *et al.* (2012) also find that using the proportional rule instead of the probabilistic CSF reduces overbidding. Masiliunas *et al.* (2012) further document that overbidding is also reduced when subjects play against computer opponents with pre-determined actions that subjects know when they make their choices.

Overall, the results of Chowdhury *et al.* (2012), Masiliunas *et al.* (2012) and Fallucchi *et al.* (2012) suggest that overbidding in contests can be explained in part by the facts that (i) subjects have a hard time calculating the expected payoffs, (ii) the costs of deviation from the Nash equilibrium are relatively low, and (iii) there is not enough feedback for subjects to learn how the contest works.

4.6 *How to Reduce Overbidding*

We discussed in Section 3 that effort expenditures in contests are wasteful, in a sense that higher overbidding rates imply lower payoffs. Therefore, given the high rates of overbidding reported in Table 1, it is important to examine how one can reduce overbidding in contests. Recently, Price and Sheremeta (2012) showed that when subjects earn their endowments before participating in a lottery contest, their subsequent efforts in contests are lower than when endowments are given to them freely as 'house money' (i.e. the money subjects risk comes from the experimenter rather than their own pockets). Furthermore, Price and Sheremeta (2011) show that subjects exert lower efforts when, instead of receiving money as a lump sum, they receive a small portion each period. Therefore, one way to reduce overbidding would be to let subjects earn their money and/or make this money available to them gradually during the duration of the entire experiment.

Another way to reduce overbidding is to promote pro-social behavior among contestants. One such mechanism is communication. Cason *et al.* (2012), for example, find that when two contestants (or two competing groups) are allowed to communicate, they usually collude by exerting very low efforts (close to zero). Even when communication is not possible, there are other mechanisms through which subjects can still learn to reduce their efforts. Savikhin and Sheremeta (2013), for example, find that subjects reduce efforts in a lottery contest if they simultaneously participate in a public good game. Mago *et al.* (2012) find that subjects exert lower efforts in contests when their identities are reveled through photo display. The authors argue that photo display reduces social distance and enhances pro-social behavior, leading subjects to behave more cooperatively.

Related to the question of how to reduce overbidding, and perhaps an even more fundamental question is whether subjects can avoid a potentially wasteful competition in a contest altogether. Kimbrough and Sheremeta (2012, 2013) propose side-payments as one such mechanism, where one player (proposer) can offer a side-payment to another (responder) in order to avoid potentially wasteful overbidding. Their experimental results indicate that subjects learn how to avoid contests even in the case when side-payments are not contracted. Kimbrough *et al.* (2011, 2013) suggest a random device (a coin flip) as a conflict resolution mechanism. They find that, instead of competing in a contest, subjects often use a fair coin flip (even in the case when one player is relatively stronger than another or when the outcome of the coin flip is not binding).

5. Heterogeneous Behavior in Contests

Figure 5 displays a typically observed distribution of effort levels by subject. The data are taken from Chowdhury *et al.* (2012). Subjects are ordered by increasing average effort choices, which are indicated by diamonds. The boxplots display within-subject variation of effort. The Nash equilibrium prediction is that all subjects should choose the same effort of 15 (i.e. $e^* = v(n-1)/n^2 = 15$), since in the experiment there are $n = 4$ players competing for a prize of $v = 80$. It is important to emphasize again that there are no asymmetric equilibria in a lottery contest and the symmetric equilibrium is unique.[13] Contrary to the theoretical predictions, Figure 5 illustrates substantial between-subject heterogeneity (see the distribution of the diamonds) and within-subject heterogeneity (see the boxplots).

Similar results are also found in Sheremeta and Zhang (2010), Sheremeta (2011), Masiliunas *et al.* (2012), and other studies reported in Table 1. An obvious and interesting question is: What

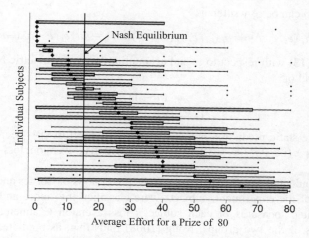

Figure 5. Distribution of Efforts in a Lottery Contest.
Note: The data are taken from Chowdhury *et al.* (2012).

can explain the between-subject and within-subject heterogeneity? In Sections 5.1 and 5.2, we provide different preference-based and demographic-based explanations for between-subject heterogeneity.[14] In Section 5.3, we provide explanations for within-subject heterogeneity.

5.1 *Heterogeneous Preferences*

In Section 4.2, we suggested that in addition to monetary utility subjects may also have a non-monetary utility of winning. Moreover, as shown in Figure 2, some subjects have a higher valuation for winning than others. Therefore, one explanation for between-subject heterogeneity is heterogeneity of preferences toward winning (Sheremeta, 2010). Another explanation comes from the discussion in Section 4.3. Specifically, we have suggested that subjects have other-regarding preferences, which are correlated with efforts in contests (Herrmann and Orzen, 2008; Balafoutas *et al.*, 2012; Mago *et al.*, 2012); and therefore, differences in these preferences can explain heterogeneous behavior of contestants.

In addition to differences in other-regarding preferences, it is well documented that subjects have heterogeneous preferences toward risk, with most subjects being risk-averse (Holt and Laury, 2002). The equilibrium effort in (3) is based on the assumption that contestants are risk-neutral, but the standard result from the theoretical literature is that (unlike in first-price auctions) risk aversion implies *lower* efforts in contests (Hillman and Katz, 1984; Skaperdas and Gan, 1995).[15] These predictions are supported by several experimental studies (Millner and Pratt, 1991; Schmidt *et al.*, 2005; Sheremeta and Zhang, 2010; Cason *et al.*, 2011; Sheremeta, 2011), which find that risk-averse subjects exert lower efforts in lottery contests than risk-neutral or risk-seeking subjects. So in addition to heterogeneous preferences toward winning and others' payoffs, heterogeneous behavior in contests can be also explained by differences in risk preferences.

Cornes and Hartley (2012) propose yet another explanation based on loss aversion theory of Kahneman and Tversky (1979). They incorporate loss aversion into a standard contest model by assuming that player *i* puts a weight of $\lambda > 1$ if he loses the contest. In such a case the expected payoff (2) can be re-written as

$$E\left(\pi_i\left(e_i, e_{-i}\right)\right) = p_i\left(e_i, e_{-i}\right)\left(v - e_i\right) + \left(1 - p_i\left(e_i, e_{-i}\right)\right)\lambda\left(-e_i\right) \tag{13}$$

Differentiating (13) with respect to e_i and accounting for the symmetric Nash equilibrium gives the effort level of

$$e_\lambda^* = \frac{(n-1)}{(\lambda - 1)(n-1)^2 + n^2} v \tag{14}$$

The comparative static prediction is that the equilibrium effort (14) decreases in the loss aversion parameter λ (i.e. $\partial e_\lambda^* / \partial \lambda < 0$). Note that, as with risk-aversion, loss-aversion implies underbidding.

Kong (2008) conducted an experiment to test the predictions of Cornes and Hartley (2012). In the first stage of the experiment, subjects were classified into more and less loss-averse according to elicited measures of each subject's loss aversion (Kahneman et al., 1990). Comparing efforts of the two groups, Kong (2008) finds that, as predicted by Cornes and Hartley (2012), more loss-averse subjects exert lower efforts in contests. However, for any degree of loss aversion, there is significant overbidding (not predicted by loss aversion). Therefore, although loss aversion cannot explain the overbidding phenomenon, it can explain heterogeneous behavior of individuals in contests.[16]

5.2 Demographic Differences

So far we have discussed preference-based explanations for subjects' heterogeneous behavior in contests. But perhaps the demographic differences are even more important. When a subject comes to a laboratory experiment, she comes as an individual with certain demographic and individual characteristics that may have even influenced her decision to participate in the experiment in the first place. So, it should not be surprising that in the experiment subjects behave differently, although ex ante they have symmetric roles. Although there is no systematic study examining how demographic and individual differences impact behavior in contests, there are several studies that may help shed some light.

Perhaps one of the most important demographic differences that impact individual behavior in contests is gender (Brookins and Ryvkin, 2011; Price and Sheremeta, 2012; Mago et al., 2013).[17] Price and Sheremeta (2012), for example, find that on average women exert 25% higher efforts in lottery contests than men. Figure 6 displays the 3-period moving average effort by gender across all 30 periods of the experiment. The Nash equilibrium prediction is that both women and men should choose the same effort of 22.5 (i.e. $e^* = v(n-1)/n^2 = 22.5$), since in the experiment there are $n = 4$ players competing for a prize of $v = 120$. It is clear, however, that both women and men overbid relative to the Nash equilibrium. Moreover, women persistently exert higher efforts than men throughout the experiment. Similar results are reported by Mago et al. (2013) in the setting of the best-of-three contests and Brookins and Ryvkin (2011) in the setting of incomplete information contests. These findings are also consistent with research on gender effects in auctions. Ham and Kagel (2006) and Casari et al. (2007), for example, find that women overbid more than men in common value auctions. Chen et al. (2013) find that women bid significantly higher and earn significantly less than men in the first-price auctions. Finally, Ong and Chen (2012) find that women overbid more than men in all-pay auctions. It is intriguing that gender effects are similar in contests and auctions; however, more research is needed to examine the exact causes of such effects. Disregarding

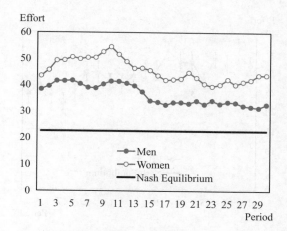

Figure 6. Average Effort by Gender.
Note: The data are taken from Price and Sheremeta (2012).

the causes for this gender difference in behavior, the fact that women overbid more than men can partially explain heterogeneous efforts in contest experiments.[18]

Another demographic difference that can explain heterogeneous behavior in contests is religiosity. Price and Sheremeta (2012) find that subjects who indicate that 'religion is very important in daily life' make 26% lower efforts in contests (see Figure 7). It is possible that more religious subjects are more risk averse and thus exert lower efforts in contests (Hilary and Hui, 2009). However, Price and Sheremeta (2012) find that religiosity is a significant predictor of effort expenditures even after controlling for risk preferences. Another possibility is that more religious subjects are more pro-social (Ahmed, 2009; Benjamin *et al.*, 2012) and more compassionate toward their counterparts (Batson *et al.*, 1993; Regnerus *et al.*, 1998), and thus they may yield the competition in contests in favor of others. Disregarding the exact

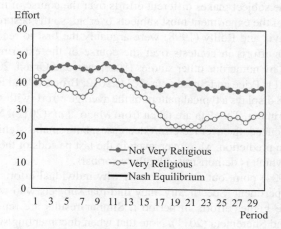

Figure 7. Average Effort by Religiosity.
Note: The data are taken from Price and Sheremeta (2012).

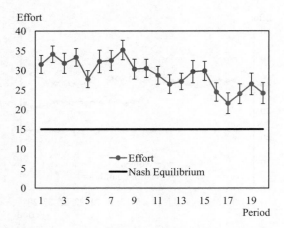

Figure 8. Average Effort over 20 Periods of Experiment.
Note: The data are taken from Mago *et al.* (2012).

reasons why religiosity impacts individual efforts in contests, it can help explain the observed heterogeneity of behavior.

5.3 *Learning and Hot Hand*

Previous Sections 5.1 and 5.2 provided a number of alternative explanations, based on preferences and demographics, for between-subject heterogeneity. In this section we focus on reasons for within-subject heterogeneity of effort.

In Section 4.1, we have suggested that the QRE model can help explain overbidding in contests. According to the QRE model, a player draws an effort level e_i from a mixed strategy distribution σ_i (see equation 5). Therefore, within-subject heterogeneity of effort can be explained by the QRE model. It is unlikely, however, that mistakes and errors are the only reasons why the same subject makes different efforts over the course of the experiment.

At the beginning of the experiment most subjects overbid, so the best response is to reduce individual effort. Davis and Reilly (1998) were arguably the first to recognize that subjects learn to reduce their efforts in contests over the course of the experiment. Their findings have been replicated by numerous other studies (Herrmann and Orzen, 2008; Fonseca, 2009; Sheremeta, 2010, 2011; Price and Sheremeta, 2011, 2012; Brookins and Ryvkin, 2011; Mago *et al.*, 2012). Figure 8 displays a typical pattern of the average effort (with standard errors) over the span of the experiment. The data are taken from Mago *et al.* (2012). Note that as subjects become more experienced, the average effort decreases, but remains significantly higher than the Nash equilibrium prediction. Moreover, even in the last periods of the experiment, efforts are heterogeneous, which is demonstrated by the error bars.

Schmitt *et al.* (2004) point out another reason why individual efforts may fluctuate over the course of the experiment. Specifically, they find that subjects who won in period t-1 are more likely to make higher efforts in period t. Similar results are reported by Sheremeta and Zhang (2010) and Sheremeta (2011). Note that when documenting such correlations, the authors usually control for strategic uncertainty by including efforts as dependent variables. Sheremeta and Zhang (2010) point out the similarities of correlation between winning in period

t-1 and higher efforts in period t to a 'hot hand' phenomenon found in the gambling literature – belief in a positive autocorrelation of a non-autocorrelated random sequence (Gilovich *et al.*, 1985; Chau and Phillips, 1995; Croson and Sundali, 2005). Therefore, it appears that both learning and hot hand response by subjects may help explain within-subject variation of effort.

5.4 *How to Reduce Heterogeneity*

In the context of labor markets, where contest-like incentive schemes are commonly applied, a high variance in individual effort can impose a substantial cost on employers and decrease the overall efficiency of the work place (Lazear, 1999, 2000). Therefore, it is imperative to find ways how to reduce heterogeneity of individual behavior (Bull *et al.*, 1987; Eriksson *et al.*, 2009).[19] There is no trivial solution to this problem. As we pointed out in Sections 5.2 and 5.3, the likely causes of heterogeneous behavior in contests are differences in individual preferences and demographic differences. It is hard to imagine a mechanism that would homogenize individual preferences toward winning, inequality, risk and losses. Perhaps even harder (if not impossible) would be to eliminate demographic differences. Nevertheless, we want to point out three alternative mechanisms that may reduce heterogeneity of behavior that is due to subjects making mistakes in contests: (i) group decision making, (ii) feedback, and (iii) simplified payoff functions. All three mechanisms are targeted to reduce subjects' cognitive load and enhance subjects' learning of the contest environment (Devetag and Warglien, 2003; Burks *et al.*, 2009).

It is well documented that groups are better at making decisions that are more in line with game-theoretic predictions than individuals (Charness and Sutter, 2012). One implication of this result is that groups should choose more homogeneous efforts in contests since theory predicts a unique equilibrium defined by (3). Sheremeta and Zhang (2010) test this conjecture by comparing efforts chosen by groups of two subjects versus efforts chosen by individual subjects. They find that group efforts are more homogeneous and result in 25% lower efforts than individual efforts. As a result, groups receive significantly higher and more homogeneous payoffs than individuals. Sheremeta and Zhang suggest that groups perform better because they reduce individual mistakes through group communication and they learn faster than individuals.

Another mechanism that may help subjects to learn faster is feedback. Mago *et al.* (2012) experimentally examine different levels of feedback in contests. In some experimental sessions, subjects only receive feedback about whether they won the contest or not. In other sessions, subjects receive full feedback about all group members' efforts. Mago *et al.* find that providing information feedback about others' efforts makes effort levels more uniform within a given group, and thus reduces between-subject heterogeneity. Fallucchi *et al.* (2012) find that not only does feedback reduce heterogeneity, but it can also reduce overbidding in the long run (i.e. when the experiment is repeated for 60 periods).

Finally, it is possible to reduce between-subject as well as within-subject heterogeneity by using a more simplified payoff function. We have already discussed in Section 4.5 that using the proportional rule, instead of the probabilistic CSF, reduces overbidding (Chowdhury *et al.*, 2012; Fallucchi *et al.*, 2012; Masiliunas *et al.*, 2012). Moreover, Chowdhury *et al.* (2012) find that not only does the proportional rule reduce overbidding, but it also significantly decreases between-subject and within-subject heterogeneity. This is mainly because the proportional rule gives subjects an opportunity to better learn the payoff structure of the contest, and thus subjects learn to make fewer errors.

6. Discussion and Conclusion

Contests are prevalent in the fields of economics, management, biology, law and political science and have attracted the attention of many theorists. It is difficult, however, to test theoretical predictions in the field because efforts are unobservable. For that reason, researchers have turned to controlled laboratory experiments that allow measuring the actual efforts in contests, while controlling for relative abilities of contestants and the amount of noise in the contest; for a review of experimental literature, see Dechenaux *et al.* (2012).

In this paper, we provide an overview of experimental literature on lottery contests and point out the two main phenomena observed in almost all contest experiments: (i) *overbidding* relative to the standard Nash equilibrium prediction and (ii) *heterogeneous behavior* of *ex ante* symmetric contestants.

We provide a number of explanations in Sections 4.1–4.5 for the overbidding phenomenon, including (1) bounded rationality, (2) utility of winning, (3) other-regarding preferences (spite, inequality-aversion), (4) probability distortion, and (5) the shape of the payoff function. Obviously, these explanations are not exhaustive. Other potential candidates, for example, are regret (Engelbrecht-Wiggans and Katok, 2007; Filiz-Ozbay and Ozbay, 2007) and overconfidence (Camerer and Lovallo, 1999; Park and Santos-Pinto, 2010). Although both of these factors are likely to add to the observed overbidding, no experimental study has systematically examined regret and overconfidence in relationship to behavior in contests.[20] This is an interesting avenue for future research.

Based on the sample of contest experiments that we review, the median overbidding rate is 72%. Moreover, in some studies the overbidding rate is so high that subjects on average earn negative payoffs. Given such high empirical rates of overbidding, it is imperative to develop and investigate different mechanisms that can reduce overbidding (i.e. conflict de-escalation) or maybe even prevent conflicts altogether (i.e. conflict resolution). We suggest several mechanisms in Section 4.6 through which overbidding can be reduced, including restricted distribution of pre-experimental endowments, communication, and social identity. We also suggest several conflict resolution mechanisms, such as side-payments and the use of randomization devices. The field of conflict resolution is very new and there are many interesting questions for future research pertaining to both conflict de-escalation and conflict resolution.

It is important to emphasize that overbidding in contests can also be used to increase economic welfare. In many applications, high contest expenditures may be viewed as preferable from the standpoint of the contest designer. For instance, in labor tournaments (Lazear and Rosen, 1981), effort is viewed as valuable because it contributes to the firm's output. In sports competitions (Szymanski, 2003), efforts have large positive externalities on fans and viewers. Similarly, in contests used to finance public goods (Morgan and Sefton, 2000) and raise money for charities (Landry *et al.*, 2006), efforts provide significant positive externalities. Finally, overbidding in contests is good news for prize-linked savings mechanisms that use lottery contests to stimulate savings (Tufano, 2008).

Unlike overbidding, heterogeneous behavior of individuals is mostly viewed as negative, because such behavior creates unnecessary uncertainty and imposes a substantial cost on the contest designer (Bull *et al.*, 1987; Lazear, 1999, 2000; Eriksson *et al.*, 2009). In Sections 5.1–5.3 we provide explanations for heterogeneous behavior in contests based on (1) differences in preferences toward winning, inequality, risk and losses, and (2) demographic differences. There are other potential candidates to explain heterogeneous behavior of contestants that have not been explored yet. First, it is possible that there are different types in the population of subjects (for example, see Herrmann and Orzen, 2008). Second, it is well documented that emotions are predictable and predictive of individual behavior in experimental games (Xiao and Houser, 2005; Schniter *et al.*, 2011, 2013); therefore, individuals experiencing different emotions may exert different efforts in contests. Theoretically, we should expect individuals experiencing hate and revenge to exert higher effort (Amegashie and Runkel, 2012) and individuals experiencing guilt and shame to exert lower effort (Behrendt and Ben-Ari, 2012) in contests. Also, it is well documented that subjects have different personality traits, such as the Big Five personality characteristics (Kurzban and Houser, 2001; Borghans *et al.*, 2008), and different cognitive abilities, as measured by IQ and SAT scores (Frey and Detterman, 2004). Future research should examine how these differences impact individual behavior in contests.

In Section 5.4 we discussed several mechanisms that can reduce heterogeneity of behavior that is due to subjects making mistakes in contests, such as group decision making, feedback, and simplified payoff functions. The idea is that mechanisms that reduce cognitive load (Devetag and Warglien, 2003; Burks *et al.*, 2009) and enhance subjects' learning of the contest environment should induce more homogeneous behavior. Given the potentially negative consequences of effort heterogeneity, future research should search for new mechanisms to induce more homogeneous behavior in contests.

On a more fundamental level, it is important to closely examine the main underlying factors that can explain individual behavior in contests. For example, although the factors contributing to the overbidding phenomenon (such as utility of winning, spite, status-seeking, mistakes, probability distortion, etc.) are frequently cited, it remains an open question as to whether some of these factors are correlated and if so, which are the most important ones. The overall impact of this correlation on individual and group behavior remains unknown. Similarly, probability distortion may be correlated with mistakes, risk-aversion, and loss-aversion; however, it is important to know which factors are the most important in explaining individual behavior in contests. The answers to these questions would significantly advance our understanding of the field.

Acknowledgements

Much of this survey is based on the work I have done with various coauthors over the course of more than five years. What I learned during those years of collaboration helped me to shape my understanding of the field. I gratefully acknowledge and thank all my coauthors who worked with me on various contest projects. I thank Subhasish Chowdhury, Cary Deck, Shakun Mago, Curtis Price, Jared Rubin, Anya Samak, Ted Turocy, Casper de Vries, Jingjing Zhang, the seminar participants at Chapman University, the University of California at San Diego, the University of Texas at Dallas, and participants at the 2012 International Foundation for Research in Experimental Economics Conference and the 2012 North America Economic Science Association meetings for their comments and valuable feedback. I retain responsibility for any errors.

Notes

1. It is still possible that subjects who are assigned *ex ante* symmetric roles in contests may still differ in their skills (abilities) of playing the experimental game (i.e. differences in

cognitive ability, understanding the incentives, learning, etc.). However, the luxury of experimental approach is that these 'hidden abilities' can be measured and controlled for in the laboratory using different methods and elicitation procedures.

2. In the context of R&D and patent races, however, a social planner may desire the positive externalities generated from increased research spending.

3. Similar phenomena are also observed in all-pay auctions with complete information (Davis and Reilly, 1998; Gneezy and Smorodinsky, 2006; Lugovskyy *et al.*, 2010; Kovenock *et al.*, 2010; Klose and Sheremeta, 2012; Ong and Chen, 2012; Mago and Sheremeta, 2012; Deck and Sheremeta, 2012) and incomplete information (Barut *et al.*, 2002; Noussair and Silver, 2006; Dechenaux and Mancini, 2008; Müller and Schotter, 2010; Hyndman *et al.*, 2012). For a review, see Dechenaux *et al.* (2012).

4. Collusion is clearly an issue in the context of auctions (see Klemperer, 2002). A common way to deal with this is to randomly re-match subjects after each period of play. However, there is no general agreement on how matching protocol influences individual behavior. In public good games, for example, some studies find more cooperation under random matching, some find more under fixed marching, and some fail to find any difference at all (Andreoni and Croson, 2008; Botelho *et al.*, 2009).

5. We have also included a dummy-variable for those experiments that last for only one period. The dummy-variable is positive, but insignificant.

6. In interpreting these results some caution is advised since changing the endowment also changes subjects' wealth levels. If individuals have more wealth, they may be more willing to spend more of it regardless of the level of mistakes. Future research is needed to clearly separate these effects.

7. There are two potential explanations as to why subjects make mistakes. First, it is possible that subjects hold incorrect beliefs about the actions chosen by their opponents. Second, subjects may simply make errors in their own actions. The first explanation is less likely to be true. The main reason is that the best-response functions in contests are structured in such a way that if a subject believes that the opponent is going to either make higher or lower than the equilibrium effort, his best response is to always exert lower than the equilibrium effort. Therefore, errors in beliefs cannot explain overbidding. There is also substantial evidence of overbidding in sequential contests (Fonseca, 2009). In such contests, subjects first observe the actions of their opponents and then make their decisions. However, even when subjects have perfect information about the actions of their opponents, they still choose to bid more than the equilibrium.

8. Similar findings on the impact of the number of contestants on the overbidding rate are documented by Anderson and Stafford (2003), Sheremeta (2011) and Morgan *et al.* (2012).

9. Delgado *et al.* (2008) suggest that another explanation for overbidding, besides a utility of winning, is a disutility of losing. They provide evidence for the disutility of losing in the context of a first-price auction. Currently, there is no study examining the disutility of losing as a possible explanation for overbidding in contests. What is even a more interesting question is how to distinguish the utility of winning from the disutility of losing. These are interesting questions for future research.

10. Sheremeta and Wu (2011) and Eisenkopf and Teyssier (2013) report similar findings in the context of rank-order tournaments.

11. Obviously, if in addition to distorted probabilities subjects also derive an additive utility of winning as in Section 4.2, then the updated equilibrium effort $e_{wd}^* = 0.13(v + w)$ could

be still greater than $e^* = 0.25v$, depending on the relative magnitude of the utility of winning (i.e. $e^*_{wd}/e^* = 0.52(1 + w/v)$).

12. Note that the proportional rule eliminates the utility of winning and thus less overbidding also might be due to the absence of the utility of winning,

13. It is possible for multiple (asymmetric) equilibria to arise if one formally introduces behavioral considerations into a theoretical model of contests (see, for example, Gill and Stone, 2010; Chowdhury and Sheremeta, 2011; Cornes and Hartley, 2012; Minor, 2012).

14. Part of the observed heterogeneity can be also explained by the QRE model. In the QRE subjects draw their efforts from a mixed strategy distribution, and thus we should observe within-subject heterogeneity. Also, if we assume that different subjects have different cognitive abilities (and thus make different levels of mistakes), the QRE could also explain between-subject heterogeneity. Currently, there is no formal analysis of the QRE which would incorporate all these elements to explain behavior in contests, and such an analysis would be an important contribution.

15. Although see Konrad and Schlesinger (1997) for a counter example.

16. For theoretical considerations of loss aversion in rank-order tournaments see Gill and Stone (2010) and for experimental investigation see Gill and Prowse (2012) and Eisenkopf and Teyssier (2013). For implications of loss aversion in all-pay auctions see Ernst and Thöni (2010), Müller and Schotter (2010), and Klose and Sheremeta (2012).

17. There is also a large experimental literature examining gender attitudes toward tournaments. Niederle and Vesterlund (2007), for example, design an experiment in which subjects can choose whether to enter a tournament or to be paid based on a piece-rate. They find that while the performance of men and women is not statistically different, men choose to participate in the tournament significantly more often than women. Niederle and Vesterlund conclude that women 'shy away from competition'. These findings have been replicated by other studies (e.g. Cason *et al.*, 2010; Balafoutas and Sutter, 2012; Price, 2012).

18. As a result of more overbidding, women receive significantly lower earnings from contests than men, suggesting that the *ex ante* decision to 'shy away from competition' (Niederle and Vesterlund, 2007) may actually be rational.

19. It is also well documented that, theoretically (Baik, 1994; Stein, 2002), heterogeneity between players leads to lower aggregate effort. These predictions are also supported by laboratory experiments (Davis and Reilly, 1998; Anderson and Stafford, 2003; Fonseca, 2009; Kimbrough *et al.*, 2011). Therefore, in addition to *ex post* negative effect of heterogeneous behavior, heterogeneity may negatively impact strategic behavior in contests *ex ante*.

20. Hyndman *et al.* (2012) study how regret aversion impacts individual behavior in all-pay auctions with incomplete information.

References

Abbink, K., Brandts, J., Herrmann, B. and Orzen, H. (2010) Inter-group conflict and intra-group punishment in an experimental contest game. *American Economic Review* 100: 420–447.

Agranov, M. and Tergiman, C. (2013) Incentives and compensation schemes: an experimental study. *International Journal of Industrial Organization*, forthcoming.

Ahmed, A.M. (2009) Are religious people more prosocial? A quasi-experimental study with Madrasah pupils in a rural community in India. *Journal for the Scientific Study of Religion* 48: 368–374.

Ahn, T.K.R., Isaac, M. and Salmon, T.C. (2011) Rent seeking in groups. *International Journal of Industrial Organization* 29: 116–125.

Amaldoss, W. and Rapoport, A. (2009) Excessive expenditure in two-stage contests: theory and experimental evidence. In F. Columbus (ed.), *Game Theory: Strategies, Equilibria, and Theorems*. Hauppauge, NY: Nova Science Publishers.

Amegashie, J.A. and Runkel, M. (2012) The paradox of revenge in conflicts. *Journal of Conflict Resolution* 56: 313–330.

Anderson, L.A. and Stafford, S.L. (2003) An experimental analysis of rent seeking under varying competitive conditions. *Public Choice* 115: 199–216.

Andreoni, J. and Croson, R. (2008) Partners versus strangers: the effect of random rematching in public goods experiments. In: C.R. Plott and V.L. Smith (eds), *Handbook of Experimental Economics Results* (Vol. 1, pp. 776–783). Amsterdam: North-Holland.

Baharad, E. and Nitzan, S. (2008) Contest efforts in light of behavioural considerations. *Economic Journal* 118: 2047–2059.

Baik, K.H. (1994) Effort levels in contests with two asymmetric players. *Southern Economic Journal* 61: 367–378.

Balafoutas, L. and Sutter, M. (2012) Affirmative action policies promote women and do not harm efficiency in the lab. *Science* 335: 579–582.

Balafoutas, L., Kerschbamer, R. and Sutter, M. (2012) Distributional preferences and competitive behavior. *Journal of Economic Behavior and Organization* 83: 125–135.

Bartling, B., Fehr, E., Marechal, M.A. and Schunk, D. (2009) Egalitarianism and competitiveness. *American Economic Review* 99: 93–98.

Barut, Y., Kovenock, D. and Noussair, C.N. (2002) A comparison of multiple-unit all-pay and winner-pay auctions under incomplete information. *International Economic Review* 43: 675–708.

Batson, C., Schoenrade, P. and Ventis, W. (1993) *Religion and the Individual: A Social-Psychological Perspective*. New York: Oxford University Press.

Behrendt, H. and Ben-Ari, R. (2012) The positive side of negative emotion: the role of guilt and shame in coping with interpersonal conflict. *Journal of Conflict Resolution* 56: 1116–1138.

Benjamin, D.J., Choi, J.J. and Fisher, G. (2012) Religious identity and economic behavior. Working Paper.

Borghans, L., Duckworth, A.L., Heckman, J.J. and Weel, B.T. (2008) The economics and psychology of personality traits. *Journal of Human Resources* 43: 972–1059.

Botelho, A., Harrison, G.W., Pinto, L.M.C. and Rutström, E.E. (2009) Testing static game theory with dynamic experiments: a case study of public goods. *Games and Economic Behavior* 67: 253–265.

Brookins, P. and Ryvkin, D. (2011) An experimental study of bidding in contests of incomplete information. Working Paper.

Bull, C., Schotter, A. and Weigelt, K. (1987) Tournaments and piece rates: an experimental study. *Journal of Political Economy* 95: 1–33.

Burks, S.V., Carpenter, J.P., Gotte, L. and Rustichini, A. (2009) Cognitive skills explain economic preferences, strategic behavior, and job attachment. *Proceedings of the National Academy of Sciences* 106: 7745–7750.

Camerer, C.F. and Lovallo, D. (1999) Overconfidence and excess entry: an experimental approach. *American Economic Review* 89: 306–318.

Casari, M., Ham, J.C. and Kagel, J.H. (2007) Selection bias, demographic effects, and ability effects in common value auction experiments. *American Economic Review* 97: 1278–1304.

Cason, T.N., Masters, W.A. and Sheremeta, R.M. (2010) Entry into winner-take-all and proportional-prize contests: an experimental study. *Journal of Public Economics* 94: 604–611.

Cason, T.N., Masters, W.A. and Sheremeta, R.M. (2011) Winner-take-all and proportional-prize contests: theory and experimental results. Chapman University, ESI Working Paper.

Cason, T.N., Sheremeta, R.M. and Zhang, J. (2012) Communication and efficiency in competitive coordination games. *Games and Economic Behavior* 76: 26–43.

Charness, G. and Sutter, M. (2012) Groups make better self-interested decisions. *Journal of Economic Perspectives* 26: 157–176.

Chau, A. and Phillips, J. (1995) Effects of perceived control upon wagering and attributions in computer blackjack. *Journal of General Psychology* 122: 253–269.

Chen, Y., Katuscak, P. and Ozdenoren, E. (2013) Why can't a woman bid more like a man? *Games and Economic Behavior* 77: 181–213.

Chowdhury, S.M. and Sheremeta, R.M. (2011) Multiple equilibria in Tullock contests. *Economics Letters* 112: 216–219.

Chowdhury, S.M., Sheremeta, R.M. and Turocy, T.L. (2012) Overdissipation and convergence in rent-seeking experiments: cost structure and prize allocation rules. Chapman University, ESI Working Paper.

Chowdhury, S.M., Kovenock, D. and Sheremeta, R.M. (2013) An experimental investigation of colonel blotto games. *Economic Theory*, forthcoming.

Cornes, R. and Hartley, R. (2012) Loss aversion in contests. Working Paper.

Croson, R. and Sundali, J. (2005) The gambler's fallacy and the hot hand: empirical data from casinos. *Journal of Risk and Uncertainty* 30: 195–209.

Davis, D. and Reilly, R. (1998) Do many cooks always spoil the stew? An experimental analysis of rent seeking and the role of a strategic buyer. *Public Choice* 95: 89–115.

Dechenaux, E. and Mancini, M. (2008) Auction-theoretic approach to modeling legal systems: an experimental analysis. *Applied Economics Research Bulletin* 2: 142–177.

Dechenaux, E., Kovenock, D. and Sheremeta, R.M. (2012) A survey of experimental research on contests, all-pay auctions and tournaments. Chapman University, ESI Working Paper.

Deck, C. and Jahedi, S. (2011) Time discounting in strategic contests. Working Paper.

Deck, C. and Sheremeta, R.M. (2012) Fight or flight? Defending against sequential attacks in the game of siege. *Journal of Conflict Resolution* 56: 1069–1088.

Delgado, M.R., Schotter, A., Ozbay, E.Y. and Phelps, E.A. (2008) Understanding overbidding: using the neural circuitry of reward to design economic auctions. *Science* 321: 1849–1852.

Devetag, G. and Warglien, M. (2003) Games and phone numbers: do short-term memory bounds affect strategic behavior? *Journal of Economic Psychology* 24: 189–202.

Eisenkopf, G. and Teyssier, S. (2013) Envy and loss aversion in tournaments. *Journal of Economic Psychology*, forthcoming.

Engelbrecht-Wiggans, R. and Katok, E. (2007) Regret in auctions: theory and evidence. *Economic Theory*, 33: 81–101.

Ericsson, K.A. and Charness, N. (1994) Expert performance: its structure and acquisition. *American Psychologist* 49: 725–747.

Eriksson, T., Teyssier, S. and Villeval, M.C. (2009) Self-selection and the efficiency of tournaments. *Economic Inquiry* 47: 530–548.

Fallucchi, F., Renner, E. and Sefton, M. (2012) Information feedback and contest structure in rent-seeking games. Working Paper.

Faravelli, M. and Stanca, L. (2012) When less is more: rationing and rent dissipation in stochastic contests. *Games and Economic Behavior* 74: 170–183.

Filiz-Ozbay, E. and Ozbay, E.Y. (2007) Auctions with anticipated regret: theory and experiment. *American Economic Review* 97: 1407–1418.

Fonseca, M.A. (2009) An experimental investigation of asymmetric contests. *International Journal of Industrial Organization* 27: 582–591.

Frey, M.C. and Detterman, D.K. (2004) Scholastic assessment or g?: the relationship between the scholastic assessment test and general cognition ability. *Psychological Science* 15: 73–378.

Gill, D. and Prowse, V. (2012) A structural analysis of disappointment aversion in a real effort competition. *American Economic Review* 102: 469–503.

Gill, D. and Stone, R. (2010) Fairness and desert in tournaments. *Games and Economic Behavior* 69: 346–364.

Gilovich, T., Vallone, R. and Tversky, A. (1985) The hot hand in basketball: on the misperception of random sequences. *Cognitive Psychology* 17: 295–314.

Gneezy, U. and Smorodinsky, R. (2006) All-pay auctions – an experimental study. *Journal of Economic Behavior and Organization* 61: 255–275.

Ham, J.C. and Kagel, J.H. (2006) Gender effects in private value auctions. *Economic Letters* 92: 375–382.

Hamilton, W.D. (1970) Selfish and spiteful behavior in evolutionary model. *Nature* 228: 1218–1220.

Harbring, C. and Irlenbusch, B. (2011) Sabotage in tournaments: evidence from a laboratory experiment. *Management Science* 57: 611–627.

Hehenkamp, B., Leininger, W. and Possajenikov, A. (2004) Evolutionary equilibrium in Tullock contests: spite and overdissipation. *European Journal of Political Economy* 20: 1045–1057.

Herrmann, B. and Orzen, H. (2008) The appearance of homo rivalis: social preferences and the nature of rent seeking. University of Nottingham, Working Paper.

Hilary, G. and Hui, K.W. (2009) Does religion matter in corporate decision making in America? *Journal of Financial Economics* 93: 455–473.

Hillman, A.L. and Katz, E. (1984) Risk-averse rent seekers and the social cost of monopoly power. *Economic Journal* 94: 104–110.

Hillman, A. and Riley, J.G. (1989) Politically contestable rents and transfers. *Economics and Politics* 1: 17–40.

Hirshleifer, J. and Riley, J.G. (1978) Elements of the theory of auctions and contests. UCLA Economics Working Papers 118.

Holt, C.A. and Laury, S.K. (2002) Risk aversion and incentive effects. *American Economic Review* 92: 1644–1655.

Hyndman, K., Ozbay, E.Y. and Sujarittanonta, P. (2012) Rent seeking with regretful agents: theory and experiment. *Journal of Economic Behavior and Organization* 84: 866–878.

Kahneman, D. and Tversky, A. (1979) Prospect theory: an analysis of decision under risk. *Econometrica* 47: 263–291.

Kahneman, D., Knetsch, J.L. and Thaler, R.H. (1990) Experimental tests of the endowment effect and the coase theorem. *Journal of Political Economy* 98: 1325–1348.

Ke, C., Konrad, K.A. and Morath, F. (2013) Brothers in arms – an experiment on the alliance puzzle. *Games and Economic Behavior* 77: 61–76.

Kimbrough, E.O. and Sheremeta, R.M. (2012) Why can't we be friends? Entitlements and the costs of conflict. Chapman University, ESI Working Paper.

Kimbrough, E.O. and Sheremeta, R.M. (2013) Side-payments and the costs of conflict. *International Journal of Industrial Organization*, forthcoming.

Kimbrough, E.O., Sheremeta, R.M. and Shields, T. (2011) Resolving conflicts by a random device. Chapman University, ESI Working Paper.

Kimbrough, E.O., Rubin, J., Sheremeta, R.M. and Shields, T. (2013) Coordination, commitment and conflict resolution. Chapman University, ESI Working Paper.

Klemperer, P. (2002). How (not) to run auctions: the European 3G telecom auctions. *European Economic Review* 46: 829–845.

Klose, B. and Sheremeta, R.M. (2012) Behavior in all-pay and winner-pay auctions with identity-dependent externalities. Working Paper.

Kong, X. (2008) Loss aversion and rent-seeking: an experimental study. University of Nottingham, Working Paper.

Konrad, K.A. (2009) *Strategy and Dynamics in Contests*. New York, NY: Oxford University Press.

Konrad, K.A. and Schlesinger, H. (1997) Risk aversion in rent-seeking and rent-augmenting games. *Economic Journal* 107: 1671–1683.

Kovenock, D., Roberson, B. and Sheremeta, R.M. (2010) The attack and defense of weakest-link networks. Chapman University, ESI Working Paper.

Kurzban, R., and Houser, D. (2001) Individual differences in cooperation in a circular public goods game. *European Journal of Personality* 15: 37–52.

Landry, C., Lange, A., List, J.A., Price, M.K. and Rupp, N. (2006) Toward an understanding of the economics of charity: evidence from a field experiment. *Quarterly Journal of Economics* 121: 747–782.

Lazear, E.P. (1999) Personnel economics past lessons and future directions – presidential address to the society of labor economists. *Journal of Labor Economics* 17: 199–236.

Lazear, E.P. (2000) Performance pay and productivity. *American Economic Review* 90: 1346–1361.

Lazear, E.P. and Rosen, S. (1981) Rank-order tournaments as optimum labor contracts. *Journal of Political Economy* 89: 841–864.

Leininger, W. (2003) On evolutionarily stable behavior in contests. *Economics of Governance* 4: 177–186.

Lim, W., Matros, A. and Turocy, T. (2012) Bounded rationality and group size in Tullock contests: experimental evidence. Working Paper.

Lugovskyy, V., Puzzello, D. and Tucker, S. (2010) An experimental investigation of overdissipation in the all pay auction. *European Economic Review* 54: 974–997.

Mago, S.D. and Sheremeta, R.M. (2012) Multi-battle contests: an experimental study. Chapman University, ESI Working Paper.

Mago, S.D., Savikhin, A.C. and Sheremeta, R.M. (2012) Facing your opponents: social identification and information feedback in contests. Chapman University, ESI Working Paper.

Mago, S.D., Sheremeta, R.M. and Yates, A. (2013) Best-of-three contest experiments: strategic versus psychological momentum. *International Journal of Industrial Organization*, forthcoming.

Masiliunas, A., Mengel, F. Reiss, J.P. (2012) (Strategic) uncertainty and the explanatory power of Nash equilibrium in Tullock contests. Working Paper.

McKelvey, R. and Palfrey, T. (1995) Quantal response equilibria for normal form games. *Games and Economic Behavior* 10: 6–38.

Millner, E.L. and Pratt, M.D. (1989) An experimental investigation of efficient rent-seeking. *Public Choice* 62: 139–151.

Millner, E.L. and Pratt, M.D. (1991) Risk aversion and rent-seeking: an extension and some experimental evidence. *Public Choice* 69: 81–92.

Minor, D. (2012) Coarse thinking and competition. Working Paper.

Morgan, J. and Sefton, M. (2000) Funding public goods with lotteries: experimental evidence. *Review of Economic Studies* 67: 785–810.

Morgan, J., Orzen, H. and Sefton, M. (2012) Endogenous entry in contests. *Economic Theory* 51: 435–463.

Müller, W. and Schotter, A. (2010) Workaholics and dropouts in organizations. *Journal of the European Economic Association* 8: 717–743.

Nalebuff, B.J. and Stiglitz, J.E. (1982) Prizes and incentives: towards a general theory of compensation and competition. *Bell Journal of Economics* 13: 21–43.

Niederle, M. and Vesterlund, L. (2007) Do women shy away from competition? Do men compete too much? *Quarterly Journal of Economics* 122: 1067–1101.

Noussair, C. and Silver, J. (2006) Behavior in all pay auctions with incomplete information. *Games and Economic Behavior* 55: 189–206.

Ong, D. and Chen, Z. (2012) Tiger women: An all-Pay auction experiment on the gender heuristic of the desire to win. *Working Paper.*

Parco J., Rapoport A. and Amaldoss W. (2005) Two-stage contests with budget constraints: an experimental study. *Journal of Mathematical Psychology* 49: 320–338.

Park, Y.J. and Santos-Pinto, L. (2010) Overconfidence in tournaments: evidence from the field. *Theory and Decision* 69: 143–166.

Potters, J.C., De Vries, C.G. and Van Winden, F. (1998) An experimental examination of rational rent seeking. *European Journal of Political Economy* 14: 783–800.

Prendergast, C. (1999) The provision of incentives in firms. *Journal of Economic Literature* 37: 7–63.

Price, C.R. (2012) Gender, competition, and managerial decisions. *Management Science* 58: 114–122.

Price, C.R. and Sheremeta, R.M. (2011) Endowment effects in contests. *Economics Letters* 111: 217–219.

Price, C.R. and Sheremeta, R.M. (2012) Endowment origin, demographic effects and individual preferences in contests. Chapman University, ESI Working Paper.

Regnerus, M., Smith, C. and Sikkink, D. (1998) Who gives to the poor? The influence of religious tradition and political location on the personal generosity of Americans toward the poor. *Journal for the Scientific Study of Religion* 37: 481–493.

Riechmann, T. (2007) An analysis of rent-seeking games with relative-payoff maximizers. *Public Choice* 133: 147–155.

Savikhin, A.C. and Sheremeta, R.M. (2013) Simultaneous decision-making in competitive and cooperative games. *Economic Inquiry*, forthcoming.

Schmidt, D., Sheremeta, R.M., Shupp, R. and Walker, J. (2005) Resource allocation contests: experimental evidence. Indiana University, Working Paper.

Schmitt, P., Shupp, R., Swope, K. and Cadigan, J. (2004) Multi-period rent-seeking contests with carryover: theory and experimental evidence. *Economics of Governance* 5: 187–211.

Schniter, E., Sheremeta, R.M. and Shields, T. (2011) Conflicted minds: recalibrational emotions following trust-based interaction. Chapman University, ESI Working Papers.

Schniter, E., Sheremeta, R.M. and Sznycer, D. (2013) Building and rebuilding trust with promises and apologies. *Journal of Economic Behavior and Organization*, forthcoming.

Schotter, A. and Weigelt, K. (1992) Asymmetric tournaments, equal opportunity laws, and affirmative action: some experimental results. *Quarterly Journal of Economics* 107: 511–539.

Sheremeta, R.M. (2010) Experimental comparison of multi-stage and one-stage contests. *Games and Economic Behavior* 68: 731–747.

Sheremeta, R.M. (2011) Contest design: an experimental investigation. *Economic Inquiry* 49: 573–590.

Sheremeta, R.M. and Wu, S.Y. (2011) Optimal tournament design and incentive response: an experimental investigation of canonical tournament theory. Chapman University, ESI Working Paper.

Sheremeta, R.M. and Zhang, J. (2010) Can groups solve the problem of over-bidding in contests? *Social Choice and Welfare* 35: 175–197.

Shogren, J.F. and Baik, K.H. (1991) Reexamining efficient rent-seeking in laboratory markets. *Public Choice* 69: 69–79.

Skaperdas, S. and Gan, L. (1995) Risk aversion in contests. *Economic Journal* 105: 951–962.

Stein, W. (2002) Asymmetric rent-seeking with more than two contestants. *Public Choice* 113: 325–336.

Szidarovszky, F. and Okuguchi, K. (1997) On the existence and uniqueness of pure Nash equilibrium in rent-Seeking games. *Games and Economic Behavior* 18: 135–140.

Szymanski, S. (2003) The economic design of sporting contests. *Journal of Economic Literature* 41: 1137–1187.

Tufano, P. (2008) Saving whilst gambling: an empirical analysis of UK premium bonds. *American Economic Review* 98: 321–326.

Tullock, G. (1980) Efficient rent seeking. In J.M. Buchanan, R.D. Tollison, G. Tullock (eds), *Toward a theory of the Rent-Seeking Society* (pp. 97–112). College Station, TX: Texas A&M University Press.

Tversky, A. and Kahneman, D. (1992) Advances in prospect theory: cumulative representation of uncertainty. *Journal of Risk and Uncertainty* 5: 297–323.

Xiao, E. and Houser, D. (2005) Emotion expression in human punishment behavior. *Proceedings of the National Academy of Sciences of the United States of America* 102: 7398–7401.

Zizzo, D. (2010) Experimenter demand effects in economic experiments. *Experimental Economics* 13: 75–98.

7

ENVIRONMENTAL MARKETS: WHAT DO WE LEARN FROM THE LAB?

Lana Friesen

School of Economics
University of Queensland
Australia

Lata Gangadharan

Department of Economics
Monash University
Australia

1. Introduction

Experimental economists have been involved in market policy experiments since the beginning of the field. Early evidence regarding the importance of market institutions, particularly the potential of posted-offer markets to result in higher prices and lower efficiency than other institutions, inspired work on the implications of such institutions in real-world markets (Plott, 1986). The area where market experiments have arguably had the largest policy impact is in the design of spectrum auctions. Experiments are an invaluable tool in this complex setting with interdependent demand that renders theory intractable and magnifies the potential importance of behavioral factors. Experiments have informed not just the choice of auction formats but have also thrown light on important details such as eligibility and activity rules. Spectrum auctions are now conducted around the world including the United States, United Kingdom, and Europe.[1] More recently, work has focused on auction design for pollution permits, especially carbon permits.

While experiments continue in the traditional areas of competition policy and auction design, market policy experiments now encompass applications as diverse as smart markets for electricity and more recently water, institutional design for emissions trading markets such as banking and enforcement, buyback schemes for conservation land, and matching

A Collection of Surveys on Market Experiments, First Edition.
Edited by Charles N. Noussair and Steven Tucker. Chapters © 2014 The Authors.
Book compilation © 2014 John Wiley & Sons, Ltd. Published 2014 by John Wiley & Sons, Ltd.

algorithms for labor markets. In our paper, we provide a review of environmental market policy experiments, which we define as experiments that involve markets with a direct environmental policy application.[2] These are experiments, which, in the terminology of Roth (1986), are conducted to "whisper in the ears of princes."[3]

Our survey focusses on experiments concerning environmental markets. Recent years have witnessed an explosion of such experiments, a trajectory likely to continue into future years. Nevertheless, even within the environmental area there is considerable diversity of application, and our survey thus illustrates the potential contribution of experiments in many diverse policy applications. We focus on this area as it is more recent and hence not the subject of many existing surveys, and because of their (potential) influence on actual policy both now and in the future. Furthermore, there exists a series of experiments building up a body of evidence about a particular policy issue. Finally, we believe that many nonexperimental economists will be unfamiliar with these applications, whereas they are more likely to know about historically strong areas such as auction design, smart markets, and competition policy.

From the perspective of policy development, experimental economics is ideally suited to examine emergent environmental markets such as emissions trading, conservation auctions, and markets for water. As environmental concerns have become more prominent in recent years, research in the area has also grown. Cason (2010), Normann and Ricciuti (2009), Cherry *et al.* (2008), Strum and Weimann (2006), Bohm (2003), Cummings *et al.* (2001), and Muller and Mestelman (1998) provide very useful and insightful surveys of how experiments have been influential in addressing environmental problems. Our paper builds on this body of research and highlights how market design has a crucial role in environmental policy making both in tackling more traditional environmental issues such as emissions trading and also in relatively less well-known but emerging areas such as conservation auctions and water markets.

While market policy experiments share the same benefits as standard laboratory experiments, most importantly, control of the environment and the associated ability to make the *ceteris paribus* changes necessary to test various hypotheses, they do typically differ in important ways. Crucially, market policy experiments usually contain a far greater level of institutional or real-world detail and greater complexity than a typical lab experiment does in order to mimic, as far as practicable, the features of the corresponding real-world market. In addition, the inspiration for the research often comes from interested parties rather than just intellectual curiosity and this can lead to short time frames in which to conduct the experiments. Finally, nonstandard subject pools are more common than in standard laboratory experiments.

These differences are intended to enhance the reliability of policy conclusions based on the experimental results, in much the same way as "wind tunnels" are used in engineering to test the practical robustness of theoretically sound bridge and other designs. In the same way, the lab enables testing of the robustness of different mechanisms (e.g. auction formats) to behavioral factors that may not be *a priori* apparent (e.g. potential for collusion). In other applications, the lab can provide "proof of concept" that a complex market can work, as in the early days of smart electricity and gas markets.

The advantages of using laboratory experiments to address policy questions are many. First, the complexity of many policy issues, such as combinatorial auction design and matching algorithms in real-world situations, is virtually impossible to model theoretically. Second, for many policy issues, the data required for empirical testing are simply unavailable, either in a timely fashion, or at all. Field testing of most policies is often not possible, and the lab provides perhaps the only opportunity to explore different policy options and counterfactuals. Third, even if theory and empirical evidence exist, laboratory experiments can test the robustness of those results to behavioral factors, sometimes uncovering unanticipated behavior that may undermine the success of a policy.

The paper proceeds as follows. We divide environmental policy market experiments in two broad categories: those on emission trading markets (Section 2), and other less traditional areas including water markets and conservation auctions (Section 3). We conclude (Section 4) with a discussion of some possible future directions for market policy experiments.

2. Emission Trading Experiments

Plott (1983) was one of the first papers to use experimental methods to examine the performance of emission permit trading in the presence of negative externalities. He compared tradable permits to emission taxes and command and control methods using the double auction trading institution.[4] Plott (1983) found that both incentive methods significantly increased efficiency compared with command and control.[5] Subsequent environmental policy experiments have focused upon the market design and its impact on different aspects such as efficiency, participation, volume of trade, price of permits, transaction costs incurred by participants, heterogeneity of market participants, uncertainty, compliance, and enforcement. In this section, we review some of the burgeoning research in this area and the lessons learnt from this body of work.

2.1 Trading Institutions

Many experiments have evaluated features of the trading institutions implemented or planned for specific environmental programs. Trading institutions can have a major impact on price accuracy and volatility in the market and the implications of this choice were clearly seen in the US federal sulfur dioxide trading program designed to reduce acid rain, instituted by the Clean Air Act Amendments of 1990.[6] The US Environmental Protection Agency (EPA) designed a new call auction for trading allowances to emit sulfur dioxide. This was one of the first few programs to allow for a tradable permit market in emissions at the national level and attracted a lot of attention from academics and policy makers around the world.

In order to encourage early, centralized trading with low transaction costs, the EPA initiated a sealed bid, discriminative price auction in which the highest bids for permits were matched to the lowest offers and the successful bidders pay their bid price. The objective was to maximize economic surplus to the seller. Each bid and ask affects transaction prices and thus creates strong incentives for traders to strategically manipulate the market. This auction was criticized for generating biased price signals as the auction rules cause sellers to choose asking prices that under-reveal their true cost of emission control because lower asking prices increase the probability that a seller trades with high-bidding buyers. Combined with the well-known result that buyers have an incentive to under-reveal demand in discriminative auctions in which they have to pay their bid price (Vickrey, 1961), the EPA rules could lead to downwardly biased prices in the market (Cason, 1993, 1995).

Cason and Plott (1996) conducted 12 sessions to evaluate the performance of the EPA auction and compared it to an alternative trading institution: the uniform price auction. In the uniform price auction, bids and asks are arrayed as demand and supply schedules, and all trades occur at a uniform market-clearing price. In this auction design, only the bids and asks at the margin affect the uniform transaction price, thus traders have an incentive to truthfully

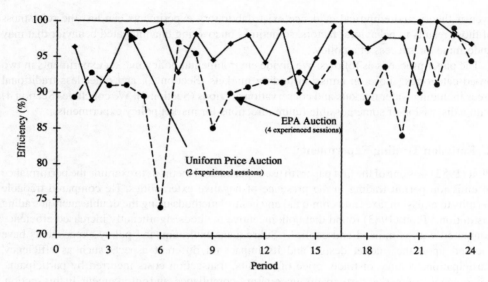

Figure 1. Average Efficiency Levels.
Source: Cason and Plott (1996), figure 5: Random draws environment.

reveal their valuations. Cason and Plott (1996) confirm the theoretical prediction that the EPA auction design creates strong incentives for both buyers and sellers to under-report their true values while the uniform price auction results in unbiased price signals and more efficient market outcomes. Figure 1 compares the efficiency of the two formats.

In 1998, when the market was more mature, Joskow *et al.* (1998) used field data from the private secondary market, where brokers were very active, and found that this market provided some information to participants in the EPA auction about the marginal value of permits. Hence, the emergence of the private market reduced the negative impact of the auction features to some degree.

Franciosi *et al.* (1999) constructed an experimental market with many features of the actual EPA market including both a mandatory auction and a continuous private secondary market. Each trading period consisted of two opportunities to trade: the private market followed by the auction. The private market used a double auction trading institution, while the auction was a sealed bid discriminative auction with a revenue rebate feature. All bids made in the auction were public information and banking of permits was allowed in some sessions. Franciosi *et al.* (1999) found that while trading improved efficiency, prices in the private secondary market did not always coincide with those in the auction even at the end of the session. With permit banking, however, permits became durable assets, and this sometimes led to speculative bubbles as evidenced by collapses in permit prices toward the end of a session. Previous experimental research (Smith *et al.*, 1988; Palan, 2013; Noussair and Tucker, 2013) has shown that asset markets are susceptible to price crashes and price bubbles. In experimental permit markets, price expectations may be difficult to form as subjects have little experience with the trading process and there is limited trading history to observe. The authors argue that in the field, this difficulty in forming price expectation could be higher due to the uncertainties about technology and about the strength of property rights.

Franciosi *et al.* (1993) compared the performance of revenue-neutral auctions (RNA), where the revenue from permit sales is returned to auction participants based on some assignment of property rights, to standard uniform price auctions, where all bidding revenue accrued directly to the seller.[7] Although the pricing mechanism in RNA is identical to the uniform price auction, the revenue-neutral aspect is a nontrivial feature that could alter the performance of the institution. The authors found that the RNA markets perform as well as the uniform price markets in both trading prices and efficiency levels. However, as is expected, the two institutions differed in terms of the distribution of gains from trade, with bidders who are large net sellers relative to their initial endowments gaining the most from the revenue rebate feature.

Cronshaw and Brown-Kruse (1999) designed an experiment to capture most of the features of the mandatory emissions allowance market under the 1990 US Clean Air Act, including the mandatory transfer of a fraction of permits to the market each period, a discriminative call auction, banking of permits, and the availability of permits at a fixed price.[8] Cronshaw and Brown-Kruse (1999) found that subjects were able to achieve about two-thirds of the gains theoretically available from banking alone and an additional 39–78% of the potential gains when trading was allowed.

Researchers at McMaster University conducted a series of laboratory experiments to testbed proposals by the Canadian government for a nitrous oxide allowance trading program in Southern Ontario. The proposal intended to create two trading assets: coupons and shares. Each coupon would entitle the holder to discharge 1 ton of nitrous oxide within a year, while shares entitle the holder to a stream of coupons for future years. Coupons would be valid indefinitely and would be distributed to firms in proportion to their holding of shares, where shares may be allocated on the basis of grandfathering, for example. The market institution proposed was unstructured, with private negotiated trades in coupons and shares expected to occur. Muller and Mestelman (1994) conducted experiments where subjects are allowed to trade coupons and shares simultaneously. The experimental design followed Cronshaw and Brown-Kruse (1999) except they utilized the open outcry market institution to resemble the institution proposed for Southern Ontario.[9] They find higher cost savings than in laboratory implementations of the US EPA institutions using the same parameters. Transaction prices, however, show a mediocre performance, as in some sessions prices do not converge to the competitive equilibrium levels. This could be because of the lack of public information about trading prices that results from the open outcry institution, which disseminates a lot less information than in an alternative trading institution like a double auction market.

The Regional Clean Air Incentive Market (RECLAIM) was another tradable permit program implemented at a regional scale, in Los Angeles to reduce the emissions of sulfur and nitrogen oxides. A unique feature in this program was that firms would follow an overlapping compliance schedule.[10] Carlson *et al.* (1993a, b) showed that issuing permits with overlapping compliance cycles would avoid the need for banking of permits, a more palatable option for some environmental groups, which saw banking of permits as a way of postponing pollution.

Cason and Gangadharan (1998) compared the performance of an electronic bulletin board system (BBS) designed by the regulatory authorities in RECLAIM to help participants find trading partners and reduce search costs, to a computerized double auction market. The BBS allows firms to indicate trading interests by electronically posting offers to buy or sell permits. Other firms can scroll through these offers and contact the offering firm to negotiate a transaction. In contrast, the computerized double auction has no bilateral negotiation, has a successive improvement rule, and the bids and asks are binding on the proposer. Some of the benefits of bulletin board institutions include providing easier access to a larger number of buyers and sellers and timely and more accurate price information. Information available through the BBS can provide easily accessible indicators of market conditions and reduce market uncertainty. An important advantage of the BBS is that it can handle trade of heterogeneous goods. Overall, the authors find that the bulletin board sessions performed as well as the continuous double auction in terms of price accuracy and volatility.

This paper also studied the impact of the trading restrictions in the RECLAIM program, which were imposed across two zones of the Los Angeles Basin to avoid trades that lead to emissions migration that could harm air quality.[11] Consistent with theoretical predictions, prices were significantly different in two zones when trading was not allowed. When trading across zones was permitted, prices equalized across zones and gains from trade with interzone trading were 4% to 17% higher than gains from trade with no interzone trading.

Ishikida et al. (2001) also report experiments that were used to testbed the RECLAIM program. The authors focus on the special features of this market: a small number of participants, no history of market trades, and buyers and sellers transacting in portfolio of trades. They found that under such conditions a two-sided combinatorial market design outperforms a uniform price double auction mechanism. The authors argue that the combinatorial feature of the allocation process allows inframarginal portfolio traders to reveal their true values without risking financial exposure.

Shobe et al. (2009) report experiments based on trading rules and policies relating to the first mandatory emissions cap and trade program for greenhouse gases in the United States—the Regional Greenhouse Gas Initiative (RGGI), launched in 2009, which covers10 northeastern states from Maryland to Maine. This program has a declining cap on annual emissions from electricity generators in the region. The treatments compare the performance of four different auction types (uniform, discriminatory, clock, and clock with excess demand) in the presence of a loose cap and a tight cap. A loose cap is defined as one that has a generous allocation of permits relative to recent emissions history. They find that auction revenues tend to be lower when the cap is loose and that discriminatory auctions yielded higher revenues than the uniform and clock auctions, though this advantage of the discriminatory auction disappears over time. Goeree et al. (2010) compare auctions with grandfathering as a means of allocating the initial pollution permits. The RGGI requires the use of auctions for allocating at least 25% of the permits. In contrast, the participants in the European Emissions Trading System are required to use auctions for at most 5% of the allocations. Goeree et al. (2010) find that using auctions leads to a higher consumer surplus and lower product prices.

Burtraw et al. (2011) compare the price discovery properties of six different auction mechanisms: sealed bid discriminatory, sealed bid uniform pricing, continuous discriminatory, continuous uniform pricing, multiround clock uniform pricing, and multiround clock uniform pricing with end of round information about excess demand. The authors implement an unannounced shift in cost conditions after three rounds resulting in an upward shift in the overall distribution of permit values. They focus on the extent to which each of these auction mechanisms track the increased equilibrium price, as the speed of price discovery under changing market conditions is important in environmental markets. The uniform pricing format outperforms the discriminative pricing mechanisms. In fact, the continuous discriminatory pricing auction yielded the worst price tracking performance. In general, prices were not near the equilibrium levels and after the demand shift, prices did not increase to the predicted level. In addition, tacit collusion occurred in the continuous bidding auctions with bidding observed at the reserve price early in the auction and some bidders not putting in a bid until the final seconds of the round.[12] The sealed bid auctions prevented this problem, as no information was available during the auction. The sealed bid uniform price auction showed the best price tracking properties alongside the multiclock auctions. The multiclock auctions, however, have a tendency to encourage collusion, hence the authors recommend the use of a simple uniform price auction for the RGGI program.

Porter *et al.* (2009) examine three different auction mechanisms (a combinatorial sealed bid auction, a sequential English clock, and combinatorial English clock auction) to maximize revenue and efficiency in Virginia's nitrous oxide auction, which was selling allowances for two fiscal years (2004 and 2005). Each state has a nitrous oxide emissions budget and can allocate its allowances to sources. Most of the emissions are grandfathered, however, new sources have to buy allowances in an auction. In situations when demand is more elastic, they find that the clock auctions perform better. They also describe the choices made for the auction in the field, which was informed by the results obtained in the laboratory. For example, in the field, a Web-based auction was chosen to maximize participation, however, instead of the complex combinatorial auction, they decided to have two separate and simpler sequential auctions of the two vintages due to the short time frame to train bidders.

Rich and Friedman (1998) discuss a pilot permit-trading program implemented in five cities and under consideration for use throughout China. Their experiments show that the trading rules designed by the Chinese EPA (a matching market institution) could lead to low efficiency and under-revelation of bids and asks. The matching market model used by the Chinese regulators maximizes the volume of emissions reduction given the revealed ability (or willingness to pay) of the buyers for the emissions permits. This auction was intended to increase trading volume.[13] The auction rules match the highest bid with the highest ask not exceeding that bid, then the next highest bid with the highest remaining ask less than that bid and iterates until the bids are exhausted. As in the case of the US federal SO_2 program, this auction design creates strong incentives for traders to misrepresent their valuations with buyers substantially understating their willingness to pay and sellers understating their willingness to accept.

In the last decade or so, given the interest in reducing emissions at the global level, several papers have explored the implications of different trading rules on the outcomes in the international carbon market. Research conducted by Bohm (1997), Bohm and Carlen (1999), Carlen (1999), Soberg (2000), Klasssen *et al.* (2005), Mougeot *et al.* (2011), and Cason and Gangadharan (2011) in this area shows that the design details can be important in the global arena as well.

As is clear from the discussion above, regulators must make numerous design choices when implementing new permit markets, and many of these design choices affect the transaction costs incurred by market participants. Regulators must also decide how to endow firms or consumers with permits. Cason and Gangadharan (2003) examine how transaction costs interact with the initial permit endowment to influence the cost-effectiveness of the overall emissions abatement. With zero transaction costs, the initial endowment affects only equity, and not the cost-effectiveness of the final competitive allocation of permits following trading. In the presence of transaction costs, however, cost-effectiveness can be significantly compromised depending on the endowment mechanism used.

A related application is designing trading institutions in the market for fishing quotas. Anderson and Sutinen (2006) use the case of the Rhode Island lobster fishery to examine different trading rules that could reduce price volatility in the market for quotas. They compare double auction and centralized call market trading rules and also introduce an initial lease period, such that permanent transfers of allowances are not allowed in the first few years after the program is introduced. Permanent transfers are allowed only after traders have had some experience with temporary lease transfers. This gradual phasing in of allowance trading is shown to be very effective in accelerating price discovery, improving equilibration, and preventing bubbles and crashes in the market. Tisdell and Ifekhar (2013) compare the performance of simultaneous and combinatorial fishery quotas markets. In simultaneous markets, markets for individual species or fishing sites operate at the same time. In a combinatorial auction, a fisher would trade combinations of quotas for different fish species or fishing sites in the same market. The authors find that combinatorial auctions are more efficient. Moxnes (2012) investigates two systems for fishery regulation: individual transferable quotas and auctioned seasonal quotas and introduces trade of both fishing quotas and fishing vessels. Both systems show similar outcomes in the experiment, however, the auctioned seasonal quotas allows for taxation of resource rent. The government can absorb some of the risk in this system in case the price of fish falls or the costs increase, hence the financial risk to the fishing firms is lower.

2.2 *Uncertainty and Enforcement*

Like all markets, emission markets are exposed to significant economic uncertainty, however, in addition, these markets are also affected by considerable scientific and political uncertainty. This uncertainty could have an impact on investment levels and on compliance strategies chosen by firms and the corresponding enforcement schemes implemented by regulators. Permit banking is one way to minimize unexpected short or long positions at the end of a trading period and can therefore reduce uncertainty and risk in the emission market.

Ben-David *et al.* (2000) explore the effects of uncertainty in tradable permit markets on prices, trading volume, and the firms' ability to realize cost savings. Treatments involve two separate types of uncertainty: uncertainty regarding the timing of permit allocation reductions and uncertainty regarding the magnitude of the reduction. They find that firms respond to uncertainty by adopting a "wait and see" approach with respect to certain decisions that can be feasibly postponed. While this does lead to a reduction in ex ante expected cost savings, it may ex post be optimal in view of the irreversibility of investment in abatement technology. Of course, by waiting for more information, firms could be forgoing abatement during earlier periods that could in turn lead to more expensive compliance efforts later. Due to the uncertainty in the permit market, firms could also be uncertain about their future role as potential buyers or sellers of permits and this reinforces the "wait and see" strategy.

Cason *et al.* (1999) introduce uncertain declines in the allocation of emissions allowances over time in their experiment and find relatively low efficiencies in these markets when there is uncertainty. Kusakawa and Saijo (2003) find that investment uncertainty could also reduce efficiency in emission markets. Ben-David *et al.* (1999) explore the relationship between investment and market performance. They provide subjects with a choice of three technologies and examine the impact of technological cost heterogeneity on the operation of the permit market. They find that heterogeneity can lead to reduced trade volume and lower efficiency. Gangadharan *et al.* (2013) examine whether emission markets encourage optimal investment in the presence of uncertainty and the extent to which such investment affects market efficiency. In a treatment with both investment and banking, the proportion of permits "overbanked" is reduced relative to the treatment with only banking. This could imply that overbanking may be less of a problem in the field (where investments are presumably possible) than in the laboratory (where they frequently are not).

Cason and Gangadharan (2006) examine the interaction between three key features of tradable permit markets: banking, uncertainty, and enforcement. They allow for the possibility of correlated random shocks to emissions to incorporate uncertainty and study the impact of these shocks on permit prices and on compliance strategies. Their dynamic enforcement strategy uses audit probabilities that depend on past compliance and inspections. They find that the impact of emission shocks on prices is significantly stronger when subjects are not allowed to bank permits, so banking helps to stabilize permit prices (see Figure 2). However, banking leads to lower compliance with regulations because the benefits to under-report emissions are greater when unused permits can be banked for future use or sale. This highlights a tradeoff between banking and compliance, which regulators may need to consider in field implementations.

Murphy and Stranlund (2006, 2007) on the other hand, design an experiment in which emissions are deterministic, banking is not allowed, and audits are random with a known and constant probability. In their first paper, they examine the effects of changing enforcement strategies on the permit market and isolate the indirect effects of enforcement on compliance behavior. In their 2007 paper, their main focus is on how compliance decisions differ under market-based and command and control regulation. They find substantial differences in compliance behavior, with firm-level characteristics an important determinant of enforcement behavior under command and control, whereas the marginal productivity of enforcement does not depend on these firm-level characteristics under an emissions trading program. This suggests that enforcement policies need to be tailored to the mechanism being used to regulate emissions.

Stranlund *et al.* (2011) report results from experiments focusing on enforcement and compliance, when banking of permits is allowed. In contrast to Cason and Gangadharan (2006), however, they examine the separate roles played by reporting (when a firm under-reports its emissions) and permit (when the firm does not hold enough permits to cover its emissions) violations in dynamic emission markets. They find that reporting violations are significant while permit compliance remains high. They argue that policies that set very high permit violation penalties hence serve little purpose and that the main issue that needs addressing is the one relating to self-reporting. Policies that encourage truthful self-reporting would be valuable in the field.[14]

Enforcement can be a bigger concern when trading is between international parties. Who in this case should be held liable for overselling permits beyond the quotas: the buyer or the seller country? Cason (2003) found that when sellers commit to honor their obligations, market performance is improved as compared to situations when such commitments cannot be made or are not observed. Godby and Shogren (2008) compare seller and buyer liability rules and find that emissions trading with a buyer liability rule would lead to less environmental protection and at greater costs, which is consistent with their theoretical predictions. Increasing the monitoring probability did not change this main result. One of the arguments in favor of the buyer liability rule is that it could encourage poorer countries to participate in a global emissions market as they would be the sellers in the market. The buyers, the argument goes, are rich countries who can shoulder the liability burden better. This aspect was, however, not explicitly designed into the experiment.

There is significant potential for using experimental research to explore compliance and enforcement in environmental markets, as evidence regarding compliance lags theoretical

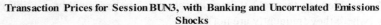

Transaction Prices for Session BUN3, with Banking and Uncorrelated Emissions Shocks

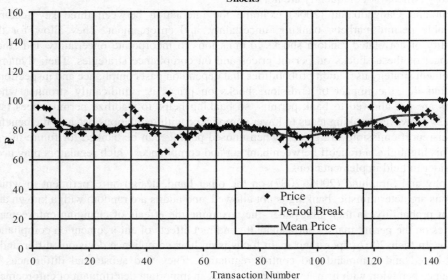

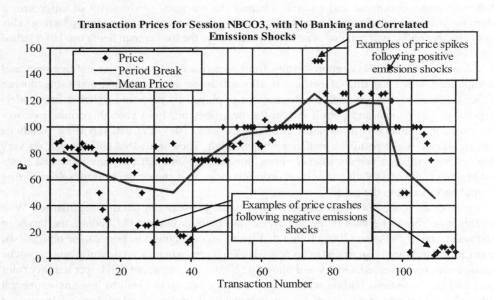

Figure 2. Impact of Banking on Permit Prices in the Presence of Uncertainty.

Source: Cason and Gangadharan (2006), figures 2 and 3.

work in this area. Field data on compliance can be hard to find and in self-reporting programs, data may not be fully reliable. Hence, experiments can make a substantial contribution in this area.

2.3 *Market Power*

Most of the theoretical literature on environmental markets assumes competitive markets. Nevertheless, the ability to exercise market power under alternative trading institutions has been studied extensively, with the double auction mechanism considered the most robust to market power (e.g. Smith, 1981).[15] Ledyard and Szakaly-Moore (1994) adapted Smith's parameters to an environmental market framework and found that strong monopolists were able to achieve about 25% of the potential monopoly price increase even in the last period of the experiment. Brown-Kruse (1995) also detected market power in laboratory markets related to emissions trading. In their experiment, single buyers (or single sellers) of emission permits on one side of the market faced 10 sellers (or 10 buyers) of one permit each, however, an important difference to previous experiments was that the dominant firm had information about the cost schedules of the remaining participants. In the last period of their sessions, monopolists achieved an average of 40% of the potential price gain and monopsonists 166% of the potential price reduction. Godby (1999) replicated many of these results. An asymmetric information hypothesis (where the dominant firm knows the production and abatement costs of fringe firms but not vice versa) would then be useful in explaining why these experiments favor the market power model. Naturally occurring economies often include large firms that could have informational advantages to smaller firms. Hence, real-world applications of double auction markets may not be very resistant to monopoly pricing.

Muller *et al.* (2002) conduct experiments in which they aggregate the five buyers into a single monopsonist or the five sellers into a single monopolist. They also find that the double auction's apparent robustness to market power pricing outcomes is not as general a result as the previous experimental literature by Smith (1981) would suggest, with market power outcomes frequently observed. However, widespread price discrimination implies that trading efficiency is not hampered as market price in the double auction converges to (near) competitive equilibrium price over time, whereas income distribution effects emerge as the most important consequence of imperfect competition as equilibrium quantity is less than competitive equilibrium.

Soberg (2000) examines the impact of market power in emissions trading markets, when the trading institution is one-sided (such as the offer auction and the bid auction). He also finds that the main impact of market power is on income distribution issue not efficiency, with price being near the competitive equilibrium price but the quantity traded is less than competitive equilibrium. Permit trading, whether under a single-sided or double auction, yields an approximately cost-effective allocation of emissions despite monopolization of the permit market.

Cason *et al.* (2003b) examine whether a dominant firm can exercise market power in the context of a laboratory testbed relating to a nitrogen reduction program. They use the double auction trading institution and parameters that approximate the abatement costs of sources in a proposed tradable emissions market for the reduction of nitrogen in the Port Phillip Watershed in Victoria, Australia. In Port Phillip Bay, there is one large emitter of nitrogen that accounts for 94% of emissions and many small emitters. Their results suggest that even though prices vary considerably, a monopoly supplier of permits was not able to dominate a potential tradable emissions permit market in this region.

3. Other Environmental Policy Experiments

More recently, environmental policy experiments have emerged in diverse fields outside the traditional domain of emission trading markets. In this section, we discuss applications to water markets (spurred by development of smart electricity markets), land buybacks for environmental purposes (applications of auction work), and various eco-labeling schemes.

3.1 Water Markets

In recent years, sophisticated water markets have developed around the world. While researchers and policy makers agree that such markets enhance the efficiency of water use, by encouraging water conservation and by moving water from low- to high-value uses, debate continues about ways to improve the trading process. Water markets will continue to grow in importance due to increased scarcity and rainfall variability.

Murphy *et al.* (2000) demonstrate the viability of smart markets for water, which allow for the pricing and allocation of resources in technologically interdependent environments, using California as a case study. Individual water users provide information on willingness to pay or willingness to accept, and this along with budget and capacity constraints are inputs for the optimization algorithm that computes the prices and allocations that maximize the gains from trade. The authors design a sealed bid uniform price double auction mechanism with location-specific bids for the simultaneous allocation of water and transportation capacity rights among the three groups of buyers, sellers, and transporters. The market results in highly efficient allocations even with uncertain water supply, relatively thin markets, and volatility in the quantities traded. Given the problems associated with the development of water markets in California (third-party impacts, manipulation by a few dominant parties), smart markets provide a viable alternative that can incorporate the same allocation criteria that the regulator uses, yet be adaptable to changing information and market conditions.

A follow-up paper, Murphy *et al.* (2009), incorporates instream flow values into the water allocation mechanism by allowing active participation by an environmental trader. The quality of the instream flows can affect nonconsumptive uses of water such as the survival of native fish species. The smart market mechanism leads to mutually beneficial trades that also satisfy environmental constraints. The authors find that while active participation by an environmental trader can lead to efficient and stable outcomes, it also leads to strategic behavior as the trader has incentives to misrepresent their true willingness to trade. In addition, while efficiency is higher due to resource allocation between upstream and downstream users, some benefit more than others leading to concerns over regional impacts.

Duke and Gangadharan (2008) also consider a market where environmental concerns generate restrictions on water trades. They evaluate the performance of the Sunraysia Salinity Levy, a differential salt impact levy introduced by the Victorian Government in Australia in 2002 to manage salt concentrations in rivers resulting from water trades (SRWA, 2002).[16] Only buyers pay the levy, but the magnitude depends on the location of the buyer and the seller along the river. The levy is imposed only on buyers who buy water from lower impact zones, thereby creating a disincentive for water trades that increase salinity concentrations but no incentive for water trades that decrease salinity concentrations.[17] Duke and Gangadharan

(2008) compare the salinity levy to an alternative salinity tax with no geographical restrictions and to a baseline water market with no salinity regulation. Their results show that both the salinity levy and salinity tax lead to significant environmental improvement as compared to the water market with no regulation. The salinity tax leads to lower water prices and more water trades in the early periods compared to the levy. The tax also reduces the cost of salinity control for the regulator and has a superior environmental outcome as compared to the levy. This testbed experiment confirms that economic incentives do improve the environmental outcome, however, using an instrument that creates barriers to trade across zones may not be the most cost-effective method. Hence, trading restrictions need to be considered with care.

In a related paper, Duke et al. (2008) study the use of simultaneous double auctions for both water permits and salinity rights in the Murray River and examine whether these simultaneous markets can efficiently allocate salinity, abatement, and water rights between irrigators. The subjects in the experiment respond to the incentives and choose to spend money on technological improvements, which could lead to private abatement in the salinity market. This showed regulators that when given a choice, individuals adopt new methods to reduce their impact, and that with appropriate incentives in the salt and water market, less water is used.

Tisdell et al. (2004) explored the impact of the trading market institution (open call or closed call auction) on the level of environmental damage caused by water extraction. They also examined the impact of providing information about the environmental consequences of extraction (at the individual and aggregate level), allowing traders to communicate with each other, and the option to verbally sanction others. They found that the open call market (where bids were common knowledge) provided the worst return per unit of environmental damages. Aggregate information treatments were more effective than providing individual information, and providing opportunities for communication also reduced water extraction.

In further work, Tisdell (2007) examined different policy options to reduce total suspended solids in water catchments in Queensland, Australia. He compared closed call tenders and cap-and-trade (both of which are market-based), to a command and control mechanism, finding that the cap-and-trade system led to high rates of convergence of prices to equilibrium predictions. Similar to the early results in emissions trading, he found that market mechanisms helped in minimizing the cost of obtaining the environmental outcome.

Lefebvre et al. (2012) examine how water rights with different security levels can help farmers to manage better and more flexibly, the risks associated with stronger and more frequent water restrictions. The holders of "high security rights" are served first in case of scarcity, and the remaining volume of water determines the allocation to owners of "low security rights." The western part of the United States has a differentiated water right system. Two Australian states, Victoria and New South Wales, initiated a differentiated water right system, respectively, in 1994 and 2000. In other states, water allocations are simply proportional to water rights, without differentiation. Uncertainty relating to water allocation can often motivate farmers to hold more rights than necessary. With differentiated rights, they could instead buy more secure rights. The authors examine two main treatments: the number of security levels for water rights (one or two) and the presence of transactions costs in the water rights and allocation markets. They find that security-differentiated water rights can improve the performance of water markets but the outcome is dependent on market transactions costs. The differentiated system offers opportunities for risk allocation, irrespective of the transactions cost scenario: less risk-tolerant farmers can trade off lower average profits for lower variability of profits, by constituting the right portfolio of high-security and low-security shares. Hence, as risk becomes a major concern for farmers, differentiated markets become a valuable water policy option. The differentiated system can also increase farmers' profits, provided transactions costs in the rights market are lower than in the allocation market.

Garrido (2007) tests two specific market regulations included in the water reforms in Spain. He examines whether prohibiting senior water rights holders from selling to junior users leads to inefficiencies in the market. He also explores if allowing intertemporal use of water storage facilities could reduce stocks and water price instability. Currently, any water left in the reservoir is common property, and this "use it or lose it" rule leads users to exhaust their entitlement before the end of the season. Garrido has four treatments: two comparing restricted versus unrestricted trading, and two in which the storage facilities can be used for private water savings across periods or not. He finds that unrestricted trading is beneficial and that permitting users to use the storage facility leads to higher water levels in the reservoir and lower price instability. Hence, property rights over saved water can have important implications on the use of water during the water shortage periods.

3.2 *Conservation Auctions and Agricultural Policy*

Another application of auctions is designing buybacks of land for different conservation purposes. For example, Cason *et al.* (2003a) conduct testbed auctions for the Victorian Bush Tender program in Australia, which aimed to reduce the aggregate nitrogen load in the Port Phillip watershed. The experiments aimed to identify information conditions that allow the regulator to award land management contracts to maximize pollution abatement for a fixed auction budget. Of particular concern was the incentive for landholders' to truthfully reveal their opportunity cost of land management changes that mitigate the environmental impacts of nitrogen pollution. The auctions had multiple rounds of sealed bids, used a discriminative pricing rule, and the regulator's budget constraint was fixed but unknown to landholder sellers (as in practice). The primary treatment variable was whether the environmental benefit (quality) of the sellers' proposed land use changes is revealed to landholders prior to submitting their offers. Revealing the benefits may increase the perceived fairness and transparency of the auction, educate landholders about the most beneficial land use changes, or promote philanthropic behavior among landholders. On the other hand, revealing information may lead to strategic bidding behavior. They find that revealing the benefits led to lower abatement and higher landholder/seller profits. Lower seller profits are better from the government's perspective, as sellers are not "overpaid" to deliver improvements in environmental quality.

In follow-up work, Cason and Gangadharan (2005) compare the impact of discriminative versus uniform price auctions on landowners' profits and the environmental benefits acquired for a given, fixed auction budget. They find that while the uniform price auction creates a greater incentive to reveal costs than the discriminative format, due to the heterogeneity of landowners' cost some landowners are "overpaid" in the uniform price auction because they receive payments that exceed their opportunity cost. Hence, the discriminative price auction has superior overall market performance. Cason and Gangadharan (2004) discuss some implication of different design features for conservation auctions.

Cummings *et al.* (2004) test design features for the Georgia irrigation auction used to pay farmers to suspend irrigation in drought years. They compared uniform and discriminative pricing formats, as well as different tie-breaking rules (inclusive or random) to inhibit collusion, and information conditions regarding provisionally accepted offers (either the permit ID number or the highest accepted price). The goal was to maximize the number of acres taken out of irrigation within a fixed budget constraint. Field experiments with farmers were also conducted. The random tie-breaking rule, and announcing only the permit ID numbers of provisionally accepted offers, resulted in a lower average cost for the regulator. These two features, along with the discriminative price format, which performed similarly to the uniform price format in the experiments but was preferred for political reasons, were adopted in the actual field auction conducted in 2001.

Parkhurst *et al.* (2002) use experiments to demonstrate how an agglomeration bonus for voluntarily conserving adjoining land could assist efforts to create contiguous conservation corridors on private land. Including an agglomeration bonus significantly decreased the fragmentation of the conserved land compared with simple incentives without a bonus where in fact, conserved land remained completely fragmented. Furthermore, allowing for preplay communication resulted in about 80% of pairs coordinating on the first-best outcome. This first paper uses a normal form coordination game, but in later work, Parkhurst and Shogren (2007, 2008) check the robustness of their results in a more realistic, but complicated, spatial coordination setting. The agglomeration bonus remains an effective policy tool in this more complex setting once participants gain experience.

A small literature exists that considers various aspects of agricultural policy, with most of the focus on the design of support payments. Bastian *et al.* (2008), Nagler *et al.* (2009), and Phillips *et al.* (2010) all find support for the theoretical prediction that decoupled support payments are nondistortionary as compared with production-based subsidies. As with other market policy experiments, Bastian *et al.* (2008) incorporate some relevant real-world features in their design such as a posted bid auction, spot delivery, and matching the guaranteed price to historical target price level. Motivated by policy changes introduced in 2002, McIntosh *et al.* (2007) investigate supply responses to countercyclical payments given to farmers (in addition to direct payments) in a world of price uncertainty. They find that such payments lead to inefficient production decisions and (possibly) higher government payments, but greater income certainty for risk-averse farmers. Bahrs *et al.* (2008) investigate different trading mechanisms for subsidy entitlements (decoupled payments) in situations of excess demand or excess supply (of entitlements) and uncertainty about the true value of the entitlement. Wu and Roe (2005) experimentally evaluate proposals to prohibit the use of tournament-like performance contracts for agricultural producers. They find that agent welfare is higher under fixed performance contracts than tournament-based contracts except when the variance of the common production shock is large. Furthermore, on average, agents exerted higher effort with fixed contracts.[18]

3.3 *Other Market Experiments that Inform Environmental Policy*

Eco-labels and eco-standards have become very popular in recent years, and now appear on dishwashing liquids, detergents, appliances, and houses, to give a few examples. Consumers, while willing to pay for better environmental quality of products in some cases, are also suspicious of the labels that private firms put on their products. Hence, there is pressure on governments to regulate these labels, for example by mandating third-party certification of environmental quality. Cason and Gangadharan (2002) study a posted price market for experience goods, in which consumers find it difficult to identify the environmental quality (low or high) of the good prior to purchase. They compare a lemons market (with no information) to three treatments, which allow for reputation building, unverified claims (i.e. "cheap talk"), and voluntary but costly quality certification. They find that while seller reputation and unverified claims can sometimes increase the provision of high-quality goods, the only reliable way to improve product quality is to use certification.

Burfurd *et al.* (2012) examine the impact of policies to achieve optimal levels of investment in energy efficiency in rental markets. Field evidence shows that rental properties often have lower levels of energy efficiency than owner-occupied buildings, a gap, which policy makers are currently considering policies to reduce. They examine the following policy treatments: mandatory and voluntary energy-efficiency ratings (similar to energy-efficiency stars for appliances), a regulatory minimum upgrade treatment (similar to energy-efficiency standards for appliances), and a cost-share arrangement designed to increase the property owner's incentive to invest in energy efficiency. Mandatory information and voluntary information policies deliver comparable empirical performance (and are superior to the other policies) in terms of efficiency, upgrade levels, and upgrade prices. Figure 3 presents the raw data on upgrades and prices.

4. Conclusion and the Way Forward

Every year governments around the world spend significant public resources on policy making. The success or failure of a policy, be it in the area of competition, the environment, or matching markets, can, however, depend critically on the design of the policy and how individuals respond to it. Much of the research relating to market policy has focused on intricate aspects of the design. These have provided significant insights for researchers and policy makers on what trading institutions to use, what kind of trading rules to incorporate, what features to allow, and what to be cautious about.

Behavioral aspects of these policies have received less attention, and this is particularly evident in the environmental area (Shogren and Taylor, 2008; Shogren *et al.*, 2010). For example, do different kinds of individuals respond differently to the same policy, and if so, what are the implications for policy design? There may also be spillovers from the market arena to other areas in which individuals interact, which could influence the final outcomes of the policy. A recent example of research that explores the performance of markets in the presence of behavioral factors is Cason and Gangadharan (2013) who consider whether competitive interactions affect agents' propensity to cooperate, using a double auction market and a public goods game. They find that although participants often cooperate when given an opportunity, the frequency of cooperation is lower when they also compete in the market. Communication improves cooperation in all environments, particularly when the market is present. Hence, spillovers though they exist, are not very high, suggesting that it could be possible to encourage cooperative efforts without reducing competition and efficiency.

While many experiments have explored the effectiveness of emissions trading, few experiments since Plott (1983) have investigated the impact of different tax regimes. This could be partly because pollution taxes are considered politically infeasible in many countries. Kallbekken *et al.* (2011) examine markets where there is a negative externality and find evidence of tax-averse voting behavior. This opposition to taxes is not because of lack of understanding of the effects or the efficiency properties of the tax. Framing the policy as a tax instead of a fee lowers support for it, whereas specifying how the revenue from the tax would be used increases support. Specifically, support for the policy is higher when revenues are used to reduce inequality.

Other recent research also demonstrates that providing a specific context in the experimental market (as compared with neutral framing) can improve decision making in the experiments

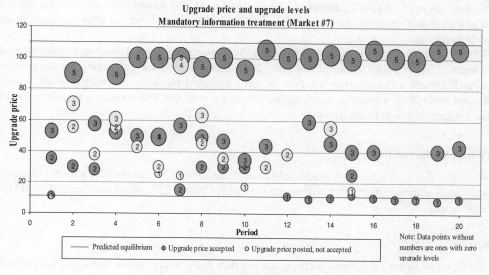

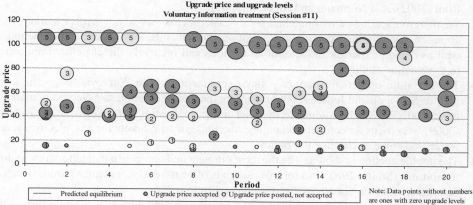

Figure 3. Information and Labeling.

Notes: In the mandatory information treatment, properties with a high upgrade level (circles with 5 written inside them) are rented at approximately E$110 and the ones with a low upgrade level (circles with 1 written inside them) are rented around E$10. With full information, market transactions are therefore consistent with the separating equilibrium and the theoretically optimal prices. The properties with a medium upgrade level (3 written inside the circle) are rented for upgrade prices in the middle of this range, consistent with a pooling equilibrium. In the voluntary information treatment, though performance is similar, there are relatively more instances of the pooling equilibrium being played throughout the 20 periods.

Source: Burfurd *et al*. (2012), figures 4B and C.

(Cummings *et al.*, 2004; Tisdell *et al.*, 2004; Ward *et al.*, 2008) or have a detrimental impact as in Cason and Raymond (2011) where using an environmental context lowered compliance with the policy.

Behavioral motivations can therefore affect the implementation and outcomes from efficient policies. Market policy experiments provide an ideal method for examining the magnitude of such effects and exploring whether cleverly designed markets can mitigate such issues. As environmental concerns continue to grow, so will the importance and relevance of environmental market experiments.

Acknowledgements

We thank Tim Cason for his valuable comments and Kristy Coulter for very capable research assistance. Funding from the Cooperative Research Centre (CRC grant number 20110044) is acknowledged.

Notes

1. Reviews of the extensive spectrum auction design literature can be found in Plott (1997), Roth (2002), and Normann and Ricciuti (2009).
2. We therefore exclude environmental policy experiments that do not involve markets (e.g. common pool resources, nonpoint pollution mechanisms, compliance experiments) as well as market experiments without an obvious and relatively direct policy implication (e.g. valuation studies).
3. The literature on general market policy experiments is vast. Surveys of specific areas include Staropoli and Jullien (2006) regarding the design of wholesale electricity markets, Roth (2002, 2008) who summarizes market design applications, and Normann and Ricciuti (2009) who focus on competition policy, auctions, smart markets for gas, electricity, and water, and some environmental policy.
4. The double auction is shown to be the most efficient and competitive of laboratory trading institutions (Smith, 1962) and for this reason is often used as a benchmark from which to determine efficiency of alternative trading institutions.
5. Efficiency in experiments is defined as the actual gains from trade as a proportion of the maximum possible gains from trade.
6. Price accuracy refers to mean price deviations from the predicted competitive equilibrium by period for each experimental session. Price volatility refers to variability of price about the mean price as measured by a coefficient of variation.
7. The distinguishing feature of the RNA is the system for distributing the receipts from the auction. Each bidder receives a payment equal to the market value of their grandfathered holding of permits. RNA rules were considered for the EPA auctions in the initial discussion stages, with a variant involving a discriminative pricing rule ultimately adopted.
8. In order to facilitate trade between permitted facilities and to allow new firms to enter the market the EPA withholds 2.24% of total allowances to sell at auction.
9. The open outcry market is similar to the pit trading on commodity exchanges, and permits multiple trades among agents and contracts to be negotiated privately.
10. Cycle 1 firms have an annual compliance year of January 1 through December 31, while Cycle 2 firms have an annual compliance year of July 1 through June 30. Transactions can be conducted with firms in either cycle.

11. Tradable permit schemes with no geographic restrictions can result in concentrated emission hot spots when the pollutant does not mix uniformly in the air or water shed.

12. With continuous bidding, subjects could view the status of their bids and see if they were provisionally winning or not and increase their bids before the end of the round.

13. Permit trading in China would involve an offset ratio greater than 1, implying that the seller eliminates more than 1 ton of emissions for each 1 ton permit acquired by a buyer, so increasing trading volume would help the regulator meet its goal of reducing total emissions.

14. See Friesen and Gangadharan (2012) for a comparison of voluntary and compulsory self-reporting policies.

15. This was because in the double auction, nonmarket power firms can withhold demand, hence indirectly forcing the firm with market power to lower prices. Smith (1981) described this apparently unorganized, collective behavior among buyers as a form of tacit collusion. The result was near-competitive market prices, although traded quantities were reduced. Smith and Williams (1989) also replicated these results.

16. Excess water can enter the groundwater system via vertical drainage; depending on soil type, gradient, and distance from the river, salt contained in the soils and groundwater is moved toward the river.

17. Irrigators located in the "High Impact Zone" can only buy water from sellers also located in this zone. Irrigators located in the "Low Impact Zones" can purchase water from sellers in any impact zone but must pay a salt levy per unit of water traded if they buy water from a lower impact zone (SRWA, 2002).

18. There is also a literature on eliciting willingness to pay for various agricultural commodities such as hormone-free beef and non-GM products, but as the link with market policy is less direct, we do not discuss these here.

References

Anderson, C. and Sutinen, J. (2006) The effect of initial lease periods on price discovery in laboratory tradable fishing allowance markets. *Journal of Economic Behavior and Organization* 61: 164–180.

Bahrs, E., Kroll, S. and Sutter, M. (2008) Trading agricultural payment entitlements: an experimental investigation of bilateral negotiations. *American Journal of Agricultural Economics* 90: 1201–1207.

Bastian, C.T., Menkhaus, D.J., Nagler, A.M. and Ballenger, N.S. (2008) Ex ante evaluation of alternative agriculture policies in laboratory posted bid markets. *American Journal of Agricultural Economics* 90: 1208–1215.

Ben-David, S., Brookshire, D., Burness, S., McKee, M. and Schmidft, C. (1999) Heterogeneity, irreversible production choices, and efficiency in emission permit markets. *Journal of Environmental Economics and Management* 38: 176–194.

Ben-David, S., Brookshire, D., Burness, S., McKee, M. and Schmidt, C. (2000) Attitudes toward risk and compliance in emission permit markets. *Land Economics* 76: 590–600.

Bohm, P. (1997) Joint Implementation as Emission Quota Trade: An Experiment among Four Nordic Countries. Copenhagen: Nordic Council of Ministers.

Bohm, P. (2003) Experimental evaluations of policy instruments. In K.G. Maler and J.R. Vincent (eds.), *Handbook of Environmental Economics* (Vol. 1). North Holland: Elsevier.

Bohm, P. and Carlen, B. (1999) Emission quota trade among the few: laboratory evidence of joint implementation amount committed countries. *Resource and Energy Economics* 21: 43–66.

Brewer, P.J. and Plott, C.R. (1996) A binary conflict ascending price (BICAP) mechanism for the decentralized allocation of the right to use railroad tracks. *International Journal of Industrial Organization* 14: 857–886.

Brown-Kruse, J., Elliott, S.R. and Godby, R. (1995) Strategic manipulation of pollution permit markets: an experimental approach. McMaster Working Paper Series, 95–10, Department of Economics, McMaster University.

Burfurd, I., Gangadharan, L. and Nemes, V. (2012) Stars and standards: energy efficiency in rental markets. *Journal of Environmental Economics and Management* 2: 153–168.

Burtraw, D., Goeree, J., Holt, C., Myers, E., Palmer, K. and Shobe, W. (2011) Price discovery in emissions permit auctions. In R.M. Isaac and D.A. Norton (eds.), *Experiments on Energy, the Environment, and Sustainability (Research in Experimental Economics)* (Vol. 14, pp. 11–36). Bingley, UK: Emerald Group Publishing.

Carlen, B. (1999) Large-country effects in international emissions trading: a laboratory test. Mimeo, Department of Economics, Stockholm University.

Carlson, D., Forman, C., Olmstead, N., Ledyard, J., Plott, C., Porter, D. and Sholtz, A. (1993a) An analysis of the information and reporting requirements, market architectures, operational and regulatory issue and derivatory instruments for RECLAIM: report submitted to SCAQMD, contract no. R-C93074. Technical Report, South Coast Air Quality Management District.

Carlson, D., Forman, C., Olmstead, N., Ledyard, J., Plott, C., Porter, D. and Sholtz, A. (1993b) An analysis and recommendation for the terms of the RECLAIM trading credit. Technical Report, South Coast Air Quality Management District.

Cason, T.N. (1993) Seller incentive properties of EPA's emission trading auction. *Journal of Environmental Economics and Management* 25(2): 177–195.

Cason, T.N. (1995) An experimental investigation of the seller incentives in the EPA's emission trading auction. *The American Economic Review* 85(4): 905–922.

Cason, T.N. (2003) Buyer liability and voluntary inspections in international greenhouse gas emissions trading: a laboratory study. *Environmental and Resources Economics* 25: 101–127.

Cason, T.N. (2010) What can laboratory experiments teach us about emissions permit market design? *Agricultural and Resource Economics Review* 39: 151–161.

Cason, T.N. and Gangadharan, L. (1998) An experimental study of electronic bulletin board trading for emission permits. *Journal of Regulatory Economics* 14: 55–73.

Cason, T.N. and Gangadharan, L. (2002) Environmental labeling and incomplete consumer information in laboratory markets, *Journal of Environmental Economics and Management* 43(1): 113–134.

Cason, T.N. and Gangadharan, L. (2003) Transactions costs in tradable permit markets: an experimental study of pollution market designs. *Journal of Regulatory Economics* 23(2): 145–165.

Cason, T.N. and Gangadharan, L. (2004) Auction design for voluntary conservation programs. *American Journal of Agricultural Economics* 86(5): 1211–1217.

Cason, T.N. and Gangadharan, L. (2005) A laboratory comparison of uniform and discriminative price auctions for reducing non-point source pollution. *Land Economics* 81(1): 51–70.

Cason, T.N. and Gangadharan, L. (2006) Emissions variability in tradable permit markets with imperfect enforcement and banking. *Journal of Economic Behavior and Organization* 61: 199–216.

Cason, T.N. and Gangadharan, L. (2011) Price discovery and intermediation in linked emissions markets: a laboratory study. *Ecological Economics* 70: 1424–1433.

Cason, T.N. and Gangadharan, L. (2013) Cooperation spillovers and price competition in experimental markets, forthcoming, *Economic Inquiry*.

Cason, T.N. and Plott, C. (1996) EPA's new emissions trading mechanism: a laboratory evaluation. *Journal of Environmental Economics and Management* 30: 133–160.

Cason, T.N. and Raymond, L. (2011) Can affirmative motivations improve compliance in emissions trading programs? *Policy Studies Journal* 39: 659–678.

Cason, T.N., Elliott, S.R. and Van Boening, M.R. (1999) Speculation in experimental markets for emission permits. *Research in Experimental Economics* 7: 93–119.

Cason, T.N., Gangadharan, L. and Duke, C. (2003a) A laboratory study of auctions for reducing pon-point source pollution. *Journal of Environmental Economics and Management* 46(3): 446–471.

Cason, T.N., Gangadharan, L. and Duke, C. (2003b) Market power in tradable emission markets: a laboratory testbed for emission trading in Port Phillip Bay, Victoria. *Ecological Economics* 46(3): 469–491.

Cherry, T.L., Kroll, S. and Shogren, J.F. (2008) *Environmental Economics, Experimental Economics*. London and New York: Routledge.

Cronshaw, M. and Brown-Kruse, J. (1999) An experimental analysis of emissions permits with banking and the Clean Air Act Amendments of 1990. In C. Holt and R.M. Isaac (eds.), *Research in Experimental Economics* (Vol. 7, pp. 1–24). Stamford, CT: JAI Press.

Cummings, R., McKee, M. and Taylor, L.O. (2001) To whisper in the ears of princes: laboratory economic experiments and environmental policy. In H. Folmer, H.L. Gabel, S. Gerking and A. Rose (eds.), *Frontiers of Environmental Economics*. Cheltenham, UK and Northampton, MA: Edward Elgar.

Cummings, R., Holt, C. and Laury, S. (2004) Using laboratory experiments for policymaking: an example from the Georgia Irrigation Reduction Auction. *Journal of Policy Analysis and Management* 23(2): 341–363.

Duke, C. and Gangadharan, L. (2008) Salinity in water markets: an experimental investigation of the Sunraysia salinity levy, Victoria. *Ecological Economics* 68(1–2): 486–503.

Duke, C., Gangadharan, L. and Cason, T.N. (2008) A test bed experiment for water and salinity rights trading in irrigation regions of the Murray Darling Basin, Australia. In T.L. Cherry, S. Kroll and J.F. Shogren (eds.), *Environmental Economics, Experimental Economics* (pp. 77–99). London and New York: Routledge.

Franciosi, R., Isaac, R.M., Pingry, D. and Reynolds, S. (1993) An experimental investigation of the Hahn-Noll revenue neutral auction for emission licenses. *Journal of Environmental Economics and Management* 24: 1–24.

Franciosi, R., Isaac, R.M. and Reynolds, S. (1999) Experimental research on the EPA's two-tier system for marketable emissions permits. In C. Holt and R.M. Isaac (eds.), *Research in Experimental Economics* (Vol. 7, pp. 25–44). Stamford, CT: JAI Press.

Friesen, L. and Gangadharan, L. (2012) Designing self-reporting regimes to encourage truth telling: an experimental study. Working Paper, University of Queensland.

Gangadharan, L., Farrell, A. and Croson, R. (2013) Investment decisions and emissions reductions: experimental results in emissions permit trading. In M. Price and J. List (eds.), *The Handbook of Experimental Economics and the Environment*. Forthcoming.

Garrido, A. (2007) Water markets design and evidence from experimental economics. *Environmental Resource Economics* 38: 311–330.

Godby, R. (1999) Market power in emission permit double auctions. In C. Holt and R.M. Isaac (eds.), *Research in Experimental Economics* (Vol. 7, pp. 121–162). Stamford, CT: JAI Press.

Godby, R. and Shogren, J. (2008) Caveat emptor Kyoto: comparing buyer and seller liability in carbon emissions trading. In T. Cherry, S. Kroll and J. Shogren (eds.), *Environmental Economics, Experimental Methods*. New York: Routledge.

Goeree, J., Palmer, K., Holt, C.A., Shobe, W. and Burtraw, D. (2010) An experimental study of auctions versus grandfathering to assign pollution permits. *Journal of European Economic Association* 8(2–3): 514–525.

Ishikida, T., Ledyard, J., Olson, M. and Porter, D. (2001) Experimental test bedding of a pollution trading system: Southern California's RECLAIM emissions market. In R.M. Issac (ed.), *Research in Experimental Economics* (8th edn, Vol. 8, pp. 185–220). Bingley, UK: Emerald Group Publishing.

Joskow, P., Schmalensee, R. and Bailey, E. (1998) The market for sulfur dioxide emissions. *American Economic Review* 88(4): 669–685.

Kallbekken, S., Kroll, S. and Cherry, T. (2011) Do you not like Pigou, or do you not understand him? Tax aversion and revenue recycling in the lab. *Journal of Environmental Economics and Management* 62: 53–64.

Klaassen, G., Nentjes, A. and Smith, M. (2005) Testing the theory of emissions trading: experimental evidence on alternative mechanisms for global carbon trading. *Ecological Economics* 53: 47–58.

Kusakawa, T. and Saijo, T. (2003) Emissions trading experiments: investment uncertainty reduces market efficiency. In T. Sawa (ed.), *International Frameworks and Technological Strategies to Prevent Climate Change* (pp. 45–65). Tokyo: Springer-Verlag.

Ledyard, J.O. and Szakaly-Moore, K. (1994) Designing organizations for trading pollution rights. *Journal of Economic Behavior and Organization* 25: 167–196.

Lefebvre, M., Gangadharan, L. and Thoyer, S. (2012) Do security-differentiated water rights improve the performance of water markets? *American Journal of Agricultural Economics* 94(5): 1113–1135.

McIntosh, C.R., Shogren, J.F. and Dohlman, E. (2007) Supply response to countercyclical payments and base acre updating under uncertainty: an experimental study. *American Journal of Agricultural Economics* 89: 1046–1057.

Mougeot, M., Naegelen, F., Pelloux, B. and Rulliere, J. (2011) Breaking collusion in auctions through speculation: an experiment on CO2 emission permit markets. *Journal of Public Economic Theory* 15(5): 829–856.

Moxnes, E. (2012) Individual transferable quotas versus auctioned seasonal quotas: an experimental investigation. *Marine Policy* 26: 339–349.

Muller, R.A. and Mestelman, S. (1994) Emissions trading with shares and coupons: a laboratory experiment. *The Energy Journal* 15: 185–211.

Muller, R.A. and Mestelman, S. (1998) What have we learned from emissions trading experiments? *Managerial and Decision Economics* 19: 225–238.

Muller, R.A., Mestelman, S., Spraggon, J. and Godby, R. (2002) Can double auctions control monopoly and monopsony power in emissions trading markets? *Journal of Environmental Economics and Management* 44: 70–92.

Murphy, J. and Stranlund, J. (2006) Direct and market effects of enforcing emissions trading programs: an experimental analysis. *Journal of Economic Behavior and Organization* 61(2): 217–233.

Murphy, J. and Stranlund, J. (2007) A laboratory investigation of compliance behavior under tradable emissions rights: implications for targeted enforcement. *Journal of Environmental Economics and Management* 53: 196–212.

Murphy, J.J., Dinar, A., Howitt, R.E., Rassenti, S.J. and Smith, V.L. (2000) The design of "smart" water market institutions using laboratory experiments. *Environmental and Resource Economics* 17: 375–394.

Murphy, J.J., Dinar, A., Howitt, R.E., Rassenti, S.J., Smith, V.L. and Weinberg, M. (2009) The design of water markets when instream flows have value. *Journal of Environmental Management* 90: 1089–1096.

Nagler, A.M., Menkhaus, D.J., Bastian, C.T., Ballenger, N.S., O'Donoghue, E. and Young, C.E. (2009) Are production decisions decoupled under a bond scheme? Experimental evidence. *Review of Agricultural Economics* 31: 222–230.

Normann, H.-T. and Ricciuti, R. (2009) Laboratory experiments for economic decision making. *Journal of Economic Surveys* 23: 407–432.

Noussair, C. and Tucker, S. (2013) Experimental research on asset pricing. *Journal of Economic Surveys* 27(3): 554–569.

Palan, S. (2013) A review of bubbles and crashes in experimental asset markets. *Journal of Economic Surveys* 27(3): 570–588.

Parkhurst, G.M. and Shogren, J.F. (2007) Spatial incentives to coordinate contiguous habitat. *Ecological Economics* 64: 344–355.

Parkhurst, G.M. and Shogren, J.F. (2008) Smart subsidies for conservation. *American Journal of Agricultural Economics* 90: 1192–1200.

Parkhurst, G.M., Shogren, J.F., Bastian, C., Kivi, P., Donner, J. and Smith, R.B.W. (2002) Agglomeration bonus: an incentive mechanism to reunite fragmented habitat for biodiversity conservation. *Ecological Economics* 41: 305–328.

Phillips, O.R., Nagler, A.M., Menkhaus, D.J. and Bastian, C.T. (2010) Experimental work on subsidies, moral hazard, and market power in agricultural markets. *Contemporary Economic Policy* 28: 488–501.

Plott, C. (1983) Externalities and corrective policies in experimental markets. *The Economic Journal* 93: 106–127.

Plott, C. (1986) Laboratory experiments in economics: the implications of posted-price institutions. *Science* 232: 732–738.

Plott, C. (1997) Laboratory experimental testbeds: application to the PCS auction. *Journal of Economics and Management Strategy* 6(3): 605–638.

Porter, D., Rassenti, S., Shobe, W., Smith, V. and Winn, A. (2009) The design, testing and implementation of Virginia's NOx allowance auction. *Journal of Economic Behavior and Organization* 69: 190–200.

Rich, C.S. and Friedman, E. (1998) The matching market institution: a laboratory investigation. *American Economic Review* 88: 1311–1322.

Roth, A.E. (1986) Laboratory experimentation in economics. *Economics and Philosophy* 2: 245–273.

Roth, A.E. (2002) The economist as engineer: game theory, experimentation, and computation as tools for design economics. *Econometrica* 70: 1341–1378.

Roth, A.E. (2008) What have we learned from market design? *The Economic Journal* 118: 285–310.

Shobe, W., Palmer, K., Myers, E., Holt, C., Goeree, J. and Burtraw, D. (2009) An experimental analysis of auctioning emissions allowances under a loose cap. Resources for the Future Discussion Paper 09–25, Washington.

Shogren, J.F. and Taylor, L.O. (2008) On behavioral-environmental economics. *Review of Environmental Economics and Policy* 2: 26–44.

Shogren, J., Parkhurst, G. and Banerjee, P. (2010) Two cheers and a qualm for behavioral environmental economics. *Environmental and Resource Economics* 46: 235–247.

Smith, V. (1962) An experimental study of competitive market behavior. *Journal of Political Economy* LXX(2): 111–137.

Smith, V. (1981) An empirical study of decentralized institutions of monopoly restraint. In G. Horwich and J. Quirk (eds.), *Essays in Contemporary Fields of Economics*. West Lafayette, IN: Purdue University Press.

Smith V. and Williams, A. (1989) The boundaries of competitive price theory: convergence, expectations and transactions costs. In L. Green and J. Kagel (eds.), *Advances in Behavioral Economics* (Vol. 2). Norwood, NJ: Ablex Publishing.

Smith, V., Suchanek, G. and Williams, A.W. (1988) Bubbles, crashes, and endogenous expectations in experimental spot asset markets. *Econometrica* 56: 1119–1151.

Soberg, M. (2000) Imperfect competition, sequential auctions and emissions trading: an experimental evaluation. Discussion Paper, Statistics Norway, Research Department.

Staropoli, C. and Jullien, C. (2006) Using laboratory experiments to design efficient market institutions: the case of wholesale electricity markets. *Annals of Public and Cooperative Economics* 77: 555–577.

Stranlund, J., Murphy, J. and Spraggon, J. (2011) An experimental analysis of compliance in dynamic emissions markets. *Journal of Environmental Economics and Management* 62: 414–429.

Strum, B. and Weimann, J. (2006) Experiments in environmental economics and some close relatives. *Journal of Economic Surveys* 20: 419–457.

Sunraysia Rural Water Authority (SRWA) (2002) Refinement of the river salinity zoning system. Victorian Government Document.

Tisdell, J. (2007) Bringing biophysical models into the economic lab: an experimental analysis of sediment trading in Australia. *Ecological Economics* 60(3): 548–595.

Tisdell, J. and Ifekhar, M.S. (2013) Fisheries quota allocation: laboratory experiments on simultaneous and combinatorial auctions. *Marine Policy* 38: 228–234.

Tisdell, J., Ward, J. and Capon, T. (2004) Impact of communication and information on a complex heterogeneous closed water catchment environment. *Water Resources Research* 40(9), doi:10.1029/2003WR002868.

Vickrey, W. (1961) Counterspeculation, auctions and competitive sealed tenders. *Journal of Finance* 16: 8–37.

Ward, J.R., Connor, J. and Tisdell, J. (2008) Aligning policy and real world settings. In T.L. Cherry, S. Kroll and J.F. Shogren (eds.), *Environmental Economics, Experimental Economics* (pp. 100–130). London and New York: Routledge.

Wu, S. and Roe, B. (2005) Behavioral and welfare effects of tournaments and fixed performance contracts: some experimental evidence. *American Journal of Agricultural Economics* 87: 130–146.

8
EXPERIMENTAL MARKETS WITH FRICTIONS

Gabriele Camera

University of Basel
Chapman University

Marco Casari and Maria Bigoni

University of Bologna

1. Introduction

A large portion of economic discussions in academic and policy circles revolve around dissecting the pros and cons of different market outcomes without considering in great detail how those outcomes can be achieved, if they can be achieved at all. 'The market' is simply treated as a black box: if any gains from trade exist, then such gains are instantaneously and fully exploited through effortless interactions guided by Adam Smith's invisible hand.

But economic interactions rarely fit this idealized view: exploiting gains from trade is far from being a smooth process. Laboratory experiments have provided a valuable tool to study economic interactions and the process of exchange in the presence of 'frictions'. This paper surveys recent experimental work on markets with frictions.

There is a variety of reasons why exploiting gains from trade may not be easy. In traditional economies based on community-type interactions, economic exchanges occur within a stable social circle, which allows community members to realize all potential gains without great difficulties. Common resources such as pastures, forests, fisheries, irrigation systems have been traditionally managed based on a repeated interaction among a defined group of well-known community members (Ostrom *et al.*, 2000; Casari, 2007). In contrast, in developed economies many transactions take the form of *impersonal* exchanges. By this, we mean exchanges that are decentralized and – unlike personal exchange – do not involve high levels of information about others' past behavior (Granovetter, 1985; North, 1990; Seabright, 2004).

Impersonal exchange is central to economic development because it offers an important advantage over personal exchange: it expands the set of potential economic interactions,

A Collection of Surveys on Market Experiments, First Edition.
Edited by Charles N. Noussair and Steven Tucker. Chapters © 2014 The Authors.
Book compilation © 2014 John Wiley & Sons, Ltd. Published 2014 by John Wiley & Sons, Ltd.

which in turn allows a society to benefit from specialization and trade. But shifting exchange from a personal to an impersonal sphere of interaction also carries a disadvantage: it does away with the reciprocity mechanisms that are available when individuals engage in recurrent relationships within a small group of well-known counterparties – such as the circle of usual trading partners or the members of a clan, for instance. This inability to trigger reciprocal mechanisms magnifies the incentives for opportunistic behavior, especially when (i) it is possible to break promises, (ii) there is lack of information about past behaviors of others, (iii) there are difficulties in communicating or in coordinating trade, or when (iv) enforcement and punishment institutions are poorly functioning. Any of these features contributes to create barriers to trade, for example, by exacerbating lack of trust in others; see Ostrom (2010). We will use the word 'frictions' to denote any collection of impediments to exchange – such as the aforementioned ones. If frictions cannot be overcome, then the additional opportunities for mutual gain offered by impersonal exchange may remain out of reach.

Over the course of history, societies have developed a whole host of institutions both formal – regulatory, enforcement, legal – and informal – such as network formations, reputation building, and social customs – specifically designed to support decentralized economic exchanges that would otherwise be unattainable. For example, the steady economic expansion during the commercial revolution in Medieval Europe from the XIII century on witnessed the development of an array of formal and informal institutions aimed at capturing new exchange opportunities. This fundamental shift in the quantity and scope of trade relied on the creation of the Merchant Law, the design of banking and financial instruments in Venice and Genoa, the expansion of monetary exchange, the creation of trading organizations such as the Hanseatic League. This process took centuries (Spufford, 2003; Greif, 2006).

The economic literature has adopted a variety of models to characterize market frictions, and understand their impact on economic efficiency. Frictions can be found in many economic models, going from models of informational asymmetries (Akerlof, 1970) to models of sticky prices (Calvo, 1983), from models of limited communication (Townsend, 1987) to life-cycle models (Samuelson, 1958). In the following section, we review a basic framework, which is based on random, pairwise trade meetings. Such focus is motivated by the fact that models built around random and pairwise trade meetings characterize a class of theoretical environments that encompass a large segment of research both in microeconomics and in macroeconomics. The paper then proceeds as follows: Section 3 presents a literature review of the recent experimental work in this area. Section 4 presents a new experiment on the role of communication in markets with frictions. Section 5 concludes.

2. Modeling Decentralized Frictional Markets

In this paper we focus on a class of environments that make frictions explicit by adopting three basic features:

  (i) The economy has a fixed population and an infinite horizon, with trade interactions taking place over a sequence of periods;
 (ii) Trade is decentralized in the sense that every interaction is anonymous, whereby in each period individuals are randomly paired to play a game;
(iii) There are severe communication, informational, enforcement and punishment limitations.

Models with such features have been adopted in microeconomics, to study economic governance (Dixit, 2003), the organization of commerce (Milgrom *et al.*, 1990), and social norms (Kandori, 1992; Ellison, 1994). Random-matching models are also used in the macroeconomics and finance literatures to study unemployment (Diamond, 1982; Mortensen and Pissarides, 1994), monetary exchange (Kiyotaki and Wright, 1989), and over-the-counter markets (Duffie *et al.*, 2005).

One of the central features of these theoretical models of frictional economies is that reciprocal mechanisms of exchange are unavailable; consequently, agents must find other ways to ensure that the opportunities for mutual gain offered by impersonal exchange do not remain out of reach. Another important feature of these economies is that they generally admit multiple equilibria, possibly including one implementing the efficient outcome. The basic idea is formalized in Kandori (1992) and Ellison (1994), who study cooperation in prisoners' dilemma games that are embedded in a random matching model; they demonstrate how groups of self-regarding, patient individuals can overcome short-run temptations to deviate from the efficient outcome even in the presence of severe communication, informational, enforcement and punishment limitations. Full cooperation can be maintained if *all* members of the economy participate in punishing a deviation by defecting forever. This community punishment scheme is decentralized.

To be sure, such a social norm of behavior requires a great deal of coordination. Yet, the theoretical literature does not discuss how agents may end up coordinating on a strategy, and in particular on a common punishment scheme. In fact, the literature often assumes, implicitly or explicitly, that a population coordinates on the best equilibrium, including the efficient outcome if available (e.g. Milgrom *et al.*, 1990; Aliprantis *et al.*, 2007). This assumption has far from trivial policy implications, hence it is meaningful to look deeper into the empirical validity of such theoretical view. In fact, one would imagine that economy-wide coordination on a strategy may be very challenging when the number of agents is large and communication is constrained.

Several questions arise: how, in practice, do groups of individuals reach efficient outcomes when theoretically feasible in markets with frictions? What strategies do they adopt to sustain it? What institutions promote efficient outcomes and can these institutions emerge endogenously? And how does the size of a group impact outcomes and strategy adoption?

A flurry of experimental studies has been recently conducted to provide an answer to some of these questions. In this paper we will focus on *indefinitely* repeated games with random matching, a design that can be seen as the closest empirical counterpart of the above-described theoretical economies. In such experimental markets, trading is modeled as a social dilemma so that maximum welfare corresponds to maximum cooperation. A group of subjects face an indefinite sequence of opportunities to cooperate (= trade). In each period, subjects randomly encounter an anonymous trade counterpart. Participants cannot rely on relational contracting because in such experimental economies they cannot identify others and do not know their histories of actions. For all these reasons, following the terminology proposed in Camera and Casari (2009), we will say that interaction takes place among *strangers*. Such a design captures the gist of interactions taking place in societies where, due to a variety of reasons, people may not know each other and may not trust each other (e.g. consider the role played by globalization and technology).

The section that follows presents a methodological overview of recent experiments with indefinite repetition and random matching. Then, we survey experimental studies that look at some of the institutions that can reduce the negative impact of frictions on cooperation: monitoring, personal punishment, monetary exchange, and communication. Finally, we will report results of an experiment specifically designed to assess whether and how different types of communication can help to sustain efficient, cooperative outcomes in frictional markets populated by strangers.

3. A Review of Recent Experimental Work on Markets with Frictions

One of the most important traits of models of markets with frictions is that the economy has an infinite horizon. Clearly, experiments cannot have an infinite duration, and generally, sessions do not last more than a few hours and subjects receive their payment at the end, so it does not matter to which specific period of the experiment the payment refers to.

Experimentalists have followed different approaches to implement models of infinite duration in the lab. A first approach is to have a pre-set – and long 'enough' – number of repetitions that is publicly announced. Generally, an end-game effect emerges in the last periods, hence those are dropped from the analysis (Selten and Stoeker, 1986; Normann and Wallace, 2012). This approach, however, does not allow a direct application of Folk Theorem-type results because there is a deterministic, publicly known end-period.

A second approach consists in having a pre-determined duration, hidden from participants (e.g. Wilson and Sell, 1997; Stahl, 2009). Making the ending unknown allows avoiding the insurgence of an end-game effect. In this case, participants do not know for sure whether or not the current period is the last one. The experimenter, however, loses control over subjects' beliefs on the continuation probability, because beliefs are unobserved, and may vary across periods and subjects.

A third approach is a continuation rule following an explicit random process (Roth and Murnighan, 1978). At the end of each period, a random draw determines whether the supergame ends or continues for one additional period. The continuation probability is usually constant: a supergame that has reached period t continues into period t+1 with a fixed probability δ. If subjects are risk neutral, one can interpret δ as the discount factor. The expected duration of a supergame is $1/(1-\delta)$ periods, and in each period the supergame is expected to go on for $\delta/(1-\delta)$ additional periods (e.g. Engle-Warnick and Slonim, 2006; Davis *et al.*, 2011). One way to give subjects a stronger feeling of an indefinite horizon is to let them interact sporadically over several weeks through an internet experiment (Wright, 2010).

A fourth approach is to have a two-period game, where period one is the stage game, and the second and last period represents a reduced-form continuation game (Angelova *et al.*, forthcoming; Cooper and Kuhn, 2011). In period two subjects play a coordination game where payoffs correspond to the net present value of the stream of payoffs of the indefinitely repeated continuation game. Despite the finite horizon of interaction, this set-up admits multiple equilibria (Benoit and Krishna, 1985). In this manner, subjects can deter defections in the first period by threatening to choose an action corresponding to the inefficient equilibrium in the second period. This approach drastically reduces the set of available strategies, excluding for instance tit-for-tat and t-period punishment strategies.

A fifth approach is to monotonically shrink payoffs across periods, in order to simulate discounting (Fréchette *et al.*, 2003; Cabral *et al.*, 2012). To ensure that sessions have a finite duration, this last approach has to be combined with one of the previous four.

A second important characteristic of models of frictional markets is that interactions are decentralized. In this regard, a crucial variable is thus the size of the economy, which can impact on the frequency with which the same subjects interact together. Most experiments on repeated games study two-person economies (e.g. Roth and Murnighan, 1978; Murnighan and Roth, 1983; Palfrey and Rosenthal, 1994; Dal Bó, 2005; Aoyagi and Fréchette, 2009).

The two subjects who populate the economy form a fixed pair and interact together in every period. Hence, the interaction is not anonymous, and individual histories are known.

By contrast, larger economies (N > 2) exhibit a variety of anonymity and monitoring levels. If in all periods a subject interacts with everyone in his economy, then we say that interaction takes place among 'partners' here, even if there are more than two persons there is no anonymity, because a subject knows for sure his counterpart in each period (e.g. Cason and Mui, 2010). The focus of the present study, instead, is on economies in which interaction is among strangers. Here, agents do not regularly meet the same counterpart and do not know if this happens; in each period, agents are randomly matched with each other (Schwartz *et al.*, 2000; Duffy and Ochs, 2009; Duffy *et al.*, forthcoming; Camera and Casari, 2009, 2010; Camera *et al.*, 2012). Strangers can be anonymous or not, depending on whether one can recognize someone previously encountered.

The literature has considered three basic architectures for strangers' economies: circle economies, turnpike economies and random matching economies. In a circle economy, agents are located on a circle, and the probability of an encounter between two agents declines with their distance (Dixit, 2003). In a turnpike environment, agents are arrayed along two parallel lines moving in opposite direction; hence agents who currently are in a match cannot meet at any future date (Townsend, 1980). With random matching, agents in an economy have the same probability of encountering each other, regardless of their distance (Diamond, 1982).

Strangers may observe different amounts of information about the choice of others in the economy. With *public monitoring*, subjects share the same information about the outcomes realized in the economy; for instance, they all observe a summary of all outcomes in the economy (Camera and Casari, 2009). With *private monitoring*, instead, subjects do not share the same information about the outcomes realized in the economy, because they cannot see outcomes in meetings other than their own (Schwartz *et al.*, 2000; Duffy and Ochs, 2009; Camera and Casari, 2009, 2010; Camera *et al.*, 2012). Information may also be *imperfect*, as when the counterpart's actions of are not directly observable (Aoyagi and Fréchette, 2009). Degrees of anonymity and of monitoring are two independent dimensions; hence we can have four types of situations.

There are Folk Theorem-type results proving that – even under these weaker informational conditions – agents can support equilibria with high levels of cooperation, provided that agents are sufficiently patient. The key to do so is to prevent defections by means of sanctioning schemes based on *community enforcement*; below, we explain how this can be done.

The folk theorems for two-person economies (Friedman, 1971) are easily extended to economies of strangers with *perfect* public monitoring; in such a case an agent can react to others' behavior as if facing a single counterpart. With *public monitoring*, a given outcome can be supported as an equilibrium with the same discount factor as in the standard Folk-theorem. Moreover, if public monitoring is not anonymous, then the strategy set is richer, because it includes strategies conditional on individual histories.

Folk theorem-type results exist also for environments with *private monitoring*, and where agents are anonymous. The results have been derived in the path-breaking works of Kandori (1992) and Ellison (1994), who consider economies with N>2 agents who play a prisoner's dilemma in pairs, know only the outcomes of their interactions and ignore the opponent's identity. If agents are sufficiently patient, then the efficient outcome can be supported as a sequential equilibrium. The equilibrium strategy considered is for an agent to start cooperating and to keep cooperating until an opponent defects. At that point, the agent should switch to 'defect forever'. This implies adoption of a form of 'collective punishment': everyone starts punishing everyone else after just one deviation. This *grim trigger strategy* can be similarly used in economies with public monitoring, but it works at a different speed. When agents cannot identify the defector and target him for punishment, they must resort to punish everyone, as a community. With public monitoring, information about a defection is instantaneously provided to the whole economy; hence punishment can involve everyone starting from the period immediately following a defection. With private monitoring, instead, punishment gradually spreads in the economy: the information about the initial defection spreads by contagion, meeting by meeting, until it eventually reaches everyone. To deter opportunistic behavior, agents must adopt a strategy that threatens a punishment sufficiently severe to lower the continuation payoff following a defection. If everyone adopts such a norm of community punishment, then this substantially drives down continuation payoffs, but it requires a higher discount factor than in an economy with public monitoring.

The theoretical predictions of these folk theorems for matching models have been recently tested in the lab. In an experiment Duffy and Ochs (2009) compared a fixed pairing (partner) versus a random pairing treatment (strangers). In the random pairing there was private monitoring and the conditions were set in a way that full cooperation was an equilibrium outcome. The study finds a remarkably higher aggregate cooperation in fixed than in random pairing, hence raising the point that, despite the theoretical viability of supporting cooperative equilibria with random pairing and private monitoring, this is something that empirically is difficult to attain. Duffy and Ochs (2009) employed an identical stopping probability in all treatments, which favored cooperation in fixed pairing because the expected number of encounters with the same counterpart is lower under random pairing treatment; i.e. the critical discount factor above which full cooperation can be sustained if subjects are risk neutral was lower under fixed pairings.

Camera and Casari (2009) studied in the lab the impact of private vs. public monitoring while keeping constant the expected number of future encounters in all treatments. They report that public monitoring promotes cooperation only when it is non-anonymous: high cooperation levels emerge in situations where subjects know identities and histories of opponents, but they are similar to private monitoring when subjects see aggregate outcomes without observing identities. These findings suggest that it is easier to coordinate on strategies conditioning on individual histories rather than on the grim trigger strategy. Additional support for this finding and the importance of reputational-based strategies comes also from the trust game experiment in Duffy *et al.* (forthcoming), and the experiment on color-coded reputation in Stahl (2009).

It is common practice in experimental economics to repeatedly expose subjects to the same decisional situation, i.e. to have several supergames. This allows the experimenter to study learning and other meta-supergames effects. In this respect, a variety of ways to partition subjects have been adopted, with different levels of potential spill-over across supergames. One protocol rules out that anyone may share a common past partner (Dal Bó, 2005). This procedure ensures that the decisions one subject made in one supergame could not affect, in any way, the decisions of subjects he or she would meet in the future. Aliprantis *et al.* (2006) call it 'anonymous' matching. Another protocol is 'absolute strangers' (Camera and Casari, 2009, 2010; Camera *et al.*, 2012). This procedure partitions the economy's participants in such a way that no two subjects are in the same economy for more than one supergame. Subjects may have shared a common past partner in supergames three or later. A third possible protocol is to populate all economies with the same subjects, across supergames (Schwartz *et al.*, 2000; Duffy and Ochs, 2009). There are other protocols in between absolute strangers and identical economies. In Aoyagi and Fréchette (2009) each agent plays K>10 supergames: in the first 10 they partition agents in fixed pairings, and in the remaining K-10 supergames they randomly rematch participants.

3.1 *Peer Punishment*

Limitations in punishment are a key friction that prevents market exchange from achieving efficiency. In the previous section we have focused on decentralized punishment mechanisms that involve and extend to the entire group (community enforcement, or group punishment). Here, instead, we focus on mechanisms that offer the option to punish specific individuals, to which we refer as *peer* (or personal) *punishment* as a way to differentiate such mechanisms from punishment schemes that indiscriminately target the entire community. Note also that, since peer punishment can be centralized or decentralized (e.g. Kosfeld *et al.*, 2009), here we focus on decentralized punishment mechanisms which is the version favored by almost all experimentalists.

There is a burgeoning literature on peer punishment (Chaudhuri, 2011), which is overwhelmingly focused on finitely repeated social dilemmas among partners (fixed matching) following the pioneering study in Ostrom *et al.* (1992). In such a setting, subjects have shown a surprising tendency to engage in costly personal punishment of others, especially defectors. Though this behavior is inconsistent with personal income maximization, it has been shown to be remarkably robust. Under finite time horizons, efficiency with peer punishment depends on two factors: the fine-to-fee ratio (Nikiforakis and Normann, 2008) and time horizon's length (Gaechter *et al.*, 2010).

Very few studies consider peer punishment in an indefinitely repeated setting; Dreber *et al.* (2008) study interactions among partners, and show that that the option of costly punishment increases the amount of cooperation but not the average payoff of the group. Camera and Casari (2009) study punishment in strangers' economies of indefinite duration. Every participant played a supergame of indefinite duration in a group of four subjects. In every period, the group was randomly partitioned into two pairs of subjects and every pair played a prisoner's dilemma. The interaction was anonymous and subjects could only observe actions and outcomes in their own pair. Hence, though each group interacted repeatedly, this design made it impossible for a single participant to build a reputation. In a treatment, they introduced the possibility to adopt peer punishment. This amounted to adding a costly opportunity to immediately respond to a counterpart's action by lowering her payoff. Cooperators and defectors alike could be punished. This design is useful to isolate possible elements or economic institutions that can facilitate selecting the cooperative equilibrium through community enforcement. In particular, it allows studying if and how subjects use peer punishment to complement or to substitute for *informal* sanctioning schemes that rely on future defections. A main finding is that costly peer punishment significantly promotes cooperation and efficiency. Personal punishment seems to boost cooperation only in small part by deterring defections and in large part by avoiding that cooperators switch to defection after punishing. This finding is interesting as the literature emphasizes the former aspect, though recent studies on peer punishment find support for the latter aspect, even in finitely repeated interaction (Casari and Luini, 2009).

Camera *et al.* (2012) identify the individual strategies employed by subjects and Bigoni *et al.* (forthcoming) extend such an analysis to a non-standard subject pool comprising clerical workers at a large US university. These workers were mostly long-time local residents, and exhibited a wide variation in age and educational backgrounds. This paper reports substantial differences between subject pools both in aggregate and individual behavior and both in the design with and without the personal punishment opportunity. Students exhibit higher levels of aggregate cooperation than workers, and are more inclined than workers to sanction defections through decentralized punishment and personal punishment, when available. Students and workers, however, adopt 'always defect' less frequently, when personal punishment is available.[1]

3.2 *Monetary Exchange*

Money is an institution that can help participants in markets with frictions to achieve better outcomes. There exist a handful of experimental studies involving the possibility to carry out monetary exchange in decentralized markets. In some experimental economies, money by design crowds-out consumption and *must* be used to avoid inefficient outcomes (e.g. Duffy and Ochs, 1999, 2002), while in others this is not so (Camera and Casari, 2010). Another key design difference is between commodity money, which is when money has redemption or utility value (Brown, 1996; Duffy and Ochs, 1999; Camera *et al.*, 2003), and fiat money, which is an intrinsically worthless object (Mc Cabe, 1989; Duffy and Ochs, 2002; Deck *et al.* (2006); Camera and Casari, 2010; Duffy and Puzzello, 2011).

Some experiments have compared the relative efficiency of money versus barter in models with 'double coincidence of wants' where subjects earn payoffs only if they barter or trade. By design, in these experiments subjects face complex storage problems involving multiple goods and money must be used to expand the efficiency frontier. In particular, Brown (1996) and Duffy and Ochs (1999) present a test of the commodity money, random matching model of Kiyotaki and Wright (1989). In a subsequent experiment, Duffy and Ochs (2002) study also fiat money with and without storage cost. In these economies, money could not be ignored because it could not be discarded; money was frequently held by agents when they also had the option of holding a good with a higher storage cost. Money tended to be held when it had a lower storage cost, even if this was not optimal.

Camera and Casari (2010) propose a novel experimental framework to study fiat money, based on a gift-giving or helping game nested in a random matching model. In every encounter one subject has a good that can be either consumed or given to her opponent who values it more. Social efficiency requires that everyone with a good transfers it to others; this outcome can be sustained through a social norm based on community enforcement of defections, which completely ignores money. Indeed, by design, monetary trade *cannot* sustain full cooperation. This set-up eliminates the need to barter or trade to earn high payoffs; in this manner, subjects can focus on the inter-temporal dimension of cooperation, which is central to the theory of money. By lifting the bias toward employing money to achieve efficiency, this design allows studying why a monetary system emerges, as opposed to simply describing what money does in the experiment. Intrinsically worthless tokens acquired value in the experiment. Their presence increased predictability of play and promoted trust that cooperation would be reciprocated when strangers could trade help for a token. In a subsequent study, Duffy and Puzzello (2011) add a centralized market to a gift giving game in order to test the theory in Aliprantis *et al.* (2007), where monetary trade can sustain social efficiency. The study shows that, under a certain pricing rule, monetary fosters allocative efficiency.

3.3 *Communication*

There exists a considerable experimental literature that has explored the role of cheap-talk as a tool to signal intentions. Here, we review some recent experiments about communication that involve either coordination games or social dilemmas, focusing on how communication can promote the emergence of social norms of cooperation *when subjects do not know the reputation of others*.[2] In particular, we will focus on two distinct issues, which are the ones dominating the recent literature: how communication can help to solve *coordination* problems, and how it can behaviorally discourage *opportunism* to improve outcomes in social dilemmas (e.g. Ostrom, 2010; Strassmair and Sutter, 2009). Most studies with communication adopted a partner setting and found that communication generally increased cooperation in a voluntary contributions game (Dawes *et al.*, 1977; Marwell and Ames, 1981; Isaac and Walker, 1988; Ostrom *et al.*, 1992).

Cason and Mui (2010) study a collective resistance game among three players, with finite and indefinite repetition. A leader may 'transgress' against one or both of two responders, who then may coordinate their individual responses through structured communication. They consider both three- and nine-subject economies with random matching. Adding communication facilitates coordination and always increases the chance of achieving the efficient outcome.[3]

Cooper and Kuhn (2011) look at collusion in two-period Bertrand duopoly games, with structured or free-form messages. In the first period the two subjects can send structured messages to each other before playing a social dilemma. In the second period, they play a coordination game. This second period is interpreted as the reduced-form of a continuation game with an infinite horizon. Structured communication does not raise cooperation but free-form communication does. They put forward three reasons for this effect of free-form communication: subjects (i) formulate explicit threats to punish cheating, (ii) exchange promises to cooperate, and (iii) invoke the mutual benefit of cooperation. Additionally, Cooper and Kuhn (2011) study the impact of renegotiation, by comparing economies with communication in both periods as opposed only to the first. Theory suggests that the possibility to renegotiate lowers the initial incentives to collude. Contrary to this prediction, cooperation is higher when communication occurs in both periods.[4]

Finally, Camera *et al.* (forthcoming) randomly divided a group of strangers into pairs to play a prisoners' dilemma, as in Camera and Casari (2009). Cooperation did not increase when subjects could send public messages amounting to binding promises of future play.

4. Communication in Markets with Frictions: A New Experimental Approach

Here we propose a new experiment on communication among strangers where subjects can send a *public* message to the entire economy (not a private message to their opponent). Three elements characterize this study. First, cooperation is part of equilibrium, unlike other communication experiments, such as the finitely repeated public goods game in Wilson and Sell (1997) where only defection is consistent with Nash equilibrium. Due to indefinite repetition, instead, our design admits multiple equilibria, ranging from full defection to full cooperation. This raises the issue of coordination *along with* the issue of opportunism. In coordination games there is no incentive to misrepresent intentions, even when there is conflict of interest (e.g. battle of the sexes). Here, by contrast, communication can be used in opposing ways: as a coordination device, for those who are motivated by long-run efficiency, and as a tool for deception, for those tempted by short-run gains.

Second, we compare the effects of free-form and structured communication, which does not allow conveying individual histories, strategies, approval or disapproval. Structured messages are not necessarily credible (see the discussion in Farrell and Rabin, 1996), self-signaling or self-committing; on the contrary, they can be outright deceptive. A contribution of this study is to quantify the incidence of deception by an appropriate design of structured communication. Third, we consider a market with frictions as interactions are anonymous and decentralized.

Table 1. Treatments and Sessions.

	No-communication		Messages		Multiple Messages		Chat
Communication frequency	n/a		Every period		Every 4 periods		Every 4 periods
Message space	n/a		Y, Z, not sure		Y, Z, not sure (4 iterations)		Free-form text
Session dates	27.4.05	1.9.05	15.2.07	28.4.10	19.2.07 23.4.10		23.2.07
No. of periods	129	125	109	42	35	39	159

Notes: Exchange rate: $.13 for every 10 points. The sessions run on 27.4.05 and 1.9.05 are also analyzed in Camera and Casari (2009).

4.1 *Experimental Design*

We ran experiments under four anonymous communication formats: *No-communication, Messages, Multiple Messages,* and *Chat* (Table 1). The stage game is a prisoner's dilemma where a subject choose between Y (*cooperate*) and Z (*defect*). Individual payoffs are 25 points under mutual cooperation, 10 under mutual defection, 5 or 30 under discordant choices. An experimental session involved twenty subjects who interacted in economies of four subjects.[5] Each subject participated in five supergames,[6] where a supergame could comprise many periods. In each period subjects were randomly matched in pairs within their economy. Subjects could observe all past actions taken in their economy but could not see individual histories (= public monitoring), i.e. monitoring was anonymous. Subjects could identify neither their current nor past opponents. Hence, subjects could not use strategies based on reputation.

A supergame consists of an indefinite sequence of periods where the continuation probability is $\delta = 0.95$, which enables to sustain the efficient outcome as a sequential equilibrium (for all $\delta > 0.25$). This rule induces an expected duration of a supergame of 20 periods.

In three treatments, subjects could communicate at the beginning and then also during the supergame. Communication was free-form in the *Chat* treatment, structured in all other treatments.

4.1.1 *Messages Treatment*

In every period subjects had the opportunity at no cost to suggest a play (Y, Z, not sure), by making a message public in their economy. A message included three parts: a suggestion (Y, Z, not sure) for the subject herself, for her anonymous match, and for everyone else.[7] The default message 'not sure' appeared as a blank space, and could also be sent by clicking a 'No Suggestion' button. We refer to it as a *neutral* message, to which different subjects could attach a different meaning, and refer to Y and Z as *explicit* messages. When choosing their action, subjects could see everyone's messages, but were unable to identify the sender of the message.

4.1.2 *Multiple Messages Treatment*

Subjects entered a pre-play communication stage at the start of period one, and then every four periods. The communication stage comprised four steps. In step one, subjects sent a message as described in the *Messages* treatment. Then, subjects saw all messages sent in the economy, and had the opportunity to revise their step-one message. Steps three and four followed the same procedure. This protocol gave subjects the same (expected) number of opportunities for communication as in the *Messages* treatment and could help them to achieve a consensus and so facilitate coordination on play.

4.1.3 *Chat Treatment*

Subjects entered the pre-play communication stage at the start of period one, and then every four periods. Communication was free-form and took place through a chat box that remained open for 2 minutes.[8] The procedure aimed at avoiding direct identification of subjects during the communication stage.

Introducing communication does not remove the equilibrium multiplicity of the baseline game. Subjects can simply choose to ignore messages. Due to public monitoring, the possibility to send messages does not increase the speed with which a defection can be communicated to others. However, public messages can facilitate a reversion to cooperation after a defection.

4.2 *Four Results*

Result 1: Structured communication did not significantly raise cooperation relative to No-communication. In contrast, free-form communication supports almost full cooperation.

The level of cooperation in an economy is the fraction of Y actions in that economy. Instead, the level of coordination on cooperation in an economy is the fraction of periods in which all subjects in that economy cooperated. These measures of cooperation are reported in Figure 1, for the four treatments. A Kruskal–Wallis test does not reject the null hypothesis that

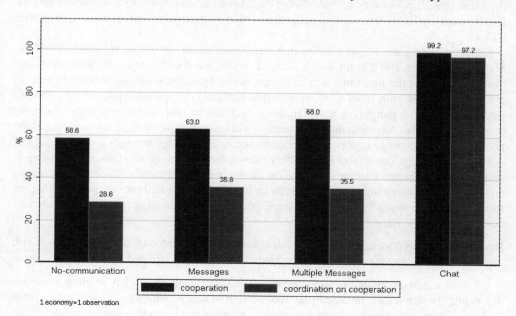

Figure 1. Cooperation Rates by Treatment.

observations from the *No-communication*, *Messages*, and *Multiple Messages* are drawn from the same population with respect to average cooperation rates in all periods (p-value > 0.1, n = 150). This result is confirmed by pairwise comparisons with the *No Communication* treatment (Mann–Whitney tests, n1 = n2 = 50, p-value > 0.10).[9] Similarly, we fail to find evidence that structured communication significantly increases the level of *coordination on cooperation* with respect to the *No Communication* treatment (35.7% vs. 28.6%, Kruskal–Wallis test on three treatments, n = 150, p-value > 0.1; Mann–Whitney pairwise tests, n1 = n2 = 50, p-value > 0.10).

More evidence comes from measuring cooperation through linear regressions, which fail to find evidence that structured communication increases cooperation relative to *No-communication*. Cooperation rates at the economy level are regressed against treatment dummies and other variables for supergames, and duration of previous supergames (see Supplementary Materials).[10]

By contrast, the *Chat* treatment exhibits average cooperation rates more than 30 percentage points higher than all other treatments; this difference is significant (Kruskal–Wallis test on the four treatments, n = 175, p-value < 0.01; pairwise Mann–Whitney, n1 = 25, n2 = 50, p-value < 0.01). An independent coder analyzed the chat messages to assess whether subjects communicated contingent strategies. In every economy subjects discussed a plan of action directed toward achieving cooperation. However, only in 40% of the economies subjects discussed a possible punishment strategy to be implemented in the event of a deviation from the plan of action. This suggests that communicating contingent strategies is not essential to achieve 100% cooperation.

Result 2: The possibility of renegotiation did not significantly reduce initial cooperation.

Periodic opportunities to communicate can facilitate re-coordination on cooperation after defections. Such possibility to 'renegotiate' weakens the credibility of punishment threats. Hence, theory predicts lower initial cooperation rates in treatments with communication than without.

Cooperation in period 1 was 70.5% in *No-communication*, 78.0% in *Messages*, 76.5% in *Multiple Messages*, 100.0% in *Chat*. A Kruskal–Wallis test does not reject the hypothesis that observations from the first three treatments are drawn from the same distribution (n = 150, p-value > 0.10). Results from a linear regression explaining cooperation rates at the economy level in period 1 highlights a non-significant increase in both treatments with structured communication (see Supplementary Materials). This does not support the conjecture that the possibility to renegotiate lowers initial cooperation rates. Result 2 answers a methodological question raised in Cooper and Kuhn (2011) about the possibility of studying collusion in finitely repeated games to draw inference on infinitely repeated games. Some of their results on the effects of communication still hold in an indefinitely repeated setting. In particular, we confirm that the possibility of renegotiation is not detrimental to cooperation, as opposed to a no-communication setting.[11]

Result 3: Structured messages signaled intentions: subjects tended to act in accordance with their own public messages. Moreover, subjects' choices were affected by others' messages.

Subjects seized on communication opportunities when available, widely sending messages that explicitly stated their intended play (66–88% of instances with a message Y or Z, Table 2). In particular, with structured communication, subjects rarely made statements of defection (5.1%, 154/3020 for *Messages*, 20/440 for *Multiple Messages*, Table 2).

Table 2. Communication as a Signal of Intentions.

Subject's message about her intended play	Cooperation frequency	Cooperation frequency conditional on the messages sent by others	
		Zero, one, or two Y messages	Three Y messages
Messages			
Not sure	0.449	0.401 (800)	0.620 (221)
Y (cooperation)	0.641	0.577 (1273)	0.783 (572)
Z (defection)	0.071	0.058 (120)	0.118 (34)
Total	0.547	0.484 (2193)	0.712 (827)
Multiple Messages			
Not sure	0.547	0.524 (21)	0.563 (32)
Y (cooperation)	0.752	0.730 (159)	0.769 (208)
Z (defection)	0.150	0.125 (8)	0.167 (12)
Total	0.700	0.681 (188)	0.714 (252)

Notes: Table 2 only considers (i) messages sent by the subject about her intended play and (ii) the concordance between the message and the action immediately following the message. The number of observations is reported in parenthesis.

In all treatments, there is coherence at the individual level between the statements made public and choices subsequently taken. In the *Messages* treatment, while a subject who publicly signaled her intention to cooperate (message 'Y') did cooperate in 64.1% of periods immediately following communication, a subject who signaled defection (message 'Z') cooperated only in 7.1% of cases (Table 2). In the *Multiple Messages* treatment there is an even stronger coherence between messages sent and subsequent choices. As a consequence, subjects could rely on public statements made by others about their intended play to forecast behavior in the economy. Our data show that actions are a function of the type of messages seen.

A subject cooperated more frequently the greater was the number of cooperative messages observed. For example, in the *Messages* treatment, those who sent a neutral message ('not sure') cooperated in 62.0% of cases when everyone else sent a cooperation message and 40.1% otherwise (Table 2). Subjects who sent a neutral message cooperated less than the economy's average. We say that a message is *informative* if it is positively or negatively correlated with a specific action.

Linear regressions confirm that, in the *Message* and *Multiple Messages* treatments, the greater is the number of cooperative messages observed, the higher is the cooperation rate for the representative subject (see Supplementary Materials). This finding supports the interpretation that sending a message of cooperation was perceived as signaling truthfully the intention of the sender.

Result 4: Subjects used structured communication for two opposite goals: either to coordinate on cooperation or to capture short-run rents through deception.

Because in the experiment messages were informative, they shaped beliefs. From Result 3, one can conjecture that the more cooperative messages were made public, the stronger was the belief that a social norm of cooperation could be supported. This means that subjects could make several uses of communication. The socially desirable, or benevolent, use is to help coordination on cooperation by reinforcing the belief that the sender of a cooperative message will cooperate. However, there is also a socially undesirable use of communication. Subjects could behave deceptively by sending a cooperative message to reinforce the belief in a cooperative outcome while intending to defect.

The data provide evidence on these conflicting uses of public messages. Based on the messages sent and observed, we can quantify a lower bound for the incidence of deceptive and benevolent use of communication. For this purpose, we define two types of subjects. A *deceptive subject* is someone who, at least once during the supergame, signaled her intention to cooperate, observed that everyone else also shared a similar intention, and defected the period immediately following such communication. A *benevolent subject* either cooperated in all those periods of a supergame when all other subjects signaled the intention to cooperate; or cooperated in all periods of a supergame when she signaled a cooperative intention. Clearly, not all subjects fit either type because either behaved differently or never faced a situation in which they could behave deceptively or benevolently.[12]

The prevalent use of communication in all treatments is benevolent. In the *Messages* treatment 41.9% of subjects were deceptive and 49.5% were benevolent when given the opportunity (number of observations 52/124, 95/192, respectively); in the *Multiple Message* treatment 27.7% were deceptive and 68.0% were benevolent (31/112, 134/197). This finding suggests that what prevented structured communication from facilitating the implementation of a social norm of cooperation is not entirely explained by limitations in the message space. As we have seen messages are empirically informative and not necessarily theoretically credible. The crux of the matter is that there were subjects who made a deceptive use of communication. Deception diluted the meaningfulness of the public messages of cooperation, and reduced the value of making public the intention to cooperate.

Finally, signaling intentions through structured communication did not have positive impact on profits in the economy. We regress the average profit in each economy on the average number of public statements that were explicit about the sender's intended play (Y or Z messages 'for oneself'), controlling for supergame order and length. None of these coefficients is significant in the *Messages* and *Multiple Messages* treatments (see Supplementary Materials).

5. Discussion and Conclusions

This paper has surveyed recent experiments on a segment of the economics literature about decentralized markets with frictions; specifically, models characterized by random, pairwise interactions taking place over an indefinite time horizon. Our review of the literature indicates how experiments can fruitfully investigate the effects of frictions and the impact of institutions – such as money, peer punishment, and communication – on the efficiency of the outcomes. We have then presented results from a new experiment on the effects of free-form and structured communication in the random matching model of social dilemmas in Camera and Casari (2009).

The focus on pre-play communication in this paper is motivated by the observation that the experimental literature has identified cheap talk as an institution that promotes social efficiency even when the socially efficient outcome is not a Nash equilibrium. One would thus expect cheap-talk to have a similar or even more beneficial impact in settings where the socially efficient outcome *is* a theoretical equilibrium, albeit one that is empirically infrequently observed.

The new experiment discussed here introduced free-form and structured communication consisting of anonymous public messages. We find that some types of communication did not help cooperation *even if the efficient outcome was an equilibrium*. This result is novel and can be ascribed to the conflicting short and long-run incentives confronting subjects. The design allows us to assess the impact of different roles of public statements: for coordination on efficient play and for deception (= falsely signaling intentions). Deceptive and benevolent uses of communication coexisted, with the prevalent use of communication being benevolent. The presence of deception destroyed trust among those participants who used communication to coordinate on cooperation and maximize long-run gains. In a way, deceptive communication diluted the effectiveness of making public cooperative statements as a way to coordinate on efficient Nash play.

Our findings for structured communication mirror some of the results obtained in finitely repeated social dilemmas, where cheap-talk can have no impact or even a negative impact on social welfare. This suggests that the same behavioral mechanism tied to communication in finitely repeated games – where defection is the unique equilibrium – is also present when the game is indefinitely repeated, so that cooperation *is* also an equilibrium. In a way, it is surprising that the behavioral impact of structured communication is unaffected by the change in equilibrium set, especially because of the associated introduction of a non-trivial coordination problem. Only in the chat treatment communication played a positive role. Perhaps the possibility to convey strategies and verbally punish defectors helped the implementation of a norm of cooperation.

To the best of our knowledge, this is the first study that investigates communication in an economy of strangers that lasts indefinitely. It leaves open several questions, such as which elements of communication can promote efficiency with pairwise, random interaction.

Acknowledgements

We thank two anonymous referees and the editors for several helpful suggestions. Financial support for the experiments was provided by Purdue's CIBER. Camera thanks the NSF for research support through the grant CCF-1101627.

Notes

1. It must be noted that there can be also an 'antisocial' use of peer punishment, i.e. a use which goes in a direction opposite to increasing the incentives to adopt strategies that are socially optimal (e.g. see Faillo *et al.*, 2013).
2. For an overview of the effects of communication in experiments, see Sally (1995), Crawford (1998) and Ostrom (2010). Most of the literature on reputation scores and internet auctions is outside the area of interest.
3. Other recent studies on communication are Bochet *et al.* (2006), which studies different forms of communication in a public good game, and Bigoni *et al.* (2012), which studies communication with indefinitely repeated interactions.
4. In that study, cooperative messages should not be credible because only defection is consistent with Nash equilibrium.
5. The sessions were run at Purdue University's VSEEL lab and involved 140 subjects. Average earnings were $24.08 and average session duration was slightly below 3 hours, including instruction reading and a quiz.

6. Subjects were informed that no two participants ever interacted together for more than one supergame. Subjects may have indirectly shared a common past opponent only after the second supergame.

7. We refer to the first part of the message (message sent 'for oneself') as signaling the sender's intention of play; the other parts of the message suggest play to others. The analysis focuses on the first part of the message.

8. We thank John Kagel for having kindly provided the chat program.

9. Unless otherwise stated, in the Result section the unit of observation is an economy in a supergame. The results of the statistical tests in the paper rely on the assumption that all observations are independent. All tests are two-sided.

10. Structured communication brings about an *increase* in the cooperation rate, which is not significant in the *Messages* treatments and only weakly significant in the *Multiple Messages* treatment. The difference in cooperation rates between *No-communication* and *Multiple Messages* is significant according to a probit regression but not according to the above non-parametric test. While in the regression one observation is a single choice by a subject in a period, in the test it is the average choice in an economy. So, the regression gives more weights to longer supergames.

11. Andersson and Wengstrom (2012) also investigate the effects of renegotiation and report that, in a two-stage game, pre-play communication only has a significant impact on subjects' cooperation when no renegotiation is possible.

12. This definition pins down a lower bound for deceptive behavior. For example, someone who sends a cooperative message, then observes two others who sent a cooperative message and one who sent a defection message is not classified as being deceptive even if she defects in the following period. Similarly, we cannot say whether a subject is benevolent if she never sent a cooperative message and she never observed three cooperative messages. Hence, we have fewer than 200 observations per treatment that we can use to classify subjects as deceptive or benevolent type.

References

Akerlof, G.A. (1970) The Market for 'lemons': quality uncertainty and the market mechanism. *Quarterly Journal of Economics* 84(3): 488–500.

Aliprantis, C.D., Camera, G. and Puzzello, D. (2006) Matching and anonymity. *Economic Theory* 29(2): 415–432.

Aliprantis, C.D., Camera, G. and Puzzello, D. (2007) Contagion equilibria in a monetary model. *Econometrica* 75(1): 277–282.

Andersson, O. and Wengstrom, E. (2012) Credible communication and cooperation: experimental evidence from multi-stage Games. *Journal of Economic Behavior & Organization* 81(1): 207–219.

Angelova, V., Bruttel, L.V., Guth, W. and Kameke, U. Can subgame perfect equilibrium threats foster cooperation? An experimental test of finite-horizon folk theorems. *Economic Inquiry*, Forthcoming.

Aoyagi, M. and Fréchette, G. (2009) Collusion as public monitoring becomes noisy: experimental evidence. *Journal of Economic Theory* 144(3): 1135–1165.

Benoit, J.P. and Krishna, V. (1985) Finitely repeated games. *Econometrica* 53(4): 905–922.

Bigoni, M., Fridolfsson, S.O., Le Coq, C. and Spagnolo, G. (2012) Fines, leniency and rewards in antitrust: an experiment. CEPR Discussion Paper No. DP7417.

Bigoni, M., Camera, G. and Casari, M. (forthcoming). Strategies of cooperation and punishment among students and clerical workers. *Journal of Economic Behavior and Organization*.

Bochet, O., Page, T. and Putterman, L. (2006) Communication and punishment in voluntary contribution experiments. *Journal of Economic Behavior & Organization* 60(1): 11–26.

Brown, P.M. (1996) Experimental evidence on money as a medium of exchange. *Journal of Economic Dynamics and Control* 20(4): 583–600.

Cabral, L., Ozbay, E. and Schotter, A. (2012) Intrinsic and instrumental reciprocity: an experimental study. Unpublished manuscript, New York University.

Calvo, G.A. (1983) Staggered prices in a utility-maximizing framework. *Journal of Monetary Economics* 12(3): 383–398.

Camera, G. and Casari, M. (2009) Cooperation among strangers under the shadow of the future. *American Economic Review* 99(3): 979–1005.

Camera, G. and Casari, M. (2010) The coordination value of monetary exchange: experimental evidence, Krannert Working Paper # 1239, Purdue University.

Camera, G., Casari, M. and Bigoni, M. (2012). Cooperative strategies in groups of strangers: an experiment. *Games and Economic Behavior* 75(2): 570–586.

Camera, G., Casari, M. and Bigoni, M. Binding promises and cooperation among strangers. *Economics Letters*, forthcoming.

Camera, G., Noussair, C. and Tucker, S. (2003) Rate-of-return dominance and efficiency in an experimental economy. *Economic Theory* 22(3): 629–660.

Casari, M. (2007) Emergence of endogenous legal institutions: property rights and community governance in the Italian Alps. *Journal of Economic History* 67(1): 191–226.

Casari, M. and Luini, L. (2009). Cooperation under alternative punishment institutions: an experiment. *Journal of Economic Behavior & Organization* 71(2): 273–282.

Cason, T.N. and Mui, V.-L. (2010) Coordinating resistance through communication and repeated interaction. Unpublished manuscript, Monash University.

Chaudhuri, A. (2011) Sustaining cooperation in laboratory public goods experiments: a selective survey of the literature. *Experimental Economics* 14(1): 47–83.

Cooper, D.J. and Kuhn, K.-U. (2011) Communication, renegotiation, and the scope for collusion. Unpublished manuscript, Florida State University.

Crawford, V. (1998) A survey of experiments on communication via cheap talk. *Journal of Economic Theory* 78(2): 286–298.

Dal Bó, P. (2005) Cooperation under the shadow of the future: experimental evidence from infinitely repeated games. *American Economic Review* 95(5): 1591–1604.

Davis, D.A.I. and Korenok, O. (2011) A simple approach for organizing behavior and explaining cooperation in repeated games. Unpublished manuscript, Virginia Commonwealth University.

Dawes, R.M., McTavish, J. and Shaklee, H. (1977) Behavior, communication, and assumptions about other people's behavior in a commons dilemma situation. *Journal of Personality and Social Psychology* 35(1): 1–11.

Deck, C.A., McCabe, K.A. and Porter, D.P. (2006) Why stable fiat money hyperinflates: evidence from an experimental economy. *Journal of Economic Behavior and Organization* 61(3): 471–486.

Diamond, P.A. (1982) Aggregate demand management in search equilibrium. *Journal of Political Economy* 90(5): 881–894.

Dixit, A. (2003) On modes of economic governance. *Econometrica* 71(2): 449–481.

Dreber, A., Rand, D.G., Fudenberg, D. and Nowak, M.A. (2008) Winners don't punish. *Nature* 452: 348–351.

Duffie, D. and Garleanu, N. and Pedersen, L.H. (2005) Over-the-counter markets. *Econometrica* 73: 1815–1847.

Duffy, J. and Ochs, J. (1999) Emergence of money as a medium of exchange: an experimental study. *American Economic Review* 89(4): 847–877.

Duffy, J. and Ochs, J. (2002) Intrinsically worthless objects as media of exchange: experimental evidence. *International Economic Review* 43: 637–673.

Duffy, J. and Ochs, J. (2009) Cooperative behavior and the frequency of social interaction. *Games and Economic Behavior* 66: 785–812.

Duffy, J., Xie, H. and Lee, Y. (forthcoming). Social norms, information and trust among strangers: theory and evidence. *Economic Theory*.

Duffy, J. and Puzzello, D. (2011) Gift exchange versus monetary exchange: experimental evidence. Unpublished manuscript, University of Pittsburgh.

Ellison, G. (1994) Cooperation in the prisoner's dilemma with anonymous random matching. *Review of Economic Studies* 61: 567–588.

Engle-Warnick, J. and Slonim, R.L. (2006) Inferring repeated-game strategies from actions: evidence from trust game experiments. *Economic Theory* 28: 603–632.

Faillo, M., Grieco, D. and Zarri, L. (2013) Legitimate punishment, feedback, and the enforcement of cooperation. *Games and Economic Behavior* 77(1): 271–283.

Farrell, J. and Rabin, M. (1996) Cheap talk. *Journal of Economic Perspectives* 10: 103–118.

Fréchette, G.R., Kagel, J.H. and Lehrer, S.F. (2003) Bargaining in legislatures: an experimental investigation of open versus closed amendment rules. *American Political Science Review* 97(2): 221–232.

Friedman, J.W. (1971) Non-cooperative equilibrium for supergames. *Review of Economic Studies* 38(113): 1–12.

Gaechter, S., Nosenzo, D., Renner, E. and Sefton, M. (2010) Sequential vs. simultaneous contributions to public goods: experimental evidence. *Journal of Public Economics* 94(7): 515–522.

Gibson C., Ostrom, E. and McKean, M.A. (2000) *People and Forests: Communities, Institutions, and Governance.* M.A. McKean (eds.). Cambridge, MA: MIT Press.

Granovetter, M. (1985) Economic action and social structure: the problem of embeddedness. *American Journal of Sociology* 91(3): 481–510.

Greif, A. (2006) *Institutions and the Path to the Modern Economy: Lessons from Medieval Trade.* New York: Cambridge University Press.

Isaac, R.M. and Walker, J.M. (1988) Communication and free-riding behavior: the voluntary contribution mechanism. *Economic Inquiry* 26(4): 585–608.

Kandori, M. (1992) Social norms and community enforcement. *Review of Economic Studies* 59: 63–80.

Kiyotaki, N. and Wright, R. (1989) On money as a medium of exchange. *Journal of Political Economy* 97(4): 927–954.

Kosfeld, M., Okada, A. and Riedl, A. (2009) Institution formation in public goods games. *American Economic Review* 99(4): 1335–1355.

Marwell, G. and Ames, R.E. (1981) Economists free ride, does anyone else? Experiments on the provision of public goods, IV. *Journal of Public Economics* 15(3): 295–310.

McCabe, K.A. (1989) Fiat money as a store of value in an experimental market. *Journal of Economic Behavior and Organization* 12: 215–231.

Milgrom, P., North, D. and Weingast, B. (1990) The role of institutions in the revival of trade: the law merchant, private judges, and the Champagne fairs. *Economics and Politics* 2: 1–23.

Mortensen, D.T. and Pissarides, C.A. (1994) Job creation and job destruction in the theory of unemployment. *Review of Economic Studies* 61(3): 397–415.

Murnighan, J.K. and Roth, A.E. (1983). Expecting continued play in prisoner's dilemma games: a test of several models. *Journal of Conflict Resolution* 27: 279–300.

Nikiforakis, N. and Normann, H. (2008) A comparative statics analysis of punishment in public-good experiments. *Experimental Economics* 11(4): 358–369.

Normann, H.-T. and Wallace, B. (2012) The impact of the termination rule on cooperation in a prisoner's dilemma experiment. *International Journal of Game Theory* 41(3): 707–718.

North, D.C. (1990) *Institutions, Institutional Change and Economic Performance.* Cambridge: Cambridge University Press.

Ostrom, E. (2010) Beyond markets and states: polycentric governance of complex economic systems. *American Economic Review* 100: 641–672.

Ostrom, E., Walker, J. and Gardner, R. (1992) Covenants with and without a sword: self-governance is possible. *American Political Science Review* 86: 404–417.

Palfrey, T.R. and Rosenthal, H. (1994). Repeated play, cooperation and coordination: an experimental study. *Review of Economic Studies* 61(3): 545–565.

Roth, A.E. and Murnighan, J.K. (1978) Equilibrium behavior and repeated play of the prisoner's dilemma. *Journal of Mathematical Psychology* 17(2): 189–198.

Sally, D. (1995) Conversation and cooperation in social dilemmas: a meta-analysis of experiments from 1958 to 1992. *Rationality and Society* 7(1): 58–92.

Schwartz, S., Young, R. and Zvinakis, K. (2000) Reputation without repeated interaction: a role for public disclosures. *Review of Accounting Studies* 5: 351–375.

Samuelson, P.A. (1958) An exact consumption-loan model of interest with or without the social contrivance of money. *Journal of Political Economy* 66: 467–482.

Seabright, P. (2004) *The Company of Strangers.* Princeton, NJ: Princeton University Press.

Selten, R. and Stoecker, R. (1986) End behavior in sequences of finite prisoner's dilemma supergames. *Journal of Economic Behavior and Organization* 7: 47–70.

Spufford, P. (2003) *Power and profit: the merchant in Medieval Europe*. New York: Thames & Hudson.

Stahl, D. (2009) An experimental test of the efficacy of simple reputation mechanisms to solve social dilemmas. Unpublished manuscript, University of Texas at Austin.

Strassmair, C. and Sutter, M. (2009) Communication, cooperation and collusion in team tournaments – an experimental study. *Games and Economic Behavior* 66: 506–525.

Townsend, R. (1987) Economic organization with limited communication. *American Economic Review* 77: 954–971.

Townsend, R. (1980) Models of money with spatially separated agents. In J. Kareken and N. Wallace (eds.), *Models of Monetary Economies* (pp. 265–303). Minneapolis, MN: Federal Reserve Bank of Minneapolis.

Wilson, R.K. and Sell, J. (1997) Liar, liar . . . cheap talk and reputation in repeated public goods settings. *Journal of Conflict Resolution* 41(5): 695–717.

Wright, J. (2010) Punishment strategies in repeated games: evidence from experimental markets. Unpublished manuscript, University of Singapore.

Supporting Information

Additional Supporting information may be found in the online version of this article at the publisher's website:

Appendix: Instructions for treatment Messages
Table S1: Treatment and communication effects
Table S2: Effect of signaling cooperative intentions on cooperation
Table S3: Structured communication and profits

9

EXPERIMENTAL RESEARCH ON ASSET PRICING

Charles N. Noussair

Tilburg University

Steven Tucker

The University of Waikato

1. Introduction

This paper reviews some of the more extensive and productive lines of experimental research on asset market behavior. The ability of experiments to observe and exogenously control key aspects of a market, such as the information that traders and dealers possess, the fundamental value of the asset, and the microstructure of the market, have attracted numerous researchers to the method. This paper does not purport to be an exhaustive survey, but rather an attempt to concisely distill some of the more influential results, and to illustrate to the nonspecialist reader the diversity of topics that have been pursued. Our choice of topics to cover also reflects an attempt to minimize overlap with two other papers in this special issue that consider closely related topics. The paper by Palan (2013) surveys work that uses and extends a particular paradigm of long-lived asset first studied in Smith *et al.* (1988). The survey of Deck and Porter (2013) considers prediction markets, a special type of contingent claims futures market that is designed with the intention of providing probabilistic predictions about future events.[1]

The scope of the term "*asset market experiments*" has some ambiguity. While no one property always distinguishes an asset from other goods, one of the following two features typically exists in the experimental studies of asset markets that appear in the literature, including those discussed below. The first feature is that asset markets allow opportunities for speculative behavior. That is, the same individual can both purchase and sell, and whether an agent is a buyer or a seller can depend on prevailing market conditions at the moment and her beliefs about future conditions. Speculation can either take place within a market period, or between periods in cases where the assets traded have a life extending over multiple periods. This feature contrasts with markets for perishable goods, with a life of one period, which

---

A Collection of Surveys on Market Experiments, First Edition.
Edited by Charles N. Noussair and Steven Tucker. Chapters © 2014 The Authors.
Book compilation © 2014 John Wiley & Sons, Ltd. Published 2014 by John Wiley & Sons, Ltd.

cannot be resold after they are purchased. The second feature is that asset markets often trade a good that has a value that is not common knowledge at the time that trade takes place. In some studies, traders may have different information about this value than others, and some may have more accurate information than others. These two features generally distinguish asset market paradigms from the experiments surveyed in the other papers in this special issue, with the exception of the two papers mentioned in the first paragraph.

This survey is organized as follows. Section 2 describes the early experimental work in which the basic methodology and baseline findings for later work were established. Section 3 discusses a very productive line of research involving issues related to market microstructure. Section 4 considers parimutual betting markets, a special type of contingent claims market. Section 5 focuses on studies documenting the heterogeneity of the participants in the experiments. Section 6 explores the effects of releasing public information on market activity. Section 7 discusses experimental work relating to the Capital Asset Pricing Model, and section 8 consists of a few concluding remarks.

2. Early Work

Forsythe *et al.* (1982, 1984) and Friedman *et al.* (1984) describe the behavior of experimental markets for assets with a life of two and three periods (a period is defined as a unit of time between two dividend payments).[2] Though these horizons are short, traders do face a situation where they have incentives to arbitrage intertemporally and to form expectations about prices in future periods. After a number of replications of two- or three-period asset markets, prices in the last period converge to approximately the rational expectations equilibrium level. However, convergence is slower and less reliable for period prices, the farther the period in question precedes the final one. The rational expectations equilibrium prices cannot be discovered until the price for the last period stabilizes, and the price discovery process unravels backward. The presence of futures markets aids and accelerates convergence to rational expectations equilibrium (Forsythe *et al.*, 1984; Friedman *et al.*, 1984). The limits of the robustness of these finding are highlighted by Anderson *et al.* (1991) who replicate the Friedman *et al.* experiment with slight changes to the operationalization of the environment. They observe support for the rational expectations equilibrium only when traders are highly experienced.

Markets for longer-lived assets have a strong tendency to generate price bubbles and crashes, prolonged deviations from fundamental values, typically at prices that are greater than fundamentals. A crash is a sudden and rapid fall in prices. This result is originally due to Smith *et al.* (1988), but it has been widely replicated and shown to be robust to numerous modifications of the experimental design. In the original design of Smith *et al.*, markets are created for assets with a life of a finite number of periods (usually 15 or 30 periods). The asset pays a dividend in each period, which (other than in a few sessions where there is a final fixed terminal value for the asset) is the only source of intrinsic value. The dividend payment is identical for all traders and the distribution of dividends is common knowledge to all traders. The time series of transaction prices in markets with this structure does not track the fundamental value, but rather is characterized by price bubbles and crashes. However, as in markets for shorter-lived assets, futures markets lead to closer adherence of spot prices to fundamental values (Noussair and Tucker, 2006). This literature is reviewed in detail by Palan (2013).

In many asset markets, some traders have better information about the value of the asset than others. One function of a market, and indeed the primary purpose of a prediction market, is to reveal this information with the market price. Several early experimental studies indicate that markets have a strong tendency to disseminate private information provided that enough individuals hold the information. For assets that have a life of only one period, and have a common though uncertain value, Plott and Sunder (1982) observe that when insiders who know the true value of the asset are present, prices in continuous double auctions reveal the insider information. This result shows that there exist conditions where it is possible to use a decentralized market to disseminate privately held information. This is consistent with the efficient market hypothesis (Fama, 1970), the notion that any privately held information is revealed in the asset price.

Later studies illustrate the limits of the ability of markets to reveal information as the informational environment becomes more complex and the task the market must accomplish becomes more complex. Plott and Sunder (1988) study the issue of whether markets can aggregate privately held information. They endow insiders with a portion of the information needed to determine the true value of the asset. Only the aggregation of all the information held by insiders would allow the state of nature, and therefore the fundamental value of the asset, to be deduced with certainty. The results on information aggregation are mixed in this relatively challenging environment. In a setting in which there are markets for contingent claims and dividends differ between agents, prices tend toward the level corresponding to rational expectations. However, when only one security is exchanged, prices do not correctly reflect the available information. Forsythe and Lundholm (1990) show for the same environment, however, that sufficient trader experience, in conjunction with common knowledge of payoffs, enables the market to reliably aggregate and reveal the inside information.

Copeland and Friedman (1987, 1991) consider the effect of sequential, in contrast to simultaneous, information arrival in a double auction market for an asset with different values in different states. They consider both a homogeneous setting in which one random event determines whether the state is good or bad from all types, and another, heterogeneous environment, in which different events determine the payoffs for different individuals. Copeland and Friedman (1987) find that models postulating strong-form efficiency are more accurate predictors of prices than some alternatives, that is, semistrong, ordinary rational expectations, private information, and clairvoyant rational expectations models. They also find that sequential information arrival is less conducive to accurate pricing than simultaneous arrival. They confirm that models that assume rational expectations outperform models that assume that private information is not reflected in prices. Copeland and Friedman (1991) propose a model of partial information revelation, and show that it outperforms full information revelation models. The model they propose assumes that traders can extract some, but not all, private information from market prices. More precisely, the key assumption is that prices allow agents to infer that the state is one member of a set rather than a single state.

Huber *et al.* (2008) study the value of private information from another aspect. They consider the relationship between information and higher returns, that is, whether individuals with better information about the asset's value earn more than those with less precise information. They study three settings. One is a call market, in which the intrinsic value of the asset in each period is determined by 10 random draws from a binary distribution. The degree of insider information is varied by having different individuals know differing numbers of draw outcomes (the least informed knowing 1 draw, the most informed knowing 9 out of the 10 draws). The second treatment is the same except that a double auction trading mechanism is used to trade the asset. The third treatment also has a double auction system, but differs from the second in that the value of the asset is determined by a sequence of dividends determined via a random walk process. The degree of insider information is the number of future dividends known (the least informed knowing one future dividend, the most informed knowing nine future dividends with a total market length of 30 periods). The information is cumulative so that there is an ordering of agents with respect to how informed they are. They find that more information is not always better from the point of view of the individual trader. Rather, only those insiders who are much better informed than others can outperform other traders.

Another type of failure of the markets to aggregate information arises when the price behaves as if it is revealing information that is not actually held by any traders. If the presence of insiders is uncertain, market activity can lead to convergence of prices to levels that are consistent with the presence of insiders, even when no insiders actually exist. This occasional failure of markets to reveal the absence of information is termed an information mirage (Camerer and Weigelt, 1991). Individuals may trade on the basis of inferences they make from the market activity they observe, generating prices that appear to reveal insider information that does not actually exist. Camerer and Weigelt usefully distinguish between mirages, which are caused by uncertainty about the information of others, and bubbles, which appear to be caused by uncertainty about the rationality of others.

3. Market Microstructure

The studies above all allowed for direct trade between buyers and sellers of securities. However, many asset markets involve designated market makers who act as intermediaries. The interaction between these market makers and informed as well as uninformed traders has been the subject of a rich theoretical literature, with early seminal contributions by Kyle (1985) and Glosten and Milgrom (1985). The predictions of their models initially motivated a line of experimental work that has continued for the last decade and a half.

Schnitzlein (1996) studies an environment in which there are three types of agents, that is, three market makers, four liquidity traders, and a single insider. The liquidity traders are computerized and trade independently of the asset value, their demand and supply determined according to a Poisson arrival process. The asset value is drawn from an approximate normal distribution, and the actual realized value is known to the insider, but not to market makers. He studies behavior under call and continuous auction trading (a distinct system from the open double auction markets described earlier) mechanisms. Noise traders experience losses, and these losses are greater under the continuous auction. Insiders make more trades under the continuous auction and dealer profits are greater in the continuous auction. The insider trading increases price efficiency, indicating that some information leakage occurs. As a consequence, the continuous auction exhibits greater price efficiency.

Lamoureux and Schnitzlein (1997) study a similar setting in which in some treatments, traders can bypass dealers and trade with each other through a bilateral search mechanism if they so choose. Their markets are also characterized by four liquidity traders, one insider trader, and three dealers. Liquidity traders are required to make net purchases and sales up to a certain level to avoid penalties. The distribution of the asset value is normal. Dealers cannot observe activity in, and may not participate in, the search market. The results show that when traders cannot bypass dealers, dealer profits are high. These dealer profits decrease to very low levels when traders can trade with each other directly. In all treatments, liquidity traders lose money on average and insiders make high profits because their information is very valuable. Market efficiency is similar whether or not there are private two-party trades that take place in the search market.

Theissen (2000), in related work, compares call markets, continuous double auctions, and dealer markets in terms of informational efficiency, in a setting with sequential information arrival. He finds that, while opening prices in the call market are closest to the true value of the asset, the call market underreacts the most to new information. The dealer market demonstrates the lowest price efficiency at the unit of the individual transaction, but is nonetheless very efficient at the level of average period price, as the deviations tend to average out. Thus, from the point of view of choice of market organization, there is a tradeoff between cost of operating the institution and informational efficiency of the resulting prices, since the dealer market is the most informationally efficient, but also has the highest costs.

The question of what disclosure requirements to impose on dealers has also been investigated. Bloomfield and O'Hara (2000) report two experiments in which they consider whether transparent markets are competitive with nontransparent markets. In the first experiment, there are two high-transparency dealers who are required to report their trades, and two low-transparency dealers who are not. In the second experiment, dealers can endogenously select whether or not to be transparent. They advance five hypotheses, based on a dynamic game-theoretic model. These are that in the first period low-transparency dealers are more likely to set the inside spreads than high-transparency types and thus clear more of the order flow while earning lower profits that period. However, after the first period, they earn greater profits and estimate the true value of the security with greater accuracy.

In the experiment, the values of the securities are random over a uniform distribution. In each round, four dealers set bid and ask prices for the securities. Additionally, there are four traders of three different types, that is, one informed trader, one active trader, and two computerized liquidity traders. The results show that low-transparency dealers outperform high-transparency types. They can set prices to make it more likely that they have the inside spread, while high-transparency dealers are constrained by their informational disadvantage. A paradox arises in that all dealers would be better off if they were all transparent, but each individual dealer has an incentive to defect to low transparency. Thus, dealers would collectively benefit from an environment with a regulatory requirement for transparency.

Flood *et al.* (1999) consider pretrade, as distinct from posttrade, transparency. They construct a market in which there are seven competing dealers who trade a single security with informed and liquidity traders. They compare relatively transparent with more opaque markets. In their transparent market setting, all bids and asks are presented on the trading screens of every market maker, and in the opaque treatment, they are not. The market takes place in continuous time, and uses professional security traders rather than a traditional student subject pool. They find that transparent markets have the effect of increasing volume by a factor of three. Search costs have a great impact in the opaque market, and in addition to reducing volume, also lead to dealers making trades at prices that are not the best currently available for them. Dealer spreads narrow to attract informed traders. Dealer spreads are wider in markets without public information than those with such information, but the differences decrease over time. Strikingly, however, markets with no disclosure are more efficient than those with public disclosure, though transparent markets are more liquid.

Krahnen and Weber (2001) consider the effects of market maker competition and adverse selection on market behavior. They compare monopolistic markets, in which there is one specialist per asset, with more competitive organizations. There are informed buyers who receive a noisy signal about the value of the asset. They adapt the design of Plott and Sunder (1988), developed to study information aggregation. Some traders receive private information that one of three possible states is not the true state. While no individual knows the true state, the private information given to all traders would allow an individual with access to all the information to determine the state, and thus the asset's value, with certainty. Within this structure, they compare both monopolistic and competitive market maker regimes to a continuous double auction in which traders conclude trades with each other directly. They also vary how much information market makers have relative to traders. They find that market maker competition reduces the size of the bid-ask spread and increases trade volume. Competitive market makers often lose money, while monopolistic ones earn considerable rents. Inside information on the part of traders translates into greater profits, in particular when market making is competitive.

Schnitzlein (2002) studies an environment where there is uncertainty about the number of insiders in the market. This is a challenging environment for theoretical models to explain. The markets constructed for this experiment are order-driven dealer markets. In both treatments, the probability that any given trader has inside information indicating the true value of the asset is 1/2. In one treatment, the actual number of insiders is made public (ND), and in the other treatment it is not (NI). Schnitzlein finds that insiders behave strategically. In the setting without disclosure, the insiders compete less aggressively than under disclosure. Monopoly insiders delay their trades more under NI than under ND, presumably to conceal their presence, and trade profitably with noise traders. Insider behavior changes as a function of the number of insiders, under ND, but not under NI. Insiders trade off the size of profit opportunities with waiting time: the greater the opportunity, the more quickly they take it. This strategizing is effective and dealers seem to have difficulty telling whether there are insiders and how many there are. A larger number of insiders slows convergence to efficient pricing. Price efficiency is lower when there is uncertainty about the number of insiders than when the number of insiders is public. When the number of insiders is publicly known, they compete aggressively. They thereby tend to reveal their information, and dealers adjust their behavior. Dealers are unable to make such inferences when the number of insiders is not known.

Cason (2000) considers the effect of allowing dealers to communicate with each other. He also studies the consequences of allowing the traders, rather than the dealer, to submit price quotes. As in the other studies in this section, he employs a setting in which trade must go through dealers, some traders are informed, and some others are uninformed. He finds that in the baseline setting in which communication is not possible, bid-ask spreads are small and prices are informationally efficient. When dealers can communicate, they succeed in colluding and realize much greater profits. The resulting prices are uninformative, so there is a large impact on market efficiency. However, even if dealers can communicate, the ability of traders to submit limit orders restores dealer competition and informational efficiency. Allowing traders to initiate orders makes bid-ask spreads tighten to the same level as the case without dealer communication in which dealers submit quotes. Dealers make negative average profits, as the bid-ask spread is not large enough to make up for their losses on transactions with informed traders.

Kirchler et al. (2011) consider the influence of market microstructure on the effectiveness of the imposition of a Tobin tax. A Tobin is a tax on financial market transactions, imposed with the goal of reducing speculation, on the presumption that such speculation increases price volatility. Kirchler et al. consider whether the tax has differential effects on market activity when there are market makers compared to when market makers are absent. Their design, which has currency markets as its motivation, consists of two markets that operate simultaneously. In contrast to the studies described in the rest of this section, the fundamental value process evolves over time and follows a geometric Brownian motion. The Tobin tax is very small, at 0.1% of the transaction value. They find that in a market with no market makers, the imposition of the Tobin tax in one market increases volatility. In a market with market makers, it has the opposite effect. If both markets are taxed, there are no effects of the tax on volatility. Efficiency is similar in all treatments. The Tobin tax reduces trade in the taxed market and increases it in the simultaneously operating untaxed market. Trading volume exhibits a modest and insignificant drop when the tax is introduced in both markets. Tax revenue is greater when there are market makers.

These results are consistent with earlier work of Hanke *et al.* (2010) who find that a Tobin tax reduces volume of trade in the taxed market, shifts some volume to other untaxed markets, and is ineffective at raising revenue if there are alternative untaxed markets. This study also reports that market efficiency in taxed markets is reduced when tax havens exist, and that the tax appears to reduce speculation. A higher tax rate leads to a corresponding increase in tax revenue by roughly the same proportion, but otherwise does not exert an effect any different from a lower tax rate.

DeJong *et al.* (2006) consider the simultaneous operation of an asset and a derivative option market in the presence of an insider. The option has a strike price equal to the expected value of the asset. The option market is open concurrently with a market for the underlying traded asset. Treatments with and without the traded option are compared. Because the stock return is normally distributed, the option value has a skewed distribution. Some traders have inside information about the actual value. The results indicate that the insider trades aggressively in both the stock and the option, leading to feedback effects between the two markets. Price convergence takes place in both markets simultaneously. When the intrinsic value of the option is positive, informational efficiency is higher in the market for the stock, and volatility is lower.

4. Parimutuel Betting Markets

A number of interesting experiments have explored the behavior of parimutuel betting markets. These are markets in which individuals have an opportunity to place bets on one or more outcomes, and the bets determine the betting odds. Once bets are placed, they cannot be revoked. Most of the studies focus on settings in which individuals have private information correlated with the eventual outcome. As in the studies on asymmetric information described earlier, a major focus is on the extent to which this private information is aggregated into market prices, which in these markets are expressed as the odds on each outcome. At the level of individual decision making, a primary focus is to study the conditions under which players will engage in herding and in contrarian behavior.

Herding is defined as betting in disagreement with one's private signal but in favor of the consensus based on prior bets. This is optimal in cases when the informational content of the prior bets weighs in favor of one outcome to a greater degree than one's private signal weighs in the favor of another outcome. However, it can also be incorrect to herd if the information implicit in others' bets does not outweigh the information contained in the private signal for a rational agent. Contrarian behavior involves betting against one's own private information and against the consensus. Contrarian behavior is of special interest because it can generate or accentuate the favorite long-shot bias.

This bias is the tendency for betting odds to overstate the probability of a long shot being the outcome, making it more profitable in expectation for other bettors to bet on a favorite than on a long shot. This is because the market odds reflect contrarian bets and overprice long shots as well as underprice favorites. Along with contrarian behavior, various plausible betting heuristics, such as betting with equal probability on each outcome regardless of payout and perceived winning probability, or betting based on idiosyncratic tastes for the outcome (favorite number, preferred color of horse, acquaintance with jockey, etc . . .), can also accentuate the favorite long-shot bias. A favorite long-shot bias can also arise as a consequence of the transformation of probabilities (Kahneman and Tversky, 1979; Prelec, 1998), risk-seeking preferences, or the presence of utility for beating the odds by betting on a successful long shot.

The source of the favorite long-shot bias has been the specific topic of a number of experimental studies. Piron and Smith (1995) report an experiment that they interpret as supporting the idea that the transformation of probabilities, rather than the existence of utility from beating the odds, is a cause of the favorite long-shot bias. Hurley and McDonough (1995) consider whether the favorite long-shot bias is a result of the fact that the racetrack earns a fraction of the amount bet. They present a model in which, with zero take for the market maker, there is no bias, but a positive take generates a bias. However, their experiment, which compared treatments with markets with and without market maker costs, yielded no difference between the two treatments, and thus their model was not supported. That is, they concluded that the favorite long-shot bias is not driven by costly information and transaction costs.

Drehmann et al. (2005) conduct a large Internet-based field experiment, in which players play a betting game with the structure of a parimutuel betting market. Players endowed with private information are offered, sequentially, one opportunity to place a bet on one of two possible outcomes, or to refrain from betting. The odds, the prices for a bet on each outcome, are updated after each bet so that they reflect the conditional probability of each outcome. Thus, the price equates the expected payoff of betting on each of the two available alternatives based on the public information only. Therefore, it is always optimal to bet in agreement with one's private information. There are a number of treatments that vary the displays that bettors are presented with, whether an option not to bet is available, and whether prices are set assuming the presence of error in the bets of prior bettors. However, all treatments have in common the feature that it is always optimal, in terms of maximizing expected value, to bet on the outcome that is in agreement with one's private signal. Despite this, only two-thirds of decisions are consistent with private signals. There is little herding, but abstention from making a bet, as well as contrarian behavior, is common.

Similar results are obtained by Cipriani and Guarino (2005). They also report an experiment, in which each bettor in a sequence possesses some private information about whether an asset's value is likely to be 0 or 100. They can bet on the outcome, by either buying or selling based on the information they have and (in some treatments) on the history of betting decisions of prior bettors in the sequence. They conduct one treatment in which the price is fixed at 50, and one in which it is flexible, varying according to prior betting activity in a manner analogous to Drehmann et al.'s (2005) experiment. In the flexible price treatment, it is always optimal to bet in favor of one's private signal. Indeed, they find that the flexible price condition leads to a lower incidence of herding than the fixed price treatment. However, they observe a high incidence of abstention from betting as well as of contrarian behavior. The results are similar whether or not the history of preceding bets is provided. In both this study and in Drehmann et al. (2005), contrarian betting impedes the ability of the market to aggregate information.

Koessler et al. (2012) introduce a design feature that greatly reduces the incidence of contrarian behavior. They construct a parimutuel market in which players move in a fixed sequence, as in the last two studies. However, at the time each individual makes a bet, all players must submit a belief assessment about the state. That is, they much assess the probability that each of the two outcomes will be realized. Beliefs are remunerated based on how far they are from the actual outcome, according to a function that ensures that it maximizes expected payoff for an agent to truthfully report his actual belief. Koessler *et al.*'s experiment has three treatments. In the Bet treatment, individuals only submit bets. In the ObsPred treatment, one group of players submits bets, and another group of observers, endowed with private signals and who can observe the history of trades, submits beliefs. In the BetPred treatment, the same players make bets and submit beliefs. When bettors submit beliefs, in BetPred, contrarian behavior decreases sharply compared to the other treatments. Under BetPred, the market also aggregates more information, primarily by reducing contrarian betting, and exhibits a much smaller favorite long-shot bias. Beliefs are also more accurate when bettors, rather than observers, are submitting them. It appears that eliciting beliefs from bettors directs more of their attention to the probability of each outcome eventually being realized. This may cause relatively less weight to be placed on the high payout associated with the long shot in the (unlikely) event that it wins, reducing the tendency to bet on it.

The parimutuel market experiments described above are highly structured in terms of the precise sequencing of bets, and the constraint that each individual can only submit one bet. Such structure facilitates the study of individual decisions and the testing of theoretical models of decision making. In many parimutuel betting markets in the field, however, such specific structure is not present. Rather the market is open-ended, and an individual can place many bets at the timing of her choosing. The laboratory experimental study of open continuous parimutuel betting markets was initiated by Plott *et al.* (2003). In their experiment, they conduct several markets that operated simultaneously. In each market, the experimenter sells contingent claims on a different outcome. Individuals are endowed with some private information about the likelihood of the outcomes and a fixed budget with which they can purchase tickets. While the market is open, any individual can at any time purchase as many tickets he wishes at a fixed price per ticket. All ticket purchases are public information, each market shows the number of tickets it has left for sale, and the odds are posted periodically. Tickets purchased cannot be resold. There are two treatment conditions, "Not Sets," in which individuals' private information would allow them to eliminate some outcomes with certainty, and "PIC," where private information allows updating of probabilities, but not the elimination of any of the possible outcomes. A favorite long-shot bias appears in both settings, though information aggregation is better in Not Sets than in PIC. Strategic behavior, in the form of waiting until late in the period (including the submission of bets just before the market close) and attempts to bluff and mislead early in the market period, are common and appear to accentuate the favorite long-shot bias.

Axelrod *et al.* (2009) modify the Plott *et al.* (2003) design in two ways. They impose a cost of delay, to encourage earlier betting, with the goal of reducing early-period strategic waiting and bluffing. This is done by increasing the price of each bet at a constant rate over the course of the market period. They also divide the period into two rounds of betting, and after the first round, the current interim odds are posted. The authors find that the process of information aggregation is more rapid with these modifications. The favorite long-shot bias is present in the first round, but largely disappears in the second round, suggesting that it is a disequilibrium phenomenon, that is, a transitory pattern that fades away if the process of market clearing is permitted to continue unimpeded.

Roust and Plott (2005) propose and test a further enhancement of this system. In their betting markets, there are two stages. In the first stage, players can buy contingent claims on each outcome with fixed budgets of fiat money (which has no value other than as a means to purchase the claims). Prices are constant over the course of this stage. Because the money has no other use, there is an incentive for individuals to spend all their budgets, and this likely reduces informational size of each subject. The number of claims purchased is not disclosed until the stage ends, so there is no incentive to bluff and mislead within stage 1. The second stage of the market is a parimutuel betting market with regularly increasing prices over time, as in Axelrod *et al.* (2009). This two-stage system reduces the incidence of bubbles and information mirages relative to, and achieves better values of measures of information aggregation than, the systems studied by Plott *et al.* (2003) and Axelrod *et al.* (2009).

5. Participant Characteristics

5.1 *Behavioral Traits*

The behavior of markets is influenced by the characteristics of traders. One of the factors that has been associated with asset mispricing in the field is trader overconfidence. Deaves *et al.* (2009) consider the role of overconfidence in price determination in laboratory markets. They measure three types of decision biases related to overconfidence in a sample of participants in experimental markets. These are calibration-based overconfidence, the better-than-average effect, and the illusion of control. They find that the measures are only weakly correlated with each other, and that the calibration-based measure is the one that correlates most strongly with the number of trades an individual concludes. Men are not more overconfident than women, but there are cultural differences. Women and men trade the same amount in Canada, but women trade less than men in Germany. In general, overconfidence leads to poorer performance.

Biais *et al.* (2005) consider the relationship between overconfidence, defined as the tendency to overestimate the precision of one's own information, and trading activity. They also look at self-monitoring, which is a form of social awareness, and its connection to trading behavior. They consider the environment of Plott and Sunder (1988) with the addition that they allow short-selling. They conduct both call markets and continuous double auction markets. A confidence interval task is employed to measure miscalibration. They ask participants 10 questions, requiring subjects to provide upper and lower limits for their answer so that there would be a 90% chance that the true numerical value lies between the two limits. They find that the extent of miscalibration is uncorrelated with the IQ of participants. In their markets, prices depart considerably from full information levels. When the true liquidation value is high, the relatively high transaction prices reveal the state. However, when prices seem to indicate a convergence to the value associated with the middle state (the second highest of the three possible liquidation values), the price pattern reflects the true state in only 52% of cases.

In the experimental market, men trade more than women. Miscalibration is correlated with poorer performance in men, but not in women. On the other hand, greater IQ is correlated with higher earnings for women, but not for men. The authors hypothesize that miscalibrated people make the price shoot toward one of the states more quickly, and this leads miscalibrated traders to earn lower profits. Self-monitoring, the awareness of one's own actions, is presumed to be correlated with a better ability to trade, and greater earnings. This is also measured in this study, using survey questions. The authors find that miscalibration does lower trading profits, and self-monitoring improves profits for men, but not for women. The effect appears to mostly be due to miscalibrated and poorly self-monitoring individuals falling into the trap of falsely thinking that prices are in the middle state.

Weber and Camerer (1998) construct an experiment to study the disposition effect. The disposition effect is a tendency, first identified in field data by Shefrin and Statman (1985), for individuals to sell assets that have increased in value more readily than those that have declined in value. Weber and Camerer hypothesize that subjects would sell more shares when the sale price is above the purchase price than when it is below, and that they would sell more when price has increased since the preceding period, than when it has decreased. They further hypothesize that the disposition effect would be smaller when the asset is automatically sold, than when the trader makes a conscious decision to sell, and that trading volume is positively correlated with the size of price changes. The rationale for this last hypothesis is derived from a theory of Andreassen (1988) that a large price change focuses trader attention on the stock, and the fact that the pattern is observed in field data. They support all four hypotheses in an experiment in which there are six asset markets operating simultaneously.

Bossaerts *et al.* (2010) report an experiment in which ambiguity aversion can have a direct measurable impact on market behavior. In their setup, ambiguity aversion has an impact that is distinguishable from that of risk aversion. Ambiguity is created by making the state probabilities (governing the actual value of the asset) unknown. Ambiguity-averse individuals are those who gravitate toward portfolios for which the state probabilities are known. The experiment of Bossaerts *et al.* consists of a sequence of periods in which two assets, stocks and bonds, each with a life of one period, trade. Bonds pay a fixed dividend and stocks have two possible terminal values, depending on the state of the world, which is unknown at the time the market is operating. Short-selling is permitted.[3] There are two endowment configurations, one of which is chosen to make a reversal in the state probability/price ranking relatively likely. Sessions in which probabilities are known are paired with session in which they are unknown.

The market data confirm that ambiguity aversion is widespread. Many individuals refuse to hold an ambiguous portfolio, and there is a great deal of heterogeneity in the level of ambiguity aversion that individuals exhibit. One reason that this is important is that asset prices are typically assumed to reflect aggregate beliefs. If people who are ambiguity-averse do not participate in the market, their beliefs have no influence on prices. A second reason that heterogeneity in ambiguity aversion is important is that inframarginal ambiguity-averse individuals affect the amount of risk held by other agents, even though they have no direct effect on prices themselves.

5.2 *Traders' Emotional States*

Three recent studies explore the role of emotions in generating bubbles in experimental asset markets. All three papers consider markets with the structure of Smith *et al.* (1988), which is discussed in detail in Palan (2013). Andrade *et al.* (2012) induce mood exogenously with film clips before the market opens. Subjects watch video clips that are: (a) exciting and arousing, (b) neutral, (c) fearful, or (d) sad. They find that the high-intensity, exciting video clips are associated with larger bubbles than the other three treatments. The other three are not different from each other.

Lahav and Meer (2010) conduct two treatments, which they call positive and neutral treatment. Like Andrade *et al.*, they induce mood by showing film clips to subjects before the market opens. Positive affect was induced with comedy routines by Jerry Seinfeld, and in the neutral treatment, no clip was shown. They find that the positive treatment is characterized by greater bubbles and higher prices than the neutral treatment. This is the case even though the neutral treatment still bubbled.

Hargreaves-Heap and Zizzo (2011) conduct an experiment in which a bubble market is created and emotions are tracked over the course of the session. They consider the emotions of anger, anxiety, excitement, and joy. Their experiment consists of four conditions in which the participants complete two sequential asset markets. In two of the treatments, the participants rate on a Likert scale from 1 to 7 how intensely they currently feel each of the four emotions at the beginning of each period. In one of these conditions, subject can engage in nonprice chat and in the other they cannot chat. They report that eliciting emotions or the ability to chat does not have an effect on market prices, but they find that the level of excitement reported is positively correlated with price level. They also find that buying assets is linked to excitement and selling assets is connected to anxiety. They do not find a correlation between emotional state and trading profits.

5.3 *Trader Strategies*

Haruvy *et al.* (2012) apply the model of DeLong *et al.* (1990) to describe data from an asset market experiment with the structure of Smith *et al.* (1988). The DeLong *et al.* model postulates three trader types: fundamental value, momentum, and rationally speculating traders. The fundamental value trader makes purchases if prices are below fundamentals and sells if they are above. The momentum trader follows previous trends, purchasing if prices have been increasing in the recent past and selling if prices have been decreasing. The rational speculator anticipates future price movements and purchases (sells) if she expects prices to rise (fall). Haruvy *et al.* (2012) test whether this structure predicts the observed treatment differences in an experiment in which the experimenter purchases and resells units of asset. The model predicts a reshuffling among traders that induces a repurchase to exacerbate bubbles and a share issue of sufficient size to induce prices to track fundamentals. The predictions are strongly supported in the data both at the market and at the individual levels.

Bhojaj *et al.* (2008) consider a setting in which there are both smart-money traders and sentiment traders. The market is conducted under high- and low-share endowment conditions, as well as high- and low-cash endowment conditions. In the first experiment reported in the paper, there is one robot sentiment trader and nine human smart money traders. The sentiment trader purchases a fixed quantity each period at the prevailing market price. The humans have the typical incentives to maximize their total wealth. In early periods, humans tend to front-run the sentiment trader by buying early, but then delay selling off, so that prices exceed fundamental value. Large endowments or tight margin restrictions temper the bubble and crash pattern. The traders from the first experiment also participate in a second experimental series where they are endowed with cash but no asset, so that some traders must hold short positions if any trade is to occur. Here, relaxing margin restrictions increases bubble magnitude, since individuals use the borrowed cash to front-run more. The authors conclude that loose margin restrictions impede convergence to the equilibrium outcomes.

In related work, Bloomfield *et al.* (2009) study whether uninformed traders exhibit distinct patterns of behavior, compared to noise traders. Noise traders are a convenient modeling device that allows dealers to make money to compensate for their losses due to superior information that informed traders have. They have three types of traders in their markets, that is, liquidity, informed, and uninformed. Liquidity traders have a requirement to buy and sell a certain number of units, generated randomly each period. Uniformed traders are the same as liquidity traders except for the transactions requirements. Last, informed traders have perfect information as a group, but individually know the true state plus/minus a random number.

They find that uninformed traders act like contrarian traders, taking positions on the other side of the market than the informed, and therefore lose money. Their willingness to engage in trade increases the volume in the market. They thus effectively serve as noise trader, behaving like noise traders specified in theoretical models. Due to their contrarian bidding strategies, market efficiency is reduced. In this study, a Tobin tax is also considered. In contrast to the work of Hanke *et al.* (2010), the tax is implemented in a market with asymmetric information. Bloomfield *et al.* find that the Tobin tax reduces the trading activity of informed and uninformed types by the same proportion. The tax does not affect market efficiency.

6. Public Information Release

In addition to being able to endow individuals with private information, and studying the endogenous dissemination of the information through trading activity, an experimenter can make information public exogenously and study the impact of the information release. A number of studies have investigated related issues. Gillette *et al.* (1999) study how information release affects prices, transaction volume, and traders' dividend expectations. They consider both markets using double auctions and call market mechanisms. There is a terminal liquidation value for the asset that is common to all units and traders, but is unknown during the time the market is open. Public signals that allow the final value to be estimated with greater precision, are released every third period over the total 15-period horizon. As the information is released, incentivized expectations of the final dividend are elicited. The authors find that information release fails to homogenize expectations. Instead, expectations and prices underreact to the information signals. Average forecasts are unbiased, but are quite heterogeneous. They do tend to reflect an extrapolation of prior trends. This is consistent with data from markets in which prices exhibit bubbles and crashes, in which traders' own price forecasts (Smith *et al.*, 1988; Haruvy *et al.*, 2007) also reflect an anticipation of the continuation of future trends. Prices deviate from fundamentals more than forecasts do, because expectations adjust too slowly. Trading volume is positively correlated with trader heterogeneity.

Kirchler *et al.* (2010) consider the framing of information and its potential effect on asset prices. In their market, the asset fundamental is drawn from a normal distribution. In some treatments, however, subjects are given some additional percentile information about the distribution, with different subjects sometimes receiving different information. In some conditions, this information is positive. This is the case, for example, when the information indicates that there is a 5% chance that the value of the asset would exceed a given amount (this level is considerably greater than the mean value). In contrast, in a negatively framed information release, the information given is a percentage that the asset return would be lower than a certain amount. This information is redundant since it can, in principle, be calculated from the normal distribution that participants already know. Nevertheless, the percentile information affects subjects' decisions and market prices considerably. Positively framed buyers purchase assets, while negatively framed buyers sell them. The data also confirm the disposition effect identified in earlier work. The overall conclusion is that irrelevant information can influence asset prices.

Gneezy *et al.* (2003) consider the effect of the frequency with which information is released and the frequency with which a portfolio can be adjusted. They measure the effect of these variables on the performance of an individual's investment portfolio. The asset traded has a life of one period and can pay a fixed positive dividend in each period with probability 1/3, independently drawn each period. Trading follows double auction rules. There are 15 total periods in the experiment. There are two treatments. In the High-Frequency (H) treatment, traders can adjust their portfolio in each period, and traders are informed at the end of each period about the value of the asset in that period. In the Low-Frequency (L) treatment trading can only take place every third period, and then only in blocks of three units. They find that more information and more flexibility result in less risk taking, and lower prices. Prices are greater than the expected dividend value in all treatments.

Corgnet *et al.* (2012) consider the effect of ambiguous, and sequentially released, information regarding the dividend distribution. Their markets consist of three periods where information was provided at the conclusion of the first and second periods about the asset's dividend that would be determined at the end of the third period. In their control treatment, the distribution of the dividend is made known via public observation of the randomization devices, and thus their associated probabilities. Conversely, in the ambiguous treatment, the dividend distribution is not made known. Rather, ambiguity is created using a process similar to Ellsberg (1961). Differently colored marbles are drawn from an opaque bag and the distribution of colors is not announced. Their results do not support the existence of an ambiguity premium and more surprisingly, the markets with ambiguity exhibit smaller deviations from the asset fundamental value.

7. Studies of the Capital Asset Pricing Model

The standard model relating the return/risk profiles to market prices is the capital asset pricing model (CAPM). Bossaerts and Plott (2004) construct an experimental environment in which the model can be applied. In their setup, there are two risky securities, A and B, as well as one risk-free asset called notes. There are separate markets for each of the three securities. Notes can be sold short, while the other two assets cannot. There are three possible states and no traders have inside information. Trade proceeds according to a process in which agents can submit limit orders at any time the market is open, and the orders are entered in the order book. If a limit order crosses the best limit order on the other side of the market, it is converted to a market order, and a trade is concluded. Both risky securities yield greater expected return than the safe asset, while security A has a greater mean and variance of dividend payment than B. The asset has a life of one period and the environment is repeated under stationary conditions for up to eight periods within the same session. A large number of traders (by experimental standards) participate in each market: usually a number between 30 and 60 individuals.

The authors test three predictions of the CAPM model. The first is that prices would reflect risk premia. The second is that the ranking of state price probabilities would be the inverse of the ranking of aggregate wealth in those states. Under the CPAM model, which assumes quadratic utility, the risk premia are proportional to the covariance between a security's return and the return of the market portfolio. This corresponds to the condition that the portfolio's Sharpe ratio, the ratio of mean return to variance of return, be as great as possible. Thus, the third prediction for the experiment is that the observed Sharpe ratio would be at the greatest feasible level.

The data show substantial risk premia indicating that agents are risk-averse. A session conducted in Bulgaria at very high stakes relative to the outside income of the subject pool yields similar results. The second prediction receives some support from the direction of price movements over time. The third prediction is also consistent with the pattern of convergence. Nonetheless, two sessions yield considerable mispricing. A second treatment, in which the realization of the state is drawn without replacement, reveals that the cause of the mispricing is a belief on the part of some traders that the state probabilities are not independent. Rather, some participants are subject to the gambler's fallacy that realizations that have not occurred for a long time are due to occur. An augmented CAPM model (CAPM $+ \varepsilon$) is proposed (Bossaerts *et al.*, 2007) that reconciles some key features of the data from this line of research. Whether the CAPM, a competitive model that assumes price taking, predicts well in a thinner market is taken up by Bossaerts and Plott (2002). They find that convergence to the CAPM-predicted portfolio holdings and prices is slower in thin than in thicker markets.

Asparouhova *et al.* (2003) consider the dynamics of market adjustment in this type of market. They organize their analysis around five conjectures. The first is that the excess demand for a security is positively correlated to the change in its transaction price. The second is the that there is an absence of indirect effects of complementarity or substitutability between assets, which means that a price change in one of the securities is uncorrelated with price changes in the other two securities. The third is that a Walrasian system of stochastic differential equations can characterize the process of mean reversion to equilibrium pricing. The fourth is that the order book contains information that correlates with the level of excess demand. The fifth is that the order book contains information that correlates with transaction prices, but which cannot be accounted for by excess demand. Asparouhova *et al.* find strong support for the first conjecture, but also observe a negative relationship between excess demand for one security and the transaction price change on the other. Stability conditions are satisfied in the experimental data. The order book does contain information about excess demand conditions.

8. Conclusion

We have reviewed several of the most longstanding lines of research in experimental finance. This survey is not intended to be exhaustive, but rather to provide a sampling of some of the more important developments in the area. While data sets from nonlaboratory financial markets are very extensive and detailed, there remain some key parameters that are unobserved and thus must be estimated. Experimental methods offer a complementary methodology that allows some key underlying determinants of prices, such as fundamental values or insider information, to be observed and varied exogenously. Thus, in our view, experimental studies can complement empirical work, particularly in the area of theory testing and development. We also believe that in the future experimental finance will push into the areas of financial engineering and market regulation.

Notes

1. For surveys of this and other early work in this area, see Sunder (1995) or Duxbury (1995).
2. The continuous double auction trading institution, first subject to laboratory investigation by Smith (1962), allows any individual to trade with any other. Any player wishing to make a purchase or sale may submit an offer to the market, which is then made public. Then, any player may conclude a trade by accepting one of these offers. This system is conducive to price-taking behavior (Smith, 1982).
3. Short-selling, given a sufficiently large capacity to take short positions, tends to reduce price levels (see, for example Haruvy and Noussair, 2006).

References

Andrade, E., Lin, S., and Odean, T. (2012) Bubbling with excitement: an experiment. Working Paper, University of California-Berkeley.

Andreassen, P. (1988) Explaining the price-volume relationship: the difference between price changes and changing prices. *Organizational Behavior and Human Decision Process* 41: 371–389.

Anderson, S., Johnston, D., Walker, J., and Williams, A. (1991) The efficiency of experimental asset markets: empirical robustness and subject sophistication. In R.M. Isaac (ed.), *Research in Experimental Economics* (pp. 107–190). Greenwich, CT: JAI Press.

Asparouhova, E., Bossaerts, P., and Plott, C. (2003) Excess demand and equilibration in multi-security financial markets: the empirical evidence. *Journal of Financial Markets* 6: 1–21.

Axelrod, B.S., Kulick, B.J., Plott, C.R., and Roust, K.A. (2009) The design of improved parimutuel-type information aggregation mechanisms: inaccuracies and the long-shot bias as disequilibrium phenomena. *Journal of Economic Behavior and Organization* 69(2): 170–181.

Bhojaj, S., Bloomfield, R., and Tayler, W. (2008) Margin trading, overpricing, and synchronization risk. *Review of Financial Studies* 22(5): 2059–2085.

Biais, B., Hilton, D., Mazurier, K., and Pouget, S. (2005) Judgmental overconfidence, self-monitoring, and trading performance in an experimental financial market. *Review of Economic Studies* 72: 287–312.

Bloomfield, R. and O'Hara, M. (2000) Can transparent markets survive? *Journal of Financial Economics* 55: 425–459.

Bloomfield, R., O'Hara, M., and Saar, G. (2009) How noise trading affects markets: an experimental study. *Review of Financial Studies* 22(6): 2275–2302.

Bossaerts, P. and Plott, C. (2002) The CAPM in thin financial markets. *Journal of Economic Dynamics and Control* 26: 1093–1112.

Bossaerts, P. and Plott, C. (2004) Basic Principles of asset pricing theory: evidence from large-scale experimental financial markets. *Review of Finance* 8: 135–169.

Bossaerts, P., Plott, C., and Zame, W. (2007) Prices and portfolio choices in financial markets: theory, econometrics, experiments. *Econometrica* 75(4): 993–1038.

Bossaerts, P., Ghiradato, P., Guanaschelli, S., and Zame, W. (2010) Ambiguity in asset markets: theory and evidence. *Review of Financial Studies* 23(4): 1325–1359.

Camerer, C. and Weigelt, K. (1991) Information mirages in experimental asset markets. *Journal of Business* 64: 463–493.

Cason, T. (2000) The opportunity for conspiracy in asset markets organized with dealer intermediaries. *Review of Financial Studies* 13(2): 385–416.

Cipriani, M. and Guarino, A. (2005) Herd behavior in a laboratory financial market. *American Economic Review* 95(5): 1427–1443.

Copeland, T. and Friedman, D. (1987) The effect of sequential information arrival on asset prices: an experimental study. *Journal of Finance* 42(3): 763–797.

Copeland, T. and Friedman, D. (1991) Partial revelation of information in experimental asset markets. *Journal of Finance* 46(1): 265–295.

Corgnet, B., Kujal, P., and Porter, D. (2012) Reaction to public information in markets: how much does ambiguity matter? *The Economic Journal*, doi:10.1111/j.1468-0297.2012.02557.

Deaves, R., Luders, E., and Luo, G. (2009) An experimental test of the impact of overconfidence and gender on trading activity. *Review of Finance* 13: 555–575.

Deck, C. and Porter, D. (2013) Prediction markets in the laboratory. *Journal of Economic Surveys* 27(3): 589–603.

DeJong, C., Koedijk, K., and Schnitzlein, C. (2006) Stock market quality in the presence of a traded option. *Journal of Business* 79(4): 2243–2274.

DeLong, J.B., Shleifer, A., Summers, L., and Waldmann, R. (1990) Positive feedback investment strategies and destabilizing rational speculation. *Journal of Finance* 45(2): 379–395.

Drehmann, M., Oechssler, J., and Roider, A. (2005) Herding and contrarian behavior in financial markets, an Internet experiment. *American Economic Review* 95(5): 1403–1426.

Duxbury, D. (1995) Experimental asset markets within finance. *Journal of Economic Surveys* 9: 331–371.

Ellsberg, D. (1961) Risk, ambiguity, and the savage axioms. *Quarterly Journal of Economics* 75: 643–669.

Fama, E. (1970) Efficient capital markets: a review of theory and empirical work. *Journal of Finance* 25: 383–417.

Flood, M., Huisman, R., Koedijk, K., and Mahieu, R. (1999) Quote disclosure and price discovery in multiple-dealer financial markets. *Review of Financial Studies* 12(1): 37–52.

Forsythe, R. and Lundholm, R. (1990) Information aggregation in an experimental market. *Econometrica* 58(2): 309–340.

Forsythe, R., Palfrey, T., and Plott, C. (1982) Asset valuation in an experimental market. *Econometrica* 50(3): 537–568.

Forsythe, R., Palfrey, T., and Plott, C. (1984) Futures markets and informational efficiency: a laboratory examination. *Journal of Finance* 39: 955–981.

Friedman, D., Harrison, G., and Salmon, J. (1984) The informational efficiency of experimental asset markets. *Journal of Political Economy* 92(3): 349–408.

Gillette, A., Stevens, D., Watts, S., and Williams, A. (1999) Price and volume reactions to public information releases: an experimental approach incorporating traders' subjective beliefs. *Contemporary Accounting Research* 16(3): 437–479.

Glosten, R. and Milgrom, P. (1985) Bid, ask, and transaction prices in a specialist market with heterogeneously informed traders. *Journal of Financial Economics* 14: 71–100.

Gneezy, U., Kapteyn, A., and Potters, J. (2003) Evaluation periods and asset prices in a market experiment. *Journal of Finance* 58(2): 821–837.

Hanke, M., Huber, J., Kirchler, M., and Sutter, M. (2010) The economic consequences of a Tobin tax: an experimental analysis. *Journal of Economic Behavior and Organization* 74: 58–71.

Hargreaves-Heap, S. and Zizzo, D. (2011) Emotions and chat in a financial markets experiment. Working Paper, University of East Anglia.

Haruvy, E., Lahav, Y., and Noussair, C.N. (2007) Traders' expectations in asset markets: experimental evidence. *American Economic Review* 97(5): 1901–1920.

Haruvy, E. and Noussair, C.N. (2006) The effect of short-selling on bubbles and crashes in experimental spot asset markets. *Journal of Finance* 61(3): 1119–1157.

Haruvy, E., Noussair, C.N., and Powell, O. (2012) The impact of asset repurchases and issues in an experimental market. Working Paper, Tilburg University.

Huber, J., Kirchler, M., and Sutter, M. (2008) Is more information always better? Experimental financial markets with cumulative information. *Journal of Economic Behavior and Organization* 65: 86–104.

Hurley, W. and McDonough, L. (1995) A note on the Hayek hypothesis and the favorite-longshot bias in parimutuel betting. *The American Economic Review* 85(4): 949–955.

Kahneman, D. and Tversky, A. (1979) "Prospect theory", an analysis of decision under risk. *Econometrica* 47: 263–291.

Kirchler, E., Maciejovsky, B., and Weber, M. (2010) Framing effects, selective information, and market behavior: an experimental analysis. *Journal of Behavioral Finance* 6(2): 90–100.

Kirchler, M., Huber, J., and Kleinlercher, D. (2011) Market microstructure matters when imposing a Tobin tax – evidence from the lab. *Journal of Economic Behavior and Organization* 80: 586–602.

Koessler, F., Noussair, C., and Ziegelmeyer, A. (2012) Information aggregation and belief elicitation in experimental parimutuel betting markets. *Journal of Economic Behavior and Organization* 83: 195–208.

Krahnen, J.P. and Weber, M. (2001) Marketmaking in the laboratory: does competition matter? *Experimental Economics* 4: 55–85.

Kyle, A. (1985) Continuous auctions and insider trading. *Econometrica* 15: 1315–1335.

Lahav, Y. and Meer, S. (2010) The effect of induced mood on prices in asset prices: experimental evidence. Working Paper, Ben Gurion University of the Negev.

Lamoureux, C. and Schnitzlein, C. (1997) When it's not the only game in town: the effect of bilateral search on the quality of a dealer market. *Journal of Finance* 52(2): 683–712.

Noussair, C.N. and Tucker, S. (2006) Futures markets and bubble formation in experimental asset markets. *Pacific Economic Review* 11(2): 167–184.

Palan, S. (2013) A review of bubbles and crashes in experimental asset markets. *Journal of Economic Surveys* 27(3): 570–588.

Piron, R. and Smith, L. (1995) Testing risk love in an experimental racetrack. *Journal of Economic Behavior and Organization* 27: 465–474.

Plott, C.R. and Sunder, S. (1982) Efficiency of experimental security markets with insider information: an application of rational expectations models. *Journal of Political Economy* 90(4): 663–698.

Plott, C.R. and Sunder, S. (1988) Rational expectations and the aggregation of diverse information in laboratory security markets. *Econometrica* 56: 1085–1118.

Plott, C.R., Wit, J., and Yang, W.C. (2003) Parimutuel betting markets as information aggregation devices: experimental results. *Economic Theory* 22: 311–351.

Prelec, D. (1998) The probability weighting function. *Econometrica* 66: 497–527.

Roust, K. and Plott, C.R. (2005) The design and testing of information aggregation mechanisms: a two-stage pari-mutuel IAM. Working Paper, California Institute of Technology.

Schnitzlein, C. (1996) Call and continuous trading mechanisms under asymmetric information: an experimental investigation. *Journal of Finance* 2: 613–636.

Schnitzlein, C. (2002) Price formation and market quality when the number and presence of insiders in unknown. *Review of Financial Studies* 15(4): 1077–1109.

Shefrin, H. and Statman, M. (1985) The disposition effect to sell winners too early and ride losers too long. *Journal of Finance* 40: 777–790.

Smith, V. (1962) An experimental study of competitive market behavior. *Journal of Political Economy* 70(5): 111–137.

Smith, V. (1982) Microeconomic systems as an experimental science. *American Economic Review* 72(5): 923–955.

Smith, V.L., Suchanek, G., and Williams, A. (1988) Bubbles, crashes, and endogenous expectations in experimental spot asset markets. *Econometrica* 56: 1119–1151.

Sunder, S. (1995) Experimental asset markets: a survey. In J. Kagel and A. Roth (eds.), *The Handbook of Experimental Economics*. Princeton, NJ: Princeton University Press.

Theissen, E, (2000) Market structure, informational efficiency and liquidity: an experimental comparison of auction and dealer markets. *Journal of Financial Markets* 3: 333–363.

Weber, M. and Camerer, C. (1998) The disposition effect in securities trading: an experimental analysis. *Journal of Economic Behavior and Organization* 33: 167–184.

10

A REVIEW OF BUBBLES AND CRASHES IN EXPERIMENTAL ASSET MARKETS

Stefan Palan

Karl-Franzens University Graz
Institute of Banking & Finance

In 1988, Vernon Smith, Gerry Suchanek and Arlington Williams published the results of experiments which would spawn a new twig on the young tree of experimental economic research. Earlier studies had used the double auction design (Smith, 1962), studied intertemporal markets (Forsythe *et al.*, 1982) or investigated securities with homogeneous value to all market participants (Smith, 1965). Yet it was the pioneering work of Smith *et al.* (1988) (hereafter SSW) to combine all of the above. To their surprise, the design they expected to yield informationally efficient prices exhibited large bubbles and crashes. Since then, hundreds of SSW markets have been run, yielding valuable insights into the behavior of economic actors and the factors governing bubbles.

In this paper we collect and aggregate the results from 41 published and 20 working papers.[1] We thereby hope to give readers unfamiliar with this literature a convenient introduction and provide researchers with a reference resource. The study is structured as follows: Section 1 describes the baseline design. Section 2 discusses the results from 25 years of research under this paradigm. Section 3 concludes the paper.

1. Description of the Baseline Market

1.1 *Market Design*

Before discussing deviations from the canonical SSW design,[2] we will define a baseline market which will serve as a reference for the remaining discussion. In a baseline market student subjects buy and sell over fifteen two- to six-minute periods in a single closed book continuous double auction (CDA) market. All subjects have participated in the same number of previous markets of this type. The asset being traded may not be sold short or bought on margin. It pays a random, discretely and uniformly distributed, four-point, positively skewed

A Collection of Surveys on Market Experiments, First Edition.
Edited by Charles N. Noussair and Steven Tucker. Chapters © 2014 The Authors.
Book compilation © 2014 John Wiley & Sons, Ltd. Published 2014 by John Wiley & Sons, Ltd.

dividend with positive expected value after each period and has no terminal value. Its risk-neutral fundamental value declines monotonically, following $V_t = (T - t + 1) \cdot E[d]$ where T is the total number of periods, t is the current period, and d is the dividend per unit of the asset. In each period, the dividend is the same for each unit of the asset and for each subject owning an asset, and dividend income is added to subjects' cash inventories immediately. There are furthermore no explicit transaction costs, no interest on money holdings and no circuit breakers. Subjects' compensation equals their final cash position, linearly converted from experimental to real currency units, plus an optional fixed show-up fee. It is arrived at by starting with subjects' cash endowments, adding dividend income and proceeds from selling units of the asset, and subtracting costs for units of the asset purchased.

1.2 Typical Price and Volume Patterns

Initial price levels in baseline markets with inexperienced subjects covary (positively) with the ratio of total cash to asset value in the market. In many common parameterizations, prices start out below fundamental value (calculated as the sum of expected future dividends), appreciate to it by periods 2 to 4, then go on to form a bubble above it, and finally crash back down to fundamentals in periods 10 to 15. This pattern is depicted in Figure 1. Note that, while individual markets in this literature are generally characterized by large heterogeneity, the majority of baseline markets with inexperienced subjects follow this pattern.

Some authors (e.g. Porter and Smith, 1995; Miller, 2002; Porter and Smith, 2008) have conjectured that prices start out low due to risk-aversion and that when subjects become more

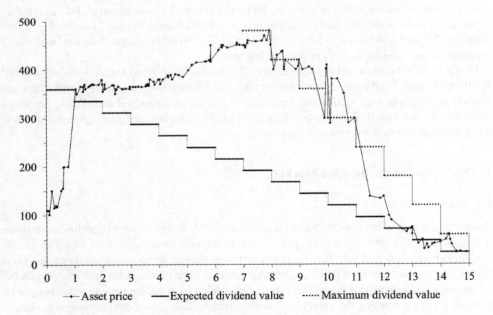

Figure 1. Typical Price Pattern in Baseline Markets with Inexperienced Subjects.
The lower (upper) step-wise decreasing function shows the expected (maximum) dividend return from holding one unit of the asset from the respective period until the end of the experiment.
Source: (Palan, 2010), Exp. 2, Round 1.

familiar with the environment, they become less risk-averse, which leads prices to start to appreciate.[3] The trend of increasing prices this creates at a time of decreasing fundamental values leads some subjects to discount the relevance of the latter and to extrapolate the price trajectory. This ignites the bubble, which flourishes until, near the end, subjects realize that prices far exceed the remaining dividend value. This in turn leads to a contraction of demand, which precipitates the crash.[4]

Unfortunately this intuitively appealing explanation has at least two deficiencies. The first is that prices as low as one-third of fundamental value at the beginning of some markets would imply implausibly high levels of risk-aversion of the (rational) sellers. The second is the unresolved question of why subjects become aware of the mispricing toward the end of a market and not at the moment when prices first start to exceed fundamentals. Part of the explanation may lie in a lack of common knowledge of rationality among the subjects.[5] Note that speculation can be a sufficient motive for even a rational subject to buy at prices greater than fundamental value if she believes there to be another to whom she can resell at even higher prices. For that to be the case, this other subject would have to either be irrational or else believe that there was a third trader to whom he could resell at yet higher prices, and so on.[6] In line with this conjecture, Cheung *et al.* (2012, May) show that inducing common knowledge of rationality leads to markets exhibiting few and small bubbles, while similarly informed and trained subjects produce substantial bubbles and crashes in the absence of common knowledge of rationality. Lei *et al.* (2001) present evidence proving that at least some subjects *do* act irrationally in SSW markets. They observe prices exceeding the maximum possible future dividend earnings in a setting where speculation is impossible. The only explanation for this result is a lack of understanding or irrationality.

Moving from prices to liquidity, the crashes in SSW markets are usually accompanied by comparatively low volume in the period of, and in the period preceding, the crash (cp. SSW, pp. 1132–1133). This reduction in volume coincides with a significant reduction of the number of bids relative to offers in the period(s) preceding the crash. More generally, there is evidence that mean prices are positively related to lagged excess bids. The early efforts of SSW at modeling this have culminated in the momentum model of Caginalp *et al.* (2000a) and Caginalp *et al.* (2000b). More recently, Haruvy and Noussair (2006) and Haruvy *et al.* (2012, November 21) succeeded in recreating the typical price pattern by simulating aggregate market prices using agents acting according to the three trader types of speculators, passive investors and feedback traders proposed by De Long *et al.* (1990). Baghestanian *et al.* (2012, September 14) classify subjects into momentum-noise traders and adaptive fundamental traders. They show that the bubble decreases in the proportion of the latter and observe that the latter also score higher on the cognitive reflection test of Frederick (2005).

2. Stylized Results

2.1 *Trader Characteristics*

The first and most solidly documented finding concerns trader experience, which in this context is defined as a subject having previously participated in a market of the same design as that currently under investigation. Experiments with multiple repetitions of a market show that bubbles shrink with experience, with prices usually largely tracking fundamental value by the third run. Experience has for this reason been considered the only factor which reliably abates bubbles, starting with the work of King (1991). His initial finding, later substantiated in King *et al.* (1993), found further support by van Boening *et al.* (1993) and Dufwenberg *et al.* (2005) (the authors of the latter two papers seem to have been unaware of the results contained in King, 1991). However, it was not until Haruvy *et al.* (2007) that the mechanism through which the elimination of bubbles with experience comes about was made the subject of detailed analysis.

Observation 1. *Sufficient experience with an asset in certain environments eliminates bubbles through the adaptive updating of expectations.*

Support: SSW first note that in their experiments with a mixture of inexperienced and twice experienced subjects, bubbles decrease in the number of twice experienced subjects in the market (SSW, pp. 1134–1135), a result echoed by King (1991), King *et al.* (1993) and van Boening *et al.* (1993). Dufwenberg *et al.* (2005) find that the mispricing in markets where either one or two-thirds of all subjects are thrice experienced is comparable to that in markets with twice experienced subjects only. Finally, Lei and Vesely (2009) show that it is sufficient for subjects to observe and earn dividends from an asset in a pre-market phase for bubbles to be eliminated when these subjects subsequently trade a similar asset in a market setting. On the contrary, Hussam *et al.* (2008) and Xie and Zhang (2012, January) find that bubbles can be rekindled or sustained when the market experiences a shock from increased liquidity, dividend uncertainty and reshuffling, or from the admission of new subjects. This evidence implies that experience is not guaranteed to readily translate between similar but nonetheless different SSW designs.

Haruvy *et al.* (2007) first discovered that the effect of experience stems from a simple process of myopic adaptation of expectations. They show that once experienced subjects seem to play a best response under the assumption that the other subjects do not adjust their behavior from the previous round.[7] The result is a steeper and faster run-up in prices at the beginning of the market, with an earlier crash than in the previous round. Applying such adaptive behavior repeatedly causes the bubble to disappear. Noussair and Powell (2010) present evidence consistent with this finding and underline it with supportive results from econometric analysis. Finally, Oechssler *et al.* (2011) report a rare counterexample where experience is not found to attenuate bubbles.[8] A second experiment observing no noticeable ameliorating effect of experience is Noussair and Powell (2010), who use a non-monotonic fundamental value structure discussed in more detail in Observation 20.

Observation 2. *Experiments with small business men and women, corporate executives and stock market dealers do not produce smaller bubbles. The evidence for non-business and -economics students is mixed.*

Support: Using a sample of professional and business people from the Tucson area, SSW observe a large bubble and no crash. King *et al.* (1993) follow up on this one-off test and experiment with corporate executives and over-the-counter traders, who are also found to produce similar patterns as typical student subjects. While this tentatively supports the generalizability of results obtained from student subjects to other subject pools, caution is in order. Ackert and Church (2001), for example, find that once experienced students majoring in business produce markedly smaller bubbles than once experienced non-business students.

Observation 3. *Trading teams reduce the bubble phenomenon compared to individual traders.*

Support: Instead of individuals, Cheung and Palan (2012) let teams of two trade with each other in SSW markets. They report that trading in teams reduces the extent of bubbles with inexperienced and once experienced subjects and in markets employing a CDA and ones using a sealed-bid/offer call auction (CA). See Charness and Sutter (2012) for a discussion of differences in individual and team behavior in economic contexts.

Observation 4. *Market size does not affect the bubble phenomenon.*

Support: Over the years, markets with widely varying sizes have been conducted. Conventionally, SSW markets are populated by between 6 (e.g. Lei and Vesely, 2009) and 15 (van Boening *et al.*, 1993) traders. However, Williams and Walker (1993) (and Williams, 2008) report results from three eight-week markets populated with 304, 244 and 310 subjects, respectively. Despite this large variation, there is no evidence of a systematic effect of the number of traders on prices.

Observation 5. *Overconfident subjects produce significantly greater bubbles.*

Support: Michailova (2011) shows that markets populated with highly overconfident traders exhibit significantly larger bubbles than ones with less overconfident subjects. She also documents that overconfidence increases from the first to the second half of the 15-period market, confirming results by Kirchler and Maciejovsky (2002). In a similar vein, Oechssler *et al.* (2011) find that the bubble probability increases by 3% for every rank the median subject believes to be better when asked – at the beginning of a market – to rank themselves among 60 subjects with respect to their expected payoffs. They also find sessions with very confident and very unconfident groups to see more trade. Finally, Ackert *et al.* (2012) report on subjects who themselves make probability judgment errors but believe others do not. They interpret this behavior as overconfidence and show that these subjects trade more and earn less than others.

Observation 6. *Subjects' emotional state affects mispricing.*

Support: Hargreaves Heap and Zizzo (2012, March) elicit to which extent subjects feel the four basic emotions of excitement, anger, anxiety and joy at the beginning of every period in SSW markets. Controlling for subject irrationality and a momentum effect they find that markets with excited subjects exhibit substantially higher prices. This result is seconded by Anrade *et al.* (2012, August), who induce different moods in their subjects prior to trading. They report that subjects exposed to an exciting and upbeat video produce significantly larger bubbles and are also more likely than others to extrapolate positive price trends from periods 1 to 3 to periods 4 and 5. In an exploratory study, Lahav and Meer (2012, May 3) find that subjects in a positive mood produce larger bubbles, with individual traders bidding for fewer assets but exhibiting a higher willingness to pay.

2.2 *Expectations*

Observation 7. *Subjects' price forecasts are biased and serially correlated. They are flat for inexperienced subjects and generally fail to anticipate the timing of the crash. Superior forecasters earn higher trading profits.*

Support: SSW note that subjects simultaneously (i) acquire experience in the mechanics of asset trading, and (ii) form expectations of price behavior in such markets. They hypothesize that bubbles with inexperienced subjects may be due to a lack of experience in the trading environment, while with once experienced subjects they might then result from expectations created in the first market. When testing this hypothesis by letting subjects gain trading experience in single period markets, they however find their hypothesis refuted since these subjects produce the typical bubble-and-crash pattern when trading in a standard market.

Subjects generally seem to form expectations by extrapolating past price patterns and by myopically updating these expectations based on their own forecast errors in the previous period or market. As a case in point, note that SSW let their subjects forecast the next period's mean contract price. The forecasts turn out to be close to the subsequently observed prices when prices remain approximately constant or when they exhibit a small trend, while lagging behind larger changes in price levels and failing to predict turning points. In markets exhibiting the typical bubble-and-crash pattern, forecasts underpredict (overpredict) prices in the boom (crash) phase and fail to predict the turning point. Following up on this, Ackert and Church (2001) regress prices on subjects' forecasts, finding that they can clearly reject the joint hypothesis of a constant of zero and a slope of one.

In the arguably most successful study of subjects' expectations, Haruvy et al. (2007) elicit mean price forecasts for all future periods at the beginning of every trading period. They report that, at the beginning of the first period of the first market, subjects ignore the fundamental value process, forecasting constant prices for all future periods. After about a third of the market has elapsed they begin forecasting increasing prices. Toward the end of the first market, subjects finally start forecasting a price peak and a subsequent slight decline, yet underestimate the violence of the crash. In the second market, subjects start out by forecasting what is largely a repetition of the first. When they observe the faster than expected price run-up early on, they react by forecasting that the bubble will rise faster and crash earlier. In the last third of this market – after the crash – they thus correctly forecast prices tracking fundamental value. In the third and fourth repetitions of the market, subjects also expect the peak to occur later than it actually does, and by the fourth market, forecasts largely track fundamental value, with prices only exhibiting minor bubble-like patterns. Analyzing predicted and actual market price changes in the first two markets, Haruvy et al. (2007) report a strong, positive relationship, although one that underestimates the magnitude of the price movements. They interpret this as evidence that subjects underestimate the correlation between their own and others' decisions, i.e. they exhibit myopia. This is mirrored by Levine and Zajac (2007, June 20), who also report that subjects' bids and asks become more similar over time, yet at the same time move away from subjects' initially more informationally efficient price expectations.

Deck et al. (2011, September) report on an overlapping generations asset market modeled after SSW. They find that subjects who only *observe* market activity and themselves have no prior trading experience rely heavily on lagged prices in their forecasts. Once subjects have gained trading experience, they expect others they observe to trade close to fundamental value. Finally, Caginalp et al. (2000a) present a momentum model able to forecast the entire 15-period price trajectory of a SSW market after a calibration using experimental data. They provide evidence for considerable predictability in these markets, finding that their model predicts similarly well as experienced human forecasters.

Observation 8. *Speculation can explain part, but not every instance, of the bubble-and-crash pattern.*

Support: Oechssler et al. (2011) report that unincentivized forecasts by their subjects suggest that these engage in speculation. When eliciting forecasts for the end-of-period price and the fundamental value, subjects in bubble markets predict prices which differ from their dividend forecasts. Oechssler *et al.* take this as evidence that subjects understand the fundamental value, but speculate on being able to resell assets they own for a price in excess of fundamental value.

Nonetheless, speculation cannot explain all observed bubbles and crashes. Lei *et al.* (2001) assign fixed roles of buyers and sellers to their subjects. This mechanism rules out resale as a motivation for purchasing. They nonetheless observe that a substantial fraction of all transactions occurs at prices below the minimum or above the maximum level of possible future dividend earnings, showing that bubbles arise, at least in part, from errors in decision-making. Hargreaves Heap and Zizzo (2012, March) underline this finding by eliciting a measure of subject irrationality after their experiment and correlating it with market outcomes. They show that the presence of irrational subjects is related to price momentum, with a relatively small number of irrational traders accounting for 'a significant amount of mispricing' (Hargreaves Heap and Zizzo, 2012, March, p. 18).

Observation 9. *Common expectations of rationality largely eliminate mispricing.*

Support: Cheung et al. (2012, May) employ an extensive set of 34 control questions to ensure that subjects understand the fundamental value process. By varying whether it is common information that everybody in the market had to answer these questions, they succeed in demonstrating that mispricing is largely eliminated under what they refer to as common knowledge of rationality. We believe it likely that the results of Lei and Vesely (2009), which we mentioned before in Observation 1, derive from a similar mechanism.

Observation 10. *Subject confusion seems to contribute to bubble formation.*

Support: Huber and Kirchler (2012) test for the role of subject confusion in bubble formation. In their first treatment they replace the fundamental value table in subjects' instructions by a graph illustrating the same information. In their second treatment, they inform subjects about the fundamental value after each period. They find that bubbles are essentially eliminated in both treatments and conclude that the bubble phenomenon is caused by subject confusion. Kirchler *et al.* (2012) tackle confusion by modifying the framing of the experiment. Instead of talking of an 'asset' or 'stock', they refer to a 'stock from a depletable gold mine'. This simple modification essentially eliminates the bubble and significantly reduces mispricing. In a follow-up experiment modeled after Hussam *et al.* (2008), they furthermore show that the bubble cannot be rekindled in their framed markets.

Observation 11. *Bubbles are reduced when subjects are provided with an alternative activity.*

Support: Lei *et al.* (2001) test whether subjects trade simply because they have no other activity to occupy their time and because of an experimenter demand effect. They refer to this conjecture as the 'Active Participation Hypothesis' and find that giving subjects an alternative activity significantly reduces Turnover, yet does not eliminate bubbles or crashes in markets with speculation. In markets with no speculation, it reduces the fraction of under- and overpriced transactions. However, Porter and Smith (1994, p. 118) make the valid point that reasoning such as that underlying the Active Participation Hypothesis 'merely predicts trade, not bubbles'.

Observation 12. *Public announcements can move prices in either direction.*

Support: Corgnet *et al.* (2010) test the impact of the public messages 'The price is too high' and 'The price is too low'. They find that the former can reduce the bubble phenomenon with inexperienced subjects and the latter can slow the experience of once experienced subjects from abating the bubble. They also provide evidence that the effect is mainly due to the content of the message and not to its level of reliability.

2.3 *Asset-to-Cash Ratio*

This section discusses the impact of differences in the relative total values of assets and cash in a market. In the studies discussed here, the asset-to-cash ratio is a function of the initial endowments, dividend payments on asset holdings, interest payments on cash holdings, the possibility of buying on margin, transaction costs, the entry and exit of traders, and changes in the asset's terminal value.

Observation 13. *Higher amounts of cash relative to the value of the assets lead to larger bubbles.*

Support: King *et al.* (1993) are the first to investigate the effect of letting subjects buy assets on margin, reporting that it increases nearly all of their bubble measures. This result finds some support in the work of Porter and Smith (1995) and Ackert *et al.* (2006). Caginalp *et al.* (1998) report that the initial ratio of cash to asset value is significantly positively correlated with initial and subsequent mean prices, which they explain using a system of differential equations. This is taken up by Caginalp *et al.* (2001), who contend that the bubble-and-crash pattern has its roots in the available liquidity, with initial overvaluation because of the usually generous endowments of cash compared to the endowments of assets, and a crash when the market value of the asset has increased to levels where the asset has become relatively expensive.[9] This implies that a smaller asset-to-cash ratio is associated with greater positive mispricing. In their most salient analysis, they show that an additional dollar in cash per asset in their experiment translates to an increase of roughly 45 cents (1 dollar) in the average price (highest observed price). This finds additional empirical support by Haruvy and Noussair (2006), who show that increasing cash endowments ten-fold leads to higher prices and greater mispricing, and Caginalp *et al.* (2002), who use a different market design yet obtain qualitatively similar results.

Kirchler *et al.* (2012) report a more nuanced analysis of the issue. They use a 2×2 design varying both the fundamental value process (declining and constant) and the change in the cash-to-asset ratio over time (increasing and constant). They observe bubbles only when combining a declining fundamental value with an increasing cash-to-asset ratio. Note that this accords well with the findings on the effect of paying interest on cash holdings (see Observation 19). Finally, Deck *et al.* (2011, September) show that in their overlapping generations experiment, bubbles and crashes coincide with the entry into and exit from the market – and the attendant in- and outflows of liquidity – of generations of traders.[10]

2.4 *Short-Selling*

Economic theory suggests that markets may be limited in their ability to reflect pessimistic information if short selling is limited, as is the case in the baseline design. A number of studies have therefore explored the effect of short-selling on the bubble phenomenon.

Observation 14. *Short-selling leads to lower prices and higher turnover. Whether it also leads to lower absolute mispricing depends on the extent of subjects' short-selling capacity.*

Support: King *et al.* (1993) find no effect of short-selling, yet later studies remark that this may be due to their design, which does not require subjects who sell short to cover dividend payments on these assets. More in line with theory, Ackert *et al.* (2006) report that the possibility to sell short in combination with borrowing restrictions eliminates bubbles by lowering prices, yet leads to higher turnover. The conclusions of Ackert *et al.* (2006) are however cast into doubt by Haruvy and Noussair (2006), who – while accepting that short selling lowers prices – question the interpretation that short selling generally eliminates bubbles. They vary subjects' capacity to sell short and find that increasing it decreases prices irrespective of whether they otherwise are below or above the fundamental value. In some of their markets, they thus observe negative bubbles. However, they replicate the finding of high turnover.[11]

2.5 Dividends

Observation 15. *Relatively later accrual of dividend payments results in smaller bubbles.*

Support: Smith *et al.* (2000) analyze three treatments with different dividend payment schemes. In the first, they have no dividends during, and a single lump-sum payment at the end of the market (A1). The second employs a baseline dividend setup, i.e. dividends after each period (A2). The third uses a baseline dividend setup augmented by a lump-sum dividend at the end of the market (A3). They find that the bubble phenomenon is most pronounced in A2 and least pronounced in A1, with A3 in between. The only session in Lei *et al.* (2001) to have both period-end dividends and a lump-sum payment at the end (i.e. analogous to market A3 of Smith *et al.*, 2000, with all other markets in their paper resembling design A2) is TwoMkt5, which also exhibits the lowest mispricing of all comparable designs in their figures 2 and 3.

Analogous evidence is provided by Caginalp *et al.* (2001), who find that paying a lump-sum dividend at the end of a market instead of at the end of each period within the market leads to markedly reduced bubbles. Out of the six hypotheses they consider, they interpret this finding as most closely in line with their 'dividend hypothesis', defined as: 'the more frequently that dividends are paid, the more that traders will focus on myopically on the short-term, and less on long-term intrinsic value'. (Smith *et al.*, 2000, p. 574). They argue that the data is in line with this hypothesis in the modified form of: '[. . .] that the presence of a large, final dividend helps traders focus on longer term strategies, and away from myopic short term strategies'. (Smith *et al.*, 2000, p. 580).

Note that both of these formulations consider only the time structure of the dividend payments, but in our opinion take insufficient account of the amount of dividends being paid at specific points in time. We argue that an alternative interpretation of the findings would be a form of myopia over time-weighted payments. In other words, we suggest that subjects overweight the value of cash flows occurring relatively earlier. When thinking of the distribution of expected dividend income over time, the evidence is in agreement with bubbles increasing the more dividend mass is shifted forward in time, as opposed to the number of dividend payments alone. Note that a comparison of the cumulative distribution functions of dividend income over time yields the ordering $F_t(A2) > F_t(A3) > F_t(A1)$ for all, which corresponds exactly to the ordering of bubble extent documented by Smith *et al.*

(2000). Alas, only new experiments would be able to distinguish between these two alternative interpretations.

Apart from the question of interpreting these findings, note that the result that prices of assets with no interim dividend payments exhibit the smallest bubbles poses a challenge to the use of the SSW setup for the modeling of financial markets outside the lab. Some of the largest price bubbles in recent history were observed in technology and internet stocks, many of which did not pay dividends.[12]

Observation 16. *Dividend certainty or minor changes in the distribution of period-end dividends are not sufficient to attenuate bubbles and crashes. Major changes to the dividend amount may affect bubbles, but the direction of this effect is unclear.*

Support: Porter and Smith (1995) replace the typical random period-end dividend with a certain dividend equal to the expected value of the canonical design 4 of SSW. They report that the bubble-and-crash phenomenon with inexperienced subjects is not significantly affected. Similarly, Lei *et al.* (2001) and van Boening *et al.* (1993) also detect no significant impact from using either a two- or a five-point symmetric dividend in the absence of further treatment variations. Interestingly, Chan *et al.* (forthcoming) report observing significantly smaller mispricing when one asset has double the dividend of the other in a setting where two assets can be traded simultaneously. In contrast to this, the Hussam *et al.* (2008) results suggest that large changes in the dividend and the asset-to-cash ratio together can exacerbate bubbles. Taken together, these last two studies indicate that large shocks to the dividend do carry the potential to affect the bubble.

Observation 17. *Subjects commit probability judgment errors when confronted with very low dividend payout probabilities.*

Support: Ackert *et al.* (2009) run two parallel markets with assets at the end of each period having a very low probability (0.02) of paying a large dividend. The 'untruncated asset' can – luck permitting – pay the dividend after every period, while the 'truncated asset' can do so a maximum of three times. Even though these two assets' expected values differ by less than the tick size (except in very rare circumstances), Ackert *et al.* find that subjects are willing to pay substantially more for the untruncated asset.

Ackert *et al.* (2012) follow up on this and replicate the finding that some subjects exhibit the probability judgment error. By eliciting predictions about other subjects' bids, they also show that some can be classified as 'rational speculators' in that they expect others to fall prey to the probability judgment error while they themselves do not. Ackert *et al.* show that these rational speculators earn superior returns, while subjects at the other end of the spectrum earn significantly less than average, despite trading more.

2.6 *Fundamental Value*

The baseline design is characterized by a monotonic, linearly decreasing fundamental value path. While such a pattern is representative of some real-world assets,[13] prominent others offer constant or increasing fundamental values over at least parts of their (economic) lives. The studies described in this section implement constant, increasing and non-monotonic fundamental value paths by combining dividends (positive returns) and holding fees (negative returns) at the end of each period, optionally accompanied by a lump-sum payment at the end of a market.

Observation 18. *Asset holdings costs can lead to prices which track or undershoot fundamental values.*

Support: Several authors have modified the asset's fundamental value path using holding costs for units of the asset, payable at the end of each period. In the first such study, Noussair *et al.* (2001) find that markets in an asset with constant fundamental value are not immune to bubbles, yet display only small bubbles and in only four out of their eight cases. For a similar asset, Kirchler *et al.* (2012) also find significantly reduced mispricing both with increasing and with constant cash/asset ratios. They observe bubbles only when combining a declining fundamental value and an increasing cash-/asset ratio, as in the SSW baseline. Davies (2006, August 18) reports that markets with increasing fundamental values induced by levying a 'maintenance payment' exhibit under- instead of overpricing. He conjectures that this may be caused by a lack of liquidity in the market and by failure of subjects to sufficiently upward adjust their price expectations.

Observation 19. *Interest payments on cash holdings eliminate bubbles if they are sufficiently high to induce an increasing fundamental value path.*

Support: Fischbacher *et al.* (2011) let their subjects invest in a riskless, interest-bearing bond. Wealth thus allocated is then unavailable for investment in the risky asset for the remainder of the period. They find that the effectiveness of interest policy in reducing bubbles is very limited, yet what effect they detect is due to the reduction of liquidity in the market for the risky asset. This finds support by Bostian *et al.* (2005, August 30), who show that even an interest rate of 20% is insufficient to eliminate bubbles if the fundamental value is flat. However, the additional cash inflow from interest payments significantly increases bubbles compared to a setting with an interest rate of only 10%. However, Giusti *et al.* (2012, March 12) report that interest payments eliminate bubbles if the interest rate is high enough to induce an increasing fundamental value path.

Observation 20. *Non-monotonic fundamental value structures lead to heterogeneous quality markets.*

Support: Noussair and Powell (2010) conduct an experiment with non-monotonic fundamental value paths, induced by dividends and a tax on asset holdings and a final buyout value. In the valley (peak) treatment, the fundamental value declines (appreciates) linearly until the temporal middle of the market, at which point the trend reverses. They find that prices track fundamentals more closely in the peak design, especially with experienced subjects.

2.7 *Endowments*

SSW give heterogeneous endowments to subjects in order to stimulate trading based on portfolio rebalancing. They report that subjects with relatively high cash (asset) endowments tend to become buyers (sellers), consistent with this aim. Subsequent studies investigate whether this heterogeneity plays a role in the development of bubbles.

Observation 21. *Heterogeneity of endowments is not a necessary condition for bubbles.*

Support: King *et al.* (1993) conjecture that early prices may be depressed due to risk-averse subjects who try to quickly sell their assets. Once these trades have been completed and the most risk-averse traders have become inactive, prices appreciate. This leads to capital gains expectations and an upward trend, which ultimately is the cause of the bubble phenomenon. To test this theory, King *et al.* (1993) run markets with inexperienced subjects who receive identical endowments. They find that equal endowments do not reduce bubbles.

2.8 Taxes and Transaction Costs

Observation 22. *There is no clear evidence that taxes and transaction costs mitigate bubbles.*

Support: King *et al.* (1993) implement a form of a Tobin tax (Tobin, 1978) in an attempt to curb excessive trading. They report that an exchange fee of 5.55% of the asset's initial fundamental value has a mixed effect on different bubble measures and levels of subject experience. Lei *et al.* (2002, June) introduce a capital gains tax of 50% on all positive changes in subjects' wealth positions after each period, designed not to impact their working capital during the experiment. The results show that such a tax does not noticeably reduce relevant bubble measures, even though it imposes substantial costs on traders. Two of the three Lei *et al.* (2002, June) markets exhibit pronounced bubbles. Chan *et al.* (forthcoming) similarly find no significant effect of a Tobin-style tax on observed bubbles or on relative prices in their setting with two asset markets.

Note that – given some qualifying assumptions – economic theory predicts no trade in SSW markets except for rebalancing due to differences in risk-preferences among the subjects.[14] The large number of trades and lack of a clear impact on Turnover of the substantial transaction costs imposed in the studies discussed above thus is evidence of either surprisingly large differences in risk preferences, of the intervention, despite its drastic nature, still being insufficient to temper speculation,[15] or of subject irrationality.

2.9 Limit Price Change Rule and Asset Holdings Cap

Several derivative and stock exchanges have rules limiting the maximum price change of a given contract over a given period of time.[16] Such rules are intended to limit price volatility by limiting expectations of rapid price changes and giving markets a cooling-off period when trade has been suspended. Similarly, some jurisdictions impose caps on an individual trader's maximum asset holdings. This measure aims at limiting the extent of speculation and momentum trading.

Observation 23. *Limit price change rules strengthen the bubble.*

Support: King *et al.* (1993) find that the introduction of a limit price change rule exacerbates the bubble, since it grows bigger and then collapses at about the same time as in baseline markets. They argue that this is due to subjects feeling that their downside risk is limited by the maximum limit price change per period. The effect of experience seems to be similar to that observed in baseline markets. Note, however, that while King *et al.* (1993) implement a trading halt, they do not give subjects a cooling-off period. For a recent empirical account of the performance of limit price change rules, see Deb *et al.* (2010).

Observation 24. *Asset holdings caps can reduce the positive bubble, but may cause a negative bubble.*

Support: Lugovskyy *et al.* (2012, November) test the effect of a cap amounting to 1.8 times subjects' initial asset holdings. They find that such a cap eliminates the positive bubble, but creates a negative bubble if upheld in later trading periods. They argue that the cap constrains momentum trading but also constrains fundamental traders' purchases when the asset is undervalued.

2.10 *Derivative Instruments*

Derivative instruments can for several reasons be considered candidates for improving pricing efficiency. First, they increase the completeness of the market (cp. Arrow, 1964, or Sunder, 1995, p. 464) by filling gaps in the space of state-contingent claims necessary for arbitrage. Second, assume that there were a positive number of boundedly rational subjects in an experimental market who did not understand the fundamental value process despite it being public information. If such subjects could observe the prices for future periods as revealed in derivative markets, this information about others' expectations may serve to alter their own outlook. It may for example aid them in the backward induction task necessary to derive the asset's present value. Third, the option of trading in a market other than the spot market may alleviate experimenter demand effects as described in Observation 11.

Observation 25. *Preliminary evidence suggests that futures markets may attenuate bubbles.*

Support: The cautious wording of Observation 25 is likely to be surprising to many working in the field of SSW markets. Futures markets have in this literature commonly been reported to reduce bubbles. However, we believe that the existing evidence is insufficient to reliably support this claim. We argue that this topic would benefit from additional analysis and further research and discuss the existing evidence in the following paragraphs.

Porter and Smith (1995) were the first to introduce futures trading. In their setting, subjects can trade futures expiring in period 8 of 15. Since the asset and the future are equivalent claims in period 8, they should at that time rationally command the same price. This implies that futures prices prior to the maturity period represent the market expectation of period 8 asset prices. Subjects in the futures treatment of Porter and Smith (1995) create significantly smaller Amplitude bubbles than the baseline design with inexperienced subjects. Note, however, that this finding is based on a sample of only three futures markets. Second, the Amplitude results from Porter and Smith's seemingly unrelated regression using the inexperienced futures treatment data are 0.92, vs. 1.53 in their baseline, while they average 0.976 and range from 0.344 to 1.388 in the rest of the literature,[17] suggesting that the Porter and Smith (1995) *baseline* treatment exhibits comparably high Amplitude values. They furthermore report that Turnover is significantly smaller in the once experienced futures market treatment than in the baseline (2.63 vs. 2.98). As Lei *et al.* (2001) argue in their later paper, this may however simply be due to subjects having two markets to trade in as opposed to one. Finally, Porter and Smith (1995) find no significant differences in Duration. Note that Palan (2010) replicates the Porter and Smith (1995) futures market experiment, only substituting a digital option contract for the futures contract, and finds no evidence for smaller bubbles (see Observation 26). While Porter and Smith (1995) did not have access to any of these later findings, they create a richer context in which to view their original findings.

Noussair and Tucker (2006) design a clever futures market treatment which publicly reveals subjects' future price expectations and simultaneously helps them undertake the backward induction necessary to understand the asset's dividend holding value. They create one futures market for every period and open them in reverse temporal order (i.e. starting with period 15). Only when all futures markets have been opened does spot trading commence. This implies that subjects have a full trajectory of prices for all future periods when they start (spot) trading the asset. Noussair and Tucker find that this leads spot prices to closely track fundamental value. All reported bubble measures are much smaller than in baseline studies. While this result is highly relevant as a test of economic theory, its transferability to markets outside the laboratory is limited. Particularly the feature of opening futures markets backwards through time is not practical at stock exchanges with no predetermined liquidation date for the underlying stock.

Taken together, we believe that the existing evidence – while suggestive – would benefit from additional research to determine under which circumstances and to what extent futures trading attenuates bubbles in this type of markets.

Observation 26. *Digital options trading does not attenuate the bubble-and-crash phenomenon.*

Support: Palan (2009) and Palan (2010) study the effect of offering subjects the chance to trade in a cash-or-nothing option market, in a design modeled after the Porter and Smith (1995) futures market. He reports that digital options do not decrease the extent of the bubble-and-crash phenomenon.

2.11 *Institution of Exchange*

Observation 27. *A two-sided sealed-bid call auction does not significantly attenuate the bubble.*

Support: Van Boening *et al.* (1993) compare markets using a CA with the more common CDA. They find no attenuation of the bubble phenomenon under the former, but report that the latter yields a lower Amplitude. Xie and Zhang (2012) also conduct CA sessions, yielding results comparable to those from a CDA. Finally, Cheung and Palan (2012) find no qualitative differences between their results from CDA and CA markets.

Observation 28. *A tâtonnement trading institution reduces bubbles.*

Support: Lugovskyy *et al.* (2010) compare markets employing a tâtonnement trading institution with markets using CA and CDA institutions. They argue that the former allows for gaining experience within as opposed to across market sessions. Their findings show that bubbles are significantly reduced under the tâtonnement institution and in some analyses perform better even than once and twice experienced CA and CDA markets from comparison studies.

2.12 *Compensation and Incentives*

Tournament incentives – i.e. compensation tied to the rank obtained within a group, instead of to the absolute performance – are a reality faced by many actors in financial markets. In particular fund managers are frequently evaluated by their fund's performance relative to that of their peers or to a benchmark, with new fund inflows usually being concentrated in the most successful funds (cp. e.g. Chevalier and Ellison, 1997).

Observation 29. *The majority of tournament incentive designs are associated with larger bubbles.*

Support: James and Isaac (2000) conduct an experiment where they alternate baseline (B) and tournament incentive markets (T) as follows: BBTTBT. They report that tournament incentives lead to mispricing even with subjects who have already converged to fundamental value in the baseline design. Isaac and James (2003) corroborate the earlier findings and observe greater mispricing under tournament incentives even in two period markets and in markets where one person is exempt from the tournament compensation (i.e. receives compensation linear in final wealth). However, they find that tournament effects largely disappear when only 50% of all subjects are subject to tournament compensation.

Robin *et al.* (2012) also employ tournament incentives but in addition distinguish between short- and long term bonus payments. They find that bonus payments after every period significantly increase Amplitude, while the long-term incentives appear to yield (not significantly) smaller bubbles even than the baseline.[18] Cheung and Coleman (2011) give their subjects periodic cash and asset infusions, which depend on subjects' paper earnings over the preceding periods. They find that market prices can become entirely decoupled from fundamental values, rising right through the end of the market despite the concurrent deterministic decline in the fundamental value. This effect holds also in markets with a constant fundamental value.

2.13 *Social Comparison*

Observation 30. *Markets with public information about the most successful subject exhibit higher prices than markets informed about the least successful subject.*

Support: Schoenberg and Haruvy (2012) provide their traders with information about the wealth of either the best- or worst-performing subject in the market. They find that upward reference information results in higher average and maximum prices and longer bubble durations than downward reference information. When mixing upward and downward informed subjects, Schoenberg and Haruvy (2009) show that the former earn less, trade (not significantly) more and pay (not significantly) higher prices. See Weiss and Fershtman (1998) for a general survey of the treatment of social comparison in the economic literature.

2.14 *Communication*

Observation 31. *The possibility to communicate may attenuate bubbles, but does not do so reliably.*

Support: In two treatments of Oechssler *et al.* (2011), there is a 0.5 probability of one subject receiving inside information on one out of two of their five traded assets which will pay higher liquidating dividends. When allowing subjects to communicate via public electronic chat messages *before* trading in each period, Oechssler *et al.* find that bubbles are less frequent. They suggest that this is because subjects educate each other about the fundamental value and market mechanics. This is surprising since this behavior is likely to be detrimental to the educators' profits. In contrast to this, Hargreaves Heap and Zizzo (2012) detect no general effect on mispricing of the possibility to communicate *while* trading. For a general survey of cheap talk communication in economic experiments, see Crawford (1998).

2.15 *Relative Prices in Multi-Asset Markets*

Observation 32. *The evidence regarding inefficiencies in relative prices is mixed.*

Support: Fisher and Kelly (2000) run two asset markets simultaneously. While they observe bubbles in their markets, the relative prices are largely correct. Furthermore, incentivized relative price forecasts exhibit little prediction error. Ackert *et al.* (2006) conduct experiments with concurrent trading in two essentially equally valuable assets and report that the relative price deviates from the expected ratio of unity. In a similar setting Ackert *et al.* (2009) report that subjects are susceptible to probability judgment error, find overpricing for one of the assets, and report that mispricing is more pronounced in bubble markets. In a full factorial design, Childs and Mestelman (2006) observe that rate-of-return parity obtains for identical assets traded in two different currencies, but that price deviations increase slightly when the assets' dividend variances differ, and increase considerably when their expected dividends differ. They find the greatest price deviations when the assets differ both in dividend variability and expected value.

In cases where the market correctly recognizes one of the two assets paying bonus dividends in Oechssler *et al.* (2011), the price for the others fails to adjust correctly. Apart from this, the relative prices are correct despite a number of market-wide price bubbles. Finally, Caginalp *et al.* (2002) report that prices of their 'value stock' are depressed when there is the possibility to trade a 'speculative stock'. Their results support a liquidity mechanism by which money invested in one asset suppresses the prices of the other.

Chan *et al.* (forthcoming) let subjects trade simultaneously in two asset markets, systematically varying the dividend payoff, life, tax treatment and holding period of one of the assets. While they observe significant bubbles in the individual assets, they do not find significant differences in relative prices when varying one asset's or one market's characteristics.

3 Conclusion

Despite criticism directed at the SSW design (e.g. against the declining fundamental value, the deterministic length of the market, or the perfect knowledge about the asset's expected value), it is the best-documented experimental asset market design in existence and thus offers a superior base of comparison for new work. Furthermore, these shortcomings have in turn sparked studies analyzing their impact on the observed results as well as work proposing new market structures free of these perceived problems. The wealth of findings and the continued interest in this field, as evidenced by the considerable number of working papers and recently published studies, indicates that the line of research started by SSW will continue to advance the discipline's understanding of traders' behavior in multi-period asset markets in the future.[19] We hope to contribute to this work through this review of the findings to date.

Acknowledgements

Our thanks for providing data, help and/or comments over the years of work on this paper go to Lucy Ackert, James Ang, Stephen Cheung, Brice Corgnet, Florian Ederer, Sascha Füllbrunn, Andrea Gauper, Dan Gode, Ernan Haruvy, Morten Hedegaard, Ron King, Michael Kirchler, Ulrike Leopold-Wildburger, Roland Mestel, Julija Michailova, Charles Noussair, Nicole Palan, Dave Porter, Owen Powell, Katerina Straznicka, and Shyam Sunder. Further thanks go to Ernan Haruvy for providing detailed data on Haruvy *et al.* (2007), and to Dave Porter for providing detailed data on Porter and Smith (1995). Finally, we are indebted to our very constructive referees and editors, whose input considerably improved the paper. All remaining errors are our own.

Notes

1. We follow the recommendation of Thompson and Pocock (1991) of including unpublished work in order to limit the influence of a possible publication bias.
2. The market structure which has most frequently been employed as the point of departure for subsequent studies is design 4 of SSW.
3. Another explanation of this mechanism could be that the most risk-averse traders sell their assets and become inactive, leaving only the less risk-averse subjects active in the market. Note however that Porter and Smith (1995) reject the hypothesis that low initial prices due to dividend risk aversion are responsible for the bubble phenomenon. In their dividend certainty treatment, dividend risk is eliminated, yet bubbles still form.
4. Noussair et al. (2001) describe a similar development, progressing from heterogeneous expectations or decision errors, which they argue are particularly likely at the beginning of a session.
5. See Geanakoplos (1992) for an excellent exposition of the concept of common knowledge.
6. Speculation may be profitable even when the resale price is lower than the purchase price, since the speculator can earn dividends during the time that she holds the asset.
7. Their behavior can thus be likened to the myopic actions of a level-1 player, as defined by Stahl and Wilson (1995).
8. Note however that their markets deviate from the baseline design in several respects.
9. An anonymous referee notes that in this sense, the important metric is the ratio of cash to price instead of cash to fundamental value of the assets.
10. Note that this is in line with the empirical findings reported in Gong et al. (2011).
11. Note that, albeit in a different experimental market design, Veiga et al. (2008) similarly find that short-selling reduces prices irrespective of the sign of the price deviation from fundamental value. On the contrary, Hauser and Huber (2012) report a clear effect of increased efficiency and reduced volatility when they allow short-selling, albeit in single-period markets with two assets.
12. We thank an anonymous referee for pointing this out.
13. The most prominent examples are investments in the extraction of a non-renewable natural resource such as oil, gold, etc. (cp. Palan, 2009, p. 40).
14. Cp. Palan (2009) for a discussion of the conditions under which a no-trade equilibrium obtains in SSW markets.
15. We again thank the same anonymous referee for pointing this out.
16. The New York Stock Exchange Rule 80B, for example, halts trading for one hour (30 minutes) if the Dow Jones Industrial Average declines by 10% before 2 pm (between 2 pm and 2.30 pm); for two hours [one hour] {the rest of the day} if it declines by 20% before 1 pm [between 1 pm and 2 pm] {after 2 pm}; and for the rest of the day if it declines by 30% at any time.
17. The individual values are 1.388 from Smith et al. (2000), 0.344 from King et al. (1993), 1.21 from Porter and Smith (1994), and 1.01 from Davies (2006, August 18).
18. The difference between short- and long-term bonus payments may be due to a difference in the basis for awarding the bonuses and might also be affected by the changing liquidity in the short-term bonus treatments. In the short-term bonus treatment, bonus payments are added to subjects' cash positions at the end of a period and can be used to fund purchases in the following periods, while in the long-term bonus treatment the total bonus is paid after trading has ended in the market.

19. Another sign of the community's perception of the relevance of this literature is that asset
     market experiments following the Smith *et al.* (1988) design have by now also found their
     way into economics teaching programs, cp. Williams and Walker (1993), Ball and Holt
     (1998) and Bostian and Holt (2009).

References

Ackert, L.F. and Church, B.K. (2001) The effects of subject pool and design experience on rationality in
     experimental asset markets. *Journal of Psychology and Financial Markets* 2(1): 6–28.
Ackert, L.F., Charupat, N., Church, B.K. and Deaves, R. (2006) Margin, short selling, and lotteries in
     experimental asset markets. *Southern Economic Journal* 73(2): 419–436.
Ackert, L.F., Charupat, N., Deaves, R. and Kluger, B.D. (2009) Probability judgment error and speculation
     in laboratory asset market bubbles. *Journal of Financial and Quantitative Analysis* 3: 719–744.
Ackert, L.F., Kluger, B.D. and Qi, L. (2012) Irrationality and beliefs in a laboratory asset market: is it
     me or is it you? *Journal of Economic Behavior & Organization* 84(1): 278–291.
Anrade, E.B., Odean, T. and Shengle, L. (2012) Bubbling with excitement: an experiment. Available at:
     Terrance Odean's personal website-http://faculty.haas.berkeley.edu/odean/.
Arrow, K.J. (1964) The role of securities in the optimal allocation of risk-bearing. *Review of Economic
     Studies* 31(2): 91–96.
Baghestanian, S., Lugovskyy, V. and Puzzello, D. (2012) Individual behavior in experimental asset
     markets: theory and evidence. Working Paper, University of Indiana.
Ball, S.B. and Holt, C.A. (1998) Speculation and bubbles in an asset market. *Journal of Economic
     Perspectives* 12(1): 207–218.
Bostian, A.A.J. and Holt, C.A. (2009) Price bubbles with discounting: a web-based classroom experiment.
     Journal of Economic Education 40(1): 27–37.
Bostian, A.J., Goeree, J. and Holt, C.A. (2005) Price bubbles in asset market experiments with flat
     fundamental values. Draft for the Experimental Finance Conference, Federal Reserve Bank of
     Atlanta September 23, 2005.
Caginalp, G., Porter, D.P. and Smith, V.L. (1998) Initial cash/asset ratio and asset prices: an experimental
     study. *Proceedings of the National Academy of Sciences of the United States of America* 95:
     756–761.
Caginalp, G., Ilieva, V., Porter, D.P. and Smith, V.L. (2002) Do speculative stocks lower prices and
     increase volatility of value stocks? *Journal of Psychology and Financial Markets* 3(2): 118–132.
Caginalp, G., Porter, D.P. and Smith, V.L. (2000a) Momentum and overreaction in experimental asset
     markets. *International Journal of Industrial Organization* 18: 187–204.
Caginalp, G., Porter, D.P. and Smith, V.L. (2000b) Overreactions, momentum, liquidity, and price bubbles
     in laboratory and field asset markets. *Journal of Psychology and Financial Markets* 1(1): 24–48.
Caginalp, G., Porter, D.P. and Smith, V.L. (2001) Financial bubbles: excess cash, momentum, and
     incomplete information. *Journal of Psychology and Financial Markets* 2(2): 80–99.
Chan, K.S., Lei, V. and Vesely, F. (forthcoming) Differentiated assets: an experimental study on bubbles.
     Economic Inquiry.
Charness, G. and Sutter, M. (2012) Groups make better self-interested decisions. *Journal of Economic
     Perspectives* 26(3): 157–176.
Cheung, S.L. and Coleman, A. (2011) League-table incentives and price bubbles in experimental asset
     markets. IZA Discussion Paper Series, IZA, Bonn.
Cheung, S.L. and Palan, S. (2012) Two heads are less bubbly than one: team decision-making in an
     experimental asset market. *Experimental Economics* 15(3): 373–397.
Cheung, S.L., Hedegaard, M. and Palan, S. (2012) To see is to believe: common expectations in
     experimental asset markets. Economics Working Paper Series, University of Sydney, Sydney.
Chevalier, J. and Ellison, G. (1997) Risk taking by mutual funds as a response to incentives. *Journal of
     Political Economy* 105(6): 1167–1200.
Childs, J. and Mestelman, S. (2006) Rate-of-return parity in experimental asset markets. *Review of
     International Economics* 14(3): 331–347.

Corgnet, B., Kujal, P. and Porter, D.P. (2010) The effect of reliability, content and timing of public announcements on asset trading behavior. *Journal of Economic Behavior & Organization* 76: 254–266.

Crawford, V. (1998) A survey of experiments on communication via cheap talk. *Journal of Economic Theory* 78: 286–298.

Davies, T. (2006) Irrational gloominess in the laboratory. Economics Working Paper 06–09, University of Arizona.

De Long, J.B., Shleifer, Andrei, Summers, L.H. and Waldmann, R.J. (1990) Positive feedback investment strategies and destabilizing rational speculation. *Journal of Finance* 45(2): 379–395.

Deb, S.S., Kalev, P.S. and Marisetty, V.B. (2010) Are price limits really bad for equity markets? *Journal of Banking & Finance* 34(10): 2462–2471.

Deck, C., Porter, D.P. and Smith, V.L. (2011) Double bubbles in asset markets with multiple generations. Economic Science Institute Working Paper 11-10, Chapman University.

Dufwenberg, M., Lindqvist, T. and Moore, E. (2005) Bubbles and experience: an experiment. *American Economic Review* 95(5): 1731–1737.

Fischbacher, U., Hens, T. and Zeisberger, S. (2011) The impact of interest rate policy on stock market bubbles and trading behavior. Available at: SSRN http://ssrn.com/abstract=1873943

Fisher, E.O. and Kelly, F.S. (2000) Experimental foreign exchange markets. *Pacific Economic Review* 5(3): 365–387.

Forsythe, R., Palfrey, T.R. and Plott, C.R. (1982) Asset valuation in an experimental market. *Econometrica* 50(3): 537–567.

Frederick, S. (2005) Cognitive reflection and decision making. *Journal of Economic Perspectives* 19(4): 25–42.

Geanakoplos, J. (1992) Common knowledge. *Journal of Economic Perspectives* 6(4): 53–82.

Giusti, G., Jiang, J.H. and Xu, Y. (2012) Eliminating laboratory asset bubbles by paying interest on cash. MPRA Paper, Munich Personal RePEc Archive, Munich.

Gong, B., Pan, D. and Shi, D. (2011) New investors and bubbles: an analysis of the baosteel call warrant bubble. Working Paper, Fudan University.

Hargreaves Heap, S.P. and Zizzo, D.J. (2012) Excitement and irrationality in a financial market. Working Paper, University of East Anglia.

Haruvy, E. and Noussair, C.N. (2006) The effect of short selling on bubbles and crashes in experimental spot asset markets. *Journal of Finance* 61(3): 1119–1157.

Haruvy, E., Lahav, Y. and Noussair, C.N. (2007) Traders' expectations in asset markets: experimental evidence. *American Economic Review* 97(5): 1901–1920.

Haruvy, E., Noussair, C.N. and Powell, O. (2012) The impact of asset repurchases and issues in an experimental market. Center Discussion Paper No. 2012-092.

Hauser, F. and Huber, J. (2012) Short-selling constraints as cause for price distortions: an experimental study. *Journal of International Money and Finance* 31(5): 1279–1298.

Huber, J. and Kirchler, M. (2012) The impact of instructions and procedure on reducing confusion and bubbles in experimental asset markets. *Experimental Economics* 15(1): 89–105.

Hussam, R.N., Porter, D.P. and Smith, V.L. (2008) Thar she blows: can bubbles be rekindled with experienced subjects? *American Economic Review* 98(3): 924–937.

Isaac, M.R. and James, D. (2003) Boundaries of the tournament pricing effect in asset markets: evidence from experimental asset markets. *Southern Economic Journal* 69(4): 936–951.

James, D. and Isaac, R. Mark (2000) Asset markets: how they are affected by tournament incentives for individuals. *American Economic Review* 90(4): 995–1004.

King, R.R. (1991) Private information acquisition in experimental markets prone to bubble and crash. *Journal of Financial Research* 14(3): 197–206.

King, R.R., Smith, V.L., Williams, A.W. and van Boening, M.V. (1993) The robustness of bubbles and crashes in experimental stock markets. In R.H. Day and P. Chen (eds.) Nonlinear Dynamics and Evolutionary Economics (pp. 183–200). New York: Oxford University Press.

Kirchler, E. and Maciejovsky, B. (2002) Simultaneous over- and underconfidence: evidence from experimental asset markets. *Journal of Risk and Uncertainty* 25(1): 65–85.

Kirchler, M., Huber, J. and Stöckl, T. (2012) Thar she bursts – reducing confusion reduces bubbles. *American Economic Review* Forthcoming.

Lahav, Y. and Meer, S. (2012) The effect of induced mood on prices in asset markets: experimental evidence. Available at: SSRN http://ssrn.com/abstract=2050299.

Lei, V. and Vesely, F. (2009) Market efficiency: evidence from a no-bubble asset market experiment. *Pacific Economic Review* 14(2): 246–258.

Lei, V., Noussair, C.N. and Plott, C.R. (2001) Nonspeculative bubbles in experimental asset markets: lack of common knowledge of rationality vs. actual irrationality. *Econometrica* 69(4): 831–859.

Lei, V., Noussair, C.N. and Plott, C.R. (2002) Asset bubbles and rationality: additional evidence from capital gains tax experiments. Social Science Working Paper, California Institute of Technology, Pasadena, CA.

Levine, S.S. and Zajac, E.J. (2007) The institutional nature of price bubbles. Available at: SSRN http://ssrn.com/abstract=960178.

Lugovskyy, V., Puzzello, D. and Tucker, S.J. (2010) An experimental study of bubble formation in asset markets using the tâtonnement trading institution. Working Paper, University of Canterbury, Christchurch.

Lugovskyy, V., Puzzello, D., Tucker, S.J. and Williams, A.W. (2012) Can concentration control policies eliminate bubbles? Department of Economics, Working Paper in Economics 13/12, University of Waikato.

Michailova, J. (2011) Overconfidence and bubbles in experimental asset markets. MPRA Paper No. 30579.

Miller, R.M. (2002) Can markets learn to avoid bubbles? *Journal of Psychology and Financial Markets* 3(1): 44–52.

Noussair, C.N. and Powell, O. (2010) Peaks and valleys: price discovery in experimental asset markets with non-monotonic fundamentals. *Journal of Economic Studies* 37(2): 152–180.

Noussair, C.N. and Tucker, S.J. (2006) Futures markets and bubble formation in experimental asset markets. *Pacific Economic Review* 11(2): 167–184.

Noussair, C.N., Robin, S. and Ruffieux, B. (2001) Price bubbles in laboratory asset markets with constant fundamental values. *Experimental Economics* 4: 87–105.

Oechssler, J., Schmidt, C. and Schnedler, W. (2011) On the ingredients for bubble formation: Informed traders and communication. *Journal of Economic Dynamics & Control* 35(11): 1831–1851.

Palan, S. (2009) Bubbles and crashes in experimental asset markets. Heidelberg: Springer.

Palan, S. (2010) Digital options and efficiency in experimental asset markets. *Journal of Economic Behavior & Organization* 75(3): 506–522.

Porter, D.P. and Smith, V.L. (1994) Stock market bubbles in the laboratory. *Applied Mathematical Finance* 1: 111–127.

Porter, D.P. and Smith, V.L. (1995) Futures contracting and dividend uncertainty in experimental asset markets. *Journal of Business* 68(4): 509–541.

Porter, D.P. and Smith, V.L. (2008) Price bubbles. In C.R. Plott and V.L. Smith (eds.) *Handbook of Experimental Economics Results* (pp. 247–255). Amsterdam: North Holland.

Robin, S., Strážnická, K. and Villeval, M.C. (2012) Bubbles and incentives: an experiment on asset markets. Working Paper 1235, Groupe d´Analyse et de Théorie Économique Lyon-St Étienne.

Schoenberg, E.J. and Haruvy, E. (2009) Relative wealth concerns in asset markets: an experimental approach. Working Paper, Columbia University.

Schoenberg, E.J. and Haruvy, E. (2012) Relative performance information in asset markets: an experimental approach. *Journal of Economic Psychology* 33(6): 1143–1155.

Smith, V.L. (1962) An experimental study of competitive market behavior. *Journal of Political Economy* 70(2): 111–137.

Smith, V.L. (1965) Experimental auction markets and the walrasian hypothesis. *Journal of Political Economy* 73(4): 387–393.

Smith, V.L., Suchanek, G.L. and Williams, A.W. (1988) Bubbles, crashes, and endogenous expectations in experimental spot asset markets. *Econometrica* 56(5): 1119–1151.

Smith, V.L., van Boening, M.V. and Wellford, C.P. (2000) Dividend timing and behavior in laboratory asset markets. *Economic Theory* 16: 567–583.

Stahl, D.O. and Wilson, P.W. (1995) On players' models of other players: theory and experimental evidence. *Games and Economic Behavior* 10: 218–254.

Sunder, S. (1995) Experimental asset markets: a survey. In J.H. Kagel and A.E. Roth (eds.) The Handbook of Experimental Economics (pp. 445–500). Princeton, NJ: Princeton University Press.

Thompson, S.G. and Pocock, S.J. (1991) Can meta-analyses by trusted? *Lancet* 338(8775): 1127–1130.

Tobin, J. (1978) A proposal for international monetary reform. *Eastern Economic Journal* 4(3–4): 153–159.

van Boening, M.V., Williams, A.W. and LaMaster, S. (1993) Price bubbles and crashes in experimental call markets. *Economics Letters* 41: 179–185.

Veiga, H. and Vorsatz, M. (2008) The effect of short-selling on the aggregation of information in an experimental asset market. Fundación de Estudios de Economía Aplicada (DOCUMENTO DE TRABAJO 2008-26), Madrid.

Weiss, Y. and Fershtman, C. (1998) Social status and economic performance: a survey. *European Economic Review* 42(3–5): 801–820.

Williams, A.W. (2008) Price bubbles in large financial asset markets. In C.R. Plott and V.L. Smith (eds.) Handbook of Experimental Economics Results (pp. 242–246). Amsterdam: North Holland.

Williams, A.W. and Walker, J.M. (1993) Computerized laboratory exercises for microeconomics education: three applications motivated by experimental economics. *Journal of Economic Education* 24(4): 291–315.

Xie, H. and Zhang, J. (2012) Bubbles and experience: an experiment with a steady inflow of new traders. CIRANO Scientific Series, CIRANO, Montreal.

11

PREDICTION MARKETS IN THE LABORATORY

Cary Deck

University of Arkansas
Chapman University

David Porter

Chapman University

The idea that there is wisdom from the collective has been forcefully described in *"The Wisdom of the Crowds"* by James Surowiecki (2004), who argues that the aggregation of information in groups results in better decisions than those that are afforded by any single member of the group. Markets, like opinion polls, are one mechanism for aggregating disparate pieces of information. The aggregation properties of prices were first noted by Hayek (1945) and were formally examined by Muth (1961). In particular, Hayek argues that market prices serve the purpose of sharing and coordinating local and personal knowledge, while Muth shows that markets do not waste information and that the current price contains all the information available from market participants.[1]

Essentially, markets are information processors, taking the "wisdom" from the "crowd" of traders and distilling it into a price. In a famous paper, Roll (1984) examines the market for concentrated orange juice. He found that 98% of concentrated orange juice production takes place in central Florida and its value is directly related to cold weather in the region. Roll examined futures contract prices for concentrated orange juice and found that if the closing futures price is higher than its opening price, a more accurate prediction of a freeze can be made by adjusting downward the National Weather Service's temperature forecast.

Prediction markets are special case of asset markets where the value of the traded asset is contingent upon the outcome of some uncertain event at or before some prespecified point in time and not upon a claim to some underlying asset as in a futures market for orange juice. In more concrete terms, suppose there is an asset that will pay $0 if event A occurs, $2 if

A Collection of Surveys on Market Experiments, First Edition.
Edited by Charles N. Noussair and Steven Tucker. Chapters © 2014 The Authors.
Book compilation © 2014 John Wiley & Sons, Ltd. Published 2014 by John Wiley & Sons, Ltd.

event B occurs and \$3 if event C occurs. If some traders have certain information that event A will not occur and other traders have certain information that event B will not occur, then if they pooled (aggregated) their information they would know that event C is a certainty and the asset should be worth \$3. The question is whether a market in which such an asset was trading would arrive at the \$3 price, thus effectively aggregating the information and letting everyone know that event C will occur.

One of the most well-known and well-studied prediction markets is the Iowa Electronic Market for U.S. Presidential Elections. In this market a trader can pay \$1 to purchase a pair of shares. Essentially, one share pays \$1 if the Democratic candidate wins the popular vote in the United States next presidential election and \$0 otherwise. The other share has a similar payoff structure for the Republican candidate.[2] At the time this is being written the market price for the democrat share is 0.60 indicating a 60% chance that the democratic candidate, Barak Obama, will receive the majority of the popular vote in the 2012 election.[3] Over the last several presidential election cycles, the Iowa Electronic Market has been found to outperform more traditional means of aggregating opinions of candidates such as opinion polls (Berg and Rietz (2003). In particular, they examine national polls for the 1988 through 2004 U.S. Presidential elections versus synchronous vote share market prices. The result of the exercise finds that over 964 polls during this time period, the market is closer to the eventual outcome 74% of the time in the vote share markets (see Figure 1, which is taken from Arrow *et al.* 2008). Forsythe *et al.* (1992) attribute the success of the Iowa Electronic market to the behavior of marginal traders, defined as those who set prices by placing limit orders near the current price, who do not suffer from judgment bias the way the average traders do. This work, combined with Oliven and Rietz (2004) suggests that prediction markets can be highly efficient even when there are many "irrational" traders so long as these traders are not setting prices. Similar exercises have been carried out by Wolfers and Leigh (2002) for local elections in Australia and Pennock *et al.* (2001) for box office receipts in the Hollywood Stock Exchange (HSX.com)[4] and both document the relative accuracy of prediction markets.

While many studies have found that prediction markets are reasonably accurate, the support is not universal. Jacobsen *et al.* (2000) found that prediction markets failed to forecast the outcomes of Dutch elections and Brüggelambert (2004) found relatively poor results for political prediction markets in Germany. Huber and Hauser (2005) argue that one explanation for the lack of success for European elections is the systematic overpricing of contracts on fringe parties that receive a small portion of the vote. Rietz (2005) also demonstrates a "bubble"

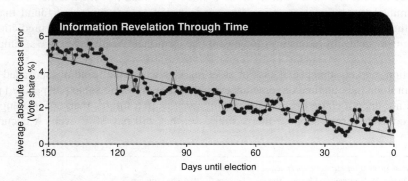

Figure 1. IEM Prediction Market Accuracies (from Arrow 2008).

phenomenon where the sum of share prices exceeds an implied probability of one; however, relative share prices remain accurate. Another mispricing phenomenon that has been observed is the tendency for prices to be biased toward a uniform price; i.e., if there are n states, the prices are biased toward $1/n$ (see Sonneman *et al.* 2008).

Prediction markets are now used in a wide variety of settings. In particular, many firms have begun experimenting with internal prediction markets to gauge forecasts of events important to the firm. For example, Chen and Plott (2002) developed prediction markets for Hewlett-Packard Corporation (HP) to forecast sales of products (monthly dollar sales or units sold, three months in the future). There were between 20 and 30 market participants who were firm employees in marketing and finance. They found that the market prices outperformed official HP forecasts. Google has been using prediction market on a large scale since 2005 with its employees. Participants in the Google markets are given an amount of artificial currency ("Goobles") to buy and sell "securities" in specific events that pays off in Goobles. The markets were designed to forecast product launch dates, new office openings, and many other items of strategic importance to Google. Cowgill *et al.* (2009) found that the while Google markets were reasonably good at predicting events, there was a tendency toward optimism. In addition, this optimism was even more pronounced on days in which Google stock did well. Forsythe *et al.* (1999) also observed that traders (in political stock markets) tend to overinvest in the outcome that they hope occurs. Such wish fulfillment can be driven both by false consensus whereby one overestimates the percentage of the population that shares one's opinion and by assimilation—contrast where new information is taken as evidence confirming existing beliefs.

The largest public prediction market in the world is Intrade.com and it offers contracts on scientific discoveries, the economy, current events, and geo-political relationships. Prediction markets have even been used to forecast outbreaks of contagious diseases (Polgreen *et al.* 2007) and the number of cattle being brought to slaughter (Gallardo and Heath 2009). Despite their widespread usage, existing prediction markets cover only a fraction of the domain in which such markets could be used to extract information. Hahn and Tetlock (2005) argue for prediction markets to be used for *setting* monetary policy. After the terrorist attacks of September 2001, a proposal was developed by the Defense Advanced Research Projects Agency to create a Policy Analysis Market (PAM) for the purpose of using prediction markets to identify likely threats to U.S. security and deploy resources accordingly. In 2008, a group of prominent economist wrote in *Science* about the promise of prediction markets and called for reducing the legal constraints on these markets in the United States to harness their power for a variety of uses (see Arrow *et al.* 2008).

One of the main obstacles to the implementation of prediction markets, other than concerns about running afoul of gambling laws, is concern about the degree to which they can be manipulated. Setting Federal Reserve Bank policy or National Security policy with systems that can be manipulated is clearly problematic. However, previous attempts to manipulate existing markets have been largely unsuccessful at creating nontransitory price movement: "The profit motive has usually proven sufficient to ensure that attempts at manipulating these [prediction] markets were unsuccessful." (Wolfers and Zitsewitz, 2004, p. 119). Wolfers and Leigh (2002) discuss failed attempts by political candidates to manipulate markets predicting their own success.[5] Also looking at political prediction markets, Rhode and Strumph (2009, p. 37) conclude that "In almost every speculative attack, prices experienced measurable initial changes. However, these movements were quickly reversed and prices returned close to their previous levels."

In order for the prices in a prediction market to aggregate information there has to be a relationship between prices and traders beliefs. From a theoretical perspective there can be a divergence between mean beliefs and the equilibrium price (see Manski 2006). This divergence is tempered when traders are risk averse (see Gjerstad 2005). In this paper we see the ability of prediction markets to aggregate information or be manipulated as an empirical question and as such our focus is on the results from laboratory experiments.[6]

1. The Success of Markets Aggregating Information

Plott and Sunder (1988) introduced what has become the classic information aggregation experiment. Like many previous experiments up to that point, their market used a double auction mechanism due to the demonstrated success this institution had in other environments and the dynamic opportunity for traders to adjust their behavior as bids and asks entered the market (as opposed to the static nature of institutions such as a sealed bid offer market where a trader could not update his choices based upon feedback from the market within the period). The traders were all endowed with a large amount of cash and a fixed number of shares. So that profits were tied only to trading and asset dividends, the cash was treated as a loan, which had to be repaid at the end of trading. Shares paid dividends to whoever held them when trading was done, but the dividend amount depended upon which of three possible states of the world (denoted X, Y, and Z) was realized and the *type* of the trader who held the asset (with type being defined by state dependent dividend payoff structure). Prior to trading, Plott and Sunder (1988) drew a ball from a bingo cage to determine the state of the world where the likelihood of each state being drawn was common information among the traders.[7] However, traders were not informed of the realization; instead each trader was told one of the two states that was not drawn. If, for example, the state was X, then half of the traders were told the state was not Y and the other half were told that the state was not Z. Thus, in aggregate the market participants knew the outcome, but no individual trader knew it. Each experimental session involved multiple sequential markets with endowments, shares, and state drawings being reinitialized before each market in the session.

In total, Plott and Sunder (1988) report the results of 11 sessions totaling 175 markets, each somewhat different from the others including the school from which the subjects were recruited, the number of trader types, the dividend values for each type, the number of traders, endowments, and shares as well as the experience level of the subjects, the duration of the experiment, and whether or not short sales were allowed.[8] This heterogeneity in the experimental design makes it somewhat difficult to identify the specific effects of any particular aspect of the market, but the researchers classify the markets into three series. In *series A*, there was only a single class of asset and there were always multiple types of traders. A rational for having multiple types is that trading should occur in equilibrium as shares are moved from those who value them least to those who value them most. If everyone had the same value for the shares, then there may be little incentive for any trading to occur. For these *series A* markets, Plott and Sunder (1988) find that information is not well aggregated and efficiency is lower than the rational expectation model would predict. However, they do find that the allocations and profits are generally consistent with the rational expectations model in the last occurrence of a particular dividend state.

Plott and Sunder (1988) find stronger support for the rational expectations model in their two other sets of markets. In *series B* the assets are state contingent. Thus rather than trading a single asset that pays off one of three possible dividend amounts, subjects are trading three

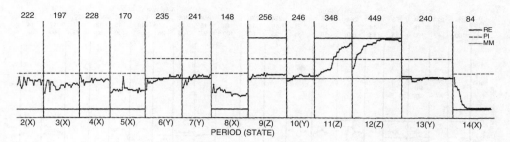

Figure 2. Market 7 from Plott and Sunder (1988).

assets, each of which payoff in a single state. For example, the X asset pays a positive dividend in state X, but does not have a payoff in states Y or Z. In *series C* there is only a single type of trader. That both of these sets of markets produce results that are generally consistent with rational expectations and have prices that reflect aggregated information are important for prediction markets, because most such markets operate with both state dependent assets and a uniform dividend structure.

"Success" in these and other laboratory markets is defined by the rational expectations model, where all of the information is aggregated into the market price, outperforming more myopic models. This should not be construed to mean that all trades occur at the price level that reflects all of the disparate information held by the traders. Indeed, when trading begins there is only private information and it takes time and trading activity for bids, asks, and contracts to reflect more than a trader's private information. For this reason, one would expect prices to move toward the full information level during the course of trading. Thus, researchers typically focus on closing prices rather than starting or average prices. The starting location and speed of convergence likely depend on a wide variety of factors from the distribution of information to the risk attitudes of the traders. Further, market prices are likely to experience variability and often do not obtain the theoretically predicted price even at the end of the trading horizon, a fact that may be lost in some of the rhetoric of prediction markets. Figure 2 shows the observed behavior in one of the *series C* sessions, where one can clearly see these behavioral patterns. This figure plots contract prices over the course of the experiment blocked by market period with the true state shown in parenthesis and the average price given above the chart. The thick/dashed/dotted lines denote the Rational Expectations/Prior Information/Maximin model price predictions.[9]

Noting that Plott and Sunder's (1988) success had come when the market involved a complete set of contingent claims or when preferences were identical, Forsythe and Lundholm (1990) set out to identify conditions under which a single security would obtain the price predicted by the rational expectations model when traders had diverse preferences. As such Forsythe and Lundholm (1990) closely follow Plott and Sunder (1988) in most respects (endowments of cash and shares, no short sales, double auction, etc.). They conducted two sets of experiments: what they call "better chance" and what one might call more challenging. As the name indicates the better chance markets "were designed to give the (Rational Expectations) model a better chance for success . . . " (p. 311). In these markets, the two dividend structures were common information, unlike in the prior study. Also unlike the prior study, subjects gained experience by participating with the same group on two different days with everyone switching dividend structures on the second day.[10]

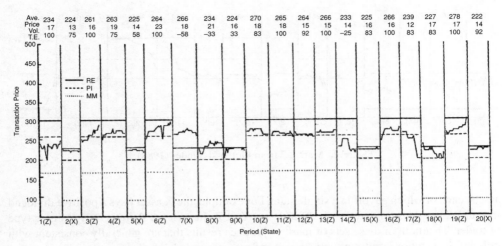

Figure 3. Market 4 from Forsythe and Lundholm (1990).

By and large, by the end of the first day (12–15 market periods) trading did not successfully aggregate information as observed prices varied little with the true state. By the second day behavior did conform to the rational expectations model, at least for closing prices in the last few market periods. However, earlier on the second day closing prices are often better described by a private information model. For example in "Market 4" with experienced traders, shown in Figure 2, the prior information model outperforms the rational expectations model in periods 1, 4, 10, 11, 12, 13, 14, 16, 17, and 18. Had this session only lasted 17 periods like the other three once experienced better chance markets, the authors would not have been able to tout the success of the rational expectations model "by the last occurrence of each state" in all these sessions. Again, when information aggregation occurs in the market, it does so through trading so the initial prices are based upon private information and other idiosyncratic aspects of the traders. During a market period prices tend to move from a common starting point toward the rational expectations price conditional on the true state. Casual inspection of the relevant figures in Forsythe and Lundholm (1990) reveal that the speed of convergence within a period varies wildly, but often the average price and the closing price are not close, see Figure 3. In this figure the legend is the same as in Figure 2, but trading volume and total efficiency by period have been added to the top of the chart.

From the better chance markets the authors conclude that experience, common knowledge of the dividend structure and of trader types, and relatively thick markets are sufficient for the rational expectations predictions to be accurate. Experience took two forms in the better chance markets: one was familiarity with the trading institution and market operations and the other was having participated as a trader with the alternative dividend structure. To explore this last feature the authors conducted some "constant type" experiments where the traders retained the same dividend structure both days, but still had common information regarding both dividend structures. The results were similar to the better chance markets and the authors conclude that switching types is not necessary for convergence.

Forsythe and Lundholm (1990) also conducted a series of experiments where they removed the common information about dividends so that a trader only knows his or her own private payoff for each state. In these "no common knowledge" treatment market prices do not reflect information aggregation indicating that common dividend information is necessary. Fortunately for advocates of prediction markets the traded assets pay the same dividend to everyone and thus the dividend structure is common information. Additionally, Forsythe and Lundholm (1990) conducted "experience and random type" sessions where subjects were twice experienced having participated in one of the pairs of better chance sessions and where the dividend type was randomly assigned in each market. In these cases, closing prices again converged to the rational expectations predictions by the end session, but average prices throughout the day and closing prices in early markets did not. From this, the authors conclude that repeated experience with the same people and a fixed dividend structure are not necessary for the success of the rational expectations model. The former is important for prediction markets given the way they are normally operationalized in practice.

More recently, Bodsky (2012) considers the case where two states of the world are possible, but traders only observe a noisy signal of the true state. In these experiments, subjects were shown two distributions of marbles, which were deposited into identical bags. One of the bags was then randomly selected and subjects had to predict which one had been chosen. Subjects were endowed with cash and shares of two types of contingent assets, one for each possible bag that could have been selected. Each subject privately observed a single draw from the selected bag and could trade with the other participants based upon this private information. This process was repeated so that each subject ultimately observed several draws from the selected bag.[11] Subjects were also asked to state their subjective probabilistic belief about which bag had been drawn. Bodsky (2012) found considerable variation in behavior, with most, but not all sessions pricing the assets near the Bayesian predictions.

2. Comparisons of Predication Markets with Other Mechanisms for Information Aggregation

The demonstrated success and popularity of (double auction) markets for aggregating information has led to it being a standard of comparison for other institutions such as surveys or scoring rules.[12] Graefe (2010) argues that prediction markets outperform surveys when judgment is needed. However, Rieg and Schoder (2011) find little justification for the use of prediction markets, which may be more costly to operate, in comparison to surveys. They use two lab experiments and an online study. Each experiment compares a double auction, a scoring rule, and a survey. In the two lab experiments, subjects predict the outcomes of soccer games while the researchers vary the diversity of information and do not allow entry/exit nor do they allow users to do research. In the online experiment, entry/exit, information diversity, and information search are not controlled. They find that all of the procedures yield similar accuracy in the lab experiments, a finding similar to earlier work reported in Rieg and Schoder (2010). However, in the online experiments, they concluded that the market is less accurate, which they attribute in part to difficulty in maintaining ongoing participation in markets. Graefe and Armstrong (2010) also compare prediction markets and surveys as well as other methods such as face-to-face meetings. In addition to finding little evidence that prediction markets outperform other methods of making a forecast, they report that participants were least satisfied with the process when engaging in prediction markets.

Healy *et al.* (2010) compare double auction markets with pari-mutuel betting, the Delphi or iterated poll method, and the market scoring rule of Hanson (2003).[13] With the Delphi method a poll is taken and the results are distributed to the respondents who can then update their responses and the process is repeated. Market scoring rules are also an iterative process.

An initial prediction specifying the likelihood of various outcomes is made by a forecaster who is rewarded based upon the weight that is put on the ultimately realized outcome. Other forecasters can then adjust the prediction and claim the reward, but must pay the reward due to the previous forecaster. Healy *et al.* (2010) find that in simple environments where there is a single event with a binary state, the double auction performs relatively well even though their markets are very thin involving only three traders. This result is also encouraging for many prediction markets, which tend to focus on single events and may operate with relatively small numbers of traders. In their study, subjects observe "several flips" of one of two possible "biased coins" and try to predict the chance that a future flip will be heads. However, Healy *et al.* (2010) also find that in more complicated environments where there are multiple correlated information states the double auction does not perform as well. Instead, they find that the Delphi method is superior not only outperforming the double auction and pari-mutuel betting, but also outperforming market scoring.[14] Of course, these results are all conditional on the very thin three person markets used in the study.

Ledyard *et al.* (2009) also looks at cases where there are multiple correlated events. The events were stochastic, e.g., in the simple environment event X occurred with a 70% chance, Y had a 20% chance of matching X, and Z had a 50% chance of occurring independently of X and Y. Different subjects observed realizations of different pairs of these stochastic processes but did not know if they were observing X, Y or Z. In their most complicated environment there were eight events (i.e., $2^8 = 256$ possible states). For their double auction markets, traders could trade simple shares for each event, thus in the complicated environment there were eight markets.[15] This institution was compared to a combinatorial call market where traders could place bids or asks for single events or combinations of event outcomes. They report that the double auction did not perform well. This result may be due in part to the implementation, but this remains an open question as the authors did not operate a noncombinatorial call market or a combinatorial double auction. The authors also considered scoring rules and opinion polls and found that market scoring performed relatively well in the complicated environment.[16]

Together these papers suggest that prediction markets are not universally the best choice. Rather, it is important to identify when prediction markets are a good choice. The answer depends at least in part on the extent of the robustness of these markets to insiders or manipulators.

3. How Do Insiders Impact Markets?

In another seminal paper, Plott and Sunder (1982) report a series of experiments on a market's ability to disseminate information more so than aggregate it. These markets were similar to those in Plott and Sunder (1988) described above in many respects (endowments of cash and shares, trading via double auction, state and type dependent payoffs, process for determining state). However, what was different was the distribution of information. In four of their five sessions, when a trader received information it perfectly identified the true state that would determine dividends. In the fifth (identified as Market 1 in the paper) informed traders observed a series of signals (draws from the bingo cage) so that they had a noisy signal of the true state. However, each informed trader observed the same set of signals and thus would have the same posterior beliefs from Bayesian updating.

In some market periods of Plott and Sunder (1982) no one received information about the true state, in others only some traders received information and in the remaining markets everyone knew the true state. If a trader has better information then other traders, the informed trader can attempt to exploit this informational advantage, but doing so will reveal (and thus eliminate) the informational advantage. For example, if an individual knows that the price of an asset is too low, then that person should purchase shares in order to take advantage of the situation. In doing so, the trader will bid up the price of the asset until the price reflects this private information. There were several idiosyncrasies across sessions, including an extra possible state in one, fewer traders in another, various numbers of markets in a session, differing patterns of information conditions, and differences in the commonality of information regarding the number of insiders. This heterogeneity again makes it difficult to identify the effects of specific aspects of the experimental design, but in aggregate the results provide general support for the rational expectations model in terms of prices, allocations, efficiency, and profits. Thus, the information that insiders possess is disseminated through the market trading process.[17]

Banks (1985) noted that Plott and Sunder (1982) did not vary the identity of the informed traders leading open the possibility that uniformed traders had simply learned who to follow rather than the market having aggregated information. To separate this explanation from the one preferred by Plott and Sunder (1982), Banks replicated their design except that the identity of the informed traders was randomized each period. The results support the claims of Plott and Sunder with respect to the pricing dynamics, but also indicate that the strength of the results in later periods may have been biased by this feature of the design.

Camerer and Weigelt (1991) also explored a market environment where insiders with perfect information may or may not be present. In most other respects their markets were similar to those previously discussed (traders were endowed with shares and cash, short sales were prohibited, trading via double auction, etc.). Traders knew their own values in each state but not the values of the other traders. In market periods in which there were insiders the identity of those insiders was determined randomly. All of these procedures were common information among the traders. They reported that in markets where insiders were present, the rational expectations model again describes closing prices reasonably well. When there were no insiders, there is no information for the market to aggregate. However, as uninformed traders do not know of the absence of insiders it is possible for them to misinterpret the behavior of other uniformed traders as revealing insider information. If an uninformed trader acts on such a mistake, this can serve as a signal to other uninformed traders thereby creating an information "mirage." However, sustained mirages were only observed in 4 of the 47 periods where such mirages are possible suggesting that information markets are not very susceptible to this phenomenon, which is good news for the functioning prediction markets.

4. Manipulation

In any market, a trader may want to manipulate the price so that he or she can subsequently take advantage of the price. For example, a trader would like to push the price of an asset down so that she could cheaply purchase a large volume, which could be sold at a profit once the price has recovered. Veiga and Vorsatz (2010) find evidence that asset market prices can be manipulated in the short run under certain conditions. In their markets there are both informed and uninformed traders, but each trader's type is private information. Thus, when a robot trader is introduced with the strategy of buying early and selling late regardless of profitability, uninformed traders cannot tell the buying behavior is not being driven by the informed traders. When the asset should have a high price this strategy pushes prices toward the correct level, but when the asset should have a low price this strategy does have a transitory effect. The automated strategy proved profitable, but still Veiga and Vorsatz (2010) report that "The presence of the robot trader does not affect the last contract price significantly." (p. 385.).

Prediction markets also face the danger that a manipulator may successfully alter the price so that policy makers who are using the aggregated information will be misled. Returning to the example of the PAM proposed by DARPA, if a terrorist could mislead the Department of Defense about how to allocate resources then such markets are of little value for national security. The same is true for other prediction markets that are taken as inputs to other decision-making problems, but the imagery is not as stark.

In a direct test with incentives for manipulation, Hanson *et al.* (2006) create a laboratory information market in which an asset has three initially equally likely dividends (0, 40 and 100). As in Plott and Sunder (1988), some participants have information that one of the dividends is not available (e.g., "not 40") and other participants have information that another dividend is not available (e.g., "not 0"). Together participants would have full information about the actual outcome. For obvious reasons, they call this their replication treatment (RT). They contrast this condition with a treatment in which there are known manipulators who get rewarded not only on their portfolio outcome but also with a bonus based on the median contract price for the period. The higher the median contract price, the higher the manipulator's bonus in this manipulation treatment (MT). Figure 4 shows the price results of these experiments.

Hanson *et al.* (2006) find that manipulators submit higher bids than nonmanipulators (in line with their incentives), but they have no effect on the information aggregation properties of the market because nonmanipulators tend to accept contracts at lower prices. It is these countervailing strategies that stymie manipulation attempts.

In a follow-up study Oprea *et al.* (2007) are the first to ask a fundamental question: Can individuals without any specific information about the underlying value of an asset, forecast

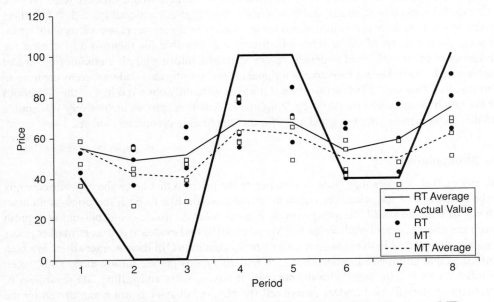

Figure 4. Comparison of Replication Treatment (RT) and Manipulation Treatment (MT) in Hanson *et al.* (2006).

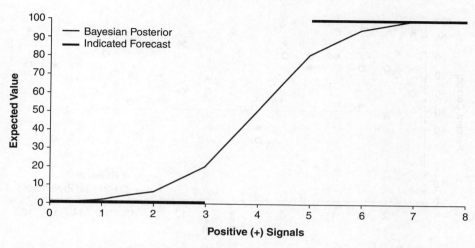

Figure 5. Expected Price conditional on Aggregate Number of + Signals (Oprea *et al.* 2007).

the actual state by just viewing the contract formation in an information as an outsider? That is, can a policymaker use the information from bids, ask and contracts in an information market to better forecast the actual state, and presumably better allocate his resources, than if he relied only on his (lack of) prior information? To do this, they create an environment in which there are but two states (0 or 100). Each trader receives a signal (+ or −). If the true state is 0, participants draw signals (with replacement) from a bag containing 1 + and 2 − marbles; If the true state is 100, participants draw signals (with replacement) from a bag containing 2 + and 1 − marbles. Armed with this information, participants trade in the market. The Basyesian posterior based on the number of gray signals in the market is provided in Figure 5.

The uninformed outside forecasters in this market are rewarded if they accurately forecast the state after the market closes. The black line in the above figure shows the predicted forecast from a fully informed Bayesian. To this setting, they introduce manipulators who are given a target randomly selected from {0,100}. The manipulators are rewarded based on both their profits in the market and how far off the average forecast (of the three forecasters) was relative to the manipulator's target. Figure 6 shows how well the forecaster performed on each treatment. They find that manipulators try to manipulate prices, but the forecasts are not impaired. This result is highly encouraging in that forecasters were able to use the market to improve their predictions and that manipulation attempts did not significantly impact this process in a negative way.

In an attempt to stress test the robustness of this manipulation process, Deck *et al.* (2012) note that the Oprea *et al.* design does not measure the intensity of the forecaster's beliefs. Thus, their design has forecasters investing in which state they believe will occur. As payoffs are quadratic, forecasters have a direct incentive to reveal their beliefs. Further, Deck *et al.* argue that the incentives of the manipulators have been heretofore relatively weak because (1) rewards from successful manipulation may be offset by losses from trading activities and (2) with multiple manipulators there is pressure to free rider. To address these two points, at most a single manipulator is active in any period in Deck *et al.* and the manipulator is only compensated based on how well she fools uninformed forecasters (i.e., manipulators were not paid on their portfolio). Finally, the manipulator is well heeled so she is not cash constrained. In other respects Deck

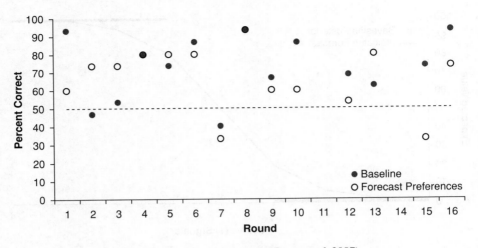

Figure 6. Forecaster Accuracy (Oprea *et al.* 2007).

et al. follows Oprea *et al.* except that traders could create shares by setting aside enough cash to cover the maximum possible dividend payment. In the treatments without manipulators, they affirm the result that forecasters can exploit information in the market to make predictions that are better than random guessing. This suggests that fixed supply of shares that has characterized most prediction market studies is not necessary. However, when manipulators are present, the forecasters do not better than random guessing, clearly demonstrating the destructive nature that a manipulator can do with sufficient incentive and wherewithal. Deck *et al.* do identify a silver lining: manipulators increase trade volume and information can be gleaned from the excess bids or asks in the market. Still, more research is needed to investigate how forecaster, traders, and manipulators might alter their behavior if it is common knowledge that previous work has identified that manipulators increase volume but information remains in the excess bids.

5. Future Work

To date, lab experiments have shown that markets do a reasonably good job of aggregating and/or disseminating information. This parallels what has been observed in the field. However, the success of prediction markets should *not* be construed to mean that in the lab markets provide fully aggregated information during the trading process or always outperform other means of aggregating beliefs. It is not as though prediction markets are a panacea while opinion polls and other methods are no better than random guesses. Rather, prediction markets provide a viable means for harnessing the "wisdom of crowds. at least under certain conditions such as when the number of traders is reasonably thick, the states are not too complex, the payoff structure is relatively simple, and the incentives and wherewithal to manipulate are relatively small.

Clearly more research is needed to fully understand the conditions under which prediction markets are robust to manipulation attempts if such markets are going to be used as decision making inputs or for the allocation of resources. One obvious gap in the experimental literature is the case where there is heterogeneity among manipulators in terms of the optimal direction they wish to push prices. Another, more critical, gap in the literature concerns the situation in which the state is endogenous or under the control of those who can trade. Again, taking the example of the PAM markets, if the market prices were observable then a terrorist could condition an attack on a low price that indicates a low probability of attack. Of course, this would make an attack more likely when the price was low, which would drive prices up making an attack less likely which would push prices back down making an attack more likely an so on.

Notes

1. Fama's 1970 article provides strong empirical support for this efficient market hypothesis, i.e., security markets are extremely efficient in reflecting the complete and accurate information about the fundamental asset value.
2. Technically, the shares payoff if that party's candidate receives the majority of the votes cast for one of those two parties. That is votes for other parties are not considered. The Iowa Electronic Market also operates markets for the vote share in U.S. presidential elections as well as markets for Congressional election outcomes and stated Federal Reserve Policies.
3. By Election Day the price had risen to 0.86 and ultimately Obama was elected.
4. The Hollywood Stock Exchange uses artificial currency in its market.
5. Hansen *et al.* (2004) were able to manipulate election predictions, but only temporarily.
6. For a more general review of prediction markets, see Tziralis and Tatsiopoulos (2007).
7. Smith (1994) makes a distinction between common information, when data are available to everyone, from common knowledge, which involves knowing that everyone knows the information, knowing that everyone knows the information, and knowing that everyone knows that everyone knows the information, and so on. It is one thing for everyone to know that a stock market bubble is about to burst; it is another to know that everyone else knows it is about to burst.
8. In this experiment, when short sales were allowed, traders had to subsequently buy shares in order to cover the short sales or had to pay an extremely large penalty.
9. The prior Information model assumes that traders update their beliefs after observing the private signal according to Bayes rule and act upon this probability to maximize their expected payoff. The maximin model assumes that traders will not purchase an asset unless the price is below the minimum possible value the trader knows the asset could take with certainty.
10. Of course there were several other differences as well including intentional ones such as the use of a mechanized device to select the true state each period and unintentional ones such as the subject pools (in this case MBA and undergraduate students at a different school). This second point is not meant as a criticism, but as a reminder that pure replication is never possible. Things like the room temperature, the gender of the researcher, or the time of day are not normally reported in experiments, but any of these features *could* add variation in observed behavior. Thus, it is important for a wider variety of researchers to conduct similar variations of important results and that one should be cautious with regards to any single study, but can feel comfortable with results that are shown to be robust. Thus, the similarity in the results between Plott and Sunder (1988) and the inexperienced subjects in Forsythe and Lundholm (1990) better chance markets despite the slight variations gives greater confidence in the reliability of the behavior.

11. This process is similar to Camerer (1987) except that information was private. The point of the Camerer experiments was to see if the market would correctly price the assets and in general the market price was similar to the price that would be obtained under Bayesian updating.

12. Chen and Pennock (2010) provide a detailed survey of the various types of institutions for aggregating information.

13. Plott *et al.* (2003) also study pari-mutual betting markets. They find mixed success for these systems in aggregating information as predicted by the rational expectations model.

14. Blohm *et al.* (2012) use experimental markets with scoring rules in a two (single market v multiple market) by three (levels of elasticity) experimental design. They find that multiple markets improve efficiency, but that the impact of a change in elasticity depends on the number of markets and the level of elasticity.

15. There was a single market for each event (event A occurs), rather than two markets (A occurs and A does not occur) as short sales were allowed.

16. Klingert and Meyer (2012) use simulations to compare continuous double auctions and market scoring. They conclude that market scoring is preferable. Jian and Sami (2012) investigate two forms of a market scoring rule, one in which people directly state their probabilistic beliefs and one in which traders reveal their beliefs by trading assets with an automated market maker. Ultimately they find that both mechanisms perform equally well.

17. Friedman *et al.* (1984) introduced a futures market for an asset that endures for three trading periods. They report that futures markets stabilize spot prices and help facilitate the leakage of insider information.

References

Arrow, K., Forsythe, R., Gorham, M., Hahn, R., Hanson, R., Ledyard, J., Levmore, S., Litan, R., Milgrom, P., Nelson, F., Neumann, G., Ottaviani, M., Schelling, T., Shiller, R., Smith, V., Snowberg, E., Sunstein, C., Tetlock, P., Tetlock, P., Varian H., Wolfers, J. and Zitzewitz, E. (2008) The promise of prediction markets. *Science* 320: 877–878.

Banks, J. (1985) Price-conveyed information versus observed insider behavior: a note on rational expectations convergence. *Journal of Political Economy*, 93: 807–815.

Berg, J. and Rietz, T. (2003) Prediction markets as decision support systems. *Information Systems Frontiers* 5: 79–93.

Blohm, I., Riedl, C., Füller, J., Köroglu, O., Leimeister, J.M., and Krcmar, H. (2012) The effects of prediction market design and price elasticity on trading performance of users: an experimental analysis. In *Proceedings of the Collective Intelligence 2012*, Cambridge, MA., Available at: http://arxiv.org/ftp/arxiv/papers/1204/1204.3457.pdf (last accessed 4 February, 2013).

Bodsky, R. (2012) Information aggregation in prediction markets: experimental evidence. Master's thesis, Chapman University.

Brüggelambert, G. (2004) Information and efficiency in political stock markets: using computerized markets to predict election results. *Applied Economics* 36(7): 753–768.

Camerer, C. (1987) Do biases in probability judgment matter in markets? Experimental evidence. *The American Economic Review* 77: 981–997.

Camerer, C. and Weigelt, K. (1991) Information mirages in experimental asset markets. *Journal of Business* 64.

Chen, K.-Y. and Plott, C. (2002) Information aggregation mechanisms, concept, design and field implementation. Social Science Working Paper no. 1131, California Institute of Technology.

Chen, Y. and Pennock, D. (2010) Designing markets for prediction. *AI Magazine* 31(4): 42–52.

Cowgill, B.O., Wolfers, J., and Zitzewitz, E. (2009) Using prediction markets to track information flows: evidence from google. Working Paper. Available at: http://bocowgill.com/GooglePredictionMarketPaper.pdf.

Deck, C., Lin, S., and Porter, D. (2012) Affecting policy by manipulating prediction markets: experimental evidence. *Journal of Economic Behavior and Organization* 85: pp. 48–62.

Forsythe, R. and Lundholm, R. (1990) Information aggregation in an experimental market. *Econometrica* 58: 309–347.

Forsythe, R., Nelson, F., Neumann, G., and Wright, J. (1992) Anatomy of an experimental political stock market. *American Economic Review* 82(5): 1142–1161.

Forsythe, R., Rietz, T., and Ross, T. (1999) Wishes, expectations and actions: a survey on price formation in election stock markets. *Journal of Economic Behavior and Organization* 39: 83–110.

Friedman, D., Harrison, G., and Salmon, J. (1984) The informational efficiency of experimental markets. *Journal of Political Economy* 92: 349–408.

Gallardo, P. and Heath, A. (2009) Execution methods in foreign exchange markets. *BIS Quarterly Review*. March 2009. pp. 83–91. Available at SSRN: http://ssrn.com/abstract=1516369.

Gjerstad, S. (2005) Risk aversion, beliefs, and prediction market equilibrium. Working Paper. Available at: http://www.aeaweb.org/assa/2006/0106_1015_0701.pdf.

Graefe, A. (2010) Are prediction markets more accurate than simple surveys? *Foresight: The International Journal of Applied Forecasting* 19: 39–43.

Graefe, A. and Armstrong, J.S. (2010) Comparing face-to-face meetings, nominal groups, delphi and prediction markets on an estimation task. *International Journal of Forecasting* 27(1).

Hahn, R. and Tetlock, P. (2005) Using information markets to improve public decision making. *Harvard Journal of Law and Public Policy* 29: 213–289.

Hansen, J., Schmidt, C., and Strobel, M. (2004) Manipulation in political stock markets—preconditions and evidence. *Applied Economics Letters* 11(7): 459–463.

Hanson, R. (2003) Combinatorial information market design. *Information Systems Frontiers* 5(1): 105–119.

Hanson, R., Oprea, R. and Porter, D. (2006) Information aggregation and manipulation in an experimental market. *Journal of Economic Behavior and Organization* 60: 449–459.

Hayek, F. (1945) The use of knowledge in society. *American Economic Review* 35: 519–530.

Healy, P., Linardi, S., Lowery, J.R., and Ledyard, J. (2010) Prediction markets: alternative mechanisms for complex environments with few traders. *Management Science* 56: 1977–1996.

Huber, J. and Hauser, F. (2005) Systematic mispricing in experimental markets—evidence from political stock markets. Working Paper, University of Innsbruck.

Jacobsen, B., Potters, J., Schram, A., Van Winden, F., and Wit, J. (2000) (In)accuracy of a European political stock market: the influence of common value structures. *European Economic Review* 44(2): 205–230.

Jian, L. and Sami, R. (2012) Aggregation and manipulation in prediction markets: effects of trading mechanism and information distribution. *Management Science* 58(1): 1–18.

Klingert, F. and Meyer, M. (2012) Effectively combining experimental economics and multi-agent simulation: suggestions for a procedural integration with an example from prediction markets research. *Computational & Mathematical Organization Theory* 18(1): 63–90.

Ledyard, J., Hanson, R., and Ishikida, T. (2009) An experimental test of combinatorial information markets. *Journal of Economic Behavior and Organization* 69: 182–189.

Manski, C. (2006) Interpreting the predictions of prediction markets. *Economics Letters* 91(3): 425–429.

Muth, J. (1961) Rational expectations and the theory of price movements. *Econometrica* 29: 315–335.

Oliven, K. and Rietz, T. (2004) Suckers are born but markets are made: individual rationality, arbitrage, and market efficiency on an electronic futures market. *Management Science* 50(3): 336–351.

Oprea, R., Porter, D., Hibbert, C., Hanson, R., and Tila, D. (2007) Can manipulators mislead market observers?" ESI Working Paper, Chapman University. Available at: http://hanson.gmu.edu/judges.pdf.

Pennock, D., Lawrence, S., Lee Giles, C., and Nielsen, F.Å. (2001) The real power of artificial markets. *Science* 291(5506): 987–988.

Plott, C. and Sunder, S. (1982) Efficiency of experimental security markets with insider information: an application of rational-expectations models. *Journal of Political Economy* 90: 663–693.

Plott, C. and Sunder, S. (1988) Rational expectations and the aggregation of diverse information in laboratory security markets. *Econometrica* 56: 1085–1118.

Plott, C., Wit, J., and Yang, W. (2003) Parimutuel betting markets as information aggregation devices: experimental results. *Economic Theory* 22: 311–351.

Polgreen, P., Nelson, F., Neumann, G., and Weinstein, R. (2007) Use of prediction markets to forecast infectious disease activity. *Clinical Infectious Diseases* 44(2): 272–279.

Rhode, P. and Strumph, K. (2009) Historical presidential betting markets. *Journal of Economic Perspectives* 18(2): 127–142.

Rieg, R. and Schoder, R. (2010) Forecasting accuracy: comparing prediction markets and surveys – an experimental study. *The Journal of Prediction Markets* 4(3): 1–19.

Rieg, R. and Schoder, R. (2011) Averaging and private information as drivers of prediction market accuracy: evidence from experimental studies. Available at: http://www.forecasters.org/submissions/RiegRobertISF2011.pdf.

Rietz, T. (2005) Behavioral mispricing and arbitrage in experimental asset markets. Working Paper, University of Iowa.

Roll, R. (1984) Orange juice and weather. *American Economic Review* 74(5): 861–880.

Smith, V. (1994) Economics in the laboratory. *Journal of Economic Perspectives* 8(1): 113–131.

Sonneman, U., Camerer, C., Fox, C., and Langer, T. (2008) Partition-dependent framing effects in lab and field prediction markets. Working Paper, UCLA.

Surowiecki, J. (2004) *The Wisdom of Crowds*. New York: Doubleday.

Tziralis, G. and Tatsiopoulos, I. (2007) Prediction markets: an extended literature review. *Journal of Prediction Markets* 1: 75–91.

Veiga, H. and Vorsatz, M. (2010) Information aggregation in experimental asset markets in the presence of a manipulator. *Experimental Economics* 13(4): 379–398.

Wolfers, J. and Leigh, A. (2002) Three tools for forecasting federal elections: lessons from 2001. *Australian Journal of Political Science* 37(2): 223–240.

Wolfers, J. and Zitzewitz, E. (2004) Prediction markets. *Journal of Economic Perspectives* 18(2): 107–126.

INDEX

A Collection of Surveys on Market Experiments, First Edition.
Edited by Charles N. Noussair and Steven Tucker. Chapters © 2014 The Authors.
Book compilation © 2014 John Wiley & Sons, Ltd. Published 2014 by John Wiley & Sons, Ltd.